Zamani

A Survey of
East African History

New Edition

Edited by
B A Ogot

D1056207

EAPH
Longman Kenya

Published for the Historical Association of Kenya

East African Publishing House Ltd
P.O. Box 30571, Nairobi

Longman Kenya Ltd
P.O. Box 45925
Shell and B.P. House (2nd floor)
Harambee Avenue, Nairobi

Longman Tanzania Ltd
P.O. Box 3164, Dar es Salaam

Longman Uganda Ltd
P.O. Box 3409, Kampala

Longman Group Ltd
London and Harlow

*Associated companies, branches and
representatives throughout the world*

© East African Publishing House and Longman Group Ltd
(formerly Longmans, Green & Co. Ltd) 1968 and 1973

All rights reserved. No part of this publication may be reproduced,
stored in a retrieval system, or transmitted in any form or by any means,
electronic, mechanical, photocopying, recording, or otherwise, without
the prior permission of the Copyright owner.

First published 1968
New Edition 1974

ISBN 0 582 60293 9

DT
365
.O33

ST. Macmillan

4-28-15

Contents

iii

Dexter Library
Northland College
Ashland, Wisconsin 54806

Introduction

The work we here introduce has been titled *Zamani* (Kiswahili for ancient times, antiquity or the past) to indicate that it deals with the early as well as the more modern history of East Africa, and it is subtitled *A Survey of East African History* to show that the subject is too vast to enable more than a summary account to be provided by the contributors in the space at their disposal. It is also a survey in so far as it is based on information available at the present time (1967). Continuing research into East African history will fill in gaps in the account and change many of the ideas and interpretations that are here put forward.

Zamani is being published for the Historical Association of Kenya, which hopes to further the study and teaching of History, and to increase public interest in all aspects of the subject. The Association plans to devote itself to the encouragement of research and to the stimulation of historical writing. This is one of the works it is sponsoring.

It is a work of collaboration and the editors are aware that it suffers from defects that all such works are prone to. Some readers may feel that it is too much like a collection of essays and that the chapters are not sufficiently connected, that contributors do not always follow up the themes discussed by their colleagues. This is partly due to the fact that, being a work of synthesis, it also embodies conclusions from the original research of many of its writers. Scholars from many disciplines, archaeology, geography and linguistics, have contributed the results of their studies and investigations into problems that the conventional historian could not have tackled, and their methods of approaching the subject have necessarily varied, both from those of their fellow scientists and from those of the historian. It will be noticed, too, that the final chapters, which bring the history of East Africa up to the present day, have been entrusted to economists and political scientists. Some past historians have been reluctant to accept such a concept of contemporary history and have frowned on its practitioners, but this attitude is now dying out. Furthermore, in a period of such crucial importance as the present, in which the foundations of post-colonial East Africa are being laid, it would have been impossible to omit consideration of how problems inherited from the past are being tackled and what informed opinion sees as the outlook for the future.

The book begins with a short discussion of the methods currently used by historians, an account of the geographical background and a discussion of early man in East Africa, after which the historians, archaeologists and linguists take over, handing over towards the end to economists and political scientists. The contributors have had complete freedom to express their own views. The responsibility for the overall arrangement is the editors'. In the belief that they aid clarity of exposition and frequently make a point better than several paragraphs, a large number of maps have been included. It will be seen that there is a dividing line in treatment, although not a break in continuity, with the nineteenth century. For earlier times contributors write of the several peoples of East Africa; later East African history more meaningfully divides into the story of what once were colonies and protectorates and now are in the process of becoming nations.

The chapters on the peoples of East Africa will show, however, that no tribe or clan can be considered in isolation from others. Neither should East African history be thought of as separate from that of the rest of Africa. Most problems discussed in the pages that follow have to be considered in an all-African context, and the solutions to them will be found in and will affect the history of the continent as a whole.

The difficulty of terminology and of classification of peoples is not exclusive to Kenya, Uganda and Tanzania. It has been necessary, as the later pages explain, to abandon certain formerly accepted terms and to introduce others. It is recognised that these are not entirely satisfactory but they are, it is hoped, freer from bias than those used hitherto. As there is no definite agreement among linguists on language classification, it has been decided to use that of J. H. Greenberg, which has the merits of attempting to be comprehensive. As is evident from the text of the amended chapters, Greenberg's system of classification is undergoing a gradual modification. (Editor's note, 1973.)

Zamani is not, of course, meant to be definitive. Research is continuing all the time. Those who have contributed to the symposium will feel encouraged if its deficiencies are recognised and noted by its readers.

If some of these should feel sufficiently interested to become historians themselves and to remedy these deficiencies it will be even more encouraging. The book is not exclusively for those studying history. Everyone, not just the historian, needs to know the history of his or her country and to take a pride in what was achieved by their ancestors.

University College,
Nairobi.
18 September 1967.

Bethwell A. Ogot,
John A. Kieran.

Preface to the Second Edition

The first edition of *Zamani*, published in 1968, was planned as a stop-gap measure aimed at producing, within a short period of six months, a work of synthesis on East African history. As a composite work involving eighteen scholars, it has surprisingly proved to be a very good introduction to the history of East Africa during the last two thousand years. It has been reprinted twice, and the demand for it still continues, not only in East Africa but also in other parts of Africa as well as overseas.

Rather than do a third reprint, we have decided to produce a Second Edition which we regard as an up-to-date synthesis of published and unpublished material on the history of East Africa from the Stone Age to the present. With the exception of chapters 15 and 16, all the other chapters have been considerably revised, about half of them completely re-written. Professor I. N. Kimambo who has replaced a former contributor, Dr B. G. McIntosh, has contributed a new chapter on 'The Eastern Bantu Peoples'. I may also add that I alone have been responsible for the preparation and editing of this edition.

University of Nairobi.   Bethwell A. Ogot
6 June, 1972.

1

The Historian in East Africa

J. A. Kieran

History

History has sometimes been broken up into social, economic, political, constitutional and other divisions, but such categorisation is for the historian's convenience only and is ignored when it seems to impede interpretation and explanation. Historians have also divided past ages into centuries although they fully realise that this is arbitrary. The subject matter of history is so vast that it has proved necessary to break it up into more manageable units, to arrange a system of classification, as for example by continents, countries and centuries.

For their further convenience, historians have generally confined themselves to seeking evidence of past developments in writings. The historian has become accustomed to handling these as his source material, whether they are found in printed or in handwritten form. He is happy and feels himself to be competent when he is searching in libraries and in archives. He knows what he is looking for there: the works of earlier historians who, like himself, have attempted to interpret, to make sense of the past, and the writings which were not always intended to serve as historical records but which today give us a picture of the daily life and events of their time. The historian knows how to deal with such evidence as he finds in such libraries and archives. The process of study- ing documents, deciding which give a true and which a false picture, evaluating the particular interest and degree of bias of the writer, and then of making a further selection, of what is most relevant and signifi- cant for the purpose our historian has in mind to accomplish—this is a task to which he is well accustomed. There are techniques which enable

1

him to detect forgeries and to decide which of the written sources he has at his disposal are genuine; his training has given him the ability to criticise the historical writings of others, and to select and organise source material so as to produce his own account and interpretation of that part of the past that interests him, one which is coherent and consistent and which gives scrupulous reference to the materials he has used. At the end, he must leave his source materials intact and accessible to other historians so that they can criticise his interpretation of the past as he will have criticised the interpretations of other historians, living and dead.

This working procedure is never easy, and it is particularly difficult in the East African situation. Documentary material for the early period is scarce, and that which does exist raises many textual problems. In chapter 5, Chittick discusses the value of the Arab geographers and the local chroniclers on whom he has drawn for his assessment of the pre-Portuguese period. Interpretation raises many problems. Sutton shows how the 'Hamitic hypothesis' has distorted much historical writing on East Africa in the past. It should be interesting for all readers of this volume to consider to what extent the later chapters by Ogot, Kiwanuka and Iliffe on Kenya, Uganda and Tanzania lay stress on factors and developments that they themselves might have ignored, while devoting less attention to topics that some might previously have considered to be of major importance.

A moment's reflection will show that written documents are not the only materials that can give information about the past, nor is writing the only medium through which individuals and peoples can give their interpretation of the past. The historian has, of course, always known this, but the ready accessibility of documentary material and his familiarity with the techniques of handling it have led him all too frequently to ignore other source materials. Man's historical experience has left discernible traces of its passage in material objects to be found in the earth, in the way society is organised, in stories and sayings, in the syntax and etymology of languages, in bodily characteristics, in the crops that man grows and the animals he herds, and in the various arts and crafts he practices. Interpretations of the past by individuals and peoples can be found in songs and dances, in works of art, in poems, legends and fables, just as in the more formalised written histories. The efficiency of writing as a means of conveying information about the past can sometimes obscure the fact that it is not the only means for such transmission. Where writing has not been of major importance in the life of a people, the historian must search for historical evidence and historical interpretation elsewhere, in the earth, in the structure of society, wherever there seems a chance of finding fresh information.

Much of this information will come from the researches of others who

2

are not historians and who are not primarily interested in history. Their methods of investigation and of recording will frequently seem strange. However, when we say that history is the study of the past, we must remember that there are many other branches of knowledge (archaeology, zoology, geology, for example) which are also concerned with the past. The information which other branches of knowledge can give the historian is frequently of the utmost value to him in reconstructing the past, while their research techniques can often indicate to him ways in which a problem might be tackled. The student of history will obviously not be able to master the various sciences which can provide information about the past so as to be competent to carry out original work in all of them, but he should know how they can help him and he should understand their methods of conducting research. Furthermore, to obtain as full and as balanced a picture of the past as is possible, it will be necessary for the historian to draw upon the conclusions of scholars in various disciplines. While a historian can appreciate the significance, for his own purposes, of information provided by someone working in another discipline, it is difficult for him, because of his incomplete grasp of the methods, techniques and principles involved, to judge whether any particular conclusions from any such other scholar are correct or incorrect. And when the historian, in making a synthesis of all available information which seems relevant to his own task of bringing the past to light, is faced with the problems of evaluating different, and sometimes apparently contradictory, pieces of information drawn from different disciplines, he has to be very careful indeed. In this situation, the colleagues of the scholars on whom he is relying should be able to advise him.

It will be remembered that historians have already learnt much from other disciplines, from geography, for instance. The movements and settlements of agricultural and pastoral tribes can hardly be understood without reference to soil and climatic conditions. Rainfall, tsetse fly belts, forests, river valleys, grasslands: all these are factors to be taken into account. Knowledge of prevailing winds, ocean currents, difficulties of landfall and the navigability of rivers explains much that relates to settlement and trade. Ojany attempts in chapter 2 to provide the geographical background necessary for the appreciation of much historical development.

There are other quarters from which help can come. The African historian will find himself more and more drawing upon the researches of archaeologists, anthropologists, linguists and students of the natural sciences. The social sciences have been breaking down old barriers associated with the former rigid classification of subjects into the sciences and the humanities, among which latter history was categorised. The African historian has the exciting and rewarding opportunity to be a pioneer in the interdisciplinary approach to problems. But all opportunities bring with them obligations. A wider choice of source materials and of techniques than is offered by the study of documents brings with it an obligation to develop some knowledge of the disciplines which have been accustomed to utilising these source materials and of the methodologies which they have worked out to make the best use of these materials. It is, of course, impossible for this to be done satisfactorily within the confines of this volume. However, it is hoped that it is possible to indicate to some extent how other disciplines and their discoveries can be of help to the historian in East Africa. And it should be stressed here that the term 'historian' does not apply exclusively to the teacher or even to the student. All of us who have ever become curious about the past experiences of our ancestors, our fellow-countrymen, our place of birth or our nation, and have attempted to find out more, and in finding out more have reflected upon it, are historians.

Archaeology

The historian does not feel too lost when he is confronted with archaeology. Here, he realises, is a definite historical science, with the same object of studying man's past, even if the methods of doing this are different, and the archaeologist in searching out the origins of man as we know him today goes further back in time. The archaeologist finds his evidence of the past in the traces that man has left in the earth. Well in advance of historians, archaeologists came to appreciate the importance of collaborating with the natural sciences. Geology was called upon for information on soil structure and for techniques; ecology interpreted man's relationship to his environment. Chemistry and physics helped with problems of dating, and medical science gave opinions on discoveries. The archaeologist took not only information but also techniques of investigation and analysis from the various sciences that could help him.

This co-operative effort is clearly seen to be necessary when one considers that the archaeologist studies what evidence remains of the material culture of past peoples and what can be deduced from this concerning them and their ways of life. The evidence for this, e.g. coins, bones, traces of metallic objects, remains of buildings, is frequently the direct study of another discipline (in these instances, numismatology, anatomy, metallurgy, architecture) and the need to extract as much useful information as possible from such evidence requires consultation between students of the different disciplines. Like the historian, the archaeologist is attempting to portray past mankind in his environment, but unlike the historian, the nature of his source material has accustomed him to consider the principles and methods of other sciences concerned with the same source material as his own.

4

The study of rock engravings and paintings and the investigation of caves above ground is an important part of the work of the archaeologist, but most of his source material comes from digging into the earth, from careful investigation, excavation and classification. From his study of the artefacts that he finds and classifies, he formulates his concept of a culture. This is largely determined by stratigraphy, the arrangement of levels of human occupation on a settlement site, each level containing survivals of the material possessions and constructions of a particular people at a particular time. The general principle is that cultures, identified by an assemblage of material possessions, will be found in layers of succession, the oldest at the bottom and the latest at the top. The archaeologist discovers such things as buildings or traces of them, burials and grave goods (objects buried with the dead), human or animal bones, coins, tools, pottery and beads. The recovery of such objects and the determination of their relationship to one another requires very careful digging, assembly and subsequent treatment of fragile or damaged pieces. Accurate determination of the successive strata or layers of human occupation, with a precise recording of the finding of various objects, is absolutely essential, so that the relationship between various objects on a site can be determined and the concept of a culture, an entity related to and associated with certain such objects, can be built up. From the allocation of objects to their various cultures, a picture can be drawn of the pattern of living at the site through successive ages. The strata themselves will show the progression, usually from the oldest levels at the bottom; bones, where found, can show what men lived at different times and what animals they kept; their pots, tools and other goods will give an idea of their daily economic life.

Classification follows the careful recovery of material and the determination of culture sequences on a single site. The archaeologist then moves into a wider field and attempts to compare his site, its strata and the objects he has found and grouped with similar sites, strata and objects elsewhere. By the comparison of settlement patterns, fashions in ornamentation, types of pottery, burial customs, etc., he hopes to learn how the cultural sequences he has established for the site he has worked on personally compare with those determined elsewhere by other archaeologists. The comparison of material and classifications of objects can then help in the identification of a culture or cultures common to those who lived at several sites. Past relationships between various cultures, suggestive of trade, conquest, migration, of an influence or contact of some kind, can also be discovered. In chapter 5, drawing on information provided by his own excavations, Chittick discusses the age and importance at various times of such places as Kilwa. Sutton (chapter 4) reports on the burial mounds of the advanced hunters, identified as the Capsian culture, and what they tell us of their way of

5

life. He also remarks on the evidence for possible contact between Engaruka and the coast, and discusses the connections there may be between certain pottery types and a cultivating, iron-using people, who may have spoken Bantu languages.

Techniques of excavation and co-operation with natural scientists in treatment of findings may be strange to the historian but the purpose behind these endeavours is the same as his own. The information that the archaeologist can pass on to the historian is limited because his acquaintance with peoples is through their material possessions and their economy, and it is from these that he differentiates them as cultures. He can discuss their patterns of settlement, their technological skills, their levels of artistry, their trade relations, whether they were agricultural or pastoral, their social and economic behaviour, aspects of life that can be reflected in artefacts. Some evidence of religious beliefs can be found in rock paintings, and remains of structures can occasionally give information about where rulers lived and how poweful they were. But much information not of such a nature as to leave traces in the earth is irrecoverable through archaeology. Evidence of political systems, languages and religious beliefs can be surmised from archaeological discoveries. Similarly, the intrusion of one cultural group upon another may be clearly discernible but the reasons for it are more difficult to determine using archaeological techniques. It is also generally true that people who lived settled lives and accumulated durable possessions can be better studied by the archaeologist than can those who wandered and whose goods perished. It should be especially noted that archaeologists hesitate to draw conclusions from an apparent lack of findings, which may result simply from an unfortunate choice of a site for excavation. Nevertheless, for the remotest past, the archaeologist is often the only one capable of recapturing history, and for more modern periods his help to the historian may be invaluable where documentation is poor or non-existent.

Anthropology

Unlike the archaeologist, the anthropologist is not primarily interested in the past, although he also studies and tries to understand cultures. He concerns himself, rather, with present-day social organisation and relations, with customs and cultural values. He investigates and explains structures of societies, forms of social organisation, institutions, ideas and forms of government, systems of marriage, inheritance and descent, religious customs and cultural values, as well as such material aspects of life as farming, cattle raising, fishing and technology. The method of anthropologists today is to live among the people they are studying, to experience their way of life at first hand, and to learn through this experience to appreciate and understand the culture as an entity with all the motivations and tensions expressed in the associated social structure. Even where the historian has a considerable acquaintance with a society as it exists today, he has much to learn from the scientific techniques of the anthropologist. As anthropologists set themselves the task of understanding, rather than merely describing, the values, institutions and ideas of societies, they are interested in finding out the form these took earlier in the societies' history, and in making conjectures about the development of societies towards their modern situation.

This social science interests the historian because the anthropologist's description and explanation of the belief and custom of today can help him visualise what the culture being described must have been like in the past. The historian needs to understand how a society functions today and what its key concepts are now, if he is to understand how it functioned at an earlier date. The historian is making use of data relating to the present day to help him understand the past, while the anthropologist is making use of data relating to the past to help him understand the present. Social anthropologists, studying the ideas, concepts and institutions of present-day societies, which are sometimes not very different from historically antecedent societies, can give the historians many insights into the reasons behind behaviour patterns and events in the past.

The historian, then, looks to the anthropologist for information about techniques of research and for evidence which can help him find traces of the past in social structures as they exist today, just as he looks to the archaeologist for information regarding traces of the past in the earth. The anthropologist can help him understand the evolution of particular institutions and ideas. Because of his interest in the ways in which various social institutions are interconnected, the anthropologist can sometimes draw the historian's attention to the fact that, while in a certain society most features form a logical and coherent whole (given the presuppositions of that society), there are, none the less, certain features which do not seem to fit in. The tentative conclusion may be that these are relics of an earlier cultural complex which has almost entirely disappeared, or, possibly, that they represent borrowings from an alien society, taken over because of their recognised value for a particular function but never wholly assimilated. Such evidence of the past with its indications of societies organised on different principles, having different economic bases, or facing problems the solution to which was attempted by a cultural borrowing of some kind, is obviously of great importance for the historian. It has been suggested that the anthropologist's appreciation that many distinct and apparently unrelated features of a society are necessarily interrelated and express the ethos of that society may enable him to state that, from the evidence that a certain feature existed within a certain society in the past, other features, evidence of which has not survived, must be assumed to have existed in association with it. This is a debatable suggestion, and the historian would be unwise to attempt to make conclusions from this principle himself or to accept conclusions based on it without taking informed advice from more than one anthropologist. One can see how tempting to the historian is the claim that, behind the isolated surviving features of vanished societies, the pattern of these societies can be reconstructed, and how dangerous it would be for him to jump to conclusions without proper consultation with the experts in the field.

A comparison of the institutions of various societies over a wide area, similar to the archaeologist's comparison of material cultures, may indicate the stimulus of one culture upon another and the lines of development and diffusion. The centre where a certain feature originated can sometimes be traced, the lines along which it spread be suggested, and the modifications it underwent in varying circumstances be indicated. Such migrations and diffusions of influence and such evidence of causal connections are bound to interest the historian. The reconstruction of a parent culture which has influenced daughter cultures may perhaps be possible, and the historian may thus be enabled to visualise the way of life of ancestral societies. This reconstruction is arrived at by studying certain modern societies, concentrating on the relics of the past which their social structures contain, understanding how these are interrelated and determining how they have borrowed and adapted from each other and from others.

Cohen here discusses the importance of the cultural system of the river-lake Nilotes in their pre-migration homeland and the larger and stronger political and social units of the Lwo. He goes on to mention the influence on the Padhola of their neighbours, and instances the Abasuba clan, a mixed group of people, mostly non-Luo, who took up the culture of the Luo of Nyanza. Sutton treats of absorption and assimilation among the early peoples of East Africa: he finds that the southern Cushites have left a deep mark on the society, economy and political structure of the highland Bantu and Nilotes. Ehret says that the Dahalo, unlike the Mbuguan and rift Cushites, who continued to practise agriculture and herd cattle, were hunter-gatherers until quite recently, explaining that they may therefore have become assimilated culturally to a larger group of pre-Cushitic hunter-gatherers.

A note of caution, however, is necessary here. Similarities between cultures may be coincidental or the result of similar response to a similar environment. It is always tempting to isolate certain features of a society which seem to support an argument, while ignoring those which do not. Sutton points out the mischief caused by the assumption that the diffusion of culture in Africa was the work of the 'Hamites', and many

8

such assumptions that institutions and concepts diffused from one or two centres have to be carefully scrutinised. Historians have not always been as cautious in using the work of anthropologists as they might have been, and the desire to fill out the pattern of the past has sometimes led them to draw conclusions which anthropologists would not have drawn from such scanty evidence. Most anthropologists, too, have been little concerned with asking questions which interest the historian, who consequently had to be content with gleanings from anthropological treatises, sometimes taken out of context or misunderstood.

Apart from information about particular societies, the general conclusions of anthropology have much to offer the historian. Investigations into human behaviour as conditioned by the prevalence of certain customs and cultural values lead some anthropologists to predict a close relationship between certain circumstances and particular human reactions. While the accuracy of certain predictions may be questionable, it is certainly true that anthropologists' detailed studies of societies can give the historian a much better appreciation of motivations, explain a good deal of what is puzzling in human behaviour, and indicate what are likely to have been the consequences of the introduction of new ideas and new institutions. This attempt at the formulation of theory and the determination of laws, with which anthropology is concerned at present, is of considerable importance to the historian, who constantly faces the problem of finding explanations for human behaviour.

In a more specialised way again, anthropology can be of help—from its study of the motivations and assumptions of societies. The historian, studying the historical traditions of a people, for example, should endeavour to find out from the anthropologist what is their concept of time. This may not necessarily be the linear progression the historian himself uses, but may perhaps be a circular concept of the constant return and reliving of historical situations. What people consider to be the relationship between past and present will naturally affect their interpretation of what has occurred in earlier centuries. Before the historian begins to study the traditions of a society, the anthropologist can help him by explaining in what ways the political, religious or social attitudes of that society and its concept of time are likely to have distorted, consciously or unconsciously, memories of past events.

Oral Tradition

The work of anthropologists has indicated the importance of oral tradition as a means of discovering the past. We are not dealing here with a separate discipline, such as archaeology or anthropology, but with

9

something which is much closer to the traditional study of history. Oral tradition is history handed down by word of mouth, the source material being the spoken rather than the written word. There are many parallels here. Just as there are various forms of documentary sources for history, so there are various forms of oral sources which can be utilised. The same broad distinction, between the deliberate work of historical re-creation and the source material which unconsciously testifies to a historical situation, holds good in oral as in written testimony. The same criteria of judgment which the historian is accustomed to use when scrutinising documents apply when he has to consider the validity and importance of oral tradition.

Oral sources which do not deliberately attempt to re-create history can include a wide range of popular material and material associated with the arts and religion: riddles, jokes, anecdotes, proverbs, poems, songs, stories set in the past often contain much of importance for the historian. Allusions, comments, casual references in a mass of other material frequently hold the key to the understanding of events. Attempts at the preservation or interpretation of history—deliberate works of historical re-creation—can include lists of kings or other notables, and similar tables of ancestry for clan groups at one level of information, and more extended histories, stories, sagas, legends and myths at another.

Just as there are certain stylised forms for writings and certain rules of expression that types of documents should follow, so oral traditions, according to their categories, will probably be cast in certain ways. One type of oral tradition, an epic poem, say, may possibly require that heroes act in a stereotyped manner, that laws concerning a certain aspect of life be associated with a certain ruler, that events follow a balanced, determined pattern, and that individual characteristics be subdued to the demands of artistry. Alterations, omissions, repetitions, apparent falsifications in the historical record of events may be related to such artistic exigencies. Consequently, the historian, studying oral tradition, has to find out, often with the assistance of the anthropologist, into what category or categories his source material falls, and what distortions he can expect to find and must allow for. A process akin to the editing of a text is necessary. All those who know the tradition should be asked for their versions, which can then be compared. The search for and the indication of variants, and the identification of corruptions, show the way in which the tradition has been handed down, the very variations, distortions and corruptions themselves being important as examples of the way in which a historical interpretation of the past has been formulated. However, oral traditions pass through a more human, potentially more emotional channel of communication than do written documents: the historian who is recording them is taking them from a live individual who is speaking to him, one who is not passive as a book or document is:

10

two people are communicating in a particular situation, and their interaction may affect the transmission and thereby the text of the tradition. An informant, whose task and honour it may be to hand on tradition, either as an official duty or by popular consent, may attempt his own elucidation and explanation, and his historical interpretation has to be distinguished from the text itself. Any commentary he may be making must be understood to be such and not be treated as part of the older oral text that he is transmitting.

The historian, it will have been noted, has in many ways to treat his oral sources as he would a document, and for his own convenience of handling he is likely to reduce them to written form. When his investigations have produced a written text, with variations, corruptions and commentaries on the text itself and notes on the situation in which it was transmitted to him, he can then go on to criticise what has been written down as he would criticise any documents that he handles. The distinction here between the recovery of oral tradition and its subsequent interpretation by the collector should be observed. As far as possible, the material, once recovered, should be made available to other historians for their interpretation and commentary as well as his own.

One of the most important criteria for evaluating the reliability of the text concerns the status of the oral informant and of his predecessors. There is an obvious difference between traditions carefully preserved and transmitted by specialised informants and those remembered by the common people. G. S. Were comments in chapter 9 that more is known about royal dynasties than about peoples. The position and function of the informant has to be clarified so that allowance may be made for his interest as an individual and as a member of a profession. The function and purpose, the reason for the preservation of the tradition must also be investigated. The old criterion, *'cui bono?'*—to whose advantage?—will have to be used as a touchstone. Does the tradition actively uphold, rationalise, support or glorify some institution or existing balance of advantage? Fabricated genealogies or stories of origins are not uncommon, as Chittick indicates (chapter 5). Traditions can be distorted for political reasons, to glorify a clan or family, for religious reasons, to claim early acceptance of a religion which has great prestige, or simply, as indicated above, from a desire to produce an edifying, dramatic or artistically satisfying story.

The anthropological approach to oral tradition can never be far away. Both when establishing a definitive text and when criticising it, a thorough knowledge of the society to which the tradition relates will be necessary. Form, content, manner of transmission and significance attached to the tradition will depend on the political and social features of the society. Myths will be understood only when their function and role in society is grasped. As in the case of all other historical evidence, wide comparisons with other material of a similar nature from surrounding areas will illuminate the study of the tradition, highlighting connections and parallels.

But the amount of material of this nature which may be recovered is likely to vary. Organised societies have taken great care of their traditions or, at least, certain individuals and classes considered it worth their while and had the power to take great care of what they wished to be considered as their traditions. Narratives recognisable as obvious historical accounts will be less easily discoverable among nomadic societies or groups less tightly organised. The complexity of less obviously historical material is daunting. Traditions, too, it should be remembered, belong to a clan or a tribe rather than to a stretch of country. Most tribes know their own history, not the history of those who preceded them. As Were says in chapter 9, very little is known or remembered of the period immediately preceding the coming of the Bachwezi. Conversely, a group, dominant militarily or culturally, may impose its own traditions on another so that what at first appears to be the history of the tribe or clan may, on closer examination, prove to be merely the story of this aristocracy. In any case, most oral traditions in East Africa will be found to go back no further than the sixteenth century.

But whatever the difficulties of tracing, defining and evaluating oral traditions, the historian has the advantage of working in a field where he is not attempting to grasp the principles and methods of investigation of a separate discipline or science: he applies to oral testimony the traditional methods, the criteria of judgment, and the techniques he uses with written evidence.

Linguistics

Language itself is a part of a culture complex, and it can be studied in an attempt to discover what its form and content, its grammar and vocabulary, can tell us about the historical experience of the people who speak it. The study of oral tradition treats language as the medium through which information is conveyed: the study of linguistics, for historical purposes, considers the language itself as the historical survival, to be looked at as the historian, using information provided by the anthropologist, looks at other social institutions. If a language is to fulfill its purpose as a means of communication, it must contain words and grammatical concepts sufficient to deal adequately with the situations likely to arise in the cultural complex that possesses the language concerned. Expressing nominal, verbal and other grammatical functions, these concepts come into existence because the realities they represent are experienced in societies which have to find conventional symbols for expressing them. Multiplicity of synonyms for certain objects and processes indicates their importance in political, religious, economic and social life. Cultural change, bringing new ideas, concepts and institutions, is reflected in the changes necessary in a language so that the new conditions of life may be expressed.

The historian, therefore, finds his source material in the traces which historical experience has left in language. The importance of a concept or object in a particular society can be assessed by the frequency or absence of words to describe that concept or object, and the subtlety of differentiation applied to its various facets. The vocabulary of a language is a record of its past, and frequently, of how society has reflected on its past, attempting to see sense and order in it.

Distribution of languages is of great significance to the historian, as are the relationships between languages. Peoples who speak languages of the same family may be assumed to be themselves connected or to have been in close contact at some time in the past. The assumption is that variations between languages of the same family can show how long ago the break in contact occurred—the greater the difference, the longer the time since the ancestors of those speaking these languages today separated. Careful comparisons can indicate migratory patterns and the spread of influence of a language as a whole or of certain concepts held by the society which spoke it. The plotting of the geographical distribution of language families can sometimes show an original centre of language diffusion, a homeland, and indicate the migration of those who spoke it or its derivatives. The spread of certain language families may represent derivation from a common ancestral language with changes induced by varying historical experience or it can imply a pervasive cultural diffusion. This applies to particular words as well. The study of the borrowing of words from other languages can show how a neighbouring influence has pervaded one aspect of culture, how a certain feature has itself been borrowed or imposed on others. Ehret, for example, uses linguistic evidence to show that Cushitic influences were weaker on the Plains Nilotes than on those of the Highlands. Extensive variations between the modern Southern Cushitic languages lead him to conclude that the ancestors of those who speak these languages today were in East Africa for a long time, possibly 4 000 years. Their influence on the Bantu can be seen in the Bantu languages. Cohen mentions the Lango as a people, not originally Nilotic, who adopted a Nilotic language, and he refers to Lwo arrivals in Kitara who adopted a Bantu language and gave up their own.

Comparison of the syntax and etymology of related languages may sometimes make possible reconstruction of their ancestor language. This parent language can then tell the historian much of the way of life

13

of the people who spoke it—of their activities, priorities and preconceptions. For an example, see Ehret's findings regarding the proto-southern Cushitic community (chapter 8).

One major problem associated with linguistics in Africa is that advanced research depends on accurate classification of African language families. Much basic research for this still remains to be done, and where it has been completed, linguists are in disagreement over what it shows. The determination of etymologies, the reconstruction of syntax, the degree of importance to attach to various linguistic features, all present difficulties. Language studies, however, are a valuable means of recovering the past.

Genetic Studies

The passage of time and the experiences they have undergone have left their impression on the constitution of all living beings. Such traces can be recognised and differentiated by scientists, and when they have been brought to the notice of the historian they can tell him something of the experiences and incidents to which they are surviving witnesses. The way in which man has adapted to the circumstances of his environment and the way in which he has adapted animals and plants to meet his needs can be seen in inherited characteristics.

As far as man himself is concerned, results of the work of physical anthropologists, biochemists, biologists, physiologists and doctors have been disappointing. Attempts to classify the peoples of Africa according to skin colour, bone structure, etc., have not been successful. Human remains provided by archaeology have not been sufficiently numerous to enable any worthwhile conclusions to be reached. Sutton, when discussing the Capsian culture (chapter 4), remarks that the caucasoid physical type he tentatively identifies with the southern Cushites appears to be of Ethiopian origin. There is not the data at present for more detailed speculation.

It was hoped at one time that the investigation of man's genetic inheritance would provide more information than has been the case. Genes determine characteristics that are handed on from generation to generation. The frequencies of genes in a population as a whole can be determined and expressed, so that, in theory, comparisons on the basis of different genetic inheritance should show significance correlations, where peoples have common ancestors or ancestors between whom there has been considerable intermarriage. Again, theoretically, it might be possible to identify degrees of intermarriage and to plot migrations and movements on a map. This may eventually happen when the technique is more refined.

The study of man's susceptibility to disease and consequent adaptive resistance to it has been put forward as a source of historical information. Associating the sickle-shaped red blood cell, as distinct from the round, with a degree of immunity to malaria, it was argued that this was to be found in Negroes and was also present in other African groups in proportion to the degree of their intermixture with Negroes. Further medical research now throws considerable doubt on all these assumptions. Nevertheless, it seems reasonable to expect human biology and associated sciences to produce in the course of time some more sophisticated tools for detecting the effect of history.

Genetic studies are more useful, from a historical point of view, when they relate to plants. The historian is interested in plants from the time of their domestication, after which, he assumes, their movements and the appearance of new cultivated varieties may be identified with the people of whose economy they form a part. Botanists can suggest where the first centre of domestication was—broadly speaking, this having been the region where the largest numbers of the wild ancestors of the domesticated plant can be found today. The spread of staple crops, with consequent effects on population and cultural developments, can be indicated by the plant geneticist. More detailed studies by the botanists are eagerly awaited. Sutton discusses food production and its importance, especially that of the banana and its route into the interior (chapter 4). Chittick (chapter 5) alludes to the possible connection between Indonesian influence and the banana.

Less attention has been paid to the origins of cattle, sheep, horses and goats than to those of plants. It may prove possible to reconstruct the process by which wild animals were domesticated and subsequently bred for man's purposes. The tracing and dating of centres and times of domestication, of routes of migration and of the evolution of specialised varieties is obviously of great importance. Unfortunately, this is likely to prove difficult owing to man's continued interference in the breeding of domesticated animals. The study of blood grouping in cattle has, so far, not proved useful in such research.

Dating

In such ways as these, then, the historian can learn about the past. Various techniques and methods of research can indicate a succession of developments which are of interest to him. The problem of fitting successive events into a firm chronological structure still remains. Reports from archaeologists concerning cultural levels can enable a relative chronology to be determined, indicating that cultures followed each other in a certain sequence. Linguists can identify the relative ages of languages,

15

and anthropologists and botanists can trace evolution and development. The succession of generations and rulers can be found in oral traditions. But this relative dating is not sufficient for the historian who demands precision and a scale against which information from varying sources can be set so that he can place evidence acquired by different scientific techniques as precisely and accurately as possible in its historical framework.

Archaeology has come forward with radiocarbon dating. Carbon 14 is found in carbon dioxide in the atmosphere. It is a radioactive isotope, produced by cosmic rays, and is absorbed by plants, and consequently by all living organic matter, including animals, during their lifetime. Absorption stops when the organism dies, and the carbon 14, already absorbed, begins to disintegrate at a fixed rate from the time of death. From laboratory examination of samples of various forms of organic matter, a calculation as to the time elapsed since the death of the organism can be made. For example, a bone sample can tell when an animal died, while a wood sample shows when a tree was cut down. Dates cannot be announced with absolute precision but, calculated with a statistical provision for error, have a probability range of between fifty and three hundred years. Contamination of the atmosphere by increased radioactivity may, however, have falsified some calculations, and some other chemical and physical assumptions may have to be revised. Other methods of dating, using physics and chemistry, are used, but the radiocarbon method appears, at present, to be the one most helpful to the historian.

Lexicostatistics is the statistical study of the vocabulary of languages with the intention of determining their antiquity. This study is based on the assumption that all languages have a basic vocabulary which changes slowly at a rate which is the same for all languages at all times, and which can be expressed as a formula. The percentages of the reconstructed basic vocabulary of the parent language possessed by derivative languages are indications of the relationship of the latter to each other and to the parent language, and suggest their respective ages. Glottochronology, a subdivision of lexicostatistics, is attempting to express rates of language development by formulae precise enough to enable dates for change to be calculated. Such statistical treatments of language have not been pushed very far on the African continent as yet and the method has not met with universal acceptance.

Natural phenomena can, sometimes, be dated. Astronomers can determine the paths taken by eclipses that occurred at various times throughout history, and fix the time when an eclipse affected a particular part of the earth's surface. If oral tradition remembers this occurrence, the events associated in tradition with the eclipse can also be dated.

Statistical calculations can also help the historian to exploit fully the

16

information at his disposal. By a system of averaging, the length of a generation (usually taken as the time between the birth of a man and the birth of his first child) can be worked out for a particular society, and dates estimated for events associated with certain generations. This assumes, of course, that problems of nomenclature of generations (i.e. several generations bearing the same name at intervals) are overcome so that the progression in time is clear. Where the number and names of successive age sets are remembered, the same system of averaging can be applied.

Some have attempted to apply this concept of averaging to reigns, to work out the average length of reign, and when the number of reigns is known, to suggest dates. This is a much more doubtful method. Periods of commotion, with rulers dying violent deaths, or long periods of peace without usurpers or rivals are likely to upset the calculation. The question of the rules of succession has to be gone into very carefully.

Method

The growing tendency in historical studies today is for the historian not only to accept information from the scientists but also to adopt some of their methods of research. An example of the adoption of such methods is the recognition of the value of the statistical approach. Attempts to determine dates, particularly where these are probabilities, not certainties, show the importance of statistics to the historian, who must know the margin of error within which he is working. The concept of probabilities and the calculation of degrees of certainty fall within the province of the statistician, and where the historian finds himself dealing with pieces of information of varying degrees of reliability he will have to know to what extent it is safe to draw conclusions from them. Techniques of sampling and measuring will be helpful. Complex data, drawn from the natural and social sciences, not necessarily in the literary form to which the historian is accustomed, will have to be dealt with. He will be handling tables, graphs, charts and formulae. Many factors will have to be studied quantitatively, and this will take the historian into the realm of mathematics. In his attempts to be as accurate and unbiased as possible in his assessments and to avoid the reproach that he is giving unscientific, subjective conclusions, he will follow methods already worked out by the natural scientists in their striving for objectivity.

Terminology that the historian has been accustomed to use in the past somewhat loosely, without much examination of what is meant by time-worn concepts, will have to be re-examined; new definitions will be necessary. The historian must not only learn to deal with the formulae, graphs and tables of the scientists, but must also grasp the precise meaning of the terms they use and employ them himself. What, for instance, is meant by 'tribe', 'culture' or 'society'? Much of the historian's disappointment with the results of physical anthropology and genetic studies in mankind seems to have arisen from his failure to understand the terms being used, the tentative nature of the suggestions put forward, and his consequent attempt to make assumptions that the researchers in these disciplines would not venture to make. Any attempt to reach conclusions from the work of archaeologists, anthropologists, linguists, botanists and others, that these researchers would reject on the evidence before them, is a temptation that must be resisted. The reconciliation of conclusions reached by scholars in various disciplines, researching along different lines, in subjects with different methods and different concepts of what can safely be inferred from research, will be one of the hardest tasks of all. More and more scientists in related disciplines, though, are becoming interested in the problems of the historian, and are starting to ask the questions that interest him. He has no longer to resign himself to picking up the occasional, infuriating, passing reference to historical antecedents in the works of researchers not primarily concerned with history. Co-operation between those researching in related studies in the attempt to find the answer to specific historical questions has been tried elsewhere, with varying degrees of success, it is true, but this still looks like one of the most hopeful ways of finding out about East Africa's past.

The greater precision and objectivity which the adoption of a more scientific method make possible accompanies the opening up of a wider field of study, stretching out far beyond the libraries and the archives. In the future, other possibilities for the recovery of historical information may become apparent. Medical science, chemistry and physics will most probably have more to offer. Metallurgy, as another instance, should produce some significant discoveries. More sophisticated methods of handling information are likely to appear; the advent of the computer, for example, has already had an important impact on the study of geography but has not yet affected the study of East African history to any noticeable extent. None of these developments changes essentially the historian's task or takes away from him his employment. Neither do they relegate to obscurity the study of written and printed documents which remain one of the finest sources of information. The historian's obligation is still that of discovering and utilising all available source material to give the most accurate interpretation possible of the past. Scholars in other disciplines may help him with information: the responsibility for its analysis and utilisation rests with him.

Further reading

BLOCH, M. *The Historian's Craft*, Manchester University Press, Manchester, 1954.

GLUCKMAN, M. *Politics, Law and Ritual in Tribal Society*, Basil Blackwell, Oxford, 1965.

GREENBERG, J. H. *Studies in African Linguistic Classification*, Compass Publishing Co., New Haven, Conn., 1955.

MOHRMANN, C., SOMMERFELT, A. and WHATMOUGH, J. (Eds) *Trends in European and American Linguistics, 1930–1960*, Spectrum, Utrecht/ Antwerp. H. Hoijer, Anthropological Linguistics.

VANSINA, J. *Oral Tradition: A Study in Historical Methodology*, Routledge and Kegan Paul, London, 1965.

MURDOCK, G. P. *Africa: Its Peoples and their Culture History*, McGraw-Hill, New York, 1959.

MCCALL, D. F. *Africa in Time-Perspective: A Discussion of Historical Reconstruction from Unwritten Sources*, Ghana University Press/Boston University Press, Legon, Boston, 1964.

LYSTAD, R. A. (Ed.) *The African World: A Study of Social Research*, Pall Mall Press, London, 1965.

VANSINA, J., MAUNY, R. and THOMAS, L. V. (Eds) *The Historian in Tropical Africa: Studies presented and discussed at the Fourth International African Seminar at the University of Dakar, Senegal, 1961*, International African Institute/Oxford University Press, London, 1964.

POSNANSKY, M. (Ed.) *Prelude to East African History*, Oxford University Press, London/Nairobi, 1966.

Journal of African History, III, 2, 1962, (Special Number: Third Conference on African History and Archaeology, School of Oriental and African Studies, London, July 1961) Cambridge University Press, London.

2

The Geography of East Africa

Francis F. Ojany

If joined together, [history and geography] crown our reading with delight and profit; if parted, [they] threaten both with a certain shipwreck.

Heylyn, *Cosmographia, 1649*

Geography is the branch of learning that concentrates on understanding the many facets of the earth. Commonly this study is focussed on a piece of the land or country. The subject then examines the complicated inter-relationships of all the aspects of the country. These facets include rocks, relief, climate, vegetation, soils, land use (including agriculture) and population. Many historians have now realised that these facets either singly or in combination have influenced the course of history. One leading historical geographer (W. E. East) even asserted that 'almost all events of historical importance are caused or conditioned by geographical factors'. Thus, it is not possible to appreciate the history of East Africa without an intelligent grasp of the salient features of its geography. The latter has provided the stage on which the events have been taking place, and has very decidedly conditioned its historical and political development.

The position and size of the East African countries

Together, the three East African countries of Kenya, Tanzania and Uganda form a compact block of terrain totalling some 636 707 square

20

miles [1 635 075 km²] of land and 42 207 square miles [109 316 km²] of water and swamp. The region is situated in the eastern part of Equatorial Africa, and extends from latitude 4° 30′ N. to latitude 11° 45′ S. and from longitude 29° 28′ E. to 41° 55′ E. Thus, the region extends from the shores of the Indian Ocean to the western arm of the great African Rift Valley. This great rift valley forms one of the most important features of the region. The presence of the Indian Ocean waters also had an early influence on the history of our area.

Table 1 The size of the East African countries

	Area in square miles [km²]		
	Land/surface	Water/swamp	Total
Tanzania:			
Mainland	341 150 [883 578]	20 650 [53 483]	361 800 [937 061]
Zanzibar	640 [1 658]		640 [1 658]
Pemba	380 [984]		380 [984]
Uganda	74 748 [193 597]	16 386 [42 440]	91 134 [236 037]
Kenya	219 789 [569 253]	5 171 [13 393]	224 960 [582 646]
Total	636 707 [1 649 071]	42 207 [109 316]	678 914 [1 758 387]

The geology of East Africa

Figure 1 shows the main types of rocks and faults that occur in East Africa. The chief rock formations are the ancient rocks, which include a complicated group known generally as the Basement System rocks, the Karagwe-Ankolean, the Nyanzian-Kavirondian-Toro rocks, the Dodoman and other older rocks which in the map are shown as 'Acid gneisses, migmatites and associated granites and granodiorites'. These rocks form the foundation of the African continent and are known to be extremely old. In western Kenya, the Nyanzian-Kavirondian rocks have been shown to be at least 3 000 million years old; the Dodoman and earlier rocks are therefore much older still. These archaean rocks were originally sedimentary formations that were laid down in great geosynclinal formations which covered much of our region and indeed much of Africa at the time. Later, but still during archaean times, these rocks were involved in intense earth movements during which they were folded, altered and considerably graniticised. As a result of these processes, the rocks became harder and much more resistant in their physical characteristics.

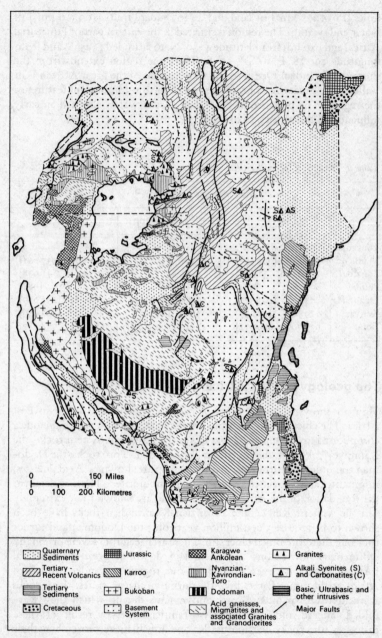

Quaternary Sediments	Jurassic	Karagwe - Ankolean	Granites
Tertiary - Recent Volcanics	Karroo	Nyanzian - Kavirondian - Toro	Alkali Syenites (S) and Carbonatites (C)
Tertiary Sediments	Bukoban	Dodoman	Basic, Ultrabasic and other intrusives
Cretaceous	Basement System	Acid gneisses, Migmatites and associated Granites and Granodiorites	Major Faults

Figure 1 East Africa: geology

Granites and other granite-like rocks (sometimes known as mobilised granites), are the other archaean rocks in the region. They are best seen in the areas marginal to Lake Victoria. These are commonly assumed to be of igneous origin although they may have been altered considerably by metasomatism. They are much more resistant to erosion and today they form a picturesque tor landscape, especially between Mwanza and Musoma and around Bukoba, and to the north and north-west of Kisumu.

Since the Karroo (Carboniferous) era, the coastline of eastern Africa has been subjected to a series of marine transgressions as can be seen from the record of the Jurassic, Cretaceous, Tertiary and Pleistocene sedimentary formations in the area. From the Tertiary to the Pleistocene, East Africa was included in major tectonic activities involving continental uplift, warping, tilting and faulting. As would be expected with resistant rocks, many responded to these stresses by breaking and not folding. Warping (here down-warping) affected the Lake Victoria basin in particular and this is interpreted as marking the ultimate phases in the process of 'basin and swell structure' so typical of the African structural environment. Tilting is illustrated best by the drainage system of Uganda as evidenced by the very gentle gradient typical of most Ugandan rivers. Back-tilting, involving stream reversal, on the other hand, is best seen in the neighbourhood of Lake Kyoga which was brought into being following the reversal of the Kafu river during the formation of the Western Rift Valley. Before these events, Kafu, like other main Ugandan rivers, probably drained into the Atlantic Ocean. Faulting produced the present-day rift valleys of East Africa and although it is known that the original tectonic valleys are ancient features, going back into pre-Cambrian times, the present picturesque features with their steep and fresh scarps are clearly post mid-Pleistocene, i.e. less than 500 000 years in age.

The tertiary and later earth movements were accompanied by much volcanic eruption which drastically modified the geography of East Africa. Most of the lava was emitted along old lines of weakness as fissure eruptions although central-type eruptions were also represented, as evidenced by the imposing composite cones of Mounts Kenya and Elgon. Some of the best agricultural lands as well as the better climatic regions are in these volcanic areas; the consequences in the distribution of man in the region will be examined later.

Rocks are important not only in soil formation, but also as sources of valuable minerals. In this connection, the East African rocks have proved disappointing so far in that they do not seem to be well endowed with minerals of economic value. The pre-Cambrian rocks in Tanganyika have yielded a valuable output of diamonds—mainly from the Shinyanga and Mwadui areas. Also in western Kenya, meagre outputs of

23

gold and copper have been worked but the reserves would seem to be very limited. Uganda has recently found more valuable deposits of copper in Kilembe and this mineral now plays an important role in the national economy. The Karroo Beds of Tanganyika are known to contain considerable reserves of coal but the technical problems involved in exploiting the mineral have so far been prohibitive. The carbonatites of Uganda supply a cement factory in Tororo while along the East African coast, another important rock for cement manufacture is the Pleistocene coral limestone. This rock is crushed for cement production near Dar es Salaam and Mombasa and the potentialities are known to be considerable.

The volcanic rocks are also significant in the economic field. The trona (soda deposits—mainly soda ash and common salt) from Lake Magadi in Kenya is the most important in this connection. Between 1919 and 1953, almost two million tons [tonnes] of soda ash were produced and in the twenty years since 1933, nearly a quarter million tons [tonnes] of common salt have been produced. In Uganda, the Katwe Salt Works, near Lake Edward, have also been worked for a considerable period. Of the Pleistocene rocks, we should note the diatomaceous earth which is worked for diatomite at Kariandus in the Kenya section of the Rift Valley. Also a number of the volcanic rocks such as trachytes and phonolites are widely used locally for building stones and for ballast while occasional occurrences of obsidian and flint in the younger rocks were used by early man to make his implements. A number of volcanic rocks were also used for the same purpose.

The relief of East Africa

One of East Africa's natural resources is the charm of its relief. The grandeur of the Rift Valley across the whole region provides the most splendid scenic beauties. Many of the internal drainage basins in this rift valley we now know provided the few habitation sites suitable for early man.

Broadly speaking, the greater part of East Africa forms an upland plateau region of over 3 000 feet [1 000 m] above sea level. This upland region rises to 19 340 feet (5 895 m) on the Uhuru peak of Mount Kilimanjaro to provide the highest landmark in Africa. Thus, although East Africa is in an equatorial region, altitude enables large parts of it to experience very little of the unpleasant conditions of the true equatorial zones.

In detail, East Africa has a complicated and highly diversified topography which, however, can be broken down into a series of plateau-like surfaces ranging in height from about 1 200 feet [400 m] above sea level,

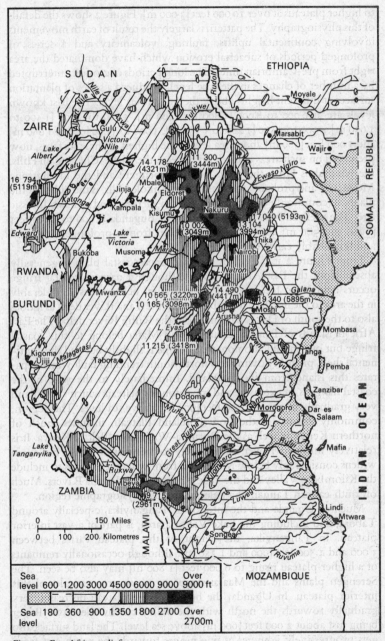

SUDAN

ETHIOPIA

ZAIRE

Moyale

Gulu

Marsabit

Wajir

Lake
Albert

Kafu

14 178
(4321m)

11 300
(3444m)

16 794
(5119m)

Mbale

Eldoret

17 040 (5193m)

Jinja

Nakuru

Katonga

Kampala

Kisumu

13 104
(3994m)

10 002
(3049m)

Thika

Edward

Lake
Victoria

Nairobi

Bukoba

Musoma

Mara

RWANDA

Natron

BURUNDI

Mwanza

14 490
(441m)

10 565 (3220m)

19 340 (5895m)

10 165 (3008m)

Moshi

L. Eyasi

Arusha

Mombasa

11 215 (3418m)

Kigoma
Ujiji

Malagarasi

Tabora

Pemba

Zanzibar

Dodoma

Morogoro

Dar es
Salaam

Lake
Tanganyika

Mafia

Rukwa

Mbeya

9 715
(2961m)

ZAMBIA

Lindi

0   150 Miles

Mtwara

0   100   200 Kilometres

MALAWI

Songea

Ruvuma

MOZAMBIQUE

SOMALI REPUBLIC

INDIAN OCEAN

Sea
level 600 1200 3000 4500 6000 9000 Over
9000 ft

Sea   180 360 900 1350 1800 2700 Over
level   2700m

Figure 2 East Africa: relief

25

to higher plateaus at over 10 000 feet [3 000 m]. Figure 2 shows the details of this physiography. The pattern is largely the result of earth movements involving continental uplifts, faulting, volcanicity and a series of prolonged periods of subaerial erosion which have dominated the area right from pre-Cambrian times. The long periods of erosion, interrupted by a number of changes in the base level, produced a series of plantation surfaces at different heights above the present sea level. The best known levels are at 6 000 to 8 000 [1 800 to 2 400 m], 5 000 to 5 500 [1 500 to 1 650 m], 4 000 to 4 500 [1 200 to 1 350 m], 3 000 to 3 600 [900 to 1 080 m] and 1 000 feet [300 m] above sea level. The highest of these surfaces, now preserved on such areas as the Kisii plateau, the Kitale-Cherangani Hills, the Machakos Hills, the crests of the Kipengere and the Livingstone Mountains and probably the crest of the Ankole Hills, is the oldest of the plateaus (commonly called the Gondwana surface), and is of late Jurassic age. The well-known, uplifted plateau of Buganda (4 000 to 4 300 feet [1 200 to 1 300 m] above sea level), results from a prolonged standstill and is probably early Tertiary in age.

From Figure 2 it is evident that a proper coastal plain is generally absent from the East African coast, although a narrow coastal fringe occurs below 600 feet [180 m]. This narrow belt widens considerably in the area to the north of Mombasa along the Tana River delta as it does also to the south of Dar es Salaam about the Rufiji River delta. The East African islands of Pemba, Zanzibar and Mafia belong to this coastal fringe but one should also note that Pemba is slightly beyond the continental shelf, probably owing to a north-south trending fault which separates this island from the mainland. Immediately to the west of the coastal fringe is an extensive and monotonous plateau which rises inland very gradually to about 3 000 feet [900 m] above sea level. This region, commonly known as the Low Foreland Plateau, includes much of northern Kenya as well as the Duruma-Wajir Low Belt of Kenya. It is relatively much narrower immediately to the west of Tanga but again widens considerably below Morogoro from where it extends to include the Kilombero Valley and the valleys of the Great Ruaha Rivers. Much of south-eastern Tanganyika belongs to this physiographic region.

Much of Uganda and the interior of Tanganyika, especially around Tabora, and including the Lake Victoria area, is part of a vast interior plateau. In Tanganyika, the height of this plateau varies between 3 000 and 4 500 feet [900 and 1 350 m], although occasionally remnants of a higher plateau rising to 6 000 feet [1 800 m] may also be seen. The Serengeti plains and the Maasai steppe or plains are examples of this interior plateau. In Uganda, the height of the plateau decreases very gradually towards the north with the valley cut by the Aswa River being just about 2 000 feet [600 m] above sea level. The land surface also gets progressively younger as one moves towards the north-east from an early Tertiary surface in Buganda to a Miocene level in Kyoga and finally a Pliocene level in Acholi. Some authors delimit the land immediately marginal to Lake Victoria as a separate region but this distinction may be unnecessary from the point of view of physiography. The slight downwarp towards the lake basin—the latest of the 'swell and basin' structure of Africa—has been noted. The present basin is almost certainly a post mid-tertiary feature.

Besides the Interior Plateau, much of Central Kenya, parts of the Northern and Southern Highlands of Tanganyika, a great part of south-western Uganda and the imposing horst block of the Ruwenzori mountains form highland areas which are clearly in a separate class. These highlands rise from about 4 500 [1 350 m] to 19 340 feet [5 895 m], the highest point on the Kibo peak of Kilimanjaro. Although these highlands are largely due to the great thickness of volcanic materials extruded since mid-Tertiary times, ancient upland massifs are also still preserved, and these erosional upland plateaus form the Gondwana planation surfaces that we have already noted. The Central Highlands of Kenya are bisected almost equally by the meridional trench of the eastern branch of the East African Rift Valley. The highlands on either side of the Rift Valley are dominated by individual ranges which deserve noting. The Aberdare Range, rising to over 13 000 feet [3 900 m], and the Ngong Hills dominate the eastern portion. The western sections of these volcanic cones were downthrown together with the Rift Valley. To the north-east of the Aberdare Range is the majestic volcanic pile formed by the composite volcano of Mount Kenya, with the Nyeri corridor forming a useful gap between the two. Continuing in the same direction is the Nyambeni Range, a relatively smaller cone that may have been formed by a feeder connected to the main Mount Kenya reservoir.

The western portion of the Central Kenya Highlands is dominated by the Mau Range with its prominent escarpment, the Kericho Highlands, and the Tinderet Hills, which continue through the Uasin Gishu Plateau to link with the other central volcano of Mount Elgon. These volcanic highlands join imperceptibly with the resistant residual hills of the Cherangani in the Elgeyo-Marakwet areas to form one extensive highland environment. Portions of these upstanding areas have also been downthrown into the floor of the Rift Valley in a similar way to the Eastern Highlands.

The highlands of Northern Tanganyika are mainly of volcanic origin and are dominated by a number of peaks amongst which Ngorongoro Crater at 10 165 feet [3 098 m], Jaeger Summit at 10 565 feet [3 220 m] and Loolmalasin at 11 965 feet [3 647 m] are the most important. The area illustrates especially well the altitudinal influence of climate, in that, although the surrounding area is almost arid, the highland region has

27

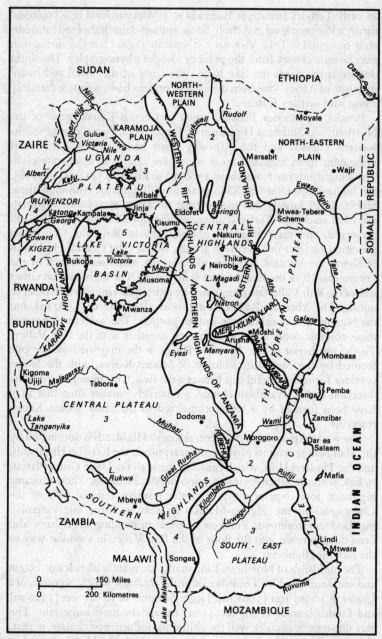

Figure 3 Major physiographic regions

developed a temperate climate in the heart of the tropics. Mount Kilimanjaro is really made up of three different volcanic cones each of which erupted at a different time but along one line of structural weakness. Shira Cone (at 13 140 feet [4 005 m]), probably erupted during the Miocene era. It was followed by the Mawenzi Cone (now 16 900 feet [5 151 m]) probably during Pliocene times; Kibo Cone (now 19 340 feet [5 895 m]) is clearly the youngest, and is generally believed to be a Quaternary feature. The different ages of these three peaks are clearly confirmed by their varying degrees of erosion. Shira, the oldest, is much dissected and reduced by erosive agencies while Kibo is still relatively intact.

Like central Kenya, the Southern Highlands of Tanzania have a complex topography in which Gondwana planation surfaces and Cainozoic lava highlands occur together. The Kipengere Range, the Livingstone Mountains in the Njombe area, the Udzungwa Range in Iringa and the Fipa Plateau between Lake Rukwa and the southern portion of Lake Tanganyika are ancient massifs in which some of the oldest erosion surfaces to be found in Africa are still preserved. Volcanic materials, on the other hand, are confined to the Rungwe Mountains between Mbeya township and the northern tip of Lake Nyasa. The eruption extruded from the point of intersection of a number of faults as can be seen from Figure 1. Such an eruption is quite common in volcanic areas where lines of weakness also occur. The highlands of Kigezi in Uganda are, of course, part of the volcanic province of Rwanda while the highlands to the west of Bukoba are due to the hard and resistant Karagwe-Ankolean rocks which outcrop in these parts. The Ruwenzori massif is an unusual horst block that was uplifted during the time of tectonic disturbances and is now preserved in the floor of the western Rift Valley.

The East African Rift Valley deserves further attention. Over much of central Kenya its average width is between 20 and 40 miles [32 and 64 km] and its floor varies from 1 230 feet [375 m] above sea level in Lake Rudolf to about 6 000 feet [1 800 m] around Nakuru. From here, the level of the floor drops southwards to 1 900 feet [579 m] in Lake Magadi. Past the Kenya border, the rift bifurcates, with the southern continuation delimiting the Northern Highlands of Tanzania, making them into another horst-like massif. We should note also that the Pangani River valley is essentially a continuation of the same system of the East African Rift Valley, the resistant Usambara and Pare mountains forming another mountain block, although details of the fault trends involved have not yet been fully investigated.

The western arm of the Rift Valley is complicated. From the point of tectonic intersection centred around the Rungwe Mountains, the north-eastern trough forms the Great Ruaha Valley while the north-western arm contains Lake Rukwa and the Karu Plains. Another parallel counterpart of this arm defines the Lake Tanganyika trough. It is this Lake Tanganyika trough which continues northwards to include Lake Albert at 2 030 feet [619 m] above sea level. The magnitude of the downthrow in the valley now infilled by Lake Tanganyika may be judged from the fact that Lake Tanganyika is the second deepest lake in the world.

The general form of the Rift Valley floor also merits examination. Its entire length is studded by a number of saline lakes which are known to be remnants of much larger water bodies that collected in this depression during the wetter phases (pluvials) associated with the last glaciation. In Kenya the lakes are Rudolf, Baringo, Nakuru, Elmenteita, Naivasha and Magadi. Just beyond the Kenya border is situated Lake Natron and further down along the south-western arm of the rift is situated Lake Eyasi, with Lake Manyara occupying the south-eastern arm. The western branch of the Rift Valley has fewer but much larger lakes as can be seen in Figure 2. The reasons for this may be greater initial downthrows and a higher rainfall. The Rift Valley floor is also characterised by a number of subsequent volcanic cones of which the Menengai Crater and Mounts Longonot and Suswa are particularly important.

The East African climate

Highly varied climatic difference is one of the outstanding facts about East Africa, the result of large altitudinal range, the distribution of land and water, land barriers, air movements and ocean currents. The environment is dominated at different times of the year by a number of air-masses and the climate is largely influenced by the character of the source regions from which these originate and by the tracts of country across which they blow. The dominance of a particular air-mass over the region is controlled largely by the apparent movement of the overhead sun between the two tropics, and this provides a convenient basis for an analysis of the East African climate.

From November to March, the main air-stream affecting East Africa is from the north and north-east which, because of its source, is a dry air-mass. Its drying influence is particularly marked in the western extremities of East Africa where, as the 'Harmattan' or 'Egyptian air', it blows from a high pressure belt across the Sahara. Over the eastern parts of the area the air-mass, known as the Arabian or Indian North-East Trade Winds or as the North-East Monsoon, is a less drying maritime variety which may bring some precipitation, as we shall note later.

By April, the wind pattern has considerably changed and the region comes under the influence of the Indian Ocean South-East Trade Winds. This air-mass coming from a vast ocean area is moisture-laden and the source of the main rains over East Africa. The air-mass blows steadily, reaching its maximum force in July when there is a low pressure belt in the northern hemisphere. When these winds cross the Equator they approach the Arabian peninsula and India as the South-West Monsoon.

This alternation of wind systems provided a natural facility for the early contacts which were established between the south-west Asian sub-continent and the East African coast. The Arabs and Indians were able to take advantage of the steady North-East Monsoon winds to sail their dhows to East Africa, to trade in the area while waiting for the onset of the South-West Monsoon winds for the return voyage with their acquired merchandise. Some degree of this traffic is still undertaken, without any appreciable improvements to the manner of construction of the dhows. The historical significance of this early contact will be apparent in later chapters but we may note here the geographical origin of much permanent human record in the coastal belt of Arabic and Asiatic cultures that are very different from those of the East African interior.

(i) Rainfall

It has been shown that the South-East Trades are responsible for the main rains over much of East Africa, but the coastal zones of the region that lie to the south of the Equator also get some rain from the North-East Trades, especially where this air-mass has crossed a wide area of the Indian Ocean. Also, parts of western Uganda get some rain from Atlantic Ocean or Congo airstreams during the northern summer, and Lake Victoria is extensive enough to generate its own maritime climate.

Although the northerly air-masses are drying and not rain-bearing, they are important in that the rains are associated with the zone of convergence between the northerly and south-easterly and indeed the south-westerly (Congo) airstreams. This zone of convergence is conventionally known as the Inter-tropical Convergence Zone (ITCZ), and since its actual position over East Africa is dependent on the position of the overhead sun, the seasonal distribution of rainfall over East Africa also follows this apparent movement of the sun. As a result of the above situation, three distinct rainfall seasons occur over East Africa. A regime of equatorial character occurs broadly over much of the northern parts of East Africa to about 3°S. over the higher parts of the region and to about 7°S. along the coastal belt. In the coastal belt, a single peak, usually about May, is evident, but inland, a double peak, between

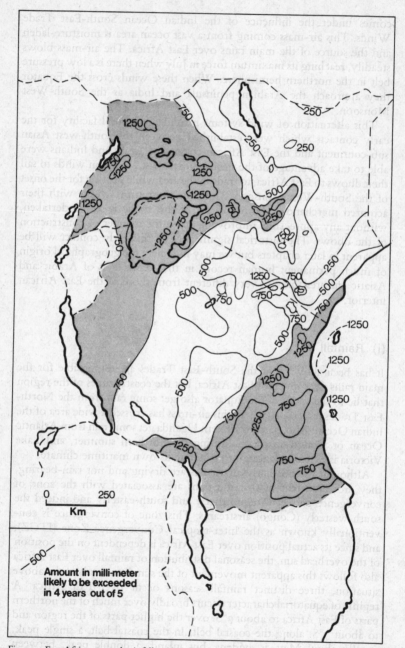

Figure 4 East Africa: annual rainfall probability

March and May and from mid-October to December, is the pattern. These are respectively the long and the short rains of East Africa. On either side of this equatorial regime, there is a tendency towards a single rainy season and a single dry season. Most of Tanzania and the coastal areas that lie to the south of Dar es Salaam, for instance, have only one rainy season extending from about December to April, the rest of the year being one long dry season. In the northern parts of East Africa, the rainy seasons also tend to coalesce to give a five months' rainy season with July as the wettest month in Uganda. In Northern Kenya the physiography, especially in the high volcanic conical hills such as Mount Kulal and the Marsabit cones, causes localised rainfall differences and such areas tend towards the equatorial-type regime with a discernible double peak, in April and November.

Relief and inland water bodies, we have noted, greatly influence the amount of rainfall received in various places. A glance at the mean annual rainfall map will confirm this fact especially if it is read in conjunction with the relief map. Highland areas stand out as better-watered islands in an essentially underwatered region. For example, in Northern Kenya, the isolated volcanic cones such as Marsabit and Mount Kulal receive much higher rainfall totals than the surrounding steppe or semi-arid and arid plains. As one ascends higher, frost may be encountered from about 7 000 feet [2 100 m] above sea level while glaciers are permanent on the three major East African mountains above about 15 000 feet [4 500 m]. Also the large water surface of Lake Victoria (26 826 square miles [68 081 km²]), modifies the local climate of the areas immediately peripheral to the lake shores, making them some of the best-watered parts of East Africa. The western, northern and the eastern shores are relatively wetter, with an annual mean from 40 to 80 inches [1 000 to 2 000 mm].

That East Africa suffers from an insufficient rainfall is an important fact worthy of emphasis. J. F. Griffiths gives a vivid picture of the seriousness of this problem when he shows that nearly two-thirds of East Africa suffers from a drought of six months or more and that only 2 per cent of the entire area is assured of a mere 2 inches [50 mm] of rainfall in every month. Given this unsatisfactory situation and given the fact that much of East Africa is essentially agricultural, mean rainfall totals are of relatively minor significance. Clearly greater consideration from the point of view of planned farming must be given to the twin factors of rainfall reliability and probability. Figure 4 gives the rainfall probability based on a five year cycle and here again the inadequacy of the rainfall is alarming. Griffiths again shows that 72 per cent of Kenya, 13 per cent of Uganda and 16 per cent of Tanzania can expect less than 20 inches [500 mm] of rainfall in four out of every five years. He also states conclusively that only 3 per cent of Kenya, 6 per cent of Uganda and 4 per cent of Tanzania can expect more than 50 inches [1 250 mm]

33

of rainfall in four years out of every five. Taking the overall picture in East Africa, 35 per cent of the area can expect less than 20 inches [500 mm] in four out of five years; 20 per cent can expect between 20 and 30 inches [500 and 750 mm]; 41 per cent of the area is likely to get between 30 and 50 inches [500 and 1 250 mm]; and only 4 per cent of the entire area can expect more than 50 inches [1 250 mm] in four years out of five. Although the above picture shows the region as unfavourably placed, it presents but an aspect of the problem. Besides this apparent water shortage, there is the related factor of unreliability, a major characteristic of the rainfall over the entire area. This unreliability concerns both the total amount and the time of arrival and is a phenomenon that applies to much of Africa. The table below will help to convey the situation better.

Table 2   *Summary of rainfall in inches [mm] over selected East African stations*[1]

Station	Maximum		Mean		Minimum	
Wajir	20	[513]	10	[249]	3	[74]
Nairobi	62	[1 570]	35	[879]	17	[437]
Mombasa	74	[1 887]	47	[1 204]	28	[709]
Kigoma	48	[1 214]	37	[935]	26	[658]
Tabora	51	[1 303]	34	[866]	15	[391]
Mwanza	59	[1 486]	41	[1 046]	28	[721]
Gulu	80	[2 035]	61	[1,544]	39	[1 004]
Fort Portal	86	[2 118]	58	[1 478]	42	[1 067]
Entebbe	89	[2 261]	59	[1 506]	38	[998]

Besides the above disadvantages, and the usually torrential nature of the rains, loss through run-off is correspondingly high and, combined with a generally high evaporation rate, further reduces the value of the rainfall for agricultural purposes.

(ii) Temperature

Besides the winds and the rainfall, other important elements of the weather which must be taken into consideration in the study of climate are temperature, humidity, sunshine and cloudiness. The first two are particularly important for human comfort. Altitude keeps temperature and humidity at a lower level, suitable for man. Coastal areas, however, are much hotter and more humid: the mean temperatures for Mombasa

[1] The source for Tables 2 to 5 is the *E.A. Economic and Statistical Review*, 1967.

and Dar es Salaam are 26.3°C and 25.7°C respectively; humidity in the area is invariably between 79 and 82 per cent. The mean diurnal and annual ranges of temperature are relatively small along this coastal belt, chiefly owing to the constantly high relative humidity. As one moves inland into the higher plateaus, the relative humidity drops as does the temperature, and the temperature ranges, both diurnal and annual, are much larger, though not as great as in the semi-desert areas. The table below gives a summary for a number of selected stations, and we should note here that the relatively lower temperatures in the interior highlands served as an attraction for European settlement in that area.

Table 3   Summary of temperature (°C) over selected East African stations

Station	Absolute maximum	Mean maximum	Mean	Mean minimum	Absolute minimum
Wajir	39.5	33.6	27.9	22.1	15.0
Nairobi	32.2	25.6	19.1	12.7	5.4
Mombasa	37.3	30.3	26.3	22.4	14.1
Kigoma	36.8	27.8	23.5	19.2	13.2
Tabora	35.7	29.5	23.1	16.7	7.0
Mwanza	35.0	27.7	22.7	17.7	10.8
Gulu	37.2	29.3	23.1	16.9	9.3
Fort Portal	31.8	25.3	19.1	12.8	5.6
Entebbe	31.7	25.9	21.5	17.1	10.4

To summarise, a major feature of the prevailing climate over East Africa is water shortage, the result of an inadequate and unreliable rainfall. Altitude modifies the climate considerably: a Tropical Highland climate over the East African Highlands culminates in permanent snow above 15 000 feet [4 500 m]. Thus the East African climate exhibits a great diversity, which although providing man with an opportunity for diversification of his activities must be regarded as essentially harsh, since so much of the environment is hot and arid or semi-arid.

Vegetation and soils

Figure 5 gives a simplified pattern of the vegetation over East Africa. It is clear that, owing largely to a lower rainfall and partly to the long established impact of man, the coastal areas of East Africa are covered not by a true Equatorial Forest vegetation but by a poorer Coastal Forest Savanna Mosaic in which the forests and the savanna grasses are less tall except along river valleys where mangrove forests and swamps also occur. Woodland Savanna Mosaic consists of scattered tree grasslands of low tree and high grass. This vegetation type is a wooded savanna complex in which either moist acacia savanna or combretum savanna may be dominant; in Kenya acacia-themeda is an important member. The Tropical Forest Savanna on the other hand is dominated in most places by elephant grass with only isolated remnants of forest. In montane and highland communities of grasslands and forests, the parts actually forested are few in contrast with wide expanses of undulating grasslands in which themeda triandra and Kikuyu grass dominate. Cedar and olive trees are much in evidence, especially in the lower sections of the forests, but bamboo forests become more important between 9 000 and 10 000 feet [2 700 and 3 000 m]. Beyond 10 000 feet [3 000 m], a mountain moorland is reached; this in turn is replaced by glaciers from about 15 000 feet [4 500 m] on Mount Kenya and 16 000 feet [4 800 m] on Kilimanjaro.

From the vegetation map, it is evident that over many of the drier parts of Kenya and Tanzania, a dry bush with thorn trees, a wooded steppe with abundant acacia and commiphora, dominates. This bush-thorn vegetation gets progressively poorer as one penetrates deeper into the drier parts of northern Kenya until a true desert vegetation is reached in the Chalbi Desert. The dry bush-thorn vegetation is better known over much of East Africa as the *nyika*—a Swahili word for 'wilderness'. It forms a rough environment which was a major obstacle to early explorers endeavouring to penetrate into East Africa from the coastal belt. In addition to the thorn bush and thicket, lack of water and scorching heat within this 'wilderness' and the malaria of the coastal belt made the explorers' task extremely hard and dangerous.

Mention has been made of the role of man in modifying the original vegetation growth. This point needs some elaboration. Man as a cultivator and pastoralist has over a long period altered his environment as simply and as cheaply as his ability and understanding has enabled him. He soon discovered that African grasses (like the 'wire grass' of South Africa) become too tough for cattle to feed on, and need to be removed; annual bush fires were clearly the most effective and simple device. The damage which fire introduced did not seem to bother him particularly. The result of all this is that the present vegetation, especially below 6 500 feet [1 950 m], is probably all derived vegetation in which a fire-resistant variety dominates.

A note must also be made here on East African soils. Soil formation is intimately related to climate, geological formations, topography, living organisms and to the time factor. Time must be available for a mature soil profile to develop. Climate is certainly the most important of the above factors because it influences the rate of weathering, leaching

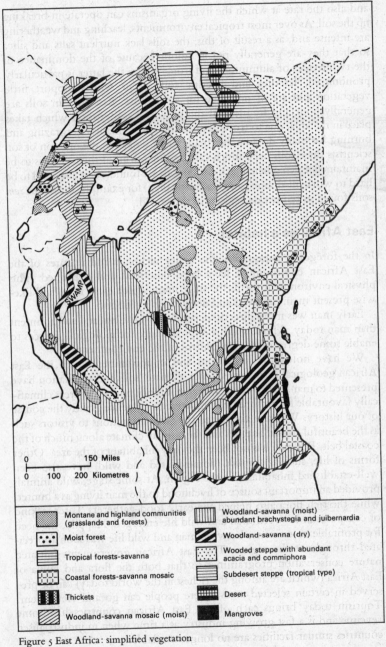

Figure 5 East Africa: simplified vegetation

Legend:

- Montane and highland communities (grasslands and forests)
- Moist forest
- Tropical forests-savanna
- Coastal forests-savanna mosaic
- Thickets
- Woodland-savanna mosaic (moist)
- Woodland-savanna (moist) abundant brachystegia and juibernardia
- Woodland-savanna (dry)
- Wooded steppe with abundant acacia and commiphora
- Subdesert steppe (tropical type)
- Desert
- Mangroves

Scale: 0 — 150 Miles; 0 — 100 — 200 Kilometres

37

and also the rate at which the living organisms can operate in breaking up the soil. As over most tropical environments, leaching and weathering are intense and, as a result of this, the soils lack nutrient salts and silica so that they are generally red in colour because of the dominance of the two oxides of aluminium and iron. Where the latter is particularly pronounced, laterites and lateritic soils occur which support little vegetation and are of no value for agriculture. East African soils are generally poor and fragile, and the powerful soil erosion which takes place in the area, due to tropical rains and also to man's overgrazing and burning for many decades, has made them worse. In the opinion of soil scientists these soils need much care and manuring if their yield is to be maintained. Even where black cotton soils are found, these also tend to be hard to work, ill-drained and less fertile than, for example, the *chernozem* soils found in temperate regions of the world.

East Africa as a habitat

In the foregoing paragraphs, the major elements and features of the East African environment have been described and explained. This physical environment forms the stage upon which early man, and likewise present man, has lived and derived his livelihood.

Early man was more directly dependent on this natural environment than man today, who has at his disposal more technological devices to enable some degree of human control of the environment.

We have noted the limitations and opportunities which the East African geological formations, relief, climate, soils and vegetation have presented to man. In this connection the interior pockets of areas climatically favourable for European living were to influence greatly the course of our history. We have also noted the other attractions to visitors such as the beautiful coastal beaches and the holiday climate along much of the coastal belt. But man has not been the only inhabitant of the area. Other forms of life, such as animals (domesticated and wild) have also been well-established inhabitants in the region. At some stage, wild animals provided an important source of livelihood to the man living as a hunter, while the rich flora also helped the early food-gatherers. Later, a kind of competition between man and wild life emerged. Happily, the need for profitable co-existence between man and wild life was soon appreciated throughout the region. The East African governments initiated nature conservation programmes so that both the flora and fauna of East Africa (which are among the richest in the world today) can be preserved in certain selected areas where people can go and view them. Tourism today brings each of the East African countries handsome revenue and is a fast growing industry at a time when in industrialised countries similar facilities are no longer available.

But the East African environment also provides a habitat for tsetse fly, which is a danger not only to man but also to his domesticated animals. The result is that large tracts of the country where these flies are found are virtually uninhabited. Different species of this fly cover two-thirds of mainland Tanzania, with the woodland tsetse *(glossina morsitans)* occupying large tracts of Central and Southern Highland Provinces.

Other species, and in particular vectors of the bovine strain, also make large parts of Lake and Northern Provinces unsafe for stock, while *Glossina pallidipes* makes large parts of the lake and the coastal areas unsafe for both man and his stock. In Kenya the shores of Lake Victoria, parts of the coastal belt and parts of the Meru and Tsavo river valleys harbour harmful species of the fly. In Uganda certain restricted parts of Ankole are known to be affected by dangerous species.

The final word about East Africa as a habitat must be an emphasis on the favourable influences which the East African highlands and their pleasant climates created in terms of habitability by the white man. The climate in parts of Kenya, Uganda and to a lesser extent Tanzania is ideal for European settlement. This fact was realised quite early, as demonstrated in the famous White Highlands and other alienated lands throughout the region. These formed the nuclei of a very well planned agricultural economy based on European farming standards which the independent African governments inherited. Also, the favourable climate encouraged non-Africans to make their homes in the region, and this, as will be shown, brought about planned urban growth and development almost unique in Africa. Many Europeans planned to live permanently in the White Highlands, in other alienated lands or in the towns of East Africa.

The population of East Africa[1]

The first census of the East African population was taken in 1948 and for those interested in the development of East Africa as one political or economic unit, it was the most important census year for the area, being the first occasion that the population of the whole of East Africa had been counted at the same time. Consequently, the 1948 population figures can be used effectively to compare the three countries. Since then, Tanzania has had another census in 1957, Zanzibar in 1958, Uganda in 1959 and Kenya in 1962. The table below summarises the population growth on a territorial basis. To enable a ready comparison of the population totals to be made, estimates have been given for each year where exact figures are not available.

[1] For a full account of the growth of the population of East Africa, see the chapter by J. G. C. Blacker in *The Natural Resources of East Africa* (see Further Reading, page 51).

39

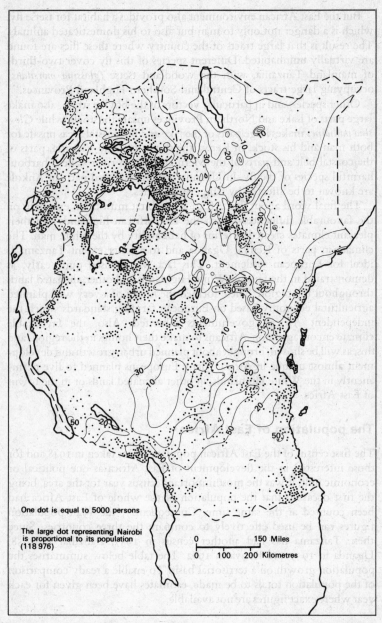

One dot is equal to 5000 persons

The large dot representing Nairobi
is proportional to its population
(118 976)

| 0 | 150 Miles |
| 0 | 100 | 200 Kilometres |

Figure 6 East Africa: population distribution as per 1948 census, and the mean annual
rainfall in inches

Table 4 Population figures in the East African countries

Mid year	Kenya	Uganda	Tanganyika	Zanzibar	East Africa
1948	5 407 599	4 958 520	7 480 429	265 000	18 111 548
1958	7 652 000	6 356 000	8 916 000	300 000	23 224 000
1960	8 115 000	6 677 000	9 237 000	308 000	24 337 000
1965	9 365 000	7 551 000	10 179 000	320 000	27 415 000
1969	10 504 000	8 526 000	12 957 000	355 000	32 342 000

The figures in the above table indicate a rapidly growing population of 3 per cent per annum in Kenya, 2.5 per cent in Uganda and 2.9 per cent in Tanzania. Zanzibar is the most densely populated area, with an average mean density of more than 360 persons per square mile [140 per km²]. The corresponding densities, in mid-1968, were: Kenya 45 per square mile [17 per km²]; Tanganyika (i.e. mainland Tanzania) 36 per square mile [14 per km²]; Uganda 108 per square mile [42 per km²]. The low figures for Kenya and Tanganyika are striking, but one must remember that large parts of these two countries are not favourable for human settlement because of the inadequacy of water.

Demographers are also interested in examining the composition of the population of a country. Table 5 gives the non-African population over East Africa between 1948 and 1965. What the figures do not show is the number of non-Africans who have since independence become citizens of the respective countries.

Table 5 Estimated non-African population in East Africa

Kenya

	Europeans	Indo-Pakistani	Arabs	Others
1948	30 800	100 000	24 400	3 400
1958	59 000	161 000	32 000	4 000
1960	61 000	169 000	34 000	4 000
1965	41 000	186 000	37 000	4 000

Uganda

1948	3 700	36 300	1 500	900
1958	10 400	69 600	1 900	2 200
1960	11 400	75 100	2 100	2 400
1965	9 000	85 900	2 100	2 200

41

Tanganyika				
1948	11 300	47 500	11 100	2 200
1958	21 200	80 900	21 400	4 100
1960	22 300	87 300	24 000	4 500
1965	17 300	85 900	25 600	4 200
Zanzibar				
1948	300	16 000	248 700[1]	290
1958	520	18 400	280 900[1]	340
1960	570	18 900	287 800[1]	350
1965	650	19 700	298 700[1]	360

[1] Includes the indigenous population, i.e. Arabs, mainland Africans and Comorians.

The numerical significance of the various non-African races in the respective countries of East Africa is, of course, related to the politico-historical development of each of these countries. It is an interesting case of history influencing human geography.

The distribution of the East African population over the entire area must now be traced. Figure 6 shows the distribution of the population using the 1948 census. The close influence of climate, and especially of rainfall, is clearly obvious from this map on which the mean annual rainfall has been superimposed. Three major regions of high population density are discernible. The concentration around the shores of Lake Victoria is particularly outstanding. Secondly, there is the coastal belt from below Mombasa to the Rufiji River including the outlying islands. Thirdly, there are the isolated islands of high densities in a number of well-watered interior highland areas. This last region includes the Kikuyu-Kamba and Embu cluster immediately to the north of Nairobi, the Arusha-Kilimanjaro-Usambara group; the cluster in the Mbeya area and the belt of high density running along the border with Rwanda and Burundi, including the Kigezi cluster and continuing as a well-defined belt with only minor interruptions up to West Nile and Madi. These clusters are even more emphatic in the 1962 population estimates plotted in Figure 7.

Urbanisation

Townscapes are, on the whole, a recent feature on the East African scene. Apart from the Bugandan capital, which had a population cluster amounting to a nucleated settlement, we must agree that East African towns as we know them today are an alien creation. The oldest towns are situated along the coast where the Arabic, Asiatic and European cultures came into contact very early. The result of this early cultural blending can be seen in the rather special urban landscapes typical of the East African coast. The majority of the African population still lives a rural

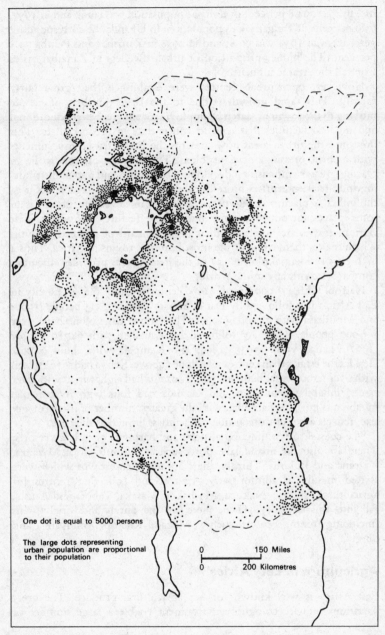

One dot is equal to 5000 persons

The large dots representing
urban population are proportional
to their population

0   150 Miles

0   200 Kilometres

Figure 7 East Africa: population distribution as per 1962 census estimates

43

life. In 1948, 94.8 per cent of Kenya's population was rural, and in 1957, 95.9 per cent of Tanganyika's population. In Uganda the corresponding percentage in 1959 was 96.8; and in 1958 in Zanzibar and Pemba 73.5 per cent. The higher proportion of urban dwellers in Zanzibar arises from all the Arabic influence.

However, once urban centres were established they grew fairly rapidly. This rapid growth is due to the large numbers of people moving to the towns in search of employment and the better educational and medical facilities that tend to concentrate in urban centres. This flow into the urban areas now presents the East African governments with a most pressing social problem. The solution appears to lie in placing greater emphasis on developing rural areas and also in distributing industrial enterprises more evenly over the whole region. As it is, the influx is placing undue pressure on urban development and is in some places introducing some undesirable features. However, East African towns are noted for their high standard of planned growth, which makes them some of the most beautiful towns in Africa. Thus a high class residential plot in any of the main towns provides amenities comparable with any in the world.

Nairobi with 478 000 people (1969 census) is easily the largest city in East Africa. It is followed by Dar es Salaam with 272 515 people (1967) and Mombasa with 236 000 (1969). These three cities alone have over 100 000 people. They are followed by Zanzibar with 68 380 people (1967), Tanga with 60 935 (1967) and Kampala with about 60 000. Besides the large urban centres mentioned above, Kenya had seven towns with over 10 000 inhabitants in 1969, Tanzania had eight towns with over 20 000 inhabitants in 1967, and Uganda had four with over 10 000 inhabitants in 1959. Tanzania, with the greatest number of towns of any size, reflects a better distribution of facilities, limited as they are.

The coastal towns function as ports and harbours or holiday resorts. There are also the inland lake ports such as Kisumu, Jinja, Mwanza, Kigoma and Bukoba. Thirdly, there are the inland towns which were started mainly as administrative centres and collecting centres for agricultural produce. Nakuru, Machakos, Masaka, Tabora and Arusha fall into this category. Then, there are the purely industrial towns (including mining centres) such as Magadi, Kilembe, Shinyanga and Singida.

Agriculture in East Africa

East Africa is well known for her agricultural produce. The great variations in her ecological environment enable a large number of

[1] Greater Kampala has a population of over 200 000.

44

different crops to do well. Colonial policies, including the decision to build railways and the introduction of both European farmer settlers in Kenya and Tanganyika and Arab clove growers in Zanzibar, helped to ensure a firm basis for agriculture. Many Kenyan settlers had no capital, so the government, in helping them with loans, committed itself to a sustained interest in their future. In Uganda there were no settlers but the generally richer soils and the Protectorate status of the country prompted the administration to encourage early African smallholders.

The hot humid coastal belt now specialises mainly in crops such as coconut, sisal, sugar cane, and cashew nuts. The cooler interior highlands (including the former white farming areas) specialise in coffee, tea, pyrethrum, wheat, barley and dairying. In the drier parts of Kenya large ranching estates are important. In Uganda, in the elephant grass zone, the main crops are cotton, robusta coffee, tea and sugar cane. The plantain banana is the main food crop here. In the short grass zone, annual cropping is the rule with cotton and groundnuts being dominant and cattle also being fairly common.

In Uganda, therefore, the main cash crops are coffee, cotton, sugar and tea; in Tanzania, sisal, cotton, coffee (mainly Arabica), cloves, cashew nuts, tea and groundnuts; and in Kenya, coffee (mainly Arabica), tea, pyrethrum, sisal, wattle bark and maize (and other cereals). Livestock products of butter, beef and milk are also extremely important in Kenya. Mineral products have been treated under geology above.

Transportation in East Africa

One of the problems which the colonising powers had to face during the scramble for Africa was the absence of any form of transport. They realised right from the start that basic transport facilities were a prerequisite for any other development. During the Berlin Conference of 1895, it was agreed that the construction of railways would help in suppressing the slave trade. It was also seen by the British as a vital means for linking with Uganda. Railway links were further seen as an important means of opening up trade, which in turn could pay for the railway.

(i) The railway system[1]

Figure 8 shows the historical progress of rail construction in the area. In Kenya and Uganda the work was done by the British, but in Tanganyika the early success story was the work of the Germans.

[1] The author wishes to acknowledge the help given to him by Mr Tom Matsalia of the East African Railways Corporation on the dates of rail construction and on Figure 8. However, the author alone is responsible for the opinions expressed here.

Developments in Kenya and Uganda

The first line of the Uganda Railway, as it was then known, was laid on 30 May 1896 at Mombasa. It reached Voi exactly one year later. Difficulties were encountered in the commiphora thicket in the Tsavo area, especially in 1898 when man-eating lions became a real menace. On 7 June 1900 they killed a railway superintendent of police. Twenty-eight Indian coolies and many Africans were also killed. The line eventually reached Nairobi on 30 June 1899. It reached Nakuru in 1900 after negotiating the difficult descent into the Rift Valley. The line finally reached Port Florence (later renamed Kisumu) on 20 December 1901.

The aim at the time was to reach Buganda. A steamer service to link Port Florence with Buganda was therefore a priority. The 1895 consignment of parts for the first boat was stolen at Lumbwa and the incident caused a delay of five years. It was not until June 1900 that S.S. *William Mackinnon* was launched on Lake Victoria. The connection with Port Bell was complete but the rail connection with Kampala, 7 miles [11 km] away was not completed until 1915. Towards the end of 1902 S.S. *Winifred* strengthened the services and in the latter part of 1905 S.S. *Sybil* was also commissioned. These steamers also served Jinja, from where a line was constructed northwards to Namasagali (the Busoga railway). It reached Namasagali in 1912.

From Nakuru it was necessary to have a link with the White Highlands. The rich farmlands of the Uasin Gishu and Kitale areas were being opened up. The line from Nakuru reached Eldoret in 1925 and was continued to Tororo in 1929. The line also reached Jinja in 1929 but the bridging of the Nile caused considerable delay, so that the line did not reach Kampala until 1931. This brought to a conclusion early efforts on the Uganda Railway. The services into the White Highlands, however, were also being extended during this period. The Nairobi-Thika line reached Thika in 1913. This line was originally a tramway and was for a while run by the Public Works Department. The Department found the operations too costly and had to hand the tramway over to the railway administration, which continued the line to Nanyuki in 1930. Meanwhile the rich soda precipitates on Lake Magadi had attracted the British Imperial Chemical Industries, which had formed the Magadi Soda Company. The company financed the construction of the Konza Magadi line as a company line which reached Magadi in 1915. In 1924, a branch line from Voi to Kahe linked with the Tanga line, and so brought the rich Kilimanjaro and Meru regions into the hinterland of Mombasa port. Further inland, the Rongai-Solai and Leseru-Kitale branch lines were opened during 1926.

The later rail developments in Uganda were all post-1950 undertak-

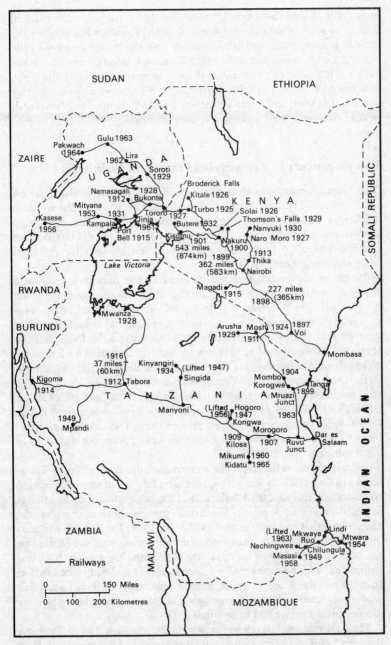

Figure 8 East Africa: dates of construction of main and branch railway lines

ings. The Kampala-Mityana-Kasese line (the copper line) reached Kasese in 1956. In the extreme north-west, the Pakwach line reached the Nile in January 1964, and in November 1969 the bridge across the Nile was opened to traffic and so brought West Nile into rail service. To the north of Jinja, one or two rational changes were effected: firstly Bukonte was linked with Jinja in 1961, shortening the Tororo-Kampala route by 50 miles [80 km]; and secondly the line from Mbulamuti to Namasagali was lifted during 1964 since it was uneconomical.

Developments in Tanganyika (Tanzania mainland)

The German contribution The early rail construction was done by the Germans. The basic economic considerations were similar to those for Kenya. The first survey work was on the Tanga line. This was started in 1891 and reached Korogwe in 1899 and Moshi in 1911. The Germans planted rubber, coconuts, sisal and cotton, and by 1903 the first sisal fibre was being exported.

Work on the central line started from Dar es Salaam in 1905 and the line eventually reached Kigoma in 1914. In the same year, the M.V. *Graft Von Goetzen* was launched on Lake Tanganyika. This provided a link with what was then known as Ruanda Urundi. The other priority line was to link Tabora with Mwanza and the Lake Victoria service. This was started in 1912 but the line had advanced for a distance of less than 40 miles [60 km] when the British defeated the Germans in 1918. During the war, the Germans tried to destroy M.V. *Graft Von Goetzen*, rather than surrender it to the British. What was left of it, the British were able to salvage and repair. The vessel was renamed S.S. *Liemba* and is still in service at the present time. The Germans also had plans to build a line from Kilwa towards Lake Nyasa but this was not accomplished.

The British contribution The granting of the trusteeship of Tanganyika to Great Britain was perhaps the most important factor in creating an awareness amongst the inhabitants of the region that they had things in common as East Africans. The British pressed ahead to complete the rail projects that had been started by the Germans. The Tabora-Mwanza line reached Mwanza in 1928, and in the following year the Moshi line reached Arusha. Later, in 1934, the Manyoni-Kinyangiri line was completed. This however proved uneconomical and had to be lifted in 1947. When the Kongwa groundnuts scheme was conceived a rail line was constructed to Hogoro through Kongwa in 1947, but when the project failed the line had to be lifted in 1956.

The next main rail development was in the southern part of Tanzania between Lindi and Nachingwea, and was opened to traffic in 1949. Ruo was then linked to Mtwara in 1954, and in 1958 a branch line was built from Chilungula to Masasi. Unfortunately, probably because of their remoteness and a restricted hinterland, these southern lines proved uneconomical. In 1963 they were lifted, although some people regarded them as a sound starting point for the eventual link with the Southern Highlands of Tanzania, Malawi and Zambia.

From the main central line, the Kilosa-Mikumi-Kidatu line was opened in 1965. The line had reached Mikumi in 1960. The other important link was from Ruvu Junction to Mnyusi, which linked the Tanga line with the central line to make the first complete grid with the Kenya Uganda system.

This completes the developments up to 1970. The system is single track, using a gauge of 3 feet 3⅜ inches [70 cm]. The growth has been quite significant. In 1933, East Africa had 2 979 miles [4 794 km] of rail line. By 1953, the service had extended to 3 100 miles [4 989 km] and in 1970, the total rail length in East Africa was 3 663 miles [5 895 km]. In 1969, the railway carried just over 7.5 million tons [tonnes] of public traffic and was served by 455 diesel and steam locomotives. Marine services had in 1970 a total of fifty-four craft, which included seven ships and two wagon ferries.

As stated above, the Ruvu Junction link with the Tanga line completed a grid. However, Lake Victoria had for a long while presented a problem since loaded wagons and engines could not continue from Kisumu through to Port Bell, Mwanza or Jinja, and a lot of time was lost in loading and offloading. This difficulty was overcome in October 1966 when two wagon ferries (M.V. *Uhuru* and M.V. *Umoja*) were introduced. At the same time, wagon ferry terminals were constructed at Kisumu, Musoma, Mwanza and Jinja.

The next major rail construction is the 1 000 mile [1 600 km] Tanzam railway which is to run from Dar es Salaam to Zambia (Kipiri Mposhi Station). This line, which will bring landlocked Zambia into the East African transport system, will be an important addition to the transport facilities in the region. It is planned on a gauge of 3 feet 6 inches [76 cm] and the Chinese People's Republic has agreed to provide the necessary loan (Zambian K286 million). The Chinese will help in the construction work and provide the locomotives and the rolling stock. The line will open up a large tract of what has been an isolated part of Tanzania. One would hope that it may at a later date be linked with the under-used Mtwara port. The railway's immediate effect will be to make Zambia's impending membership of the East African Community much more meaningful.

Another extension is planned to link Musoma with Arusha. Such a line would certainly step up the flow of traffic through Tanga.

(ii) Road, air, sea and other transport systems

Like the railways, road construction in East Africa has expanded considerably. With increasing traffic the generally poor state of the roads presents a serious concern to development planners. In 1967, there were nearly 229 000 licensed motor vehicles in East Africa. Kenya had 109 441, Tanzania 72 653, and Uganda 46 879. At the beginning, the roads acted as feeders to the railways but now road transport has developed in competition with the railways, in spite of the size of the region which would seem to favour the railway as the primary means of moving heavy traffic.

East Africa also has efficient air and sea transport facilities. Not only are the three international airports—Nairobi, Dar es Salaam and Entebbe—served by international air routes, but internal air transport is providing an important service to residents, visitors and businessmen alike. Mombasa's role as East Africa's most important harbour should be noted. Dar es Salaam is also important, as are Tanga and Mtwara although these last two ports have yet to be fully utilised. Lastly, we should not forget the vital role played by the East African postal and telecommunication services as well as the external telecommunication links.

Conclusion

An attempt has been made to describe the East African environment. The influence which this environment has played in conditioning human organisation has also been mentioned. The analysis of the influence of these factors on the course of historical development must be left to the historians. The sea, the few good natural harbours, the alternating monsoon winds, the modified tropical climate of the East African highlands, the few pockets of rich soils, have all been important in attracting European settlers to East Africa. Once the potential of East Africa as a farming area had been realised, and the demand for such crops as coffee, sisal, cotton, tea, pyrethrum, cereals, dairy produce and beef had been ascertained, the importance of East Africa as an agricultural region was established. The early establishment of the rail line ensured an early start, and we must add that to some extent the policies of the colonising countries, who intended to remain in the area for a long time to come, enabled more permanent development. The independent African governments thus inherited a well established and sound basic structure for further developments.

This survey has shown the diversity of the region. This diversity presents a wide range of opportunities and also some drawbacks. One of the main problems of the area is widespread water shortage. The presence of the tsetse fly should also be noted, as well as the generally poor soils. However, the picture commonly painted of a predominantly harsh environment has possibly been overstated.

Further reading

RUSSELL, E. W. (Ed.) *The Natural Resources of East Africa*, East African Literature Bureau, 1962.

H.M.S.O. *East African Royal Commission, 1953–1955, Report, Cmd 9475*, London, 1955.

OLIVER, R. and MATHEW, G. (Eds) *History of East Africa, I*, Oxford University Press, 1963, Baker, S. K. J., *The East African Environment*.

O'CONNOR, A. M. *An Economic Geography of East Africa,* G. Bell and Sons, 1966.

LOBECK, A. K. *Physiographic Diagram of Africa*, Columbia University Press, 1946.

KING, L. C. *South African Scenery*, Oliver and Boyd, 3rd Ed., 1963.

LEAKEY, L. S. B. *Adam's Ancestors*, Methuen and Co., 4th Ed., 1953.

OMINDE, S. H. *Population Movements to the Main Urban Areas of Kenya, Cahiers d'Etudes Africaines*, XX, Paris, 1966.

KEAY, R. W. J. *Vegetation Map of Africa South of the Tropic of Cancer*, Oxford University Press, 1959.

MONKHOUSE, F. J. *A Dictionary of Geography*, Edward Arnold, London, 1965.

EAST, W. G. *The Geography behind History*, Nelson, London, 1965.

Survey of Kenya, *Atlas of Kenya*, 1962.

Survey of Tanganyika, *Atlas of Tanganyika*, 3rd Ed., 1956.

Survey of Uganda, *Atlas of Uganda*, 1963.

East African Community, *Economic and Statistical Review*, (quarterly). (The statistics for the tables are from this source.)

3

The Prehistory of East Africa

Merrick Posnansky

Humanity during its existence has passed through several drastic and fundamental revolutions of economy and way of life but those which most readily come to mind are the more recent, the industrial and the scientific or atomic, by which mankind has harnessed the power of heat and the atom for technological progress. More fundamental, however, are those which closely affected man's very existence, the Neolithic or agricultural revolution by which man controlled his food supply, the urban revolution which led to the complexities of life in towns, and the human revolution. It is the last which is fundamental to our whole story, the revolution by which man emerged as a thinking being, capable of conceptual thought and of acquiring, assimilating, adapting and transmitting ideas from and to creatures of his own group. The human revolution was preceded by the evolution of the primates in which a hominid or group of hominids emerged capable, first of tool-using, and later of tool-making. The full description of this evolution is outside our scope though an outline must be attempted.

The Human revolution

In recent years, particularly since the accidental discovery by workmen, who thought it was a baboon, of the first of the *Australopithecines* or 'southern apes', at Taungs in the north-eastern part of Cape Province of South Africa in 1924, it has been realised that Africa can claim to hold most of the key information on human evolution. It has often been suggested that a missing link exists that would solve our problems and as each major discovery of fossil human material has been found newspapers have hailed the discovery as that of the 'missing link'. It would be far more truthful to say that it is the chain that is missing whilst the links exist. They have been joined in different ways at one time or another by the world's leading palaeontologists and it is the ease with which new chains or trees of evolution are built up which most clearly indicates how heavily we have to lean on the imperfections of the fossil record. Nevertheless, the relatively abundant discoveries of new fossil material in east, south and north Africa since 1930, and more precise dating methods, are enabling agreement to be reached as to the stages of human evolution and the timetable involved.

Man belongs to the Primates. His particular family is that of the *Hominidae*. Fossil remains have been found in East Africa that are particularly relevant to dating the sequence by which the *Hominidae* separated from the *Pongidae* (great apes, like the chimpanzee and the gorilla) and man developed from the *Hominidae* stock. It would appear from fossil evidence that the higher primates had their ultimate origin in an arc running from western Europe through Africa to south-east Asia, an area which still contains the largest number of species of present-day primates. As early as thirty million years ago two distinct groups had emerged belonging to the genus *Dryopithecus*, the ancestor of the apes and to *Ramapithecus* (and *Kenyapithecus*) an early hominid. From then on the evolution of each group went its own way. The *Proconsul* fossils, from around the Kavirondo gulf area, particularly Rusinga Island and Homa Mountain, and from Mounts Napak and Moroto in Karamoja, Uganda, belong to the *Dryopithecine* group and the *Kenyapithecus* fossils are probably related to the *Ramapithecus* group. It would appear that the differences between the two families were at that time not as marked anatomically as they are at present. There is still much disagreement between scientists as to the exact names to give to these various early fossil ancestors of man, and all we can definitely say is that fossil bones of ancestors of both the apes and hominids have been found. Unfortunately the number of fossil finds, except for the *Proconsul* material, are few and scattered over a vast period of time, with most being represented by small jaw or skull fragments and virtually no evidence of such bones as the pelvis, feet and spine which can indicate methods of locomotion and the degree of erect posture, so valuable for re-constructing their appearance and mode of life.

It would appear that from between twenty and thirty million years ago to two or three million years ago the main development was of bipedalism. Different hypotheses have been advanced to explain why an erect posture and two-legged walk (bipedalism) developed. It is possible that the reduction of forest cover in Miocene and Pliocene times, some thirty to twenty million years ago, meant that previously tree-living primates had to adapt themselves to a savanna environment. Part of this adaptation involved defence against carnivores. The small primates, poorly equipped to face the larger predators, had to look up over the tall grass on their hind legs to see if their way was clear. The departure from a forest environment possibly also led to the beginning of hunting, as the savanna provides less obvious protein than the forest with its berries, leaves and fungi.

What, however, are more important than the reasons for bipedalism are its effects. Bipedal locomotion freed the hands. The hands were able to evolve as specialised units, the thumb became separated and the fingers more adaptive. The first bipedal creatures that we know of were the *Australopithecines* of which now over three hundred specimens, comprising over a hundred individuals, have been found in South Africa, East Africa and the Tchad area.

At Olduvai Gorge in Tanzania, the most famous and certainly the most important early stone age site in the world, Dr and Mrs Leakey in 1959 excavated a magnificently preserved skull which they called *Zinjanthropus*, Man of Zinj, which is the name by which the East African coast was known in medieval times. Because of its excessively large crushing and grinding molars it was nicknamed 'the nutcracker man'. It has since been realised that this fossil belongs to the *Australopithecines*.

The *Australopithecines* had a small brain, around 27–34 cubic inches [450–550 cc] compared to our own of around 92 cubic inches [1 500 cc]. Two main groups of *Australopithecines* have been distinguished, one of a robust stock which was perhaps largely vegetarian, whilst the other was more graceful and individuals were perhaps no taller than 4 feet [1 m 22 cm], had no forehead but a ridge of bone along the skull and a marked bony brow. The lower jaw was massive, with particularly large molars, and comparatively small incisors and canines, which suggest a predominantly vegetarian diet. These teeth demanded a heavy jaw and muscles to support that jaw and the thick skull bones provided support for those muscles. Altogether fragments of nearly twenty individuals have been found at Olduvai, near Lakes Natron and Eyasi, in the Omo Valley in Southern Ethiopia, close to the Kenyan border, and most recently at a site east of Lake Rudolf. Potassium argon dating, an isotopic method in which the decay of the radioactivity of the argon in the deposit containing the fossils is measured, has been used at Olduvai to provide a date between $1\frac{1}{2}$ and $1\frac{3}{4}$ million years for the *Australopithecines*, whilst at Omo and east of Lake Rudolf new dates between $2\frac{1}{2}$ and 4 million years for fossil material indicate that the *Australopithecines* had an ancestry of several million years stretching back into Pliocene times.

Figure 9 Principal stone age sites in East Africa

Man, the tool-maker

Contemporaneous with *Australopithecus* in East Africa was another hominid called *Homo habilis*, 'the skilful man' who was the first systematic tool-maker and some authorities would say the direct ancestor of modern man. Six representatives of *Homo habilis* have been found at Olduvai. It was a creature with a bigger brain than *Australopithecus*, perhaps nearly 43 cubic inches [700 cc], and both hand and foot bones have been found belonging to it. Some palaeontologists however suggest that *Homo habilis* represents only a more developed *Australopithecine* rather than a separate genus.

The significance of the *Australopithecines* is that they have been found associated with the first true tools. There is at present no ideal way of demonstrating when an advanced hominid with erect posture walking on two feet can be called man except by pointing to the regular manufacture of tools for a preconceived purpose. Language was once thought of as one of the criteria of man but this is something on which the palaeontologists can never provide information. Language would seem to have a secondary importance; in itself it was a man-made tool for transmitting ideas. It has been suggested that as all the present peoples of the world use only a limited range of sound in their languages, and yet are capable of a wider range, that there was one single original centre of language and thus of mankind. The ability to make a wide range of sounds developed because of the greater flexibility allowed to the vocal chords when the angle between throat and mouth widened on the assumption of an erect posture. The size of brain was formerly also suggested as an indication of man but the brain size of the *Australopithecines* falls within the range of the great apes and not of modern man. Modern apes have been observed to use and to make tools. We can only accept as proof of conceptual thought the regular process of making tools and using them to carry out preconceived purposes. It is almost certain that man first progressed from a tool-using to a tool-making stage. First he would find that a sharp stone was useful for sharpening a piece of wood or cutting a bough off a tree or taking meat from the bone of an already dead creature. Later, whenever he wanted to carry out a similar task he would look around for a sharp stone. It was only a relatively short cut to improving on nature and making one's own tools.

But, why, we might ask, should this have occurred to one group of the hominids. By around two million years ago in the relatively open environment of the Transvaal and the Eastern Rift Valley region of East Africa, the *Australopithecines* had emerged as erect bipedal creatures. Their hands which were useless for defence were free to develop manipulative skills. Two of these skills which have been distinguished are the power grip, in which man tightly grips a stone, and the precision grip, when he uses his tools for delicate work by holding his tool between the thumb and forefinger. During the human revolution only the power grip was developed though during the earlier parts of the stone age the precision grip developed. Man at the beginning was not very dextrous. In the fairly open country he was vulnerable to attack and he needed to protect himself in different ways. One form of protection was to develop as a community and another was to pass from the tool-using to the tool-making stage. Both eventually became complementary features of the human revolution. Tools became extensions of the body and just as essential. Without tools to create weapons and the implements which would help procure a food supply, the *Australopithecines* would have remained just another primate group, becoming specialised to an environment and ultimately becoming susceptible and vulnerable to ecological change. The human revolution essentially implies a change from susceptibility to adaptability.

The *Australopithecines* were at first little better than scavengers competing for carrion with other scavengers like the jackal and the hyaena and making use of accessible edible fruits. One advantage may have been their bipedalism which allowed them to run away with stolen meat. Even scavenging would have needed group activity, particularly when predators were around. Primate teeth are incapable of dealing quickly with tough raw meat and long bones and it was possible that in their camp sites, where bones would have accumulated, they first realised the value of the simple everyday raw materials and the usefulness of the sharp fractures in bone. Much of their food debris began to be utilised for the jobs at hand and occasionally for defensive and offensive weapons. But our only firm evidence comes from stone tools.

At Olduvai Gorge archaeological and geological research has indicated a 300 foot [90 m] thick sequence of lake deposits which have been exposed by the cutting of the gorge. The lake basin was somewhat tilted and the waters were shallow, so that creatures lived around the edge in what was a relatively dry area. The region is now noted for its extinct volcanoes but when the lake existed at the edge of the Serengeti plain they were still active. Deposition of the fine volcanic tuffs and unconsolidated material from the foot of the volcanoes was rapid and we have no reason to suppose that the vegetation was such as to afford more than the minimum stabilisation of the loose deposits. The lake persisted from before Pleistocene times (2 to 3 million B.C.) until 50 000 to 100 000 B.C. All the time its waters fluctuated, leaving broad shore areas at times high and dry and at other times submerged by shallow waters. From the geological composition of the deposits five distinct beds have been differentiated, four of the age of the lake basin and the fifth being the infilling of the gorge cut through at the end of the

FIGURE 10 TABLE OF STONE AGE EVENTS

GEOLOGICAL PERIOD	YEARS	HUMAN & PRE-HUMAN TYPES	STONE AGE INDUSTRIES	IMPORTANT SITES	REMARKS
	1500 AD			Nyero (Uganda)	Period of latest use of stone – many rock paintings of this age
	500			Nsongezi rockshelter	Spread of Bantu-speaking agriculturalists
	0 BC	IRON AGE	(NEOLITHIC STONE-BOWL CULTURES)	Hyrax Hill Nakuru	
	1500		WILTON	Magosi	First spread of pastoralism
		CAUCASOIDS TRICKLE IN FROM NORTH EAST	KENYA CAPSIAN		
	6000		STILLBAY (POINTS)	Ishango Gamble's Cave	Specialised foraging Communities developing
		DEVELOPMENT OF PRESENT DAY AFRICAN RACES (BUSH-BOSKOPOIDS) ? BIG BUSHMEN	LUPEMBAN	Gilgil River Kinangop (Kenya)	First systematic burials
LATE	10 000	HOMO SAPIENS	SANGOAN	Nsongezi Sango Bay (Uganda)	Fire and new tool-making techniques make man more adaptable
MID	50 000		SPECIALISED TOOLS COMPOSITE TOOLS		

PLEISTOCENE

Period	Date	Hominid	Tools	Sites	Notes
EARLY PLEISTOCENE (STONE)	300 000	HOMO ERECTUS (PITHECANTHROPUS)	STANDARDISED TOOLS — ACHEULEAN (HAND-AXES etc.)	Nsongezi (Uganda) Olorgesailie (Kenya) Isimila and Olduvai (Tanzania)	Full development of hand axe industries Prehistoric fauna different from present
	750 000				First spread of man into Europe and Asia
	1 500 000	AUSTRALOPITHECINES (AND HOMO HABILIS)	OLDOWAN 'Chopping tools' FIRST TOOLS	Olduvai Peninj Garusi (fossils only) Omo East Rudolf Koobi Fora	← The human revolution →
PLIOCENE	3 000 000	RAMAPITHECUS (KENYAPITHECUS)		Omo Fort Ternan	Period of probable development of bipedal primates
MIOCENE	15 000 000 \ 30 000 000	DRYOPITHECUS (PROCONSUL)		Rusinga, Homa Mt, Napak Moroto	Partially bipedal primates emerging

mid-Pleistocene period. Earth movements were common in the area and largely explain why it disappeared, though it is probable that the infilling of several hundred thousand years played a significant part in its disappearance. As the deposits include large amounts of fresh volcanic material, the K/A or Potassium Argon method of dating has been employed for dating the sequence.

The stones found in the lowest levels exhibited a regular pattern of intentional flaking which allows them to be identified as tools. This identification is supported by the fact that the lake deposits are comparatively stoneless so that any stones had to be brought into the area, presumably for the purpose of tool-making. The associated bones comprised large numbers of small creatures, juvenile pigs and antelope, frogs, tiny reptiles and birds. Catfish, which often survive in fairly seasonal lakes and swamps, also seem to have been caught quite easily by the *Australopithecines* and even possibly by his predecessors. Of the long bones, the ends had been fractured in a way that clearly showed that the marrow had been extracted. It was significant that though many of the long bones bore signs of gnawing by carnivore teeth and all the bones were broken, the *Zinjanthropus* bones were intact, even the delicate facial bones, which would suggest that *Zinjanthropus* was not just another meal for a carnivore. Also from Bed I a windbreak of stones was found suggesting that these early 'men' built crude houses.

We can conclude that man presumably first made tools when he began to realise the usefulness of naturally sharp bones and stones. From being a scavenger he developed into a systematic hunter, though at the beginning only of small creatures like frogs, birds, lizards and the more easily caught antelopes. No evidence from either South Africa or East Africa is conclusive enough to pin-point man's emergence in either locality, though the period was the Late or Early Pleistocene and the creature who broke through the 'human barrier' probably an *Australopithecine*. The remains of the earliest *Homo erectus*, the only other contender for the title of being the first man, from North Africa, Java and China, were contemporary with developed tools already recognisable as of the hand-axe tradition, and were thus later in date than Bed I Olduvai or the Transvaal *Australopithecines*. At Trinil in Java *Homo erectus* remains have been dated by the Potassium Argon method to around 500 000 B.C.

Cultural evolution

What is apparent is that the human revolution meant that rapid evolution took place. The brain, particularly the frontal lobes, expanded in response to the calls made upon it. An eminent anthropologist, Sir W. Le Gros Clark, has aptly said: 'It was the development of the distinctly human type of social organisation which demanded an accelerated development of those parts of the brain whereby emotional and instinctive impulses can be more effectively subordinated to the good of the community as a whole.' As hunting supplemented scavenging, a greater necessity for group consciousness took place. Hunting by primitive methods was a group activity particularly when larger animals were the prey. Ideas were shared and tools made in a regular intentional pattern. One important feature of humans and near humans is that the pelvic changes necessary for bipedal movement resulted in the birth of their young in a more immature state, with a soft skull which has to mould itself through the small opening of the mother's pelvis at birth. Much of the development of the complicated brain had to take place after birth and the dependence of the young on their mothers allowed a greater opportunity for the transmission of ideas and habits. It also meant that the mother was withdrawn more and more from hunting so that man's social loyalties grew. A home-base at least for short periods became essential as man's range as a hunter became greater and mothers and babies were left behind. Hunting is often a long process and involves tracking and stalking and one difference between man and near-man is that the bipedalism of the former was perfected by this constant use of his feet.

The growth of the brain was accompanied by a progressive reduction of the jaw and of the size of the teeth, particularly of the canines. The jaw was no longer a fighting mechanism and did not require such powerful muscular attachments. Selection was no longer a natural process but depended more on man's ability to transmit ideas, on his adaptability to different environments and on his success as a hunter using his tools and co-operating with others of his group. This process we call cultural evolution. In this sense man domesticated himself. Group activity and the transmission of ideas demanded language, particularly in a creature like man who was not equipped with the speed of a cheetah or the strength and power of the lion and had to substitute guile in the collective activity of hunting.

The Stone Age

The Stone Age in East Africa can be divided for convenience into three periods: an early period, down to 60/50 000 B.C., when the Stone Age societies were characterised largely by what the archaeologists call hand-axe industries and for which our main evidence comes from the Rift Valley areas of Kenya and Tanzania and the Kagera river in Uganda; a middle period, from 50 000 B.C. to around 15 000 B.C., when man became more adaptable and more widely distributed because of his mastery of fire and of new stone tool-making techniques, and a late period when we are probably dealing with men similar to the present day races of Africa. This last period lasted until as recently as five or six hundred years ago in certain isolated areas of East Africa.

The earlier Stone Age

An important feature of the earlier period is that physical and cultural evolution were closely interrelated. The more man used tools the less he used his jaws and the more he used his brain; so by the end of the period the human beings in East Africa probably had brains very much the same size as present-day people. The pace of change was slow. The first tools from Olduvai Gorge, which have given their name to the earliest Stone Age industry[1] in Africa, the Oldowan, were simple and made for the job in hand, such as chopping bones open and cutting branches off trees for spears. The waste flakes struck off in giving a pebble or splinter of stone a sharp edge were probably used for skinning animals, cutting difficult ligaments between bones and scraping skins and sharpening sticks. Soon after a million years ago man discovered that tools with a sharp edge all round, and with a point formed by the convergence of two sharp edges, provided a highly practical all-purpose tool which the archaeologists call a hand-axe. It took another half million years before these hand-axes became fully refined. These industries are known to the archaeologists as Acheulean, after a place in France where identical hand-axes were first found over a hundred years ago. By the end of this earlier period, besides hand-axes, many other tools were being made, such as cleavers which had a straight cutting edge like a present-day axe, numerous scrapers and throwing stones, which may have been made into a throwing weapon called the bolus, and knives. Progress is measured as much by the complexity of tools, implying the number of jobs that could be done with them, as by the technological advancements in making tools.

Right throughout the Stone Age man was a parasite on the landscape. He lived by hunting and gathering. The Stone Age represents a progressive development of man as a hunter. At first he killed by driving animals into traps or muddy lake waters, or by outrunning and outwitting them. Except for scavenging large animals, which had died natural deaths or were caught unawares, he probably had to depend on smaller game. It was only by the end of the period that he could kill from afar with missile weapons. His social groups were probably small, perhaps no

[1] In this chapter the word *industry* is used rather than the more commonly used term *culture* as it is felt that it describes more closely the nature of our evidence.

more than an ideal, easily fed hunting band of twenty to thirty, and they constantly changed camp, largely keeping to lakes and rivers where animals came to drink. Man, who needs water almost daily, and who had few containers for water, was also tied to the same environments. But if comparisons with modern hunting peoples are valid it is almost certain that a greater part of his food supply came from collecting activities, digging up roots, eating berries and nuts, insects and various greens. Africa was probably then the most populous continent, though the total population perhaps rose from no more than 100 000 around half a million years ago to perhaps three or four million by the end of the stone age, the largest number a hunting economy could have supported.

When we link these population figures with the length of time involved in the Stone Age we can understand why remains of the early Stone Age are so abundant, particularly in East Africa where on sites like Olorgesailie in Kenya, Nsongezi in Uganda, Isimila (near Iringa) and Olduvai Gorge in Tanzania, stone tools are numbered in tens of thousands. Stone tools are heavy, they easily lose their edges and must have been used on the spot for butchering-up animals rather than being carried around. It is reasonable to assume that each day many tools were made and abandoned. Multiply this process by the over two million years of the Stone Age and it is easy to see why stone tools are so numerous. Unfortunately none of the wooden tools that men made, and which were perhaps more important for hunting, have survived.

By around 750 000 B.C. the principal human type was *Homo erectus* (formerly called *Pithecanthropus erectus*) and had a brain size of 67 cubic inches [1 100 cc]. He may have been preceded by another creature intermediate between the *Australopithecines* and himself, a few of the bones of which have been found in the Lake Baringo area. By this time man had spread from Africa into Asia and Europe. The process was probably a slow one with hunting groups moving north and eventually passing into the other continents. By half a million years ago early hand-axes and chopping tools occur in both southern Asia and western Europe.

It would appear that at that time the forests were too difficult to live in for these primitive hunter-gatherers. Most of the stone tools were made from fine grained rocks like quartz, quartzite and obsidian. Sites of the early Stone Age are normally discovered as the result of erosion in which present-day rivers have cut through old lake deposits or river gravels, as at Olduvai or Olorgesailie, and tools or fossils erode out of the deposits or become exposed so that the archaeologist knows exactly where to dig. Fishing, particularly for swamp fish, was probably also practised. The fossils of the animals which were the contemporaries of early man indicate varieties long extinct, like *Sivatherium* (a giraffe-like animal with horns), various large pigs and even tigers.

The middle Stone Age

By 50 000 B.C. fire was systematically in use. With its use man could drive out carnivores from rockshelters and keep himself warm in high altitudes, but most important of all it helped in hunting. He could make the gums of trees into glues for hafting shaped stones onto wooden shafts for lances, cook hitherto poisonous roots to make them edible, and extract and process the poisons of berries and insects which he then painted on his spears to make them deadly. Fire was also used for scaring animals from thickets and for felling trees. At the same time new tool-making techniques allowed him to make smaller tools by shaping the tool on the core of stone, from which he then struck off a thin almost ready-made implement. The large numbers of small tools of the period, and the distinct signs of their utilisation, suggests that the hunter had a mastery over skin and sinews and could almost certainly make suitable ropes and strings from animal products or bark. More efficient lances capable of leaving a blood spoor made hunting less hazardous. Tools became specialised and there were tools for working wood, pounding roots and working bone. Both fire and technological advances made man more adaptable and it is from this time that we find more evidence of man in the more heavily vegetated areas of western Uganda and in the thickly wooded mountain regions.

Two main cultural traditions from around 50 000 B.C. can be distinguished, one in the more wooded areas (Sangoan-Lupemban industries) where the tools are specialised for wood-working and digging up roots and include adzes and chisels; and a second (Stillbay industries) in the open country of the Rift Valley and Central Tanzania, the tools of which are smaller with leaf-like lance points being the most distinctive. The woodland peoples probably had a more vegetarian diet, judging by their tools which include large numbers of heavily abraded stones presumably for pounding roots.

The later Stone Age

By 15 000 B.C., or perhaps somewhat earlier, a new people entered East Africa, akin in physical appearance to the Caucasoid peoples of south-west Asia and North Africa. They brought with them new technological advances in stone tool-making. Instead of striking flakes from a core of rock by direct percussion, they had learnt to strike off thin blades of stone, probably by using a punch between the hammer and the core. It was realised that more efficient tools could be made by using smaller sized points or cutting components. The invention of the techniques of blade manufacture allowed small, sharp stone tool-components to be produced, which could then be used in composite tools. Instead of a large number of specialised stone tools of assorted sizes, the new tools consisted of variously-shaped small sharp blades and bladelets which, when blunted along the edge or at the end, to avoid splitting the handle or shaft in which they were placed, could be hafted to form arrows with or without barbs, to make knives and bolts for small game. Though the scrapers of the middle period of the Stone Age continued in use, new varieties, small and haftable, appear to have given a completely different appearance to the industries. The use of these tiny blades or microliths allowed man to exploit raw materials hitherto unused. Small pebbles of jasper, chalcedony, rock crystal and chert, unsuitable for a Stillbay point, could now provide a fine-grained raw material suitable for these smaller tools. Several microliths have been found mounted as barbs, and it is certain that the use of the barbed arrow and spear was one of the chief technological advances of the period. Barbs allowed the point to remain for a longer period in the animal and thus facilitated a more effective blood trail, and if the barb was poisoned it enabled the poison to invade the bloodstream. The bow and arrow was almost certainly in use, and the bow was also used for drilling holes in seeds and discs of ostrich eggshell to make beads.

Many of the sites of this late period are found under overhanging rocks, often commanding wide views of the countryside from which the hunter could spy out game. Occasionally the rockshelter was near water, as at Nsongezi on the Kagera river or Magosi in Karamoja in Uganda, in an area where natural rock cisterns retain water through the dry season. In several caves, particularly in Kenya, burials have been found. At Gambles Cave near Elmenteita the skeletons were placed in a contracted position, perhaps representing rebirth, covered in ochre to represent blood. These burials are the first indication of systematic religious practices. The burials are of Caucasoid peoples. But these new peoples, whose industries have been called Capsian after a site in North Africa, were never very numerous. They passed their ideas to their neighbours to the west and south and by 5 000 B.C. industries incorporating microliths, for a long time known as the Wilton industries, were common throughout East Africa. The most distinctive microliths were less than an inch [2.5 cm] long and crescentic in shape with the backing on the curved edge.

It is possible that the predominant population about this time was composed of what the archaeologists call 'Big Bushmen', who in physical appearance were somewhat similar to, though larger than, the present-day small Bushmen hunting peoples of south-western Africa. Skeletal remains of these men have been found in both West Africa and the Nile Valley and it would appear that they formed the basic stock of Africa from whom the present-day African races of Negro and Bushmen have developed in the last ten thousand years. During the late Stone Age, man spread over the larger part of East Africa, including parts of the East African coast.

One of the main features of the later Stone Age was that highly specialised and successful hunting societies developed. Several of these societies, such as the groups around Lakes Edward and Rudolph, were fishermen using barbed bone points as fish spears and possibly even harpoons for catching Nile perch and other fish. A date of around 6 000 B.C. has been obtained for the fishing site of Ishango at the mouth of the Semliki river on Lake Edward, where the fishing camps were covered by the grey volcanic ash of the Katwe explosion craters which were then active. Their diet included fish, fowl and game as well as oysters of different kinds. A carved bone with sets of parallel lines probably indicates that a simple calendrical or numeration system was known. Other late Stone Age peoples lived around Lake Victoria, subsisting on a diet of shells and fish and leaving behind large middens of shells. In the more forested areas, flaked stone axes were polished for tree felling, grinding stones were used for grinding seeds and heavy stones perforated by laborious pecking away from both ends with another stone were used as digging stick weights for the more systematic collection of roots. Particularly large numbers of polished stone axes, adzes and chisels, sometimes collectively known as 'celts', and occasionally made of haematite, have been found in north-western Uganda, suggesting an extension of the Uelian industries of northeastern Congo into the West Nile district. Probably towards the end of this period boats were used for fishing and travelling to the islands. Some of the industries of Karamoja are similar to those described from Somalia and Ethiopia and indicate that contact from the north-east existed. In the Rift Valley area of Kenya between Nairobi and Eldoret, where the natural volcanic glass, obsidian, is found, the late Stone Age industries are characterised by the presence of particularly long knives which were easy to strike off from cores of obsidian; one of the latest industries is known as the Elmenteitan.

Rock art

A large amount of our information about the more recent Stone Age hunter-gatherers comes from rock paintings. Rock paintings tell the archaeologist more about the spiritual and religious life of the hunters than stone tools or even burials ever can. The paintings of East Africa are all relatively recent; some are the work of Iron Age pastoral peoples. Those that survive are probably only a fraction of many that were painted, as a large number suffered from exposure to sun and rain. The paintings are largely on the underside of overhanging rocks, mostly on granites that weather, leaving numerous clefts and overhangs. Other pictures were probably painted on pieces of bone, skin, barkcloth and wood, but except for one decorated bone from Nyero in Uganda the rest have vanished. By the late Stone Age man was a skilful tool-maker and hunter. He had the technical ability to decorate, and his success as a hunter gave him both the time and the stimulus for art. As a hunter he had to observe the life of the animals he hunted. Much of his time was invariably spent in stalking prey, looking for it from raised viewpoints, and so he acquired a keen memory of the details of the animals he hunted. Why he painted is difficult to answer, but it is probable that he depicted animals sometimes to commemorate his successes and at other times hoping that by drawing the desired animal he would have luck in hunting. But the art probably formed part of his vivid folklore and it is difficult to disentangle what was considered magic and what was functional for the success of the hunt.

The paintings are dated by finding pieces of decorated rock in the deposits, at the foot of the painted overhangs, which are associated with stone tools dateable by other means. Occasionally the subject matter of the paintings (for example, cows with long horns in a rockshelter on Mount Elgon near the Enderbess area) gives a clue as to age. Very often one painting obscures another and it is thus possible to work out a relative sequence of painting at a particular site. Rock paintings have now been dated to as early as 3 200 B.C. in the Cape area of South Africa. It is possible that rock art began as early as this in East Africa but that the oldest paintings weathered away in the open environment; the surviving paintings were all probably made within the last thousand years. The paints were obtained by grinding down rotted ironstone (ochre) and mixing it with urine or fat when red was required, manganese or charcoal for black, and kaolin or guano for white. Fingers, splayed ends of sticks, and feathers were probably the most often used brushes.

The largest number of sites is in Tanzania where over a thousand are known, concentrated particularly in the Central Region in the Kondoa area though also around Singida and Lake Eyasi, where until recently the Hadza, the last hunting and gathering group, lived. In Kenya the only sites are on Mount Elgon and in Turkana and Maasailand and the latter are very recent, whilst in Uganda sites are found amongst the granite inselbergs of eastern Uganda with a single site in Karamoja. The Tanzanian sites largely depict animals and a few humans. Many lively scenes occur, in some of which the people are masked. The very latest paintings are in white whilst the earlier ones are in various shades of red, brown and orange. The earlier paintings are more lively than the later ones and in style and subject matter have affinities to paintings in Zambia and Rhodesia. The Uganda paintings are largely of schematic designs such as concentric circles and dumb-bell shapes though canoes are found at two localities. Associated with some of the paintings in Uganda are rock gongs. These consist of slabs of rock, both upright and horizontal, which have weathered off the parent rock but are still gripped or wedged by supporting rocks at one end so that they vibrate when struck. It is probable that most rock gongs are of Iron Age date though the tradition of making them may have begun in the Stone Age. Rock engravings, common in South Africa and in the Sahara, are rare in East Africa and the two main ones in Uganda consist of schematic designs.

The legacy of the stone age

By 1 000–1 500 B.C. a knowledge of agriculture and pastoralism was entering East Africa from the north. Many of the stone industries associated with the first food-producing pastoral societies are similar to the Capsian and Elmenteitan industries of the late Stone Age peoples, and like them their burials are of Caucasoid peoples. A knowledge of food production had probably been preceded by a knowledge of pottery in East Africa and in many rockshelters late Stone Age industries are associated with pottery. At first the new societies, which were characterised by the use of stone bowls, probably lived by both hunting and agriculture or pastoralism. Until around A.D. 500 the impact of the pastoralists and agriculturalists was slight and confined to the eastern Rift Valley zone as far south as Lake Eyasi.

From around A.D. 500 as iron-using Negroid agricultural peoples began to expand, perhaps from the west and south, the hunting and gathering peoples steadily became less and less important as an element in East Africa's population and were restricted to the largely bush-covered lower rainfall areas like the rift valleys, or the thick forests. Slowly many hunters and gatherers acquired the use of metal for their arrows and some groups, realising the advantages of a settled life with assured food supply, were probably absorbed amongst their Bantu-speaking neighbours. The traditions of many East African peoples speak of the inhabitants they found on arrival in their present homelands as being small hunting peoples, possibly akin to the Bushmen of southern Africa.

Much of the final disappearance of the survivors of the stone age has taken place comparatively recently. In Uganda the Ateso found hunting peoples in Teso in the eighteenth century; in north-eastern Karamoja a small group of Ik peoples still try to live by hunting and gathering. In Kenya, the Wanderobo were still common in the late nineteenth century whilst in Tanzania the Hadza are only just settling into an agricultural existence. Many present-day populations probably retain an element of the original population in their physical make-up. Agriculture allowed populations to expand whilst the hunters were never numerous and their effect on the population, even on absorption, was probably slight. Besides the few present-day survivals of hunting and gathering peoples, the legacy of the Stone Age was small. Certain specialisations, like fishing, a little forest clearance, an extensive knowledge of the useful plants and medicines that nature had to offer and perhaps in some areas a tradition of rock painting, are all that have survived.

Postscript (1973)

In 1969 at Koobi Fora, East of Lake Rudolf in Kenya Mr Richard Leakey discovered stone tools of the Oldowan industrial tradition in volcanic tuffs dated by Potassium Argon to 2.61 million years ago. These are the earliest stone tools yet known and suggest that tool making began in the Pliocene period. Numerous remains of *Australopithecines* have also been found in East Rudolf as well as further north in the Omo valley and it would appear that both the robust and gracile varieties were contemporaneous. Some of the *Australopithecines* in the Omo area may be as old as 5–4 million years old. *Homo sapiens* remains dating from 150 000 years ago have been found in the Kibish area and are the earliest yet known from Africa.

In 1968 excavations at Munyama Cave, on Buvuma island in Uganda, revealed a microlithic industry dated to 12 975 ± 80 B.C. As similar dates have also been published for late Stone Age sites in Southern Africa it is apparent that microlithic industries began far earlier than previously assumed and probably in several place in Africa and not necessarily as a result of cultural diffusion.

Further reading

CAMPBELL, B. C. *Human Evolution*, Edinburgh, 1966.

CLARK HOWELL, F. *Early Man*, Chicago, 1965.

CLARK, J. D. *The Prehistory of Africa*, London, 1970.

COLE, S. *Prehistory of East Africa*, London, 1963.

LEAKEY, R. E. F. New Perspectives on Man's Origin: current research in East Africa, *Kenya Past and Present, 1,* 1971.

LEAKEY, M. D. *Olduvai Gorge, III,* Cambridge, 1971.

LE GROS CLARK, SIR W. 'The Humanity of Man', *Nature,* No. 4792, 1961.

NAPIER, J. R. *The Roots of Humanity*, London, 1971.

PFEIFFER, JOHN E. *The Emergence of Man*, London, 1969.

PILBEAM, DAVID. *The Evolution of Man*, London, 1970.

POSNANSKY, MERRICK (Ed.) *Prelude to East African History*, London, 1966.

WILLCOX, A. R. *The Rock Art of South Africa*, Johannesburg, 1963.

4

The Settlement of East Africa

J. E. G. Sutton

This chapter outlines the making, development and blending of East African society from peoples of varied stocks and origins. This means looking back, not just to the beginning of the Iron Age, but beyond it to the first evidence of agricultural settlement and livestock husbandry in East Africa. The story is reconstructed mainly from archaeology, anthropology and linguistics.

The chapter is divided into three parts. The first discusses some general aspects of food-production in East Africa, both by cultivating crops and by keeping livestock, both with iron tools and without them. The second part explains how the peoples of East Africa are grouped and classified, especially by language. With this background, the third part is an historical reconstruction of the settlement and peopling of East Africa. Finally, for those who are perplexed by the non-mention of 'Hamites' and 'Nilo-Hamites', the appendix provides an apology.

The production of food

We have seen that the history of man as a tool-making animal goes back about two million years, according to the evidence from East Africa. For almost the whole of this period (about 99.5 per cent of human history) men were directly dependent on nature for their livelihood. Throughout the inhabited parts of the world they lived off wild produce—the animals they could ensnare or run down with wooden spears, clubs or stones, or in the later periods of the stone age shoot with bow and arrow; the fish they could spear or trap in streams, rivers, lakes or floodwaters; the eggs they could filch from nests, and the wild fruits and vegetables they could pick off trees and plants or dig from the earth. These foods and other necessities of life were prepared with tools of wood, skin, bone and stone, supplemented in time by the use of fire. Progress there was, but extremely slow by modern standards, and imperceptible in any man's lifetime. Then, during the course of the late stone age, commencing about ten thousand years ago, man began in certain parts of the world to assert himself over nature by producing his own food—that is, by the cultivation of plants and the taming of animals, bringing them under his control, making them dependent on him, modifying their forms by cross-breeding and selection, and adapting them to new environments. Some writers have referred to this as the food-producing revolution: perhaps it is more correct to regard it as an evolution, for the first steps towards cultivation and domestication must have been very gradual and largely unconscious. But, as the ideas of food-production have gained momentum, as they have spread from country to country and from people to people, their effects have been truly revolutionary. More reliable food supplies and man's greater regulation of them have encouraged larger and more settled populations, specialisation in crafts, industries and trade, and developments in social and political organisation. After the beginnings of tool-making, food-production is doubtless the most important development to have occurred in the history of mankind.

Crops and livestock

Only in a few places in the world has the evolution from gathering and hunting to agriculture and herding been played out from the first stages. For the first cultivation of any plant, the first steps towards taming any animal, could have occurred only where that plant or animal already existed in a wild state. For instance, we know that taro and bananas were first cultivated in the wet regions of south-eastern Asia, wheat and barley in the hills of western Asia, and several of the millet crops in the savannas of Africa, that donkeys were first tamed in northern or north-eastern Africa and llamas in South America, because these are the places where the ancestors of these plants and animals grew or ran wild. Then, once successfully brought under human control and care, plants and seeds could be carried to new regions by means of trade, contact with neighbours or the migration of an expanding agricultural people. Alternatively, as herds increased or exhausted the grass, they would be led in search of new pastures. Often it would be found that particular crops or animals would not thrive in a new environment with a different climate and soil. But sometimes they might be adapted, by human perseverance and ingenuity in developing new strains of the animal or plant in question.

With the spread and increasing variation of crops and domestic animals, cultivators and herdsmen learnt by experience what would succeed and what would fail in particular environments. This is well illustrated by the widely varying methods of subsistence observable nowadays in Africa, and especially in East Africa. In the northern part of the continent the principal grain crops have been barley and wheat, but south of the Sahara various types of sorghum, millet and eleusine have been found more successful. In forested regions with heavier rainfall these grain crops are comparatively less important, and more reliance is placed on planted crops, notably in East Africa the banana. Most East African peoples combine their agriculture with livestock-husbandry. This is truer of grain-cultivators than of banana-growers, whose dense populations and forest environment leave little room for grazing. Whereas cattle, except in areas of tsetse fly, are valued primarily for their milk, sheep and goats are kept for meat. Certain tribes go to the extreme of disdaining agriculture and live predominantly or exclusively off their livestock. Some do this almost by choice, notably sections of the Maasai whose fine plateau grasslands can produce enough milk for subsistence round the year. But in less favoured regions, such as the semi-desert of northern and eastern Kenya where crops will not grow, people are forced by circumstances to be nomadic pastoralists. Some of these latter regions are not suitable for cattle, and camels instead provide the mainstay of life. In most cases, exclusive pastoralism does not rule out the possibility or necessity of obtaining agricultural produce, by exchange with other tribes, for use at those times of the year when the milk yields are low. Some tribes, notably in northern Kenya, are themselves divided into interdependent pastoral and agricultural wings. The pastoral wing consists mainly of the young men who lead the herds to grazing over the plains, while the women, old folk and young children remain at home in the agricultural land, retaining just a few head of stock for family use. Pastoralists tend to occupy or roam over large areas in search of grazing and water round the year, but in fact those who live a purely or predominantly pastoral life are not very numerous. The prestige of the pastoralist is high and ownership of cattle has a social as well as an economic value; hence many people, who for their actual subsistence rely more on their fields than on their herds, maintain a strong cultural and emotional attachment to the latter. It is one thing to imagine oneself a pastoralist, another to really be one.

It is true that East Africa has not played an important role in the initial cultivation of crops from wild plants or in the first taming of animals from the wild. The staples of life in East Africa were probably all introduced from outside. The cultivation of millet and sorghum apparently spread from the Ethiopian highlands three to four thousand years ago, along with goats, sheep and cattle which had earlier been brought to Africa from western Asia. Bananas, as well as rice, certain yams and perhaps sweet potatoes, began to reach Africa about two thousand years ago along the trade and migration routes of the Indian Ocean. During the last five centuries maize and cassava have been introduced to Africa from the Americas, but few East African tribes used these on a large scale before the nineteenth or twentieth century. Recently, however, they have in many areas superseded the traditional millets as the principal crops. Nor should we consider only the main carbohydrate foods: equally important is the wide variety of pulses, and of green, stalk and ground vegetables grown in East Africa. These similarly are of diverse origins and antiquities. Food-production, therefore, did not suddenly arrive in East Africa from a single source: rather, different crops and different methods of husbandry have infiltrated from different directions at different times. Hence the complex economic pattern of modern East Africa.

Furthermore, in identifying these external origins, we are in danger of overlooking the no less important East African achievements in adapting crops and livestock to local conditions, and in creating viable economies throughout East Africa. Hardier varieties of millets, sorghum and eleusine have been developed, some of them by crossing introduced forms with indigenous wild grasses. Yet more impressive has been the region's contribution to the cultivation of bananas for cooking, brewing and eating raw: East Africa has more varieties than the rest of the world put together. Some are peculiar to particular areas, as can be seen by comparing those of Rungwe, Buganda and Kilimanjaro, where dense populations rely on bananas as the main staple.

Pastoralist and agriculturalist

Equally significant progress has been made with livestock-husbandry in East Africa, in developing breeds of cattle and small stock able to thrive locally and to withstand droughts, diseases and other hazards. It is commonly said that East African herdsmen are idle and only interested in the quantity, not the quality, of their cattle. This view is basically false and derives from a misunderstanding of the principles and problems of livestock-husbandry in the varied regions of East Africa. To provide food for a family around the year, the management of the beasts and of their breeding and grazing demands very high standards of attention and experience.

73

Another common misconception about pastoralism is to regard it as historically separate from and essentially opposed to agriculture. There has been a tendency to imagine the history of East Africa (and indeed of northern and eastern Africa in general) as a continual feud between pastoralists and agriculturalists. The herdsman as a noble warrior has been contrasted with the cultivator as a servile labourer; or, to reverse the prejudices, the treacherous and aggressive raider and cattle-thief is pitted against the more industrious and progressive farmer. It is true that there is often a sharp division between the pastures and the arable land. This is very marked in some of the northerly regions of East Africa, where open grazing stretches across the lowland plains away from the fields which are situated in the better-watered country, often around the hills and forests. Or occasionally, as in parts of Kenya and northern Tanzania, the finest pastures are the highland plateaus, whereas agricultural communities may inhabit fertile valleys and irrigated basins below the escarpments. These contrasts may lead to specialisation, but similarly they encourage co-operation. We have already observed how grain cultivation and livestock-husbandry are ideally complementary, how pastoralists and agriculturalists will exchange their respective products, and how some tribes divide into agricultural and pastoral wings as the most efficient way of utilising resources and supporting themselves. These divisions may be based on age and sex, cutting across the family. But there do arise circumstances in which tensions develop, or in which the pastoral wing, ranging further and further afield in search of grazing in the dry season, will eventually break away entirely from the agricultural nucleus to form a separate tribe living an exclusively pastoral life. It is then that pastoralism may become almost fanatical, a religion unto itself. But the uncertainties of drought, disease and cattle-theft and, most important, competition for grazing, mean that few people succeed as exclusive pastoralists. The case of the Maasai is interesting. They are popularly regarded as pure pastoralists, but in fact the rich plateau grasslands of Maasailand are sufficient for only a minority of the Maasai speakers. The rest have to supplement their milk and blood diet with grain foods or undertake intensive agriculture, as do the numerous Arusha Maasai. Some have joined Bantu-speaking agricultural tribes. All this was essentially true of the Maasai even before the alienation of parts of Maasailand by the British and Germans. As a very crude generalisation we might say that agriculture has accounted for the settlement of peoples and pastoralism for their dispersal, but in fact each very strongly influences the other.

Fertility and erosion

There is a fair correlation between maps of rainfall and of population density in East Africa. In general, the more rain, the more intensive the agriculture and the more people the land can support. But the correlations are not always so close. Some of the best watered areas are not well exploited because of thickness of forest, unsuitability of soils, unattractive climate, tsetse fly or some other cause. There are, for instance, wide parts of southern and western Tanzania with fair rainfall but sparse populations.

Both fields and pastures can and do deteriorate. Agriculture and grazing place an unnatural burden on the land. Crops exhaust the fertility of the soil in a way that natural vegetation does not; cattle devour the grass and goats the browsing, sooner and more thoroughly than do wild animals. As the woods are cut or burnt to provide fields and as domestic animals swallow the young shoots and prevent the regeneration of bush cover, the rain runs off faster, the soil suffers and the land erodes. This may lead to further clearing of the forest or bush for new fields and the abandonment of old fields to pasture, while the former pastures deteriorate into semi-desert. East African peoples have for long been aware of this, of course. Herdsmen have to move from pasture to pasture; some manage to follow a fairly regular annual pattern of movement to provide their herds with sufficient grazing, others have to be more adaptable and resourceful year by year according to circumstances. Cultivators know how many years they can harvest a crop on a particular plot of land before it must be left to recover its fertility. Banana plantations in some regions will bear a sufficient food supply for very many years. Millet fields may yield only two or three crops. Hence in many of the mediocre regions a family may require a wide area to slash and burn, or for bush-fallowing, over the years. In certain favoured places irrigation may promote more intensive cultivation.

Tools and food production

The types of land that are cultivated, the range of crops grown and general efficiency in producing food are largely determined by the tools available. Metal tools, and especially iron, are more efficient than those of stone and wood for cutting bush or forest, for sowing, planting and reaping crops and for preparing food. In many parts of the world, food production began in the late Stone Age, before the discovery of how to work metals; and this was the case in parts of Kenya and northern Tanzania.[1] In other regions of East Africa the first food production

[1] This food production without the knowledge of metals is often referred to as 'Neolithic'. As this term is sometimes used loosely and can confuse, we prefer to avoid it: instead of 'Neolithic communities', we speak of 'late Stone Age food producers'. This adequately distinguishes them from late Stone Age hunter-gatherers on the one hand, and Iron Age food producers on the other.

apparently began later, at the same time as iron-working.[1] Iron-working could not have been introduced before food production, for hunter-gatherer communities are too unsettled, and lack the resources and incentives to develop such skills. For to smelt iron from sand or rock and to forge knives, axes, hoes and other tools is a highly specialised craft and a secret to be guarded. The smith, therefore, is generally respected or even feared. The dependence of an agricultural community upon his skills often assures him a high social rank and occasionally political power. Many pastoral or semi-pastoral communities, however, notably Cushitic and certain Nilotic groups, tend to despise smiths and other craftsmen as servile castes. But their necessity is acknowledged and hence the need to maintain the iron-working clan or caste.

Though iron is not essential to food production, its coming greatly increased agricultural efficiency and encouraged the opening-up of new land which had earlier remained untouched except by hunters and gatherers. In particular, iron-working helped cultivators to tackle the regions of high rainfall and thick forests—those in which the banana has become so important as the staple of life for vast numbers of people. Iron, then, led to an increase and expansion of agricultural peoples, to a more intensive settlement of East Africa.

The peoples of East Africa

The peoples of Africa belong to three main physical types—Negroid, Bushmanoid and Caucasoid. The last covers much of northern and north-eastern Africa, as well as western Asia, India and Europe. The Negroid and Bushmanoid races are exclusively African—or were before overseas slave-trades began. It is now thought that these are two branches of an old African stock, rather than two strictly separate races. As for Pygmies, they probably do not constitute a race of their own, but another division of the Negroid specially adapted to forest conditions.

In East Africa the present peoples are almost entirely Negroid (excluding, of course, the small numbers of recent immigrants from overseas). A partial exception is north-eastern Kenya, where the Galla and Somali represent a mixture of Negroid and Caucasoid elements. Many other peoples of Kenya, northern Tanzania and perhaps western Uganda, though definitely Negroid, do betray indications of some admixture of Caucasoid blood. This suggests that semi-Caucasoid peoples (perhaps rather like present-day Ethiopians) were once more widespread in certain regions of East Africa. The Swahili peoples of the coast, moreover, have combined some Caucasoid traits through intermarriage with Arabs.

---

[1] We might note that iron was the first metal to be used in East Africa: there was no copper or bronze age as in some parts of the world.

The Bushmanoid type is not found nowadays in East Africa. However, among the Sandawe and their neighbours in central Tanzania, who are basically Negroid, some Bushmanoid traits are said to be observable. The only Pygmy Negroes now in East Africa inhabit the forests above the western rift valley on the borders of Uganda, Rwanda and the Congo. It seems clear that Bushmanoid peoples, and perhaps Pygmies as well, were more widespread in East Africa in the period before the introduction of food-production. Since then they have undergone gradual assimilation by essentially Negroid peoples, expanding in larger numbers with agriculture, domestic herds and better tools. The unassimilated Bushmanoid and Pygmy remnants were forced into the least attractive types of country.

These physical differences are not very useful for classifying tribes or groups of tribes. The distinctions between racial types are vague, and individuals vary enormously. We can only make very general observations on how the Hehe, for example, look different from the Acholi or the Kikuyu: we cannot attempt to define tribes in this way. A tribe is a tribe because it feels it is one. It must possess a common culture, and particularly a common language. It is not necessarily a single political unit. Tribes, moreover, are fluid groupings: some members are lost, others are incorporated, through the continual processes of migration and interaction with neighbours. There is no such thing as a 'pure' tribe, derived from a single founding ancestor. Again, arbitrary division or merging of tribes, for administrative convenience or through the ignorance of government officials, was not unknown in the colonial period.

Linguistic classification

The most useful and objective method of classifying tribes and larger groupings is by language, as in the scheme on Figure 12. This is based mainly on Greenberg's classification. Doubtless there are numerous modifications or refinements still to be made in the exact placing of certain groups and individual tribes. However, the general picture for East Africa should hold fairly well.[1]

The important groups that the student of East African history should note are those in block capitals below the third horizontal line in Figure 12—Bantu, Nilotic, Cushitic. The names of families and their main divisions (at the top) are only important when relating the languages of East Africa to their general African context. Similarly, the divisions of Bantu, Nilotic, etc. and the names of individual tribes are

---

[1] Thanks are due to Dr Ehret for advice on linguistic relationships and nomenclature.

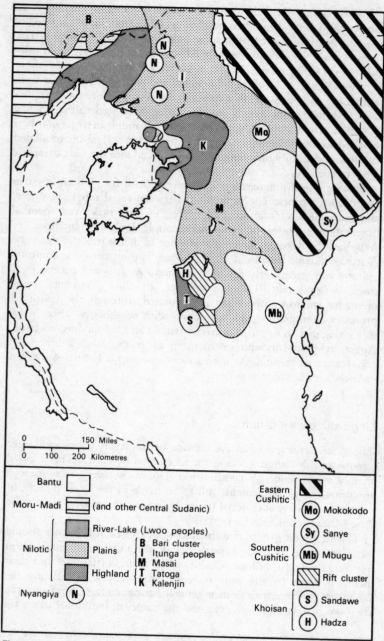

Figure 11 Peoples of East Africa: linguistic classification

included mainly for reference. For simplicity's sake, Bantu prefixes have been omitted.

A few notes are required on the classification and relationships of languages. Greenberg divides African languages into four main families, each of which is represented in East Africa. (In fact, examples of all four can be found within the Kondoa district of central Tanzania—a phenomenon that occurs nowhere else in the continent.) Between these four families no relationships can be traced. Thus Nilotic appears to be totally unrelated to either Bantu or Cushitic; but it is dinstantly related to Moru-Madi which stems from the same family. The divisions and sub-divisions which have occurred in each family are the result of long historical processes. Languages are never static: they are constantly changing or evolving. Hence, when a tribe speaking a single language splits into two or more parts, so will the language split, since each part will begin to evolve separately. Relationships and family-trees can be reconstructed by comparative studies of present-day languages. It is very difficult to work out when particular splits and changes occurred. But it is possible to date changes relatively. For instance, within Nilotic, the divisions between the three branches—River-Lake, Plains, Highland—must have occurred at some time before the Plains branch divided into three further clusters. On the other hand, the ancestors of Nilotic must have separated from those of Moru-Madi at a much earlier period. By correlating this linguistic scheme with other historical considerations it may be possible to estimate the approximate time-depth of some of these developments. This is attempted in the latter part of this chapter.

While languages have been continually evolving and splitting, many have also been dying out. For when people of two separate stocks combine to form a single tribe, whether through conquest or through peaceful assimilation, one language eventually prevails, the other dwindles and dies. Though a few words of the discarded language may be borrowed by the surviving one, genuinely mixed or hybrid languages do not emerge. Sometimes it is the language of the majority that is adopted as the common tongue, sometimes that of the minority; sometimes that of the more powerful element, sometimes that of the weaker. This depends on various social and political factors. Below we will trace examples of Cushitic-speakers who have been absorbed by Nilotic groups; and we shall see how peoples of various stocks have been and still are being 'Bantuised', that is, absorbed into Bantu-speaking tribes, forgetting their original non-Bantu speech. This reinforces the point made above that no tribes are 'pure' or derived from single ancestors. It also shows that we cannot explain tribal or group history merely by reference to the linguistic classification. The history of the Nilotes, for instance, is not just the history of the Nilotic languages; it must consider also the numerous interactions with various peoples originally of non-

Nilotic speech that have been absorbed into the Nilotes. Nevertheless, this does not detract from the point that languages and their classification, though not history in themselves, remain very important for the study of history.

To what extent do linguistic families and groups correlate with physical types and with cultural features? Of Greenberg's four language families, it will be observed that two, Niger-Congo and Chari-Nile—represented in East Africa by Bantu, Moru-Madi and Nilotic—are in general the languages of Negroid peoples; that Afroasiatic includes most of the languages of the Caucasoid and semi-Caucasoid peoples of Africa; and Khoisan those of the Bushmanoid peoples. But these general observations must be applied exceedingly cautiously. For the Niger-Congo language family does include some Caucasoid peoples, whereas there are also some Negroid peoples speaking Afroasiatic languages, notably some of those of the Cushitic division in East Africa. This underlines the importance of not muddling the labels used for physical types and linguistic groupings. We cannot talk of 'Negro languages'; nor can we use the terms 'Bantu' or 'Afroasiatic' to describe racial types.

On peoples' cultures, their economies and social and political organisations, we can also make some useful observations. If we compare Bantu and Nilotic-speakers, we notice that most Nilotes attach more importance to cattle, while Bantu on the average cultivate more. But there are some Bantu who keep large herds and despise agriculture, whereas some Nilotes have no cattle at all. Circumcision, to take another example, is commonly regarded as a Cushitic trait, for it is virtually universal among Cushitic-speakers. But when we find that a number of Bantu and Nilotic-speaking tribes in Kenya and northern Tanzania have adopted this custom, we cannot call them Cushites. They remain Bantu and Nilotes, culturally influenced by Cushites, perhaps.

One further point on the naming of linguistic groups. Many of the names are apparently geographical. 'Nilotic' for example originally meant 'of the river Nile'. But as a term for a group of related languages, 'Nilotic' does not include all the peoples living by the Nile. The Madi live on both sides of the Nile, but their language is not Nilotic. Conversely, some of the Nilotic-speakers live a long distance from the river. So, as used here, the word 'Nilotic' has really nothing to do with the river Nile. Similarly, linguistic divisions into 'western', 'eastern', etc. are not always geographically strict.

Before embarking on a general historical account of the peopling and settlement of East Africa, a few words must be said about each of the main linguistic groups.

Bantu languages

These cover the larger part of the Congo and of eastern and southern Africa. South of a line drawn from the Niger Delta to the southern Somali coast, almost all African languages are Bantu, except for the area of Khoisan speech in the far south. There are some irregularities in the Bantu line, most notably a wedge of various other languages in the highlands and rift valley of Kenya and northern Tanzania (as shown on Figure 11). The Bantu languages number several hundred. They are, as groups of languages go, very closely related, which indicates that their dispersal over a wide region began perhaps only two thousand years ago. The details and directions of this spread, in East Africa and elsewhere, are only beginning to be worked out. Most likely the main centre of the spread was in the Congo or some adjacent country. But this question of origin is less important than the clear fact that the Bantu *have expanded* —and expanded *rapidly*. By Greenberg's classification, Bantu is merely a sub-group of a branch of the Niger-Congo family. Other branches of Niger-Congo (whose relationships to Bantu are, of course, very distant) cover most of West Africa.

Nowadays about three-quarters of the combined population of Kenya, Tanzania and Uganda are Bantu.

The inter-relationships of the various Bantu languages of East Africa have not been sufficiently studied. Therefore the groupings suggested on Figure 12 are exceedingly arbitrary and based partly on geography. Some use has been made of Bryan's classification of Bantu languages.

Moru-Madi

Most of the languages of the Central Sudanic division of the Chari-Nile family are found in scattered blocks in the southern Sudan, the north-eastern Congo and the Central African Republic. The so-called 'Moru-Madi group' extends into north-western Uganda. It was probably once more widely spread in this region.

The Nilotic group

Much more extensive in East Africa is the Nilotic group, some sections of which have made fairly dramatic 'explosions' in a southward direction in the last thousand or two thousand years. We propose here a classification of the Nilotes into three branches.[1] The Highland branch of the

[1] See appendix to this chapter on the designation 'Nilo-Hamites', formerly used for some of the Nilotic groups.
The three branches of Nilotic designated here, Highland, Plains, and River-Lake, correspond to Greenberg's 'Southern', 'Eastern' and 'Western' Nilotic respectively.

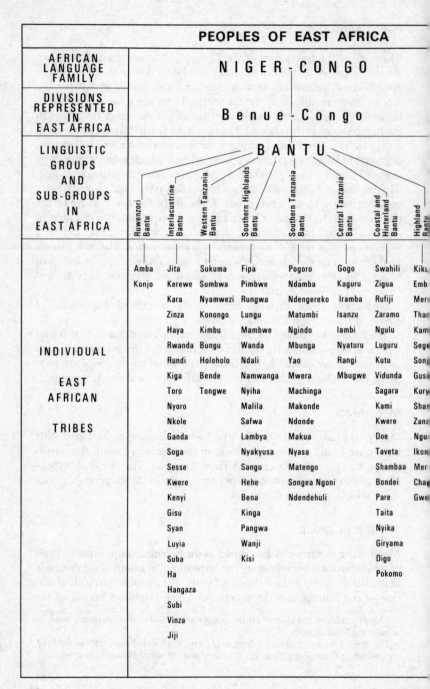

PEOPLES OF EAST AFRICA							
AFRICAN LANGUAGE FAMILY	NIGER-CONGO						
DIVISIONS REPRESENTED IN EAST AFRICA	Benue-Congo						
LINGUISTIC GROUPS AND SUB-GROUPS IN EAST AFRICA	BANTU						
	Ruwenzori Bantu	Interlacustrine Bantu	Western Tanzania Bantu	Southern Highlands Bantu	Southern Tanzania Bantu	Central Tanzania Bantu	Coastal and Hinterland Bantu	Highland Bantu
INDIVIDUAL EAST AFRICAN TRIBES	Amba	Jita	Sukuma	Fipa	Pogoro	Gogo	Swahili	Kiku
	Konjo	Kerewe	Sumbwa	Pimbwe	Ndamba	Kaguru	Zigua	Emb
		Kara	Nyamwezi	Rungwa	Ndengereko	Iramba	Rufiji	Meri
		Zinza	Konongo	Lungu	Matumbi	Isanzu	Zaramo	Thar
		Haya	Kimbu	Mambwe	Ngindo	Iambi	Ngulu	Kam
		Rwanda	Bungu	Wanda	Mbunga	Nyaturu	Luguru	Sege
		Rundi	Holoholo	Ndali	Yao	Rangi	Kutu	Son
		Kiga	Bende	Namwanga	Mwera	Mbugwe	Vidunda	Gusi
		Toro	Tongwe	Nyiha	Machinga		Sagara	Kury
		Nyoro		Malila	Makonde		Kami	Shas
		Nkole		Safwa	Ndonde		Kwere	Zana
		Ganda		Lambya	Makua		Doe	Ngu
		Soga		Nyakyusa	Nyasa		Taveta	Ikon
		Sesse		Sangu	Matengo		Shambaa	Mer
		Kwere		Hehe	Songea Ngoni		Bondei	Cha
		Kenyi		Bena	Ndendehuli		Pare	Gwe
		Gisu		Kinga			Taita	
		Syan		Pangwa			Nyika	
		Luyia		Wanji			Giryama	
		Suba		Kisi			Digo	
		Ha					Pokomo	
		Hangaza						
		Subi						
		Vinza						
		Jiji						

Figure 12 Peoples of East Africa: Linguistic Classification

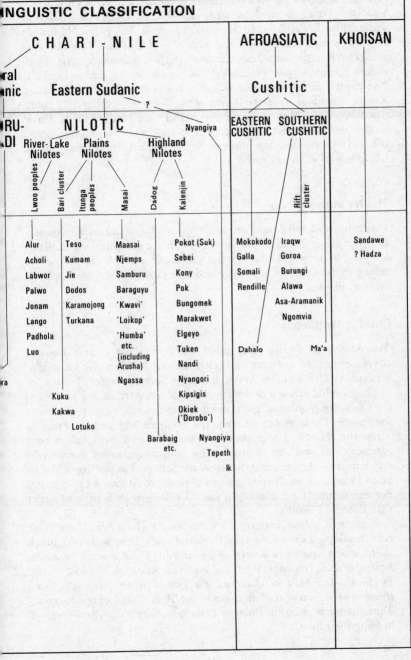

CHARI-NILE

Eastern Sudanic

?

NILOTIC

River-Lake Nilotes | Plains Nilotes | Highland Nilotes | Nyangiya

Bari cluster

Itunga peoples

Masai

Dadog

Kalenjin

Lwoo peoples

AFROASIATIC

Cushitic

EASTERN CUSHITIC | SOUTHERN CUSHITIC

Rift cluster

KHOISAN

Lwoo peoples	Bari cluster	Itunga peoples	Plains Nilotes (Masai)	Highland Nilotes (Kalenjin)	Eastern Cushitic	Southern Cushitic	Khoisan
Alur	Teso		Maasai	Pokot (Suk)	Mokokodo	Iraqw	Sandawe
Acholi	Kumam		Njemps	Sebei	Galla	Goroa	? Hadza
Labwor	Jie		Samburu	Kony	Somali	Burungi	
Palwo	Dodos		Baraguyu	Pok	Rendille	Alawa	
Jonam	Karamojong		'Kwavi'	Bungomek		Asa-Aramanik	
Lango	Turkana		'Loikop'	Marakwet		Ngomvia	
Padhola			'Humba'	Elgeyo			
Luo			etc.	Tuken			
			(including	Nandi			
			Arusha)	Nyangori			
			Ngassa	Kipsigis	Dahalo	Ma'a	
Kuku				Okiek			
Kakwa				('Dorobo')			
Lotuko							

Barabaig etc. | Nyangiya | Tepeth | Ik

83

Nilotes consists of the Kalenjin cluster in the western Kenya highlands, with the Dadog as well as small numbers of Okiek (or 'Dorobo') scattered further afield as far as central Tanzania. The Plains Nilotes fall into three main sub-groups: the Maasai in Kenya and Tanzania; the Itunga (or Karamojong-Teso) cluster of north-western Kenya and north-eastern Uganda with extensions into south-eastern Sudan; and the Bari cluster, mostly in southern Sudan, but in the case of the Kuku and Kakwa extending across the border of the West Nile district of Uganda. The River-Lake Nilotes consist of the Dinka and Nuer of the Sudan, as well as the Lwo-speaking peoples, who are divided into a number of tribes extending from the southern Sudan to northern Uganda and the lake-shore of western Kenya.

The Nyangiya group

This consists of small numbers of scattered hill-cultivators and hunter-gatherers in north-eastern Uganda. They are the unassimilated remnants of a pre-Nilotic population. It is not yet certain whether their languages belong to the Chari-Nile or the Afroasiatic family. The former appears more probable.

Cushitic languages

The Afroasiatic family (also called 'Erythraic') has several divisions covering most of northern and north-eastern Africa as well as south-western Asia. (It includes Arabic and other Semitic tongues.)

The Cushitic division of this family is entirely African. It is centred in the Ethiopian highlands, and is divided into five main groups. Of these the Eastern Cushites extend from the southern highlands of Ethiopia across the Horn and over much of north-eastern Kenya, where they (various Galla and Somali groups, that is) have expanded in relatively recent times—very recent in the case of the Somali. The placing of Moko-kodo (Yaaku), a small remnant group north of Mount Kenya, in this division is uncertain; possibly it should belong with Southern, rather than Eastern, Cushitic.

Southern Cushitic languages are confined to East Africa, and have been developing there for several thousand years. They were once much more widely spread in Kenya and in northern and central Tanzania. Several of these languages are dying out on account of absorption, mostly by Bantu. The Ma'a in Usambara, the Dahalo of the lower Tana, and speakers of several of the languages of the 'Rift cluster' of north-central Tanzania are nearing the point of extinction. The Iraqw, however, are holding their own.

Because of their antiquity and isolation, it is difficult to unravel precisely the divisions and inter-relationships within Southern Cushitic, and the exact relationship of Southern Cushitic as a whole to the rest of Cushitic in Ethiopia and adjacent lands.

The Khoisan family

The Khoisan (or 'click') family comprises the languages of the Bushmen and Hottentots of the Kalahari and adjacent parts of southern Africa. The fact that Sandawe of central Tanzania belongs to this family is one of several indicators that Bushman-type people were once more widespread in eastern and southern Africa. The position of the Hadza hunters near Lake Eyasi is less certain: Greenberg regards their language as Khoisan, but others suggest that it may be Afroasiatic. Like many other such languages, it needs more careful study.

Peopling and settlement: historical reconstruction

When the first food-producing communities began settling in parts of East Africa towards the end of the late stone age, they would have found the country thinly populated by bands of hunters and gatherers. Many of these, especially in the more southerly regions, would have belonged to the Bushmanoid stock. This is indicated by skeletons of Bushmanoid type occasionally discovered in late Stone Age sites, and by certain other lines of evidence. Commonly the most distinctive finds from the camping and cooking sites of late Stone Age hunters and gatherers are minute stone tools of types known as Wilton (see chapter 3). The Wilton extends from eastern to southern Africa, where it is connected with ancestors of the present-day Bushmen. The most usual camping-sites were under the shelter of overhanging rocks, which in central Tanzania are frequently painted with wild animals and hunting scenes. These rock-paintings also have their counterparts in southern Africa, where they are attributed to the Bushmen of earlier times. It is particularly significant that many of the Tanzanian paintings are in or next to the territory of the Sandawe, who are linguistically related to the Bushmen of southern Africa and apparently betray some physical relationship too, and who were until very recently living by hunting and gathering. The Sandawe, therefore, are the remnants of a Bushman-type population with Khoisan speech that roamed more widely in the savannas and woodlands of much of East Africa before the beginning of food-production. The Hadza are possibly another such remnant.

In some parts of East Africa there were probably hunter-gatherers of

85

different stocks. In many of the highland regions of Kenya and northern Tanzania, stories are told of dwarfs who once lived or hid in the thick forests. The reliability of these stories is difficult to assess, but they may refer to the former presence of Pygmies. Certainly the Pygmies of the Congo, who extend right up to the Uganda border, descend from populations that have for long been adjusted to gathering and hunting in the forests.

Around Lake Victoria some hunter-fisher groups were using pottery at the end of the late Stone Age. Yet more significant is the earlier evidence of advanced hunters and perhaps also fishermen in the highland savannas of Kenya and northern Tanzania. These are known from finds of stone tools of the Capsian type (see chapter 3), famous for blades, perhaps used as knives and spear-heads, made of the fine obsidian rock. These advances began reaching the Kenya highlands about ten thousand years ago. They may have connections with the middle Nile region or with Ethiopia. But their origin and the type of people responsible remain far from clear at the present stage of archaeological research.

The first cultivators and herdsmen

These advanced hunters lived in precisely those highland regions which later, towards the close of the late Stone Age, experienced the first introductions of agriculture and domestic herds into East Africa. Dating by the radiocarbon method indicates that these developments had begun by 1 000 B.C. in the Kenya highlands. That the newcomers were of a partly Caucasoid physical type is suggested by the skeletons excavated from a number of their burial sites. In fact, much of our knowledge of these earliest food-producers comes from burials; but some living sites have been discovered and investigated. The burials are usually under cairns (piled stones). Some are about 12 feet [4 m] high and about 50 feet [15 m] in diameter, but many are much smaller. They can be found either singly or in groups, occasionally numbering a hundred or more. Their distribution extends from northern Kenya to central Tanzania, the whole length of the Rift Valley and the highlands on either side, as well as across the plains that stretch away to the east and north as far as Ethiopia. Often the burials contain offerings or some of the belongings of the dead man or woman. These include grindstones and pestles, earthenware pots and stone bowls which apparently contained food. Similar objects have been found at the living sites. From this we conclude that these people probably cultivated grain crops, presumably types of sorghum and millet. Animal bones show that they kept cattle, and probably goats and sheep. Nor was hunting despised; it continued to supplement the diet. It seems that there was considerable interbreeding

86

between the newcomers and the indigenous hunters and gatherers of the highlands and adjoining plains.

A very famous communal burial site of this period is the Njoro River Cave in the elevated part of the Kenya rift valley. It was excavated by Dr and Mrs Leakey. They found that the bodies had been cremated— an unusual practice, but one which ensured that many grave-goods that would normally have rotted were carbonised and thus preserved. These include basketry, cords, gourds and a beautifully carved and decorated wooden vessel, presumably a milk container, besides the more durable objects—pots, stone bowls, grindstones and pestles. Also famous from this site are the pendants and hundreds of beads belonging to necklaces. The beads were made from bone, ostrich eggshells, nuts, sedge-seeds, and various semi-precious stones, all obtainable locally.[1]

The Njoro River Cave is only one of many burial sites of these very late Stone Age cultivators and herdsmen, one which provides, however, an unusually rare insight into their material culture and economy. Like the hunters and gatherers, they lacked all knowledge of metals. Their knives, scrapers and spears were made of stone, principally obsidian that provided beautifully sharp edges. Their axes were of polished stone, their hoes of stone or wood. They preferred, therefore, the more open country with light soils, where fields could more easily be cleared and dug and where grazing was more available. Possibly it was in this pre-iron period that the first irrigation works were constructed for agriculture in the highlands. Many systems of irrigation channels exist in Kenya and Tanzania to this day, both in the hills themselves and, more valuable, at the base of escarpments where rivers flow into the drier plains. We do not know for certain how old these complex feats of engineering may be; but it is certain that many of them are ancient, and their present users often attribute them to tribes that have now vanished or been absorbed. Of similar antiquity, perhaps, are the big dams in the plateau grasslands that doubtless provided reservoirs for watering cattle, and the deep rock-cut wells in the drier plains of north-eastern Tanzania and eastern and northern Kenya. Many of these wells are still used and enlarged by the present inhabitants of the plains—Maasai, Galla and Somali. But the reservoirs have fallen into disuse. There is a fine series of these old reservoir dams at Ngorongoro, just above the crater.

The burials with their grave-goods, the red ochre with which the corpses were often adorned, and the special placing of skulls or jaw-bones, provide clear evidence of religious beliefs connected with cults of the dead. The burials are so numerous, both male and female, that it is difficult to believe that they represent important persons only. Quite probably, the societies of the highlands, then as now, were mostly chiefless.

[1] These finds are in the Kenya National Museum.

Can we identify these late Stone Age food-producers more precisely? The Ethiopian highlands would have been the most likely direction from which seed-agriculture and domestic livestock would have spread into the highland and rift valley regions of East Africa. The Caucasoid elements in the physical type also point to an Ethiopian origin: so do the methods of burial, for cairns are constructed in Ethiopia to this day by Cushitic-speaking peoples. The practice of circumcision as an initiation rite, and certain other social and cultural traits widespread among the present peoples of the Kenya and northern Tanzania highlands, also indicate earlier Cushitic influences in these regions. The Southern Cushites (see Figures 11 and 12) provide the obvious answer. Only a few pockets survive, the largest tribe being the Iraqw (also called Mbulu); but it is clear on linguistic grounds that they are the remnants of a population that expanded from Ethiopia a few thousand years ago. Physically they should be classified as Negroid, doubtless partly through intermarriage with other stocks in East Africa, but they still seem to betray certain distinctive features that might link them with the populations of Ethiopia.

As far as we can trace it at present, this late Stone Age food production was confined to the highlands, rift valley and plains of Kenya and northern Tanzania. But it would not be surprising were we to discover that it extended into the southern highlands of Tanzania, or were evidence to come to light of food production during the same period in northern Uganda. Neither region has been well examined. Nevertheless, it seems fairly certain that most of East Africa, including the Lake Victoria region and western and southern Tanzania, remained the territory of hunters and gatherers until the beginning of the Iron Age.

The coming of iron

Iron tools and the skills of making them became known in East Africa nearly two thousand years ago. In several regions, especially the westerly ones and around Lake Victoria, the first iron-using and iron-working is believed to have been introduced by early Bantu-speaking settlers, who between one and two thousand years ago were expanding rapidly and opening up for agriculture vast areas, not only of East Africa, but also of the Congo basin and of southern Africa. This view of Bantu expansion is based partly on comparative linguistic evidence, but also on the discoveries right through these broad regions of the sites of early Iron Age cultivators who made and used distinctive styles of pottery, known to archaeologists as 'dimple-based', 'Kwale', 'channelled' and related wares. These sites have been dated by numerous radiocarbon tests to the first millennium A.D. There can be little doubt that they represent early Bantu settlements.

However, a Bantu explanation of the origins and spread of iron-working can hardly hold for the *whole* of East Africa; for in the northerly parts of Kenya and Uganda and much of the highland and Rift Valley region Bantu speech has never penetrated. (Nor, it seems, are 'dimple-based' and related types of early Iron Age pottery found there.) These regions have been inhabited by Nilotes and other peoples, who share with Bantu the general negroid physical type, but who are entirely different from them in language and early history. In some of these northerly regions the first iron users may have been the first Nilotic speakers, notably those of the Highland division, who were pressing into Kenya from the north-west in the first millennium A.D. Alternatively, it is possible that the older Southern Cushitic population of much of the Kenya and northern Tanzania highlands, which had been settled there before the Iron Age, had independently acquired iron from some source before the Nilotic incursions.

From the above it is clear that the old view of iron diffusing to East Africa from Meroe on the Middle Nile must now be rejected, or is at least far too simplistic. Instead, it is now being suggested that the knowledge of iron could have reached East Africa from a combination of directions—the Congo, the Indian Ocean and Ethiopia—during the first millennium A.D. All this shows that our knowledge of the introduction of iron, especially to the northerly parts of East Africa, is still rather vague. But some general observations can be made, notably that between one and two thousand years ago an iron technology replaced a stone one throughout virtually the whole of East Africa. It is, of course, true that even during the present millennium some people still used stone tools for certain purposes alongside iron, and that some groups of hunters and gatherers, unable or unwilling to obtain iron, continued late to flake stone for weapons and tools. Despite these qualifications, it can be said that by A.D. 1 000 nearly all East Africans had passed from the Stone Age to the Iron Age, and that many had done this several centuries earlier. Furthermore, by this time East Africa as a whole was essentially an area of food production, no longer one of pure dependence on nature. Again it is necessary to note exceptions, such as the persistence of various small hunting and gathering bands, some of them till the present day, and the tendency of many people to supplement their agricultural diet by hunting. All the same, it remains clear that between 1 000 B.C. and A.D. 1 000—the end of the late Stone Age and the beginning of the Iron Age—East Africa as a region had made the transition from a land of natural foods and small foraging populations, to one of fields and pastures controlled by man, with all the implications for population increase and human domination of the landscape.

As already seen, the earliest grain cultivation and cattle-keeping was in the highland grasslands of Kenya and northern Tanzania two to three thousand years ago before the coming of iron. Then, early in the Iron Age in the first millennium A.D., with the expansion of old populations and the arrival of new ones (early Nilotes and especially Bantu), these grain crops and domestic animals spread to other regions with more varied environments; and, because of iron tools, it was possible to begin clearing the more fertile but thickly vegetated lands for increasingly intensive agriculture. It was probably in this same period that bananas (originally a south-eastern Asian crop) were introduced to the east coast of Africa, and began to be used and adapted by expanding populations in East Africa, especially in the wetter regions like those adjoining Lake Victoria. The Iron Age saw not only agricultural expansion and diversification and population increase, but also more agricultural—and pastoral—specialisation.

The middle and later Iron Age

The processes of population expansion and economic specialisation continued through the middle and later parts of the Iron Age, that is from A.D. 1000 onwards. During this period also, further groups of Bantu and new divisions of the Nilotes (the Plains and River-Lake Nilotes) entered East Africa. The effects of these movements are discussed below in the section on intermingling and assimilation, and in chapters 7 to 10, where they are studied in greater depth. For, when we reach more recent centuries, it is possible to reconstruct history, not only from archaeology and linguistics (and very general anthropological considerations) as hitherto, but also from oral traditions. Nevertheless, as we have seen, not even the richest and longest oral records stretch back to the earlier half of the Iron Age or to the coming of the Bantu and first Nilotes.

The middle part of the Iron Age (about A.D. 1000–1500) in the interior is known, though very imperfectly, from several archaeological sites. They reveal no evidence of formal long-distance trade. (The caravan routes linking the interior and the coast developed much later, in the eighteenth and nineteenth centuries: see chapters 11 and 12.) But early indirect contacts with the coast are illustrated by occasional finds of seashells and imported beads on upcountry sites. More interesting are the indications of industrial specialisation and exchange at relatively local levels in the important commodities of salt and iron. The availability of iron ore varies from district to district; and, in recent centuries at least, some districts with good and plentiful ores have specialised in smelting and trading iron bars and hoes to less fortunate ones in exchange for food and livestock. Sources of fine salt are even rarer. Those at Ivuna near Lake Rukwa and at Kibiro by Lake Albert were being exploited by the middle Iron Age; while the exceptional salt springs of

Uvinza in western Tanzania were first known and worked right back in the early Iron Age about fifteen hundred years ago. This information on ancient salt production has been obtained from excavations at these sites: what is not yet known is how extensive the local trades were before the last two centuries.

One archaeological site of the middle to late Iron Age that requires special mention is Engaruka, at the foot of the rift wall in northern Tanzania. Here are remains of numerous homesteads and stock-pens enclosed by dry-stone walling, and of an extensive field and irrigation system. Most of this probably dates between the fifteenth and eighteenth centuries, according to excavations by the Tanzania Antiquities Department and radiocarbon dates. But it needs to be emphasised that these remarkable ruins at Engaruka in no way constituted a 'city', as some writers have romanticised them. It was not an industrial or commercial centre but an agricultural settlement, concentrated, partly perhaps for reasons of defence, but more especially because Engaruka, where a river descends from the highlands into the dry plains, is the only place in the area where agriculture is feasible—and then only through the construction of irrigation furrows. The inhabitants of Engaruka were probably a Southern Cushitic-speaking group, akin to the nearby Iraqw.

Intermingling and assimilation of peoples

Neither Nilotes nor Bantu arrived in East Africa all at the same time. Instead, we should imagine numerous Bantu and Nilotic movements throughout the length of the Iron Age—a period of almost two thousand years from the present. Some of the more pastoral Nilotic immigrants may have sped across the northern plains and grasslands as conquering waves or as desperate splinter-groups in search of land or refuge; but more often migrations were slow and gradual, involving peaceful penetration and settlement. As populations increased and more land was required, so expansion and migration proceeded, and new territory was cleared from the wild, for homesteads and fields. If this was the usual case with the Nilotes, it was even truer of the Bantu, most of whom settled in primarily agricultural regions.

The early Bantu expansion was not enacted in a complete vacuum. This is equally true of the first Nilotic movements from the north. As already stressed, there were older populations of hunter-gatherers, who would have entered into relationships with the newcomers and exchanged products. Many were absorbed into the expanding food-producing tribes; others maintained their independence by retreating into the forests and other types of country less favourable for crops and herds. There are to this day a number of groups or bands that live by

Dexter Library
Northland College
Ashland, Wisconsin 54806

hunting and gathering and exchange with their agricultural and pastoral neighbours. Some, such as the Khoisan-speaking Hadza near Lake Eyasi, have already been mentioned. There are also the Sanye and others in the plains of eastern Kenya, and the bands called 'Dorobo' in the highland forests of Kenya and northern Tanzania, who speak various Nilotic and Cushitic tongues. Not all these hunter-gatherers and forest-dwellers are in fact true descendants of the pre-food-producing inhabitants of East Africa. Some have reverted to this mode of life, for in hard times many people will take refuge in the forest or revert to a life dependent on nature. A cultivator whose crops fail, a herdsman whose cattle die or are stolen, people fleeing from wars or repudiated by their kinsmen, are liable to 'turn Dorobo', as the saying goes. 'Dorobo' may be despised by pastoral and agricultural peoples, but the honey, game-meat and other products of the forest which they trade in are appreciated. Certain 'Dorobo' groups make pots which they trade to Maasai or other neighbouring tribes. This interdependence is essential for their continued existence.

More extensive processes of assimilation by Bantu and Nilotes have taken place in the highland regions of Kenya and northern Tanzania already occupied by the Southern Cushitic-speaking food producers. The first and most important Nilotic group in these regions was the Highland branch, ancestral to the present Kalenjin tribes. Linguistic and arch-aeological studies show that at certain times in the past they have been more widespread in the highlands and rift valley than they are now (see chapter 8). The Bantu approaches to the highlands were from other directions—the south and the coastal region. The Cushites were not simply overthrown by the successive waves of newcomers; there were some very long processes of intermingling. Though, as we have seen, the distribution of Southern Cushitic languages is today very restricted, these people have left a deep mark on the customs, beliefs, economies and social and political organisations of the Bantu and Nilotes now inhabiting the highlands.

We should not envisage the history of the peopling of East Africa in the Iron Age merely as a process of Bantu and Nilotes absorbing the earlier hunter-gatherers and Southern Cushitic food producers. There was also considerable interaction, both peaceful and hostile, between various Bantu and Nilotic groups. Throughout central Uganda there has been much friction and intermingling in the last five centuries since the Nilotic Lwo peoples began pressing against the northern borders of the Bantu (see chapter 7). The expansion of the Lwo in north-western Uganda has also helped to reduce the areas of Moru-Madi-type languages, which may already have been pushed back by the more northerly Bantu. On the edges of the western Kenya highlands and southwards into Tanzania, Bantu sections have impinged upon older populations of

Highland Nilotes, resulting in assimilation in both directions over many centuries. The Bantu who live in the highlands east of the Rift Valley (Kikuyu, Kamba, Chagga, etc.) and those at its southern end (Rangi, Nyaturu, Gogo, etc.) have absorbed many non-Bantu elements. These include, besides hunter-gatherers and Southern Cushites, pastoralists of diverse origins—Highland Nilotes, Galla and other Eastern Cushitic groups, and in the last century or two Maasai of the Plains branch of the Nilotes. Whereas Nilotes have tended to dominate the highland and Rift Valley grasslands, Eastern Cushites, expanding from Ethiopia and the Horn, have for several centuries roamed the dry plains of northern and eastern Kenya and perhaps north-eastern Tanzania, stretching from the highland edges right down to the coast. Pressure from Eastern Cushites was one of the factors that induced certain Bantu groups to move from the coastal regions and river valleys into the Kenya highlands. Surrounded by Nilotes and Eastern Cushites, both jealous for the grasslands, the Highland Bantu have been mainly confined to the fertile forested hill-slopes where few cattle can be kept. But here they provide refuges for pastoralists who from time to time fall on evil days and lose their cattle or are driven by stronger rivals from the grasslands. For instance many of the highland Bantu, particularly those of Kilimanjaro and Mount Meru, have absorbed numbers of Maasai, or in some cases have themselves been absorbed by the more agricultural of the Maasai, such as the Arusha.

One further question of possible Cushitic influences needs discussion. This concerns western Uganda, north-western Tanzania, Rwanda and Burundi—what is commonly called the interlacustrine region. The peoples of this region are entirely Bantu-speaking; but a minority, which tends to form a pastoral aristocracy known as Hima or Tusi within certain of these Bantu tribes, possesses physical features suggesting that some of their ancestors may have been of partly Caucasoid type. Some writers have surmised that the region was invaded some centuries ago by Western Cushites from the south-western Ethiopian highlands, and that these invaders were responsible for the origins of the organised interlacustrine kingdoms that have persisted till this century. The presumed invaders have been associated not only with the ancestors of the present Hima and Tusi clans, but also with the legendary Chwezi, who are said to have ruled a large kingdom called Kitara centred in western Uganda some five hundred years ago (see chapter 9). Associated with the Chwezi legends are some large earthworks, which, as archaeological investigations indicate, would have been royal capitals and cattle-enclosures of that period. This theory of Western Cushitic migration to Uganda remains problematical—unproven, but not entirely impossible. Unfortunately, it has been bedevilled, not only by simplistic presentation, but also by association with more notorious theories of

93

'Hamitic' conquest and superiority (for which see the appendix to this chapter).

Lastly, Nilotes have absorbed Nilotes, and Bantu have absorbed Bantu. To take Nilotes first: from Lake Kyoga northwards there has been fusion of Itunga and Lwo-speakers (branches of the Plains and River-Lake Nilotes respectively) pressing from opposite directions in recent centuries. The Lango have come through this maintaining the Lwo speech, whereas, among the Kumam and the Teso, Itunga languages have prevailed. In the highlands and rift valley, Maasai (plains Nilotic) have assimilated some of the previously far-ranging Kalenjin (Highland Nilotic), while the Kalenjin have been constantly interacting among themselves and thus forming new tribes. Similarly, within the Moru-Madi group of peoples, the expanding Lugbara have in the last hundred years or more swallowed up part of the Madi tribe. For an interesting example of inter-Bantu fusion, we might observe the region to the east and south-east of Lake Victoria. Here Bantu who have come around or across the lake have mixed with others who have crossed from the eastern highlands through the non-Bantu zone of the rift valley. Elsewhere there have been constant and numerous inter-Bantu movements. Though, as we have seen, the main Bantu penetration into East Africa appears to have been from the west or south-west, this has not prevented secondary migrations in the opposite direction. Several tribes in central Tanzania claim to have originated through the fusion of a resident Bantu population with new arrivals, also Bantu, from the east or north-east. Some of these movements were connected with increasing populations and the need to open up more land for agriculture. Finally, the Ngoni movements, conquests and settlements in the nineteenth century (chapter 12) demonstrate how new Bantu tribes were formed in what had long been Bantu territory. It is not surprising then, that, although there have been Nilotes and Bantu in East Africa for one or two thousand years, the traditional histories of individual Nilotic and Bantu tribes usually go back only one, two or three hundred years, and never more than six hundred.

Thus we see the complex nature of tribal origins and compositions. Though we may for convenience classify tribes by their languages as Bantu, Nilotic, Cushitic, etc., the more we examine them, the more mixed we find their ancestries to be. A tribe emerges not by maintaining the pure blood of its ancestors, not by sedulously avoiding contact with its neighbours, but by successfully assimilating its diverse elements. To survive, a tribe must continually adjust itself to surrounding circumstances. This will be further borne out in the chapters that follow, covering the later histories of the main East African ethnic groups. The history of East Africa and of its component regions is not just a collection of histories of individual tribes or groups of tribes, but a story of fusion and interaction by which all tribes and groups have been constantly altered or even transformed. If we try to study tribes or groups in isolation, we will end up not with a history of East Africa, but with tribalist histories full of biases and antiquarianism.

Appendix: 'Hamites' and the Hamitic myth

In the foregoing account the reader will have noticed no mention of 'Hamites' or 'Hamitic influences'. Since these have figured prominently in other writings on the history of eastern Africa, some explanation is required. The term 'Hamitic' is highly confusing, and also hedged with racist overtones. It has been used in a variety of ways to denote linguistic, physical and cultural traits, and often more vaguely, reflecting European presumptions that light-skinned peoples are more intelligent than dark-skinned. For the 'Hamites' have commonly been envisaged as the 'more European-like' of Africans—in other words, those peoples with lighter skins, thinner lips and straighter noses inhabiting most of northern and north-eastern Africa. To these 'Hamites' have been attributed any remarkable technological feat, any notable political organisation, any trace of 'civilisation' in black Africa. For instance, old irrigation systems and dry-stone walling in the East African highlands and rock-cut wells in the plains, the coming of iron-working and the origins of the inter-lacustrine kingdoms, have all been related to 'Hamitic' invasions or influences from the north. Hence were invented theories of vanished 'Hamitic civilisations' in certain regions, theories of 'conquest of inferior by superior peoples' (as Speke surmised in the Lake Victoria region), theories of interaction and intermarriage between 'Hamites' and Negroes by which the latter were raised from utter barbarism (as Seligman imagined), and theories of imitation by which Negroes tried to improve their lot by copying the example of the 'Hamites'. As Seligman put it, 'the civilisations of Africa are the civilisations of the Hamites'; the history of Africa, he believed, could be written only in terms of 'Hamites' and their influences. Not surprisingly, the tendency in recent years has been to reject such illogical and prejudiced views of Africa and her past. Modern research shows that many of the presumed 'Hamites' existed only in the imagination of earlier writers.

It is odd, moreover, that the 'Hamites' as popularly conceived—or misconceived—should include not only the fabled founders of empires and the presumed authors of technological feats, but also peoples with very frugal material cultures and uncentralised political systems, notably some present-day pastoral tribes in eastern Africa. For the 'Hamitic problem' has been further confounded by its association with pastoralism. Large tracts of eastern and northern Africa are best suited to a herding life involving seasonal movements in search of pasture and water. This type of economy does not in general encourage the development of advanced material cultures or centralised political systems. But the pastoralist, with his proud bearing as he watches his herds and commands the plains with his spear, and contempt for his agricultural neighbours, has won a romantic admiration from some European observers. He has been hailed as innately superior, especially be he light-skinned. Clearly a definition of 'Hamite' on the basis of pastoralism or any other cultural consideration is subjective and unhelpful.

The use of 'Hamitic' to describe a physical (or racial) type can be avoided by adopting a more scientific terminology. The lighter-skinned inhabitants of northern and north-eastern Africa should properly be classified 'Caucasoid', or, where necessary, 'semi-Caucasoid' or 'Negroid-Caucasoid crosses'. But such descriptions would not extend to East African pastoralists such as Maasai, Karamojong, Turkana, Hima and Tusi, who have commonly been called 'Hamites' or 'semi-Hamites'. These peoples are decidedly Negroid, though some of them may have incorporated a small admixture of Caucasoid blood in their ancestry.

Lastly, as a linguistic term, 'Hamitic' has been used generally more scientifically and responsibly, but unfortunately in at least two main senses, referring either to a large family of languages stretching from the Moroccan to the Somali coasts, or to a division within this family covering much of Ethiopia and the Horn with scattered outposts in Kenya and Tanzania (e.g. the Iraqw). To prevent confusion, it is strongly recommended that we use Greenberg's linguistic terminology avoiding the word 'Hamitic'. We should thus refer to the main family as 'Afro-asiatic', and to the division as 'Cushitic' (as in Figure 12).[1] And, as stressed above, it is important not to confuse linguistic and physical terminology.

'Nilo-Hamites'

If 'Hamitic' is unacceptable, the same must apply to 'Nilo-Hamitic'. The peoples formerly designated 'Nilo-Hamites' belong to four or five main groupings—Kalenjin (with Tatoga), Masai, Itunga (i.e. Karamo-jong-Teso cluster) and the Bari cluster (see Figure 12). They were called 'Nilo-Hamites' because they were considered on both linguistic and cultural grounds to be mixtures of Nilotes and 'Hamites'. The 'Hamites' in this case would have been Cushitic-speakers. We would, however, strongly oppose any suggestion that the 'Nilo-Hamites' be reclassified

[1] One word of warning: Cushitic languages have no connection whatever with the Nubian and Middle Nile regions which the ancient Egyptians called Kush, and where the kingdom of Kush, based on the cities of Napata and Meroe, flourished some two thousand years ago.

'Nilo-Cushites'. Recent studies of their languages show that they are basically Nilotic, and that any Cushitic word-borrowings are superficial. Some of them, notably Kalenjin and Maasai, have assimilated numbers of Cushites and have also made cultural borrowings from them (as explained in this chapter), but this is irrelevant to a strictly linguistic classification which we insist on using here. Moreover, it is now believed that the so-called 'Nilo-Hamites' do not constitute a single branch within the Nilotes. As Dr Ehret argues, 'the Nilo-Hamitic hypothesis has made a unity of diversity'.[1] The Nilotic languages should be divided into three main branches (see page 81 and Figure 12). The River-Lake branch comprises the peoples formerly called 'Nilotes' or 'Nilotes proper'; the Plains and Highland branches are those formerly called 'Nilo-Hamites'.

Further reading

Most of the literature dealing with the settlement of East Africa is outdated, controversial or difficult for the student or general reader. However, the following contributions to the subject deserve notice.

MURDOCK, G. P. *Africa: Its Peoples and their Culture History*, New York, 1959. (Introductory chapters and those on East Africa.)

MCCALL, D. F. *Africa in Time-Perspective: A Discussion of Historical Reconstruction from Unwritten Sources*, Ghana and Boston University Presses, 1964. (A general discussion of historical reconstruction.)

OLIVER, R. and MATHEW, G. (Eds) *History of East Africa*, I, Oxford, 1963.

SHINNIE, P. L. (Ed.) *The African Iron Age*, Oxford, 1971, esp. chapter 6.

COLE, S. *The Prehistory of East Africa* (2nd edition), New York, 1963; London, 1964.

KIMAMBO, I. N. and TEMU, A. J. (Eds) *A History of Tanzania*, Nairobi, 1969.

For linguistic map and classification:

GREENBERG, J. H. *Languages of Africa*, Indiana and the Hague, 1963.

For recent archaeological work:

Azania, Journal of the British Institute of History and Archaeology in East Africa, published annually since 1966.

For Bantu expansion:

OLIVER, R. 'The Problem of the Bantu Expansion', *Journal of African History, VII*, 1966, pp. 361–76.

POSNANSKY, M. 'Bantu Genesis: Archaeological Reflexions', *Journal of African History, IX*, 1968, pp. 1–11.

[1] For this same reason the recently suggested term 'Paranilotic' for the old 'Nilo-Hamitic' seems unacceptable.

5

The Coast Before the Arrival of the Portuguese

Neville Chittick

Our written historical records for the interior of Africa go back only a century, and the oral traditions nowhere more than five hundred years or so, and that only where conditions for their being remembered are exceptional. For the history of the coast, however, we have written accounts which profess to give a record of events spanning the last two thousand years.

These historical sources fall into two groups; those written by people living outside East Africa, and those set down by chroniclers who lived on the coast itself. For the period before the arrival of the Portuguese, the first group consists mainly of the works of Arab geographers. These works, the product of the most advanced civilisation of its age, are mostly descriptions of the world as it was then known, together with some historical observations and anecdotes; others contain accounts of travels. So far as East Africa is concerned, they are based mostly on the reports brought back by merchants, but one or two are written by persons who actually sailed to these shores and so at least in part are based on what the authors saw. These accounts are of the highest evidential value, since they describe the state of affairs when they were set down and also events which had happened only a short time before. Unfortunately, however, many parts of these accounts are difficult to understand. The geographers believed that southern Africa curved round in an easterly direction to join up with countries of the Far East, and this makes accounts of the southern regions and islands confusing: Waq-Waq, for example, is usually the name of some islands off eastern Asia, but also denotes an area of Africa. Many names are corrupt and difficult to interpret, for short vowels are not usually written in Arabic, and many of the consonants are distinguished from each other only by dots, so that the placing of a dot in the wrong place, or its omission, will change the pronunciation of the name. There is often imprecision in the use of terms, too: 'Zenj' is used both for black people in general, and for a particular negroid group. Moreover the geographers were not particularly interested in the history of the regions they were describing and neither they, nor most of their informants, understood the language of the native peoples of the region.

The historical sources from outside East Africa are thus of the highest value for what they do tell us; but this is not a great deal. The most important works are those of al-Mas'udi (first half of the tenth century) and Ibn Battuta, who describes things as he saw them in about 1331.

The second group of sources comprises those accounts which were set down on the East African coast. These are mostly chronicles of individual towns, giving the names of their rulers and some account of their doings. They were written in Arabic or in Swahili in Arabic script. The only one of these chronicles which is of any antiquity is that of Kilwa, which was written around 1530 and has come to us in two differing versions, one transmitted by the Portuguese historian, de Barros, who wrote in the mid-sixteenth century, and the other copied in Zanzibar in 1877. Most of the rest of the chronicles were set down only in recent times, and none can be traced back beyond the second half of the eighteenth century. These histories from our coast have much to tell of events before the arrival of the Portuguese; one of them even has quite a lot to say of happenings before the Hijra, the flight of the Prophet Muhammad from Mecca to Medina in A.D. 622, which marks the beginning of the Islamic era.[1] But an historical document can only set out facts remembered at the time when it was written, unless the author is relying on an earlier written source. To this extent they should be treated as we would oral traditions that have been committed to writing. While all historians have appreciated that some of the stories told in these chronicles are mythical or semi-mythical, none of them has submitted these chronicles to a sufficiently critical approach. Most historians of the coast have been trained in the European tradition of recent historical scholarship in fields where we have many sources; those trained in the traditions of oral history have concentrated their attentions on the peoples of the interior.

Application of the principles of criticism used with oral traditions, together with other evidence with which we shall deal later, is leading to some important amendments to facts of the history of the coast as

[1] Years of the Islamic era are indicated by the letters A.H. *(anno Hegirae)* before the date thus: A.H. 600 (= A.D. 1203–4).

hitherto received. These new theories have not yet been entirely accepted and it will be found that in some respects the dating or account of events in what follows differs from what will be found in older books; where appropriate I have indicated the view previously taken of certain matters.

We have just referred to another type of evidence. This is that derived from archaeology, by which we mean not only the evidence of objects and structures which have been dug out of the ground, but also of inscriptions on graves and buildings, and the style of architecture of the buildings themselves. There is also the evidence provided by linguistics, by place-names, by anthropology and ethnology, but these are of small importance in the study of the history of the coast as compared with that of the interior, where other evidence is scanty.

Archaeological research in this region has only been undertaken on any significant scale in the last few years and we have already learnt much from the discoveries. Substantial evidence for the revision of aspects of coast history has come from excavations, in particular from the coins which were minted by certain of the sultans of Kilwa.

Before Islam

The original population of the coast and its hinterland consisted of peoples who lived by hunting and gathering; they were responsible for the 'microlithic' stone industries, with very small tools, typical of the late stone age. The Sanye and Boni, who live in the hinterland of the northern Kenya and southern Somali coasts, follow this mode of life and are probably survivors of these peoples. The Sanye speak a southern Cushitic language, and appear to be a relic of an early Cushitic movement into East Africa. They may have partially supplanted a population allied to the Bushmen and Hottentots who live further south at the present day but who were formerly much more widespread;[1] we cannot yet say much about the relative distribution of these peoples. Others of the early Cushites, in the interior, are believed to have had a pastoral economy, with cattle, in the first millennium.

Some historians have suggested that Egyptians, Phoenicians, Persians and others may have come to the East African coast centuries before the birth of Christ. There is, however, no real evidence that this was so; Herodotus gives a brief account of the circumnavigation of Africa by Phoenicians, who are supposed to have wintered on the continent, but this account is almost certainly spurious. The Egyptians, it is true,

---

[1] The theory is currently advanced that these are not ethnically entirely distinct from the negroid peoples, as was thought hitherto.

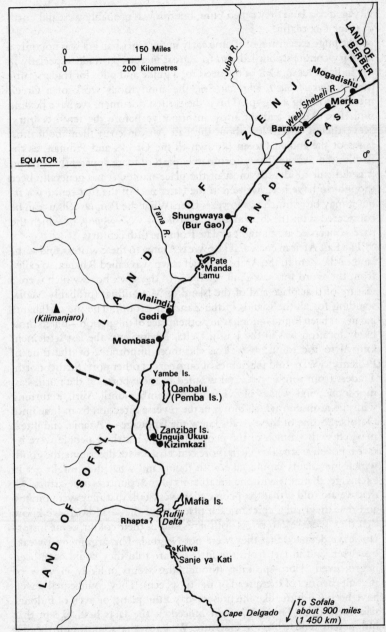

Figure 13 The coast before the arrival of the Portuguese

Within the map:
- 150 Miles
- 200 Kilometres
- Juba R.
- LAND OF BERBER
- Mogadishu
- Webi Shebeli R.
- Merka
- Barawa
- ZENJ
- BANADIR COAST
- EQUATOR
- 0°
- Tana R.
- LAND OF ZENJ
- Shungwaya (Bur Gao)
- Pate
- Manda
- Lamu
- Malindi
- (Kilimanjaro)
- Gedi
- Mombasa
- Yambe Is.
- Qanbalu (Pemba Is.)
- Zanzibar Is.
- Unguja Ukuu
- Kizimkazi
- LAND OF SOFALA
- Mafia Is.
- Rhapta?
- Rufiji Delta
- Kilwa
- Sanje ya Kati
- Cape Delgado
- To Sofala about 900 miles (1 450 km)

voyaged to a land they called Punt, but this was probably west and north of Cape Guardafui.

The huge expansion of Rome early in the Christian era was not only a military conquest, but led also to a great increase in trade, especially in the Indian Ocean. Out of the need for a guide and pilot for traders came the *Periplus of the Erythraean Sea*, the anonymous work of a Greek merchant living in Egypt. This is the earliest document we have dealing with East Africa and the most informative before the tenth century. Nevertheless, it tells less about the East African coast than about most lands of the Indian Ocean (known to the Greeks and Romans as the Erythraean Sea) and, as unfortunately parts of it are apparently corrupt, it is difficult to identify most of the place-names. It has generally been thought to have been written in the latter part of the first century A.D., but it may be as much as 150 years later. What the *Periplus* tells us can be considered with the information in Ptolemy's *Geography*, of which the parts concerned are thought to date from the fifth century.

The East African coast was known as Azania to these writers, and as the land of the Zenj to the Arabs. Its chief town was called Rhapta, so called from the word for 'sewn', in reference to the sewn boats which were a feature of that place and of the island of Menouthias (probably Mafia, standing for all the islands of the Zanzibar group). The site of Rhapta has never been found—nor has any other place of this period—but its most likely location was in the Rufiji Delta. Rhapta was the last settlement known to the south, as well as the most important, by the time of Ptolemy; we are told the names of numbers of other ports further north. Traders from south-west Arabia sailed to these ports on the north-east monsoon wind which blows from November until April, returning with the monsoon which blows in the reverse direction from June until October. Some of these Arabs knew the language of Azania, and inter-married with women of the people there. What these people were by race is not clear; the *Periplus* is more concerned with describing the goods which merchants should take with them, and what they might get in exchange, than it is with the inhabitants of the countries it describes. All that we are told is that the people were very tall, that they were pirates, and that they had a chief in each place; since they had boats we know that they were seafarers. As nothing is said of their colour, some histor-ians have deduced that they were not Negroid. This argument is weak, however, and in fact from the little we are told they could have been negro, even Bantu-speaking (though this seems unlikely in view of present theories of the spread of Bantu speech). They could equally well have been Cushitic, like the present-day Ethiopians, or even of Indone-sian extraction. This last would indeed fit the facts best, except that Indonesians tend to be short in stature. We know that some time in the first millennium A.D. many Indonesians settled in Madagascar, bringing with them food crops, notably the banana, which were to become of great importance to Africa. It is possible, too, that they settled on the coast of what is now Kenya and Tanzania, although the time of the *Periplus* is rather earlier than it is thought this immigration took place. But the fact that Ptolemy speaks of man-eating Ethiopians in the southernmost part of this region indicates that the people were dark in colour, for this is the connotation of 'Ethiopian' in Greek.

The Azanian coast was under the suzerainty of Charibael, who was ruler of Himyar in south-west Arabia; we are told that it had long been under the domination of whichever was the most powerful state in Arabia. However, the people of Mouza (the port of Mocha in the Yemen) controlled the coast under the authority of Charibael, and it is from this port that most of the ships came.

The goods that they came to barter for were those typical of the exports of East Africa throughout history, primarily the products of the animals which were so exotic to the rest of the known world. First in importance was ivory; then turtle-shell and rhinoceros horn. In addition a little coconut oil was exported; this piece of information is important, because it shows that the coconut palm had already reached the coast from the east, and also that some people at least were living in permanent settlements. It is notable that slaves are not mentioned, though we are told that they were brought from the coasts of the Horn of Africa. From that northern region, the chief exports were aromatic gums and spices.

The main goods which the traders brought to exchange for these commodities were metal tools—hatchets and daggers and awls, and lances which were specially made for this trade at Mouza. These tools would mostly have been of iron, and indicate that the inhabitants of Azania had little or no knowledge of how to smelt this metal. The traders also brought glass vessels, and, to some places, a little wine and wheat as gifts to get the goodwill of the inhabitants.

For some four centuries after the time of Ptolemy we have no reliable information about the coast. It is probable that some trade continued with the Arab world, and that there was a trickle of Arab immigration. This may be at the root of unreliable traditions of colonisers being sent by Harun al-Rashid or others, but this is by no means certain. There is a tradition from Oman, of doubtful authenticity, of an emigration from that country to the land of Zenj in the seventh century. This is the story of the brothers Sulaiman and Sa'id, joint rulers of Oman, who are supposed to have left with their followers after being defeated by an 'Umayyad army. And de Barros tells of the coming of some heretic Muslim people he calls Emozaidij, by which he probably means followers of the Shi'a leader Zaid. This probably has some historical truth, and may incorporate memory of the arrival, in the eighth or ninth century of some Zaidis on the Banadir coast, from which they were later displaced by

103

orthodox immigrants, becoming largely absorbed in the interior by the pagan inhabitants. Such movements and trade were certainly on a very small scale, for no archaeological remains of settlements of this (or the earlier) period have yet been found.[1]

In the ninth and tenth centuries we find the first information in Arabic sources, notably al-Mas'udi who died about A.D. 945; and it is from that period that the earliest identified town sites date. Most of the ships at that time came to the coast from the Persian Gulf, especially from the great port of Siraf, and from Oman. Al-Mas'udi himself made at least two journeys to the East African coast, once from each place. In this and subsequent periods the coast was usually considered as divided into three parts: Berber, which extended down to the Webi Shebeli; the land of the Zenj proper, which extended thence down to the land of Sofala, whose northern limit was probably in the region of Pangani, opposite the island of Pemba, and extended for a thousand miles [1 600 km] or so to the south. Beyond this is the shadowy, hardly-known land of Waq-Waq. Of the islands, only one is mentioned by name; this is Qanbalu, which is probably to be identified with Pemba.

The people of all this region are referred to by the Arabs as Zenj. They were governed by kings who could be elected and who maintained armies. It was a religious-minded society; we are told more than once of men preaching to the people, and some of these priests probably advised the king. Al-Mas'udi tells us that they harnessed oxen like horses, and used them both for transport and for war.[2] The Zenj cultivated bananas, millet, and, on the islands, coconuts; they also ate meat and honey. The trade in ivory flourished; it was shipped, we are told, to Oman and thence to India and China. Al-Mas'udi also mentions the production of gold in the land of Sofala and the Waqwaq.

The Zenj were probably a Bantu-speaking negroid people who are believed to have moved into this region in the first centuries A.D. Such people were almost certainly present on the coast from the Usambara mountains northwards, and in the southern part of Somalia where was situated, or was soon to come into being, the famous town of Shungw- aya. Moreover, in a passage apparently referring to the southern part of the coast, al-Mas'udi gives us two words of the Zenj language which are held to be Bantu; the identification is, however, less certain than has been maintained. He also tells us that some of the Zenj tribes are cannibals and sharpen their teeth; the latter is a trait found among certain Bantu tribes in modern times.

[1] A few finds of Greek and Roman coins have been reported from East Africa, but some are undocumented and the others have been found with later coins, and probably reached East Africa in a later period.

[2] Their social organisation seems to have resembled that of the western lacustrine states, notably Rwanda, in recent centuries, where a cattle-keeping, pastoral aristocracy ruled over a settled peasant population.

Early Muslim settlement

The number of Muslims who had so far settled on the coast must have been small; as late as about A.D. 1150 the towns of the mainland from Barawa south are described as pagan. This is according to al-Idrisi who, however, does not appear to be very reliable. We know from al-Mas'udi that in the tenth century the island of Qanbalu had a mixed population of Muslims and Zenj pagans; the former, presumably Arabs, had conquered it long enough before for the Muslims to have adopted the Zenj language. The ruling family was of the Muslim group. There are other indications of Arab immigration in this period; there was a colony of Muslims at Merka, probably dating from the tenth century, and also as we shall see at Manda near Lamu and at Unguja Ukuu in Zanzibar. Probably most of these immigrants came from the Persian Gulf; those at Merka came from the great port of Siraf, and de Barros tells us of the coming of a group of refugee people from Al-Ahsa near Bahrein on the opposite side of the Gulf, who are supposed to have founded Mogadishu and Barawa. This event, if historical, most likely occurred in the eleventh century. Traditions of the Zanzibar islands and the Mrima coast tell of people called Wadebuli trading and settling on the coast. These people probably came from Daybul, which was a great Muslim port in north-west India near the mouth of the Indus, until it was destroyed about A.D. 1250. These people were probably then sailing to the southern part of the coast too, though few seem to have settled and they were rapidly absorbed.

The earliest coastal settlements which have yet been discovered date from the ninth and tenth centuries, and we are able to supplement knowledge from historical sources with that from archaeology.

These trading towns, not only in the earliest period, but until quite recent times, were sited for preference on islands; failing this the favourite position was on a spit of land almost encircled by creeks and mangrove swamps. This was for security; with a stretch of water protecting their wealthy towns from the poorer inhabitants of the hinterland, they had no need of defensive walls, which in the earliest period are seldom found. They would cultivate on the mainland if it was close, crossing to their *mashamba*[1] in boats, but did not venture into the interior. A very similar pattern is still found in the Lamu archipelago, where all the main settlements are on islands. Indeed, in recent times of insecurity on the mainland, refugees have settled at the sites of old island towns which had been abandoned for centuries.

Though these towns looked out on the ocean for the wealth they derived from their commerce, they had to obtain from the mainland

[1] Kiswahili: cultivated land.

the goods to barter for their imports. These goods were brought to the coast by the people of the interior; there is hardly any evidence of expeditions inland until the nineteenth century. It is probable that goods which came from far off were bartered from tribe to tribe, rather than being carried by long distance caravans.

Two town sites of this period have been partly excavated. The lowest levels at Kilwa date probably to the ninth century, but it was a poor though quite extensive place. Most or all the inhabitants were pagan, but they were trading on a small scale to the Arab lands. Unguja Ukuu flourished at this period, but has not been dug; to judge by the amount of imported pottery and the finding of a hoard of gold dinars there many years ago it probably had a Muslim population. We know from a famous inscription dated the equivalent of A.D. 1107, in a mosque at Kizimkazi in Zanzibar, that a Muslim town was there at that time.

The most important early town at which excavations have been carried out is Manda, near Lamu. Though work has been on a small scale, enough has been found to show that it was a very wealthy place. Some of the buildings were of coral stone set in mortar, though many were of mud and wattle; masonry walls built against the sea are of very large coral blocks, many weighing over a ton—a massive form of construction found nowhere else in sub-Saharan Africa. From the finds we can tell something of the goods which were imported. Probably cloth was as important as anything, but of the objects which have survived, Islamic pottery, imported from the Persian Gulf, is the most important. This is found in very large quantities indeed; it is about seventy-five times commoner than at Kilwa in the same period. Some fragments of Chinese porcelain and stoneware show that trade had already begun with China, though (as in all subsequent periods also) this was not imported direct but transhipped in the Gulf and probably elsewhere earlier on its journey. Glass was also imported from the Arab countries in large quantities—much more than at any later period; it is worth remarking that glass was also mentioned in the *Periplus* as an import. Oddly enough, hardly any glass beads of this period have been found either at Manda or Kilwa, though shell beads were made in large numbers. Coins are lacking too, so trade was by barter; at Kilwa, cowrie shells were used for trade. A remarkable industry was the smelting of iron (of which only very poor ores are available near the coast) at both places, and apparently on a large scale at Manda; so that there seems to be some truth in al-Idrisi's remarks about the iron mining and working (and export of iron) of the Malindi-Mombasa region.

We learn more of the exports from Arab authors. Most of them are the time-honoured natural products of which we have already read in the *Periplus*—ivory above all, which was sent as far as China, ambergris, leopard skins and turtle-shell. But a new commodity, gold, is mentioned for the first time in the tenth century. This was known to exist in the interior of the mysterious land of Waq-Waq, far to the south, and was mined in what is now Rhodesia. For export, it was carried down to the coast of the Sofala country, and shipped from there; this trade, however, does not seem to have developed until a later date. Subsequently, as we shall see, this was to become much the most important source of Kilwa's wealth. Slaves are only once mentioned, and then only as being shanghaied after an episode of legitimate trading; but we know that large numbers of slaves must have been exported—perhaps mostly from the Horn—since there were enough Zenj in Iraq to stage a long and largely successful revolt in the ninth century.

The spread of the 'Shirazi'

No archaeological work has been done on the Somali coast, but the towns of the Banadir were probably becoming places of importance in the eleventh and twelfth centuries. Several waves of immigrants came to this region, probably mostly from the Persian Gulf, but some from southern Arabia. These groups settled among the Bantu of the area,[1] each establishing a sort of alliance with the tribe with which they were closest in contact. The immigrants brought few if any women with them, so that most of their descendants must have increasingly intermarried with the Bantu.

Many of these groups of immigrants settled in Mogadishu, which by the thirteenth century was the most important town on the coast. It was a mercantile city, governed by a council of elders, and already controlled the gold trade with Sofala. Some of these immigrants came from Persia, as we know from two thirteenth-century inscriptions in Mogadishu. Of outstanding importance was the group of people associated with the name Shirazi, though whether the immigrants were all or mainly Persian is doubtful—Shiraz was the capital of Fars, which controlled the eastern side of the Gulf where there were many Arabs too; and the name of the capital town is often given for that of the province.

Though there was at least one Shirazi family at Mogadishu, most of them seem to have settled further south, in the Shungwaya region, and at its main town of the same name.[2] Here there evolved a polity, more African in character than at Mogadishu, though apparently ruled by the Shirazi element. It was from this zone that all the great north-eastern group of Bantu tribes later dispersed under pressure from the Galla.

[1] Few if any Somali had by this time reached the region south of Mogadishu.

[2] The site of this town is traditionally at Bur Gavo, a little north of the Kenya border. But recent work indicates that this town was not occupied before the sixteenth century; probably there was an earlier site (or sites) of the town. The area concerned extends from the region of Lamu to the Juba river.

From this region of the Banadir coast the Shirazi, by then of somewhat mixed blood, began to migrate to places further south, probably in the second half of the twelfth century. They settled at various places, no doubt at various times, including probably Shanga (and Manda) in the Lamu islands, the Tanga area (Yambe Island), Pemba, Mafia, the Comoro Islands, and most important of all, Kilwa. With the arrival of the Shirazi at Kilwa, begins the period when the Kilwa Chronicle provides us with the first detailed knowledge of events and personalities. This is in a sketchy and inaccurate form, but nevertheless approaches what can be called an historical work.[1] It would not be useful here to give a detailed account of the sultans of Kilwa: this can be found in works listed at the end of this chapter.

At the start of the Shirazi dynasty, towards the end of the twelfth century, Kilwa seems to have been of little more importance than neighbouring places; indeed it is quite probable that the earliest sultans ruled from Mafia and not from Kilwa. The early coins are commoner there than at Kilwa; of these the very first to appear are minute pieces, some of silver, which bear the name of al-Hasan. The next in date have the name 'Ali ibn al-Hasan, probably his son and the founder of the dynasty as set out in the Chronicle. Succeeding sultans were much troubled by wars with the neighbouring island state of Shanga, on Sanje ya Kati, and they were twice deposed by usurpers from that place. However, by about A.D. 1230 Kilwa is of sufficient importance to be mentioned, along with Mogadishu, as a stage on the voyage to Madagascar. By the time of the death of the last of the dynasty, the grandson of the founder, near the end of the thirteenth century, Kilwa was a power to be reckoned with, second only to Mogadishu.

The Ahdali or Abu'l-Mawahib Dynasty at Kilwa

The throne of Kilwa was now seized by a man belonging to a family (Ahdali) which seems to have come from the Hadhramaut. Soon after the beginning of this dynasty there is a marked change in the archaeological record, notably in the style of architecture and in local pottery. This change is dramatically exemplified in the building of the great palace and trading emporium of Husuni Kubwa, covering over two acres and the largest single early building known in Africa south of the Sahara. These innovations were almost certainly associated with new immigrants, coming probably this time from South Arabia. They were

[1] This account, and much of what follows, sets out the author's own views on the origin and early history of the Shirazi and succeeding dynasty at Kilwa. These views (Chittick, 1965) have found wide acceptance, but it should be stated here that the hitherto received view is that the Shirazi came direct from the Gulf to Kilwa in the latter part of the tenth century, and established a dynasty which was still ruling when the Portuguese arrived.

Sunni Muslims of the Shafi'i persuasion, whereas their predecessors had been Kharijites.

It is probable at this time, too, that Kilwa gained entire control of Sofala (which name now denotes a specific town) and of other parts on the southern coast. Kilwa had earlier shared in the gold trade with Mogadishu but now had almost a monopoly. The gold was paid for mostly in cloth (much of which was manufactured at Kilwa) and glass beads, of which increasingly large numbers are found from deposits dating from about A.D. 1200 onwards. It was the huge profits of the gold trade that made it possible to carry out the great amount of building executed at this time. Previously stone houses had been rare; now they became common and, besides Husuni Kubwa, the Great Mosque was much extended at this time. Expensive Chinese porcelain, of which only tiny quantities had hitherto been imported, now became common.

Kilwa controlled Mafia and the ports of the Mozambique coast, but very little else. Zanzibar and Pemba were probably under her hegemony for a period, but in the fifteenth century Zanzibar was independent and minting its own coinage. But nevertheless much of the mercantile prosperity of the times rubbed off on other towns; it is from this period that many of the smaller ruined settlements that are scattered along the coast have their origin. Each of these was autonomous; some, like Gedi and other towns of the northern Kenya coast, were quite large, with many houses of stone. The dwellings in many others were of mud and wattle, like the houses of the coastal villages at the present day; only the main mosque and the tombs, which are often large, were of stone.

In the second half of the fifteenth century Kilwa suffered from severe dynastic intrigues, and it is probable that the rate of profit to be had from the gold trade was much reduced. She was thus already in decline when the Portuguese appeared on the scene, and was easily overcome by them. In this period, for reasons that are not clear, the focus of power and prosperity, which had first moved southwards from the Banadir coast to the Kilwa region, began to move back again, now to the northern part of the Kenya coast. This process was much accelerated after the establishment of Portuguese suzerainty; in the sixteenth century Kilwa and other places declined with extreme rapidity while those in the north suffered less, or even increased in prosperity.

Mombasa was rising in importance in the fifteenth century and, further north, Pate was becoming a substantial town. This place has established for itself an unjustifiably important place in the early history of the coast, as a result of an over-hasty acceptance of the story told in the unreliable Pate Chronicle. It was in fact non-existent or insignificant before the fourteenth century, and rose to importance only in the sixteenth and later centuries, with which period we are not here concerned.

The Fourteenth-century scene

We can form a fair idea of the aspect of the towns of the coast, their inhabitants and the way of life in the fourteenth and fifteenth centuries from the evidence of excavations, supplemented by the eye-witness accounts of Ibn Battuta and the Portuguese.

The inhabitants can be considered as falling into three classes in most of the important settlements. The ruling class (except where a recently arrived immigrant group had succeeded in making itself dominant) was of mixed Arab and African ancestry, brown in colour, well read in the faith of Islam. Such would probably be also the landowners, the skilled artisans, and most of the religious functionaries, and merchants. Inferior to them (in many cases in a state of slavery) were the pure-blooded Africans, some of them recently arrived, who performed the menial tasks, and tilled the fields. Apart from both were the transient or recently settled Arabs, still incompletely assimilated into the society.

Of occupations, that of merchant was the most prominent; many were also engaged in crewing the ships in which the merchants also sailed. Apart from agriculture (including, no doubt, the growing of cotton), the weaving of cloth seems to have been the biggest industry. Other crafts include the striking of coins and other work in copper, the carving of bone and ivory, and the working of semi-precious stones. Many must have been employed as stone masons and carvers, the standard achieved in the latter (especially in some inscriptions) being very high.

The towns must have looked much like the older places on the coast, such as Lamu, at the present day. The houses were built very close to one another, often sharing a party wall and sometimes linked together, suggesting a family relationship between the occupiers. The blocks of buildings were separated by very narrow lanes, though often there were gardens behind. They were of one storey, except in the largest towns, up to three being found at Kilwa. Roofs were flat, built of stone laid on mangrove poles which were usually squared; the weight of these massive roofs and the strength of the timbers restricted the width of the rooms, which is 8 feet [2.4 m] or a little less. The houses followed a fairly uniform plan. They were entered by a doorway leading to a sunken courtyard. Facing on to this was usually a reception room or verandah, with the main living room behind, and bedrooms to the rear of this; such a basic arrangement was often much elaborated by the addition of other rooms. The main entrances into the courtyard of the larger houses were impressive, and in the Kilwa area ornamented with borders of recessed cut stone, sometimes with herring-bone ornament, the commonest decorative motif at this period. At least one latrine, well constructed in cut stone, was included in each house, with an adjoining bidet for ablutions. Houses at Gedi were also provided with a special compartment for cooling water jars.

There were usually no windows, except in the façade facing the courtyard, so the inner rooms must have been dark, but their ceilings and thick walls would have been cool. The walls were plastered and never painted. Decoration of any sort was sparing. Ornamental niches in cut stone were sometimes set in walls or on either side of doorways, which were often beautifully assembled of cut coral. Some of the main rooms were decorated with hangings, probably carpets, and carved wooden friezes, as is attested by rows of holes for suspension pegs. In the fourteenth century decorative motifs in cut stone are found; in the succeeding century their place, in the Kilwa region, was to some extent taken by glazed bowls of Persian and Chinese wares which were set in the lower side of vaulted roofs of buildings.

Cooking was commonly done over a portable earthenware stove, with three horns on which the cooking vessel was placed, with charcoal beneath. A sort of bread was baked of rice or millet flour in an oven set in the wall (*fanuri ya mkate wa mofa*).

The upper classes ate off imported glazed Islamic ware, or Chinese porcelain; by the fifteenth century even the poorer people seem to have had their food served in an eating-bowl rather than straight from the cooking-pot. At Kilwa, at least, those who could not afford glazed imported bowls still had individual bowls to eat from.

We can supplement this picture by eye-witness accounts. Ibn Battuta early in the early fourteenth century describes Mogadishu as a town of enormous size living by trade, with many rich merchants. He writes of a curious system under which one of these men would entertain any visiting merchant, who could only buy and sell through his host. The town was famous for its woven fabrics, which were exported widely. A highly developed court life revolved round the sheikh, as the ruler was entitled. When Ibn Battuta went to the mosque in his presence, he was brought special clothes to wear. The sheikh walked through the town with a four-tiered canopy or parasol of silk carried over him, and accompanied by a band of drums, trumpets and pipes. The people were obese, from eating to excess. He describes a meal brought to him from the sheikh: rice cooked in ghee with a seasoned sauce of meat and vegetables, and side dishes of bananas cooked in fresh milk and ginger, peppers, and mangoes in sour milk.

Kilwa sounds from Ibn Battuta's description to have been rather smaller than Mogadishu. He is most struck by the piety of the sultan, who was being visited by numbers of Sherifs from Hejaz. These descendants of the Prophet Muhammad were being maintained by the sultan out of booty taken in raiding expeditions against the pagan Zenj of the interior. The Zenj, at least those of Kilwa itself, tattooed their faces, as do the Makua and Makonde at the present day; though it seems unlikely that these tribes were in the area of Kilwa at the time.

At the beginning of the sixteenth century, the Portuguese were considerably impressed with what they found in the towns of the coast. They were most struck with the luxury of the adornment of the upper classes. Clothes were of rich silk as well as cotton, though slaves wore only a loin cloth; we read of much gold and silver jewellery, earrings and bangles for both arms and legs, none of which have come down to us. We learn more of their agriculture; millet and rice were the grain crops, and we know from another source that rice was actually exported to Aden, and so must have been obtained in quantity from the mainland. Oranges, lemons, pomegranates and Indian figs as well as onions and other vegetables were grown in gardens watered from wells. Fat-tailed sheep, goats, cattle and hens were raised; of course fish also formed a large part of the diet. Bees were kept in cylindrical hives hanging from trees, much as on the mainland at the present day. The boats of the coast ran up to about fifty tons, built with planks sewn with coir cords and with matting sails. These vessels were evidently of the *mtepe* type in use until recently, whose ancestry goes back to the time of the *Periplus*.

An Islamic society

In conclusion, we should try to set in perspective this society which flourished on the eastern coast before A.D. 1500.

There is little doubt that this civilisation was the highest which existed at the time in Africa south of the Sahara. To what extent it was an 'African' society has been much argued, often in a muddled way, for to think of a cultural unity related to the continent as a whole is only confusing.

Culturally Africa falls into three or four divisions. The northern part, all that north of the Sahara, with fingers as it were, extending across the desert and up the Nile into the Sudanese belt, belongs to the Mediterranean world; Ethiopia too belongs partly to that sphere, and links more closely with the Arabian sub-continent on the other side of the Red Sea. The eastern coast and Madagascar belong to the world of the Indian Ocean. All these regions have closer links with lands overseas than with the rest of the African cultural unity. To people who have ships, the sea is a road, not a barrier: it is the land, especially waterless land and thick forest, which divides.

These cities of the coast look out over the ocean; their society was primarily Islamic, and their way of life mercantile. This does not mean to say that it was Arab; the immigrants were probably few in number, and intermarrying with African women and those already of mixed blood, their stock was rapidly integrated with the local people. Probably by the second or third generation they would have abandoned their spoken language for Kiswahili or the local language, though retaining Arabic for writing. Some elements of the African culture survived and were incorporated in the whole but were always secondary to the Islamic framework.

At the same time, the impact of this civilisation on much of the mainland coast was slight, and inland non-existent. It is unlikely that any Moslems went into the interior, save on an occasional war-like raid, dignified by Ibn Battuta as *jihad*, a holy war. Their religion never penetrated beyond the shore of the mainland, nor did their impressive skills in building have any influence in the hinterland. Buildings in stone and the burning of lime for mortar were unknown even 5 miles [8 km] from the coast.

We should picture this civilisation as a remote outpost of Islam, looking for its spiritual inspiration to the homeland of its religion, but hardly contributing to the advancement of science or of learning. Scornful of their pagan neighbours, but willing to compromise with them in the interest of profit, the citizens of these towns built up a society and culture that had much that was individual to itself, but which contributed little to the heart of Africa.

Further reading

As explained in the introduction, the account set out above differs from the hitherto received history in certain respects. The arguments supporting these differences are set out in three articles by the author, and other earlier works should be read bearing these arguments and conclusions in mind. The three articles are:

CHITTICK, N. 'The "Shirazi" Colonisation of East Africa', *Journal of African History*, *VI, 3* (1965) (pp. 275–94).

CHITTICK, N. 'Kilwa, a Preliminary Report', *Azania, I*, (1966) (pp. 1–36).

CHITTICK, N. 'A New Look at the History of Pate', *Journal of African History*, *X, 3* (1969) (pp. 375–91).

Other reference books include:

FREEMAN–GRENVILLE, G. S. P. *The East African Coast: Select Documents from the First to the Earlier Nineteenth Century*, Oxford University Press, 1962. (A convenient source-book which gives translations of most of the important documents.)

FREEMAN–GRENVILLE, G. S. P. *Medieval History of the Coast of Tanganyika*, Oxford University Press, 1962. (Sets out and analyses the versions of the Kilwa Chronicle. The archaeological sections of this work are somewhat unreliable even where they are not out of date.)

113

OLIVER, R. and MATHEW, G. (Eds) *History of East Africa I* (G. Mathew, The East African Coast until the Coming of the Portuguese), Oxford University Press, 1963. Reprinted with other early chapters as *History of East Africa: The Early Period*, Nairobi, 1967.

GRAY, SIR J. *A History of Zanzibar*, London, 1962. (A standard work, but follows the old chronology.)

GARLAKE, P. S. *The Early Islamic Architecture of the East African Coast*, Oxford University Press, 1966. (An exhaustive and well-illustrated account of the subject.)

CERULLI, E. *Somalia, Scritti vari editi ed inediti*, 3 vols, Roma, 1957, 1959 and 1964. (Contains a wealth of information; in Italian with Arabic texts.)

KIRKMAN, J. S. *Men and Monuments of the East African Coast*, Lutterworth Press, London, 1966. (Gives a popular account of the sites in their historical setting, with emphasis on Kenya. The same author's archaeological reports on Gedi and other sites may also be consulted.)

6

The Coast from the Portuguese Invasion to the Rise of the Zanzibar Sultanate

F. J. Berg

Until the beginning of the nineteenth century the East African coastal belt belonged to the rest of the continent only in a geographical sense. Before A.D. 1800 events at the coast passed almost unnoticed in the interior, while people living along the coast were rarely touched by what happened upcountry. But in the long run the destiny of the coast became indissolubly linked to that of the entire region. From our present perspective, the most significant development on the coast during the period 1500 to 1850 was the growth of long distance trade between coastal and upcountry Africans.[1] Yet, as will be seen, the origin of this caravan trade was in comparatively recent times. It seems less a logical outgrowth of past experience than a radical break with tradition, and it marked a new departure in the relationship between coast and hinterland.

Throughout most of the years prior to 1850 inhabitants of the coast were preoccupied either with their own local affairs or with successive intrusions by Portuguese and by Omani Arabs. The dominant interest of their time was not the opening of the interior to commerce, but a series of intermittent wars against foreign invaders. It may be no coincidence that the peace which the Zanzibar Sultanate brought to the coast was accompanied by a vigorous expansion of trade inland. After

[1] Some long-term, even indirect, consequences of the caravan trade are discussed in chapters 11 and 16, which deal with the Arab impact on East Africa and with pre-Independence economic and social developments.

115

1850 the future of the coast was shaped, not by local wars, but by its association with the interior. The pivot of its history, once situated in the Middle East or Europe, slowly swung inland to the uplands and plateaus of East and Central Africa.

The years 1500 to 1850, therefore, were only a prelude to what may be regarded as the modern history of the coast—its affiliation to the rest of East Africa. Essentially they belong to the self-contained, pre-modern period of coastal history, the period of warring city states whose fortunes rose and fell on the currents of international trade and politics. The coast's encounter with the interior, crucial as it was for East African history, began almost as an afterthought at the very end of this period.

Our knowledge of the commercial and political rivalries of the coastal towns and of the extent to which their people were affected by the intervention of Portuguese and Omani empire builders is often fragmentary and incomplete. Nevertheless, a broad pattern emerges from the surviving Portuguese, Arab, and Swahili sources.

It is clear that the coast settlements were, at the time the Portuguese became aware of their existence, largely independent of one another and of foreign control. Their struggle to preserve their independence against the Portuguese and later against the Arabs of Oman is the first of two great themes which run through the coast's post-Portuguese history until the middle nineteenth century. This is the theme which most directly concerned the Portuguese and about which most information survives. Swahili and Portuguese chroniclers alike gave it a prominent part in their histories.

The other theme, though perhaps equally important, was less well understood by the writers of the day and is consequently less familiar. It concerns the continual ebb and flow of preliterate peoples up and down the coast in the vicinity of the northern Swahili towns. These migrations of clans and small tribes appear to have begun soon after Portuguese fleets became established in East African waters, perhaps by the middle of the sixteenth century. Along the coast of Kenya and northern Tanzania the movement was mostly from north to south, following the ranges of hills fringing the coast. Tribal traditions are substantially agreed that the homeland of the immigrant peoples was an area known as Shungwaya, located approximately between the Tana and Juba river valleys.[1] Much less is known about tribal movements in the immediate hinterland south of Tanga, no doubt because the central Tanzanian coast was more sparsely settled by Swahili townsmen than the area to the north. Relocations and adjustments among the coastal peoples seem to have been largely complete by 1700, though conflicts between the newly

---

[1] The exact location of Shungwaya will probably be open to discussion for many years to come. It has been described as a city and as a region; very likely it was both.

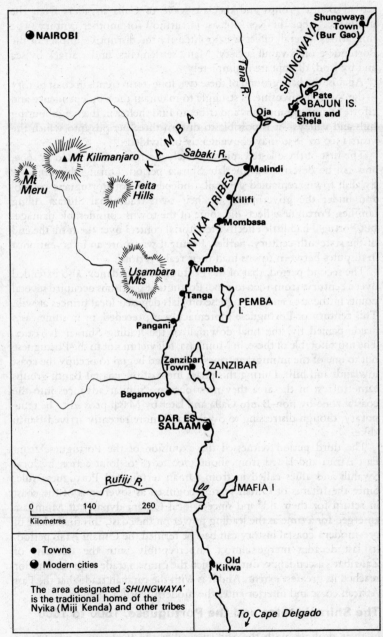

Figure 14 The East African coast to the mid-nineteenth century

117

settled Bantu groups and the last wave of Galla invaders from the north-west kept the Kenya coast in turmoil for another century. The migrations' overall effect was to intensify the disruptive impact of the Portuguese on Swahili society. Many settlements, under attack by sea and by land, disappeared completely.

Against the background of these two long-term trends in coast history —the Swahili townsmen's struggle to maintain their independence and efforts by immigrant clans and tribes to find shelter in the neighbouring hills and valleys—it is possible to discern three periods into which the years 1500 to 1850 may conveniently be divided.

The first of these lasted approximately a century, from 1500 to 1600, and can be described as the late Shirazi period. During this time the Swahili towns remained generally independent of Portuguese control and under the government of their own traditional Shirazi ruling families. Portuguese fleets did some of the towns considerable damage, but Portugal had little effective territorial control over them till the end of the sixteenth century. Earlier, Portugal was more an interventionist in disputes between towns than their real overlord.

The second period, that of the Portuguese ascendancy, also extended over a century, from 1600 to 1700. Portuguese garrisons occupied several points in the area and Portuguese officials deposed local princes at will. This century of Portuguese supremacy was preceded, or in some cases accompanied by, the final downfall of the leading Shirazi dynasties. The most notable of these, in Mombasa, fell victim not to the Portuguese but to one of the immigrant tribes which had begun to occupy the coast lowlands and hills. During this phase most of the coastal Bantu groups came to rest in the area they now occupy. Similar advances into the coastal zone by non-Bantu Galla and later by Masai proved to be temporary, though distressing to Swahili and more recently arrived Bantu alike.

The third period witnessed the expulsion of the Portuguese from East Africa and lasted from about 1700 to 1850. Joint action by local Swahili and allies called in from Oman terminated Portuguese rule. Since the Imams of Oman were recognised as sovereigns of the coast in return for their aid, and since a local Omani dynasty at Mombasa emerged for a time as the leading power on the coast, this final phase of pre-modern coastal history can best be termed the Omani Arab period. Its last decades merge almost imperceptibly with the sultanate of Zanzibar's ascendancy, during which the caravan trade with the interior reached its greatest extent. And it is with the caravan trade that the East African coast and interior enter the modern world together.

The Shirazi states and the Portuguese, 1500 to 1600

In their dealings with the Shirazi sheikhs the Portuguese possessed a number of decisive advantages. Two were theirs the moment Vasco da Gama anchored off Kilwa in 1498: an advanced naval and military technology and sufficient resources to concentrate greater power on any given part of the coast than a single Swahili city state could assemble. A third, perhaps as important as either of the others, they soon acquired. This was a strategic vision that embraced the entire Indian Ocean, transcending local East African trade rivalries and dynastic hatreds. Unlike their Shirazi opponents, the Portuguese approached political and economic problems in the Indian Ocean basin with a unity of purpose that maximised available resources. Within the first two decades of the sixteenth century they had seized or been given bases beside most of the commercial crossroads between East Africa and the Indies. To the Portuguese, East Africa was only a subsidiary part of the global picture, an important one perhaps, but by no means their primary concern. For years it was sufficient, from the Portuguese point of view, to play one coastal state against another without going to the trouble of crushing or occupying every one of them.

The Shirazi field of vision was much more restricted[1]. Though the Swahili settlements' prosperity rested upon the same Indian Ocean commercial system that the Portuguese had only recently discovered, the limited resources at their sheikhs' disposal restricted each state's political activity to the East African coast. The Shirazi political tradition, therefore, was limited to local interstate rivalries with no hope of controlling international trade and little fear of international enemies. The sudden appearance of Portuguese fleets constituted an economic and political revolution for which they were completely unprepared. Not surprisingly, the Portuguese found it possible to profit from divisions among the small coastal powers and were rarely confronted with united or co-ordinated opposition.

At the time of Vasco da Gama's arrival there were numerous Swahili states scattered along the coast, of which four—Kilwa, Mombasa, Malindi, and Pate—were predominant. Zanzibar and Pemba seem often to have been partitioned among several rulers, and when ruled by a single island-wide prince, as Portuguese records suggest happened occasionally, no important consequences resulted.

Kilwa, most geographically extended of the states, proved to be the most vulnerable. Its sheikh agreed to pay tribute to Portugal in 1502. Three years later the Portuguese detached Sofala and the Sofala-Mozambique gold trade from their new subject's dominions. Portuguese

[1] Most but not all ruling dynasties of the Swahili city states were 'Shirazi'. The Nabahani clan of Pate was of Omani origin, and the Nabahani had representatives on Pemba as well. Other Pemba notables were Shirazi, as were some on Zanzibar. Shirazi families, mostly related by ties of blood or marriage, governed Kilwa, Mombasa, Malindi, and numerous less famous settlements such as Kilifi and Oja (Ozi or Ungwana).

119

interference in domestic politics and the presence of a Portuguese garrison in Kilwa from 1505 to 1512 hastened its rapid decline. Thereafter little is heard of it; Kilwa's possessions to the south passed permanently to Portugal, and the city itself entered a period of stagnation that ended in a massacre of the population in 1587 by the notorious Zimba.[1]

With the exception of Malindi, which at once made a firm alliance with the Portuguese, the northern tier of states and the islands proved more resistant. Malindi long supplied Portugal with the territorial foothold it desired in the area and supplemented the somewhat unsatisfactory base the Portuguese established in the far south at Mozambique in 1507. Other towns, including Mombasa and Pate, were slower to submit. Mombasa, a particularly irreconcilable foe, was three times attacked and plundered by the Portuguese (in 1505, 1528, and 1589) before losing its independence. This steadfast resistance suggests that Mombasa had by 1500 emerged as the leading town on the coast, which in turn accounts for Malindi's willingness to make common cause with Portugal.

As the major northern Swahili power, Mombasa had most to lose by accepting Portuguese overlordship and, at the same time, most to fear from possible results of a coalition between Portugal and envious local rivals. Its position, however, was a strong one. Portuguese descriptions of its wealth and its proven ability to recover repeatedly from devastation suggest that it tapped a considerable part of the triangular trade between the East African ports, the Middle East, and India. Moreover, though nominally an island state, it functioned as a mainland power. Its Shirazi sheikhs were kin to rulers of smaller mainland states nearby and seem to have had access to military aid from the non-Swahili people who lived in the hills behind Mombasa Island. Such was Mombasa's resilience that an unusual combination of circumstances was necessary to bring about its overthrow.

One of these came in the guise of an ally. Two Turkish expeditions to the coast, in 1585 and 1587, caused the Portuguese to feel the security of their position in the Indian Ocean severely threatened. Far from strengthening the Sheikh of Mombasa, the second Turkish expedition provoked a major Portuguese counter-stroke against the Mombasans and their new allies. Coincidentally a warband of Zimba appeared outside Mombasa while the Portuguese fleet was blockading it. An

---

[1] The Zimba were a warrior band which first appeared in the Zambezi valley and later marched as far north as Malindi before being defeated and dispersed in 1589 by Swahili, Portuguese, and Segeju. Their origin and the cause of their irruption into East Africa have yet to be satisfactorily explained, though numerous theories have been advanced. Though their appearance coincides with the coast's 'time of troubles', during which Segeju and other Bantu tribes moved south from Shungwaya, it had no connection with this much greater migration.

120

informal division of labour between Zimba and Portuguese enabled the Zimba to occupy the city, which was then pillaged for the third time in a century. Yet the destructive power of the Zimba, as well as their cannibalistic appetite, seems to have been greatly exaggerated by Portuguese and later historians. Two years later Mombasa had recovered sufficiently to mount a major land expedition of its own against Malindi. This, however, culminated in disaster and enabled the Portuguese to seize control at last. The Mombasan army was surprised and routed at an encampment on the road to Malindi by the Segeju, a newly arrived tribe allied to the Sheikh of Malindi. The Segeju then occupied Mombasa Island, shortly afterward surrendering it to the Sheikh of Malindi and the Portuguese.

For Portugal, possession of Mombasa was the turning point in its involvement with East Africa. At a single blow the Portuguese eliminated their most important enemy and converted his stronghold into the mainstay of their authority upon the coast. In 1593, a year after the island had fallen into their hands, they acknowledged their ally, Sheikh Ahmad of Malindi, as ruler of Mombasa (the last sheikh of the old dynasty had been killed by the Segeju), garrisoned the island, and built the famous Fort Jesus. Hereafter Mombasa was headquarters for Portuguese governors on the coast and chief port of call for vessels sailing between Goa and East Africa. Mombasa's strategic location, combined with Portuguese fears of further Turkish raids from the Red Sea, persuaded Portugal to convert a system of alliances and casual collection of tribute into something more nearly resembling an East African empire. Fort Jesus, the point from which it was administered, soon became regarded as the principal embodiment of Portuguese power and the main objective of its antagonists.

The Portuguese ascendancy, 1600 to 1700

Mombasa's transformation into a dependent ally garrisoned by Portuguese soldiers removed the last challenge to Portugal's paramountcy on the coast. For nearly a hundred years afterward her sovereignty was acknowledged by the Swahili towns. The century was hardly a peaceful one, being punctuated by frequent uprisings, but until the end Portuguese supremacy was reasserted as frequently as it was resisted. This does not mean that Portuguese officials exercised day-to-day supervision over the coastal states, but simply that their rulers acquiesced in paying tribute to the king of Portugal through his representative, the captain of Mombasa.[1]

[1] Kilwa and its remaining possessions, notably the Island of Mafia, were considered for a short time to be outside the jurisdiction of the captain of Mombasa. By 1600 the city had shrunk to such unimportance that this scarcely mattered; it had drifted out of the mainstream of coastal events.

Failure to do so could and often did result in dethronement, possibly death. In addition to keeping a close watch on the 'kingdom' of Mombasa-Malindi and collecting customs there, the Portuguese maintained a customs house at Pate and intermittently kept up small communities and religious establishments in the larger towns. Generally life on the coast was not hazardous for individual Portuguese traders or adventurers, who often enjoyed excellent personal relations with the ruler and people of the communities in which they settled. This was true to such an extent that official efforts were sometimes made to restrict the activities of unapproved settlers and to concentrate them at Mombasa. Toward the end of the century greater frequency of anti-Portuguese risings dissipated much of this friendly atmosphere.

Portuguese success in overcoming opposition by the Shirazi princes, however, was counterbalanced by steady deterioration in her position elsewhere in the Indian Ocean. Dutch and English commercial competition grew more intense every year, while Persia and Oman had by 1650 ousted the Portuguese from their fortresses on the Persian Gulf. Re-emergence of strong oriental powers to the north, coupled with a drop in revenue from Indian Ocean trade and attacks on Portuguese settlements, cast a long shadow on Portuguese influence at the coast. Unaided, divided, and overawed by a locally entrenched great power, the Swahili towns could do little but submit. But against a weakened oppressor and with help from Arabia they had reason to hope that rebellion might pay. It was against a background of mounting Portuguese incapacity and increasing outside encouragement that the revolts of the last half of the century took place.

Another factor, as yet little understood, but perhaps nearly as important as the long-term decline in Portugal's imperial fortunes, was immigration by various tribes into the coastal zone. This may actually have strengthened the Portuguese position on the coast and compensated partly for decreasing assistance from Portugal and Goa to the captains of Mombasa. One earlier by-product of the migrations had been the defeat of the formerly hostile Shirazi state of Mombasa by the Segeju, and continuing unrest outside the coast towns probably hurt the Swahili more than the Portuguese. Portugal was not concerned with the defence of every town and island. That was the concern of the townsmen. For the captain of Mombasa it was enough to be sure of the security of Mombasa Island, to collect customs and tribute, and see to it that no town or sheikh made good an attempt to defy his authority. All available evidence suggests that the Portuguese took little interest in tribal movements within their sphere of influence. References to Segeju, Galla, a group behind Mombasa described as 'Mozungullos', and, at the end of the period, to the Nyika, occur in Portuguese records; but these references rarely tell much about the people to whom they apply.

The Segeju and 'Mozungullos' are exceptional in this respect, as the one group was for a while closely associated with the allied state of Malindi and the other with the Portuguese establishment at Mombasa.

However uninteresting or incomprehensible seventeenth-century folk-wanderings along the coast hills may have seemed to contemporary Portuguese officials, they were of the greatest importance to the Swahili and, of course, to the migrant peoples themselves. Nyika and Swahili traditions identify as Galla the aggressors who forced the Shungwaya tribes out of their homeland and pursued them down the coast as far as Mombasa. The traditions are so much agreed on this point, and so much substantiated by early nineteenth-century European observers, that there can be no doubt that Galla were a major disruptive factor on the coast. Nevertheless, it is known that immigrant groups fought one another as well as Galla and must have displaced the clans or tribes which preceded them. It is also possible that the original emigration from Shungwaya was more due to gradual dessication of the area between the Tana and the Juba than to Galla or even Somali pressure. In this case Galla, as the most recent and most aggressive group to press down the coast, would have been blamed retrospectively for the entire series of migrations.

Ultimately the Nyika or *Miji Kenda* tribes[1] reached defensible havens in the hills from which they were able to repel Galla attacks. By 1700, perhaps earlier, they were established in approximately the same areas they now occupy (though the Giriama have since expanded to the north) and had begun to attract Portuguese attention. Whether the 'Mozungullos' mentioned earlier by the Portuguese were absorbed by the Nyika, driven away, or were an earlier migration of Nyika is uncertain. The Segeju remained in the vicinity of Malindi about three decades after its sheikhs abandoned the town in favour of Mombasa. Then, some time after 1635, they pushed further south and settled near the coast on either side of what is now the Kenya-Tanzania border. During the last half of the century, and throughout the century following, Galla raids kept the Swahili and their neighbours in a state of constant alarm.

Because of widespread insecurity on the mainland the seventeenth century was also a time of resettlement and migration for townsmen. Inhabitants of Swahili settlements on the north coast fled south, sometimes accompanied by Nyika. Pemba, the Bajun Islands, and Mombasa absorbed some of the refugees. Most of the Twelve Tribes which comprise the present Swahili population of Mombasa occupied the island in this period, including those which formed the *Thalatha Taifa*, larger of the two Swahili federations which reconstituted the old Shirazi city state. And it is possible that many of the little Swahili

---

[1] These tribes now prefer to be known simply as the *Miji Kenda* or Nine Tribes. They include the Chonyi, Digo, Duruma, Giriama, Jibana, Kambe, Rabai and Ribe.

towns along the *Mrima*[1] of Tanzania were founded as part of the same shift of population. In an environment of deserted mainland plantations and towns, southward and island-ward migration by Swahili, and confusion in the immediate hinterland, the Portuguese were well able to maintain themselves. Absorbed as they were in maritime trade and without much interest in events outside the larger ports and sheikhdoms, the problems besetting seventeenth-century coastal society seem hardly to have attracted their attention.

The decline of Portuguese power

The only major Portuguese commitment was to Mombasa and to the great fortress which dominated it. As long as Fort Jesus and Mombasa harbour were secure, the African side of the Indian Ocean commercial system was in Portugal's grip. This, far more than tribute from small Swahili communities, was what mattered to Portugal. Under these circumstances, Portuguese interest in domestic politics and even in the course of day-to-day affairs at Mombasa was inevitable.

Seen from this point of view, the decision of Sheikh Ahmad of Malindi to occupy Mombasa and place himself under Portuguese supervision was unwise. But considering the city's strategic position, its comparative security and past fame, and the disordered state of affairs outside Malindi, it was also understandable. During his lifetime, partnership between his dynasty and the Portuguese worked well. Probably with Portuguese aid, and certainly with Portuguese approval, Sheikh Ahmad added Pemba to his dominions, sending forth a new wave of Shirazi settlers to guarantee future loyalty. These colonists may have come from the area around Malindi, which seems to have declined greatly in importance when the sheikh shifted his court to Mombasa. Malindi, moreover, had already been attacked by Zimba and was then surrounded by Segeju. It may have seemed no more attractive to its inhabitants than to their ruler.

Soon after Sheikh Ahmad's death in 1609 there began a series of disputes between sheikhs and captains of Mombasa which ended in a royal revolt in 1631. Tactless behaviour by the captains, whose actions were impossible to supervise either from Lisbon or Goa, were mostly at fault. Portuguese accounts admit that great injustices were done to the sheikhly family. The incumbent Sheikh, Yusuf bin Hasan, succeeded in surprising and destroying the Portuguese garrison. A year later he fled the city after withstanding one Portuguese siege. Yusuf's apparently voluntary departure made possible a prompt Portuguese reoccupation.

So great a blow to their prestige seems to have done the Portuguese

[1] Kiswahili: East African coast.

little immediate harm, for they continued to collect the accustomed tribute from subject states and kept their customs house at Pate. Zanzibar, whose sheikh enjoyed the privileged status of non-tributary ally, likewise remained loyal. Yusuf bin Hasan's later visits to the coast stirred up a short-lived rebellion on Pate in 1637 which was put down with aid from neighbouring towns. This was Yusuf's last serious attempt to injure Portuguese interests; the next year he was reported to have died at Jiddah on the Red Sea. He was not replaced by another sheikh, and the captain of Mombasa was thereafter directly responsible for governing the city.

Resistance to Portuguese rule eventually centred on the Nabahani state of Pate. Different members of the Nabahani dynasty had for a time alternated between loyalty and rebellion, but later sheikhs decided on resolute opposition. Pate's futile revolt of 1637 proved the forerunner of more serious attempts in 1660, 1678, 1686, and 1687. All were suppressed, though with increasing difficulty. On each occasion the Imam of Oman supplied aid to Pate, and on the first his troops besieged Fort Jesus for several months and plundered Mombasa. Omani intervention completely upset the old balance of power; it reinvigorated local resistance at the very time Portuguese strength was ebbing. The end came in 1698 when, after a three year siege, Mombasa fell to an army from Oman and Pate. A few years later Zanzibar, sole surviving Portuguese ally, was occupied by Omani troops. Excepting a brief, almost accidental reconquest of Mombasa in 1728-9, Portugal's ascendancy in East Africa did not survive the century.

The Omani Arab period, 1700 to 1850

Expulsion of the Portuguese from Mombasa was not the beginning of a corresponding Omani ascendancy. The fortunes of war in the Persian Gulf alone were sufficient to prevent this; a few decades later Oman was almost entirely overrun by Persia. As a result the Yarubi dynasty, which had been responsible for Oman's emergence as a maritime power and an active Omani policy in East Africa, fell into disrepute and out of power. Though the BuSaidi successors to the Yarubi never renounced claims to the East African coastal towns they inherited from them, they were unable to enforce these claims before the early decades of the nineteenth century. Oman's liberation of the coast was thus of little benefit to the Omani Imamate.

For this the East Africans were partly to blame. Each Swahili town prized its own freedom above all else and none was eager to see the Imam of Oman's governors step into the boots of the former captains of Mombasa. Struggles with the Portuguese had not been essentially a mat-

125

ter of Muslim against Christian, but of small states trying to break free of a domineering larger one. Mere community of religion with the Arabs was not sufficient to make forceful Omani government any more acceptable than the Portuguese regime had been. The Omani tried at first to post garrisons at strategic points along the coast, with a concentration of force at Mombasa. Though the system began to break down almost as soon as it was initiated, to a great extent because of insubordination and strife between rival garrisons, it was nonetheless galling to the local sheikhs.

Their resentment produced an embassy to Portuguese officials in Goa inviting Portugal to dispatch a fleet to East Africa and resume her old position there. Individuals from various parts of the coast had previously urged this, but in 1727 the Sheikh of Pate himself authorised a treaty of alliance with the Viceroy of the Indies at Goa. Soon after, a joint Patan-Portuguese fleet appeared off Mombasa during an outbreak of fighting between townspeople and garrison. It easily got possession of both city and fortress. The following year the Mombasans found Portuguese rule as intolerable as ever and ousted the garrison without outside help. The significance of this brief Portuguese interlude (1728–9) lies entirely in the demonstration it offers of the coast towns' determination to resist control from abroad. So long as the Imam of Oman confined his sovereignty to assistance against foreign enemies the towns were pleased to acknowledge it, but imposition of garrisons or more than nominal tribute soon set them to plotting with the Portuguese.

The revolt of 1727–8 set the seal on Oman's failure to replace Portugal as the great power on the coast. Civil wars and Persian invasions kept the imams occupied for nearly a century, and the Swahili towns were again free to forge their own destiny.

Nevertheless, Oman's unsuccessful bid to occupy Portugal's position led to a continuing involvement with East Africa. Reverses on the coast and temporary anarchy at home did not close channels which the wars against Portugal had reopened. Individual Arabs and whole Arab families remained in the coast towns after the imam's authority had lapsed. They were sometimes reinforced by additional emigration from south-eastern and southern Arabia. It is difficult to weigh the importance of their presence in the early eighteenth century, but by the end of the century a process of re-Arabisation seems to have begun on the coast, in which Arab kinship, values, and some elements of material culture gained prestige at the expense of Swahili culture. In the long run Swahili society was considerably modified by this process, a process that gained impetus after Omani authority was reasserted in the 1820s and 1830s. The Omani Arab period thus ranks with the era of Shirazi colonisation as one in which the impact of the Middle East upon the coast was highly significant.

Mombasan supremacy under the Mazrui

Omani political influence of a local kind was not absent even during the century-long gap between the frustration of Yarubi hopes and the creation of a BuSaidi realm centred on Zanzibar. The Mazrui, a clan of Omani Arabs in the service of the Yarubi Imams, established themselves as hereditary rulers of Mombasa soon after the brief Portuguese reoccupation and presided over yet another revival of this famous old city state. Under Mazrui rule Mombasa's power reached its zenith, outstripping that of the Shirazi and Malindi dynasties. For many years, Pemba and the mainland from Tanga past Malindi owed allegiance to Mombasa. Even Pate passed briefly under Mombasan influence, first as an ally and later as a virtual protectorate. The political history of the coast from 1750 to 1840 can in fact be read mainly as a struggle between two Omani dynasties, the Mombasa-based Mazrui and the Muscat-based BuSaidi, with all but the very last victories going to the Mazrui.

Yet it would be a mistake to regard the Mazrui simply as successors of the Shirazi and Malindi sheikhs. The structure of the Mombasa polity, indeed, grew more complex with each change of dynasty and each accretion of new population. What evidently had been a rather simple sheikhdom under the Shirazi evolved into an uneasy Portuguese-Malindian condominium during the Portuguese ascendancy and, finally, under the Mazrui, into an amalgam composed of two hostile groups of Swahili tribes which acknowledged members of an Omani family as heads of state because of the impossibility of coming to an agreement among themselves. Though this combination had potential for great instability, it served Mombasa well enough to dominate most of the northern coast for several decades after 1750.

The way in which various elements in the coastal political system realigned themselves between 1700 and 1750 helps to explain why this was possible. For the first time in more than two hundred years foreign powers capable of decisive intervention in local rivalries had retreated from the coast. Those Swahili states which survived the dislocations of the previous century consolidated their position. In the far south, Kilwa clung stubbornly to existence as a quiet non-participant in political affairs; its revival as chief mainland port for the East African slave trade had not yet begun. Zanzibar and Pemba, which as yet lacked a tradition of being co-ordinated polities in their own right, were content to acknowledge nominal Omani sovereignty and enjoy *de facto* independence. The mainland opposite these islands was divided among groups of small Swahili chieftaincies focused around Bagamoyo, Pangani, Tanga, and Vumba. The Vumba group had close ties with the northern states, while the groups along the Tanzanian Mrima did not.

Further up the coast states were fewer but larger. Several old settle-

127

ments, including Malindi and those between it and Mombasa, had disappeared altogether. The number of mainland towns near Pate and the Bajun Islands had likewise dwindled, most having been abandoned during the earlier time of troubles. Mombasa thus enjoyed a considerable field for expansion, there being no substantial rivals between Vumba and the Bajun Islands. Pate, predominant among the northern island states, had to reckon on the presence of well-established neighbours, of which Lamu was the most important. Still further north lay a string of settlements along the Somali coast which played as little part in events to the south as they had done during the Portuguese period.

Of the non-Swahili tribes occupying the coast those most important to the city states were the Segeju, allied to the *madiwani*[1] of Vumba; the nine Nyika tribes, associated in various ways with the Swahili of Mombasa and, to a lesser extent, with Vumba; and the Galla, who continued to menace Nyika and Swahili mainlanders alike until the 1840s. Other inland peoples occasionally appeared at the coast but seem to have had no lasting political impact upon the towns. The situation behind the Mrima coast is, however, not well known, largely because coastal settlements there neither preserved much in the way of traditions or chronicles of their own nor attracted much outside notice.

The general picture, therefore, is of a collection of small states occupying a freer, less turbulent, and poorer environment than formerly. Foreign powers had disappeared and mainland upheavals subsided, but international trade across the Indian Ocean had gone dry after two centuries of war. Among the coastal states only two were outstanding: Pate and Mombasa. Pate expended its vigour on civil wars over posession of the sheikhship. Mombasa alone conducted an active foreign policy. The Mazrui, by solving the riddle of who should govern Mombasa, bridged the gap between the city's Swahili factions and directed its energy beyond its own borders.

Mombasa, however, was fortunate in more than simply enjoying three generations of government by able Mazrui *liwalis* (governors). It also benefited from being an important refuge for townsmen from all over the coast during the seventeenth century. Clans and families from places as far distant as Kilwa and Barawa in Somalia had gradually drifted into Mombasa after the fall of the Shirazi dynasty.[2] Their presence in the city, as much as its excellent harbours and the security afforded by Fort Jesus, made it unofficial capital of the northern Swahili. When the Mazrui first arrived, native and immigrant Swahili had sorted themselves out into two antagonistic federations. One—the larger, though comprising only

[1] A Kiswahili term meaning magnates.
[2] Most of these immigrants came from places north of Mombasa. Though cases are known of individuals coming from the southern coast, all clan and tribal names of the Mombasa Swahili are of northern origin.

three tribes, the *Thalatha Taifa*—had its headquarters at Kilindini Town on the western side of Mombasa and occupied a few villages on the mainland. The smaller group—made up of nine tribes, the *Tisa Taifa*—was identified with the oldest and most recent Swahili population and lived mostly at·Mombasa Town or Mvita. The first task of the Mazrui was to make peace between the federations, something they achieved while still representing the Imam of Oman. By 1746 they asserted and successfully defended their independence from Oman and were acknowledged by the Swahili as heads of state at Mombasa. Though often strained, the unity of the Mombasan polity never broke down under their rule. Quarrels among *Thalatha Taifa* and *Tisa Taifa* and succession disputes between rival Mazrui claimants sometimes flared, but never so long or so divisively as the civil wars of Pate.

Mombasa derived one more benefit from consolidation under the Mazrui: a complete set of Nyika alliances. All nine Nyika groups, excepting the southern Digo near Vumba, looked upon certain leaders of the Swahili tribes of Mombasa as their intermediaries with the outer world. Once it was certain that these Swahili notables all owed allegiance to a single state it was possible for that state to use Nyika manpower in war and obtain the major share of Nyika trade in peace. Thus Mombasa, alone among the coastal states of the eighteenth and early nineteenth centuries, could consistently tap the resources of a significant non-Muslim, non-urban tribal area.

In 1746 Liwali Ali bin Athman al-Mazrui definitively established independence of Oman by overcoming an Omani force that had assassinated his brother Muhammad, the first Mazrui liwali to disown the BuSaidi dynasty. Mombasa then moved from strength to yet greater strength. Under Ali the city detached Pemba from Oman and nearly overran Zanzibar. Ali's successor, Masoud bin Nasir, seems to have been the first liwali to initiate an alliance with the Nabahani of Pate by acknowledging their claim to a share of the government of Pemba. Mombasa in return was able to keep a garrison in Pate. Though the agreement was soon repudiated after one of Pate's many civil upheavals (1776), the two states continued to co-operate as partners, with Mombasa enjoying precedence. The madiwani of Vumba also acknowledged Mombasa's supremacy, perhaps because of internal breakdowns in the Vumba polity in 1792 and 1824. Whatever the cause, they assisted the Mazrui in maintaining a sort of diplomatic suzerainty over Tanga and the southern Digo.

Mombasan decline and rise of Zanzibar

Not until 1810 or 1812 (the date, an important one, is disputed) did Mombasa's fortunes begin to decline. The immediate cause was a

129

proverbially disastrous defeat at Shela inflicted by Lamu upon an army dispatched by Mombasa and Pate. The battle of Shela clearly established Lamu's independence of Pate, ended Pate's career as dominant state in the Bajun Islands, and uncut Mombasa's position as senior power on the entire coast. It also opened the door to a revival of direct Omani influence from Muscat, which was probably its most important long-term consequence.

Sayyid[1] Said bin Sultan had held power in Oman for only a few years at this time, but did not hesitate to reassert his dynasty's claim to govern the East African coast. The people at Lamu, perhaps astonished and a little frightened by their success at Shela, at once appealed to him to send them a governor and garrison as protection against further attacks. Said complied with Lamu's request. This was the origin of the Omani reconquest, which Sayyid Said came near to completing in his own lifetime.

Several circumstances favoured him. Sayyid Said himself was a shrewd, determined, and—very important—long-lived ruler. He had the foresight and good fortune to make a very useful alliance with Great Britain. This proved helpful in strengthening his control of Oman and in winning British approval of his objectives in East Africa. Oman, though neither rich nor easy to govern, ranked as a great power by East African standards and could, with a second-hand naval technology borrowed from Britain, command East African waters with little difficulty. Further, several coastal states had begun to fear Mombasa more than Oman. Others, like Kilwa, had become too weak or indifferent to offer opposition to either Oman or Mombasa, and Oman had the greater resources.

Lamu's submission in 1813 gave the Sayyid a base off the northern coast. Before 1813 he held little more than Zanzibar and strategically insignificant acknowledgement of his interests by Kilwa and the Mrima towns. Then, in 1823, a dynastic quarrel at Pate gave him the opportunity of terminating Mazrui influence there. A successful campaign in the Bajun Islands encouraged the Omani forces to sail to Pemba, where Said's commander was again victorious, partly because of Pemba Shirazi discontent with Mazrui government. Though loss of Pemba (1823) isolated Mombasa, the Mazrui soon after produced an extraordinarily able liwali, Salim bin Ahmad, who was able to stave off defeat till his death in 1835. But this was only a temporary respite. There followed a succession dispute between Mazrui factions which alienated the more influential Mazrui supporters among the Swahili. In 1837, Sayyid Said's attack on the city, his fourth, gained its objective. Fort Jesus was then garrisoned by a mercenary detachment. A year later the

[1] The title 'Imam' had by this time lapsed in Oman.

130

leading Mazrui were either deported or driven from the city and local authority divided between leaders of the two Swahili federations and a non-Mazrui Arab liwali. This was Sayyid Said's major political achievement on the coast and symbolises the end of an era far better than his son Majid's later conquest of Pate. Said, meanwhile, transferred his capital from Muscat to Zanzibar Town in 1832, thereby giving his possessions an East African rather than an Arabian orientation.

The Omani Arab phase of coastal history can thus be regarded as shading off imperceptibly into a Zanzibari phase during the decade 1830 to 1840. Sayyid Said's creation of the Zanzibar Sultanate brought renewed prosperity to the coast. The southern region from Cape Delgado to Tanga rapidly developed a flourishing caravan trade in ivory and slaves with the far interior. The islands of Zanzibar and Pemba, drawing on slaves exported from Kilwa and the Mrima towns, turned into plantation societies specialising in the production of cloves. Zanzibar Town itself became an important international port. To the north there was a primary development of grain and coconut plantations—which also relied on slave labour, procured through Zanzibar—and a secondary but nonetheless important ivory trade with the interior. The entire pattern of economic growth was underwritten by Indian capitalists at Zanzibar and co-ordinated, as far as it could be, by the Sayyid's government. In some respects it can be compared to the coast's participation in the pre-Portuguese Indian Ocean commercial system; in other respects it prepared the way for East Africa's entry into the modern world. Probably no tendency in this last direction was more important than accelerated growth of the caravan trade through Zanzibari encouragement.

Origins of the caravan trade, 1800 to 1850

The question of how and where the Swahili towns got the goods which were their contribution to the Indian Ocean trade has long been one of the great uncertainties of coast history. Much has been made of the Kilwa gold trade, and it has been suggested that it was gold from south-central Africa which somehow nourished much of the coast in the days before the Portuguese. Ivory has also been singled out as a major item in the coast's external commerce, and a miscellaneous collection of relatively uncommon products ranging from ambergris to hippopotamus teeth has similarly found its way into commercial itemisations. Yet there is little indication before 1800 of the means by which the Swahili obtained goods—like ivory—with an upcountry origin, or even of there being a large enough commerce in them to support the Swahili towns.

After 1800, however, it is possible to piece together a picture of the commercial life of the coast. Quite likely the situation at the beginning of the nineteenth century resembled that of the preceding centuries in their less prosperous phases. At least what is known of this period[1] is not inconsistent with the scraps of evidence which survive from earlier times.

In the opening years of the century most coastal towns do not seem to have enjoyed a flourishing commerce. Ordinary citizens appear often to have lived by cultivating mashamba near their city, frequently on the mainland if the town were on an island. Settlements on Pemba and the Kenya coast traded extensively in grain with southern Arabia. By volume this was easily the most important international commercial activity at the coast. There was also a moderate seasonal grain trade up and down the coast between towns, islands, and the Nyika. Galla raids on mainland mashamba were the greatest obstacle to it. Some communities levied a grain tax to purchase peace from the Galla.

Indirect trade with the interior supplemented agriculture and grain shipping. The middlemen seem traditionally to have been the Nyika and their 'Mozungullo' predecessors along the northern coast; the situation along the southern coast is not known until 1840. Nyika traders bought ivory in small lots from the Kamba and a few other inland tribes, and carried it back through their own country for sale at the ports. The trade they carried on was essentially a short-range operation and seems not to have involved large numbers of people. Once at the coast the ivory was purchased by Swahili, Arab, or Indian Muslim and Hindu merchants.[2] Probably this had been the pattern of trade for centuries; certainly there is no record of anything more extensive before the nineteenth century.

Then, in the third and fourth decades of the century, the emphasis began to shift. At first initiative remained with the people of the interior. Changes reflect simply the greater number of tribes and people involved. The first recorded appearance of a Kamba caravan at Mombasa was in 1825, and this may actually be one of the earliest Kamba ventures. On the Tanzanian coast opposite Zanzibar, the earliest recorded Nyamwezi caravan appeared in 1839; possibly direct Nyamwezi contact with the coast began a decade or two sooner. Whether there had been middlemen similar to the Nyika operating between the Nyamwezi and the coast is as yet impossible to say.

In any case Swahili and Arabs soon began sending their own caravans into the interior, inspired by the commercial upturn encouraged by

[1] Most of the evidence for the pre-caravan period comes from detailed observations made by British visitors to Mombasa in 1824–5, supplemented by what is known from traditions and other sources.
[2] There were small Indian communities in the larger towns during the earliest years of the nineteenth century, considerably in advance of the influx of Indians after establishment of the Zanzibar Sultanate.

132

Sayyid Said's activity at Zanzibar. The Sayyid himself financed caravans from Zanzibar as early as 1837. Privately organised expeditions began to go upcountry from Pangani, other Mrima ports, and Mombasa at approximately the same time. This did not discourage the Nyamwezi, who continued to organise caravans during most of the century. The Kamba, however, seem to have given up their part in the trade some time in the decade 1850 to 1860, possibly because the Masai closed the northern routes at times. Swahili and Arabs, with access to the resources of Indian merchants and moneylenders, were better able to contend with such difficulties.

Though later development of the caravan trade belongs more to the Zanzibar sultanate than to the Omani period, its origins lie in the hazy transition between the two. What prompted the Kamba and Nyamwezi to begin taking their ivory direct to the coast is still unknown. But the break with tradition of coast traders themselves organising caravans into the interior is less difficult to explain: Sayyid Said's economic revival made it worthwhile. In this way, the Zanzibar sultanate helped launch the first prolonged encounter between coast and interior, pointing to the direction the future would take.

Further reading

BERG, F. J. 'The Swahili Community of Mombasa, 1500–1900', *Journal of African History*, IX, 1, 1968.

BOXER, C. and AZEVEDO, C. *Fort Jesus and the Portuguese in Mombasa, 1593–1729*, London, 1960.

CHITTICK, N. 'The Shirazi Colonisation of East Africa', *Journal of African History*, VI, 3, 1965.

FREEMAN–GRENVILLE, G. S. P. *The East African Coast: Select Documents*, Oxford, 1962.

GRAY, J. M. *The British at Mombasa, 1824–26*, London, 1957.

GRAY, J. M. *History of Zanzibar from the Middle Ages to 1856*, London, 1962.

GUILLAIN, M. *Documents sur l'histoire, la géographie et le commerce de l'Afrique Orientale*, 3 volumes, Paris, 1856–58.

KIRKMAN, J. S. 'Historical Archaeology in Kenya, 1948–56', *Antiquaries Journal*, XXXVII, 1–2, 1957.

KIRKMAN, J. S. *Men and Monuments of the East African Coast*, London, 1964.

LAMPHEAR, J. 'The Kamba and the Northern Mrima Coast', in R. Gray and D. Birmingham (Eds) *Pre-Colonial African Trade*, London, 1970.

PRINS, A. H. J. *The Swahili-Speaking Peoples of Zanzibar and the East*

African Coast (International African Institute Ethnographic Survey), London, 1961.

STRANDES, J. (trans. J. Wallwork) *The Portuguese Period in East Africa*, Nairobi, 1961.

TRIMINGHAM, J. S. *Islam in East Africa*, Oxford, 1964.

7

The River-Lake Nilotes from the Fifteenth to the Nineteenth Century

D. W. Cohen

Historians attempting to recover the early history of Africa find no more difficult problem than the reconstruction of the great population movements of the past. The migrations and expansion of the Bantu speaking peoples in southern, central, and eastern Africa have, in recent years, received considerable attention from historians, linguists, and botanists. In spite of the remoteness in time of the early Bantu migrations, considerable progress is being made in reconstructing the expansion through the correlation of linguistic, archaeological, and botanical evidence. Some historians have presented convincing evidence that the expansion of the Bantu speakers from a core area south of the Congo forest was the expansion not only of a language and its sub-languages and dialects but of a people, of an ethnic group—that present-day Bantu speakers, while clearly including some peoples who had previously spoken other languages, are largely culturally and genetically related to those early Bantu speakers.

The very wide appearance of peoples today speaking the languages called Lwo in the Sudan, Congo, Ethiopia, Uganda, Kenya and Tanzania raises questions of a similar order to those which the wide appearance of Bantu languages has raised. The Lwo problem would seem to be an easier one to sort out than the Bantu expansion; first, the expansion of the Lwo would seem to be relatively recent, and to have occurred during the last five to seven centuries; second and perhaps more important, peoples today speaking Lwo languages generally have fairly explicit tradions of long distance migration going back to a 'cradleland' in the Sudan.

While this would seem to open the way to constructing a straightforward story of the migration and expansion of a people, this is not the case. First, many groups who were probably part of the migrations from the cradleland are today embedded in Bantu and Ateker[1] speaking societies; some have probably lost their 'Lwo' identity and will remain unknown to us, others are linked with the Lwo migrations through varying kinds of evidence and many of these Bantu- and Ateker-influenced Lwo have in the past and are today playing important roles in non-Lwo speaking society. Second, the Lwo speakers who left the cradleland are noted for the ability to incorporate non-Lwo groups into their linguistic group. A striking example is the case of the people of Lango District in Uganda who today speak a Lwo language but among whom relatively few peoples descended from the cradleland Lwo settled. Most Lwo speaking groups today, then, are, in terms of the ethnic origins of their antecedents, extremely heterogeneous; that is, inclusive of families and clans from many different African 'worlds'.

The problem of reconstructing the migrations becomes all the more difficult when one attempts to establish a cultural identity for the Lwo speakers at a particular place and time. The early Lwo speakers— and we might say their descendants as well— seem to have been especially well equipped with the qualities that made the adjustment of their own culture to new conditions easy. They clearly drew on the traditions and cultures of other people when this was necessary for survival, growth, and dominance. Their social institutions, their economy, and even the ideas embodied in their religion seem to have absorbed new and different concepts and to have changed to new circumstances. Some authors[2] have pointed to 'divine kingship' and the 'cattle complex' as basic components of Lwo culture. Yet the most recent research on Lwo history is rather convincing on two points: first, that increasingly hard questions must be asked about 'Lwo divine kingship' and the 'Lwo cattle complex' and pastoral tradition; and second, that if any features seem to be rather universal among Lwo speaking groups of the past, it is their flexibility among new peoples, their ability to adapt and to absorb.

Thus attempts to see the Lwo speakers today as a self-contained ethnic group encompassing descendants of those who left the cradleland are being rapidly discarded. And even attempts to see the Lwo as an ambitious group on the march passing their cradleland culture to all whom they met on the march are coming under attack.

If we then ask where is our solid ground?—where can we put these Lwo in our reconstruction? how are Lwo speakers today to see their own history?—it is possible to say that here we have a linguistic group whose

[1] One section of the Nilotic language group including the languages spoken today by the Teso, Jie, Kumam, and Karimojong peoples in north-east Uganda

[2] Not excluding the present writer in the first edition of this volume.

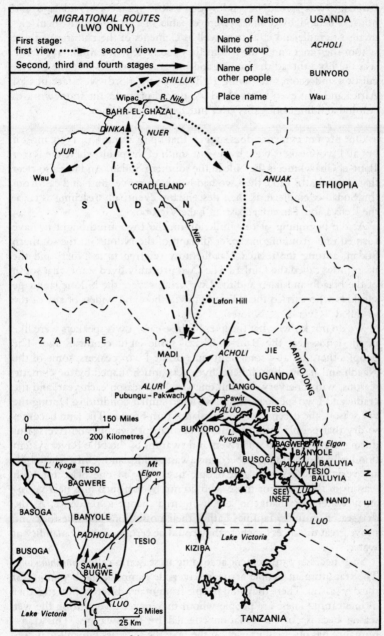

Figure 15 The migrations of the Lwo

language was spread far and wide, whose speakers—cradleland and non-cradleland Lwo alike—were capable of carrying with them elements of cradleland culture as well as elements of the cultures of those whom they met and with whom they interacted. We might say that it was the Lwo thread that joined and integrated peoples of quite diverse cultures and economies living right across the north-west face of East Africa and that even today this Lwo thread provides the framework of cultural and linguistic unity over much of eastern Africa.

Our present evidence does suggest that up to about A.D. 1300, most if not all Lwo speakers were living just south of the point where the River Bahr-el Ghazal meets the Nile in the southern Sudan. And it is also clear that around A.D. 1400, the Lwo had begun to move south and east from this Sudanic 'cradleland', their descendants eventually reaching as far as the Kenya and Tanzania coasts of Lake Victoria.

At the beginning of this millennium, the Lwo are thought to have formed one grouping in the 'cradleland of the Nilotes' in the southern Sudan, among the related Naadh (now referred to as Nuer) and the Jiaan (now called the Dinka). The Lwo probably lived somewhat south of the Naadh and Jiaan and the Lwo groups were the Nilotic language speakers who carried their dialects the farthest and widest of any of the so called 'River-Lake Nilotes'.

We do not know what the lives of these early Lwo speakers were like in the lands near the Bahr-el Ghazal some eight centuries ago. The peoples there today—some remnants of the Lwo speakers, some of the Naadh and Jiaan—live difficult lives very much shaped by the climatic seasons, with one very dry and one very wet season each year, and the cradleland Lwo speakers must have faced similar conditions. During the dry season, the green savanna grasslands turn brown. The land becomes so dry that people must migrate to permanent swamps and rivers. But during the wet season, the rivers and swamps of the Nile River system flood, and the flat savanna becomes a vast swampland. Only where hills are very near the rivers can people live safely in one place for both seasons of the year. For those who do not live on such hills near permanent water, the change in season means a change in residence. As the dry season unfolds, families gather their possessions and livestock and move great distances to where they could be certain of the availability of water.

Such necessary movement according to season is called *transhumance*. The transhumant people arrive at riverside camps at the beginning of the dry season. There they find people from many different hills together in one camp. These are people whom they never meet during the wet season because of the isolation effected by the swamps. This transhumance has no small impact on the way the societies which today live

138

in the old cradleland are organized. In the wet season, an elder rules his family on the hilltop. In the dry season, in the temporary camps, either one strong family dominates or the group as a whole falls back on its own cooperative instincts to maintain peace and harmony during the life of the camp.

While the lives of some Lwo speakers may have been moulded by the necessities of transhumant life, others living in or near the cradleland would have had the opportunity to settle on ridges close to permanent waterways and so been freed from the necessity to leave their homes during any but the driest of dry seasons. Rather, they could simply send their children down the ridges to the permanent rivers to get water and to herd cattle through the drought. Perhaps more significantly, the more permanent home would have allowed or encouraged people to expand the share of their time growing crops such as sorghum and millet. More permanent agricultural communities and the increasing scarcity of good agricultural land near water yet free from floods would probably have given impetus to the emergence of ridge chiefships, based on the control and disposition of land, such as we see in parts of the cradleland today. Such a ridge chief may have been the descendant of the first pioneer and the earliest form of 'government' may have been the governing of his own family or clan on the ridge. If ridge land were given to newcomers from other families and clans, the powers of the chief might grow correspondingly. Today in the cradleland, there are Lwo speaking communities such as these—some incorporating a number of ridges—and ruled by ridge chiefs called *jago*, a Lwo title found throughout the Lwo speaking parts of East Africa, suggesting the carriage far and wide of this title for a local chief. Today associations of ridges can encompass quite a large number of people, some cut off season-ally, some not, with a consciousness of unity against other ridge as-sociations, suggesting a pattern of social organisation of considerable flexibility.

If the pressures of environment and climate are as sharp as many suppose, then the conditions for the Lwo seven centuries ago would not be unlike those of the peoples in the cradleland today. Thus, it is likely that some Lwo speakers were at that time caught in the rugged trans-humant life of the Sudanic pastoralist, while others were more settled as farmers practising a mixed economy in the more permanent ridge communities. It is also likely that there was considerable fluidity be-tween the two extremes. The vagaries of climate, the overcrowding of ridges, disease, drought, famine, conflict and wanderlust very likely caused families to seek new abodes and new masters, at times requiring seasonal migrations and living in temporary camps, and at other times permitting more settled life. And this fluidity between the two extremes is likely to have offered to the Lwo a magnificent training ground for migration. The temporary camps that the Lwo occupied all along the myriad migrational paths from the Sudan to the Lake Victoria coast were probably organised in ways similar to those of the dry season in the cradleland. For they were camps of economic and military necessity and they were built up on existing social structure. Equally, they were practised in the welding together of disparate groups, whether in the camps or on the heterogeneous ridges, and they accepted the stranger when he came—and were likely to marry into his family as well, linking the groups indelibly. Moreover, they carried with them flexible ideas of cooperation and authority learned in the difficult conditions of the temporary camps and on the scarce land of the ridges. We can even postulate that there were, among some of the peoples of the cradleland, political notions and institutions of a fairly elaborate kind, for we know today that certain titles, institutions, and traditions such as that of the *rwot* (or *reth*-King) are found not only among most of the Lwo speaking groups of East Africa but also among groups like the Shilluk living near our reconstructed cradleland of the Lwo language.

One of the interesting problems relating to the Lwo migrations is to what extent the early Lwo speakers can be identified with the 'cattle complex'. The cattle complex, which has been the centre of life for many peoples in East Africa for many generations, and of some peoples in the Nile Valley for apparently more than two millennia, has been associated with the ancient 'Nilotic peoples' of whom the Lwo speakers are said to be a part. In the 'cattle complex' great importance is attached to cattle in all spheres of life—for meat, milk, and blood as dietary staples; for hides, bones, dung, and urine for all kinds of domestic uses; to supply the 'glue' of social relationships including marriage, friendships, settlements of legal disputes; to provide a colourful array of nicknames for men and women; to offer a cause for war and raiding; to furnish a source of pride; and to constitute a focus in the spiritual life of a people.

Traditions record that many Lwo speaking peoples did in the past have something of a cattle complex; but it is not a universal phenomenon among the Lwo. More than a few Lwo groups have no recollections of a cattle complex and no survivals that would suggest a pastoral economy. Many other Lwo speaking groups adapted easily to a life without cattle when they found conditions unfavourable to pastoralism or more favourable to other forms of economy. What is clear is that people on the march can adapt when they have to, that practising pastoralism in one place does not necessarily exclude the possibility of flexibility and change in another. That Lwo speakers appear to have adapted easily to new conditions and does not make the transformation any the less remarkable.

Early Lwo migrations: the first stage

During the fifteenth century, the Lwo, probably as a result of pressure from peoples to the east, began to leave their cradleland. There are at least two different views about how these migrations occurred. The older view is that a large body of Lwo moved north up the Nile from the cradleland, turned east, and then south. This explanation accounts for the present position of the Shilluk and Anuak Lwo peoples north and east of the Lwo source area. According to this view, the northwards moving Lwo were led by Nyikang and settled in present-day Shilluk country in the southern part of the Sudan. After they had settled, Giilo, Nyikang's brother, tried to take away the rethship from Nyikang. Giilo's side won but Giilo decided to leave anyway. They moved eastwards, some of them stopping and settling in Anuakland, which now lies on both sides of the border between Ethiopia and Sudan. Some pressed ahead in their travels, this time south-west. They passed Lafon Hill in the Sudan where another division occurred, some moving on, the main group eventually reaching northern Uganda.

Another view has the Lwo moving southwards from their cradleland to the Nile valley lands of northern Uganda, and there a division is said to have occurred. One group, under the leadership of Dimo and Nyikango, moved north to a place called Wipac on the Bahr-el Ghazal. At Wipac, there was another split, this time between Nyikango's group and Dimo's. Dimo's group moved to Wau, where they settled, and Nyikango's group moved to and settled in present-day Shilluk country, reaching there between 1500 and 1600. In this view, the Anuak are also thought to have broken off from the main body at Wipac, moving under Giilo to settle in their present homeland along the Sudan-Ethiopia border.

Both views are largely conjectural and represent efforts to synthesise fragmentary evidence covering an enormous complexity of small movements of small groups, some perhaps moving in a linear path, others only wandering here and there. Until we have more evidence on the first stage of the Lwo movements south and north from the cradleland, it might be best to say merely that the Lwo migrations from the cradleland to northern Uganda involved the movement of a number of small groups, perhaps culturally and linguistically similar, yet travelling at intervals as much as fifty or a hundred years apart. Although geographically separate, groups on the march may have preserved common traditions, particularly of rethship or rwotship. The prestige of the reth-rwot probably induced many non-Lwo speakers to join the Lwo travellers, eventually becoming linguistically and ethnically absorbed into the Lwo group, yet at the same time altering at least incrementally the culture of the Lwo speakers whom they met.

When we leave the puzzle of the first stage behind, we have rather more evidence and a somewhat less conjectural picture may be constructed. It appears that the Lwo entering northern Uganda moved in three streams, though here again one is hesitant to see these as monolithic streams of Lwo travellers. Rather they are the historian's syntheses of three complexes of small migrations. For the sake of simplicity, these may be roughly referred to as the western, the central, and the eastern streams.

The second stage

In the traditions of many Lwo speakers today, the key to the western Lwo stream would seem to be a place called Pubungu. Pubungu—Pakwach—on the Nile in northern Uganda, is recalled as a temporary camp in the traditions of many Lwo groups. The Lwo arriving at Pubungu would have been there by the mid-fifteenth century for by that time Lwo fragments were already leaving Pubungu for other horizons. Tradition has it that Pubungu was, for many of the travellers, the ideal place to settle after a long and difficult migration. Many others, however, were dissatisfied with Pubungu and wished to continue the migrations still further. Oluum is recalled as a very important man in the discussions over what to do. He had a number of sons, including Labongo (or Nyabongo), Gipiir (or Nyipiir), and Tifool, each with his own party of supporters.

The two sons, Gipiir and Tifool, eventually left Pubungu, moved westwards into the Congo, and established themselves as chiefs of the people who call themselves the Alur today. While today there are the survivals of many independent Alur chieftainships, prior to the arrival of the Lwo the Alur had no chiefs and spoke a central Sudanic language. When the Lwo arrived, they won respect as chiefs and gradually the non-Lwo Alur gave up their language for that of the Lwo, and the two groups intermarried and became one people, though the old Lwo clans remained royal ones and the previous Alur clans became subordinate.

Similarly, another group, the Patiko, left Pubungu and moved to the north-east into present-day Acholiland. There they met Ateker speaking Iseera cultivators whose origins were to the east and north-east and who preceded, but were linguistically related to, the Jie-Karamojong pastoralists who were to come to dominate north-east Uganda in later centuries. The Lwo moving into Acholiland also met Sudanic speaking cultivators expanding from the west, and are likely to have encountered at an early time small communities emerging out of earlier Iseera-Sudanic contact in the region. Recent research has shown that these Lwo and Sudanic speakers and Iseera who met in Acholiland were not of incompatible cultures and that all were predisposed to organise themselves into small groupings of several clans.

The history of Acholiland is complicated all the more by the diffuse movements of individual families back and forth throughout the region, by the later arrivals of both commoner and royal Lwo from several directions, and by the varying forms, timing, and degree of contact among Lwo, Sudanic speaking and Iseera families. But, by 1680, the Lwo clearly had a strong foothold in the region, as a consequence not only of their growing numbers, but also of their ability to absorb pre-Lwo groups into their linguistic world. Before 1700, small Lwo-dominated centralised states began to emerge in Acholiland, some ruled by migrants from Pubungu, others by later Lwo families trickling in from the north in the 'central stream' of Lwo entry into northern Uganda and by Lwo from the south from the northern margins of the Bunyoro empire.

The Acholi states appear to follow fairly similar patterns. The Acholi state is typically small, built up on the close linkage of several clans to a rwot or king and his royal family. Most of the royal families had an elaborate array of regalia, ritual, and ceremony which reinforced their generally light-handed control of day to day affairs in their domains. While to an extent the Acholi clans were self-contained, exercising many functions in their own right, the rwot appointed village chiefs, *jago*, whose role among the settled commoner families was not unlike that of the jago ridge chief in the cradleland, varying in activity according to the diversity of families in the neighbourhood. Taxes and tribute, which were collected in the form of both goods and labour, provided physical support for the king, while the association of the rwot with ancestral spirits provided an additional supplement to his base of authority. While even the fragmentary picture we have of migrations is exceedingly complex, the many states in the Acholi region are so similar as to suggest an impressive development of a 'national' culture. Equally striking are the similarities between the structures of states and the patterns of state formation and growth in Acholiland and these same factors in Alur and northern Busoga, all three areas dominated by Lwo immigrants presiding over numerous small polities.

At probably the same time that the Lwo were setting out from the Pubungu camps for the north-east, other Lwo were moving southwards, settling on the northern shores of Lake Kyoga as well as across the Nile in the bend of the Nile between Lake Kyoga and Lake Albert. This area is called Pawir or Chope. South of these Pawir settlements were Bantu speaking peoples, some of whom may have penetrated north of the Nile in the pre-Lwo period. More importantly, the Bantu speaking peoples were at the time of the first movements of Lwo speakers south of the Nile, very likely under the influence of the Bachwezi rulers of what is now western Uganda. The Bachwezi are recalled today as having achieved great fame and power in a fairly short period through superhuman qualities. They built a large, though not solid, empire between the great lakes of Uganda. Some historians say that they were early Lwo travellers who won great respect from the people they found in the grasslands of the west. Others say they were Sudanic speaking people who had spread their settlements from the northern margins of the Congo forest as far as the Lake Victoria shores. Still others say they were originally Cushitic speaking.

The important thing to consider here, however, is that these Bachwezi, after ruling for two or three generations, began to lose the support of the local population, and this at a time when the first Lwo speakers were arriving at the northern edge of their empire. The Bachwezi fled southwards, giving up their kingdom. It was the Lwo who assumed kingship over the remnants of the Bachwezi empire called Kitara. Some stories tell us that the Lwo were invited to take over as rulers by the Bachwezi before they ran away. The number of Lwo who went over into Kitara must have been few, for they soon gave up their Lwo language for the language of the Bantu speaking people whom they ruled. They began a dynasty of kings (each called *Mukama*) that lasted some eighteen generations, perhaps four or five centuries, up to its dissolution in 1967 by the Uganda government and the death of Mukama Tito Winyi IV in 1971.

The dynasty is called the Bito dynasty because the founders were of the Jo–Bito clan of the Lwo. Their kingdom came to be called Bunyoro, and while the Bito family gave up their Lwo language, they introduced many words, clans and customs which appear to have their origins in the cradleland. In Bunyoro-Kitara itself, the Bito assumed the regalia and much of the tradition of the Bachwezi while introducing ideas of government which were new to the kingdom.

Bito families established themselves as dynasties or sub-dynasties as far as Kiziba in the south near the border of Tanzania and western Uganda and in Buganda where the founder of the royal dynasty, Kimera, is said to be the twin brother of Isingoma Mpuga Rukidi, the founder of the Bito dynasty in Bunyoro. While the tradition of brotherhood seems more symbolic than real, Kimera does represent the intrusion of Bito leaders and followers at the centre of Buganda at a very early period in the history of the Ganda kingdom.

The third stage

Between 1450 and 1720, numerous families and clans of cradleland origin and Lwo speaking but of mixed origins began to leave the camps

144

and settlements along the Nile between Pubungu and Bugungu, encompassing Pubungu-Pakwach and Pawiir. Some moved north into present-day Acholiland carrying new Pawir culture among the Lwo and non-Lwo speakers in that area. Many of the families moving from Pawir founded small states in Acholi and some crossed the Nile again and established new states in Alur. What one finds in the traditions of north-western Uganda today are two layers of dynasties, one pre-1680 and one post-1680, and the more recent layer would seem to be a consequence of the movements from Pawir around 1680, set off by Nyoro invasions up the Nile.

But, still earlier, Lwo speakers left Pawir moving along the northern shores of Lake Kyoga. Other groups, for example that of Adhola, were moving southwards from Acholiland at the same time, and Lwo speakers of various streams probably met in the region of Kaberamaido, a peninsula which juts south-westwards into Lake Kyoga. Soon, the Lwo-speakers began moving east again, south-east, and then south around the north-eastern fingers of Lake Kyoga.

At a similar period, around 1500, other Lwo speakers were moving southwards through Agoro along what historians now believe is an eastern stream of Lwo expansion. Some of the Lwo moving southwards, either from Acholi or directly from the Sudan in the central or eastern streams, met Ateker speaking agriculturalists and pastoralists north-east of Lake Kyoga; these would emerge as the Langi, Jie, Karamojong, and Teso, but only among the Langi would they have a significant impact —the Langi eventually giving up their Ateker language for Lwo. Conversely, these Ateker speakers had a considerable impact on the Lwo speaking communities of eastern Acholi, noticeably affecting the Lwo dialect spoken in that area.

As the Lwo speaking migrants pushed south, they passed the foothills of Mount Elgon and crossed into eastern Busoga, camping at Budoola and Banda for two or three generations from their foundation between 1550 and 1600. Some of the clans of Adhola's group and followers met along the way, crossed back into west Budama around 1625. Tradition has it that the first clans in Budama found no one in the country when they arrived, but they recall having to fight off cattle-raiding Maasai coming from the east. These attacks forced them towards the western part of the area and obliged them to clear the thick forests there for settlement. Settlers on the eastern side had to build their houses in tight settlements surrounded by deep trenches as an extra measure of defence. The Padhola, as the descendants of these settlers are known today, had to fight off the peoples of Bunyole to the north.

By about 1700, the worst of these teething struggles with environment and enemies were over and the Padhola settlers moved quickly to open up new areas. The Padhola pioneers had chosen a thickly-forested

145

area in which to halt their migrations, and it took great efforts and great commitment to clear the frontier for cultivation. More clans and families arrived, some Lwo speaking, some Bantu speaking, some from Busoga, some from elsewhere. Most clans claimed relationship with Adhola and the picture we get is of a disparate group finding unity around a central core of Lwo speaking families and Lwo tradition. The rigours of clearance, settlement, and defence reinforced the cooperative instinct, and there were few interclan struggles over the relatively scarce land. The difficulties of clearance awarded rights to the land to the pioneer. As the population grew, a unified Lwo speaking Padhola society and a unique Padhola culture emerged from this collection of clans of various origins who were attempting to establish their 'world' in an area quite unlike that of the cradleland. The Padhola are a magnificent instance, in microcosm, of the adjustments and transformations undertaken and felt by Lwo speakers fusing with other groups under new conditions. The Lwo core seems to have dominated just because of the experience which it carried to Budama.

As the Lwo speakers were leaving the Budoola camps for Budama, others were moving westwards towards the Bantu speaking world of south Busoga. In the seventeenth century, a Lwo speaking group, the abaiseNaminha, established a small state a short distance west of Budoola, but was soon displaced by a second group from the Lwo speaking camps, the abaiseWakooli, whose dynasty became the core of an expansive state that survived into the colonial period.

Another group from the camp left in the late seventeenth century, travelling west, absorbing and surrounding themselves with Bantu speaking followers in what is today recalled in the popular tradition of Busoga as the Mukama migration. Out of the movement from east to west, there emerged in the early eighteenth century a number of small states ruled by lineages of the abaiseNgobi clan—lineages which· can be traced back to the Lwo speakers in the Budoola camps. Other Lwo trickled into Busoga from the north-east and north-west and together were ultimately responsible for the establishment of some twenty small states across the face of northern Busoga. While all were linguistically absorbed into the Bantu speaking world, many of the dynasties preserved traditions which carry them back to the Lwo camps of northern Uganda.

The Budoola camps provided still more Lwo speaking migrants for further expansion. Many of the Lwo left the Budoola camps at Budoola and Banda in the seventeenth century for Nyanza in Kenya, and were, with Lwo speakers travelling directly from northern Uganda, the spearheads of a new Lwo speaking community, the Luo of Nyanza, who today are the largest of the Lwo speaking groups.

146

The fourth stage

The migrations into the Nyanza area of Kenya constitute a fourth phase of the expansion of Lwo speakers. While the migrations to Nyanza are as complex as any that occurred earlier, comprising small groups moving at different times over different routes, it is possible, for the sake of reconstruction, to see the whole migrational picture in four rough divisions.

The first was the Joka-Jok. They were very probably in the eastern stream of Lwo speakers out of the cradleland, and this group very possibly encompasses the first Lwo speakers to reach and settle in Nyanza. They probably reached that area between 1500 and 1550.

The second major division was the Jok'Owiny. They were perhaps closely related in their migrational history with the Lwo speakers who comprised the Adhola group. Passing along the western foothills of Mount Elgon from northern Uganda, they crossed what is now Budama to the eastern side of Busoga where they joined other Lwo speakers in establishing camps at Budoola and Banda in the mid-sixteenth century. They were probably in the camps for more than fifty years, for they were moving south-westwards into Alego in Kenya by the early years of the seventeenth century. At Alego, they found a number of Bantu speaking groups whom they defeated. Some of the Bantu were absorbed into the Lwo linguistic group while others were driven off to Samia and the Bunyala coast of Lake Victoria near the Uganda–Kenya border.

The third major division was the Jok'Omolo, who passed from Banda in eastern Busoga to Nyanza in the seventeenth century. Some of these Lwo speakers had passed from Pawir, moving south of Lake Kyoga and across Busoga to Banda. Others had travelled along the foothills of Mount Elgon, reaching the Banda camps from the north-east.

The fourth major division comprised a very mixed group of peoples whom tradition recalls as 'Abasuba'. This group, like the migrating Lwo speakers, lacked any consciousness of ethnic unity, rather finding this unity later. Many of the Abasuba were refugees from the Ganda and Soga states or migrants from the islands of Lake Victoria and from Tanzania. They came as non-Lwo but eventually took up the language of the Lwo and fused with the emerging culture of Nyanza. Most of the Abasuba settlements were established in south Nyanza.

What must be remembered about the peoples of all four divisions is that they did not come as tribes.[1] They came in small groups, probably families, and these groups recognised no units larger than the clan, at

[1] Large groups, the member of which cannot reconstruct the lines of unity, but who nevertheless accept or believe that they constitute ethnic units based on a single founder.

least while on the way to Nyanza. Their first lakeshore settlements were isolated and many practised transhumant pastoralism.

With the first settlements there was a great deal of interclan warfare, a sharp contrast with contemporary Budama to the north-west where the pioneers of Padhola were too preoccupied with survival to turn on one another. In this first period, too, we see the beginnings of a shift from a primarily pastoral life of cattle keeping to a primarily agricultural existence. We can only speculate on the possible reasons for this change. One possibility is that large areas of Nyanza proved to be endemic with cattle trypanosomiasis. Perhaps, also, population growth led to gradual expansion of the Lwo speakers into higher lands very suitable for agriculture. The mixing of peoples in Nyanza may have lessened the earlier attachment to pastoralism, particularly if the early areas conquered from Bantu speakers prove, with future research, to have been agricultural zones where great value was placed on land. Whatever the reasons for the transformation, agriculture and associated disputes over land resulted in still more virulent interclan feuding among the Lwo speakers.

What seems clear, however, is that the increasing importance attached to land by the early Lwo speakers in Nyanza played a key role in forging a new unity encompassing diverse Nyanza groups, a unity which would, by the mid-nineteenth century, take the shape of a Lwo nation. The first settlers on the land were recognised by latecomers as dominant in the area. Distribution of land began to go hand in hand with the growth in the authority of one family over other families. Feelings of loyalty and cooperation gradually developed among the followers of a dominant group. They made war together, combined to defend their lands, and out of this feeling of local consciousness a tribe began to emerge. Often the tribe took the name of the dominant lineage. In this way, there developed between 1550 and 1750 a number of strong tribes in the northern and central Nyanza regions. Within these tribes, individuals, especially members of the dominant lineage, gained respect for their leadership in war and were looked to for decision-making concerning the whole tribe.

Still, with the rapid growth in population in central Nyanza, warfare among clans became more frequent. Between 1750 and 1800, many clans began to break apart and disperse, with some members crossing the Kavirondo Gulf to south Nyanza. This development weakened the clans, and the people began to look more and more for protection and rule not to their clan heads, but to the head of the dominant family in the tribe. A form of chiefship was indeed emerging. Though not unlike that which emerged elsewhere in the Lwo speaking world, the rise of chiefs in Nyanza appears to have developed directly out of local conditions.

148

Throughout this early period, and even later, wars with Masai, Nandi, and Baluyia groups gave the Luo tribes of Nyanza a feeling of unity against all other peoples. They continued to expand and conquer along the borderlands up to 1900. The arrival of an Ateker speaking Tesio branch of the Teso cut the Luo off from their Padhola neighbours and from further migrations and contributed to a stronger feeling of Luo unity. As war became less common, and as the clans of the region continued to disperse, travel became feasible and the movements of families and individuals frequent. There was extensive intermarriage and contact between oldcomers and newcomers, between communities of one region and those of another. The lines that joined the disparate elements of the society were reinforced. From many separate pieces, a people conscious of their unity emerged. It was an enormous achievement in the relatively short period of two hundred years, and while not an exclusively Lwo achievement, it was one in which the Lwo speakers played an enormous part. A new 'people' was born, providing a transitional structure between the cradleland groups and the modern concept of 'nation'.

Further reading

CRAZZOLARA, J. P. *The Lwoo*, parts I (1950), II (1951), and III (1954), Verona, Italy.

OCHIENG, W. R. Clan Settlement and Clan Conflict in the Yimbo Location of Nyanza, 1500–1915, in *Ngano*: Nairobi Historical Studies *I*, Ed. B. G. McIntosh, Nairobi 1969.

OGOT, B. A. *A History of the Southern Luo Peoples, 1500–1900*, Nairobi, 1967.

SOUTHALL, A. W. *Alur Society*, Cambridge, 1956.

Unpublished sources: Extremely important work is presently under way in Uganda in a number of areas today occupied by Lwo speaking peoples. The work of Professor J. B. Webster, John Tosh, O. Shiroya, M. Odada, J. Lamphear, O. Adefuye, Sister Maura Garry, Paul Owot, F. K. Uma, R. M. Packard, and Ron Atkinson is noted in particular, and one looks forward to the very early publication of their findings, which were invaluable in the revising of this chapter.

My own work on the early history of Busoga will be published in 1973, and will include material on the expansion of Lwo speakers into that area.

8

Cushites and the Highland and Plains Nilotes to A.D. 1800

Christopher Ehret

It is fitting that the histories of the Cushitic speaking peoples in East Africa and of the more easterly Nilotic peoples should be considered together. Their courses have so often impinged, not only in the north of East Africa along the edge of the Ethiopian highlands, but as far south as central Tanzania. Some aspects of these contacts have long been recognised, though often misinterpreted; other equally important aspects have, however, gone entirely unnoticed. Of the various Cushites of north-eastern and eastern Africa, only two groups, the Eastern and Southern Cushitic peoples, have played significant roles in the history of East Africa. Those Nilotes who have had particularly close relations with the Eastern and Southern Cushites speak languages belonging to the Highland and Plains branches of the Nilotic language group. The Highland group of peoples has had an especially complex history of Cushitic contacts.[1]

It should already be evident that the naming of peoples in this chapter is based on language criteria. A people is called Cushitic because as a people they speak a Cushitic language; or they are called a Kalenjin people because their speech belongs to the Kalenjin group of languages. Neither features of culture nor physical types are meant to be implied by the names.

[1] For a classification of these groups and a listing of the East African peoples belonging to each, the reader should refer to chapter 4.

The Nilo-Hamitic hypothesis

The older view of the contacts between the Highland and Plains Nilotes and the Cushites may be characterised as the 'Nilo-Hamitic' hypothesis. By 'Hamitic' was implied the Cushites, among others. Behind the hypothesis lay recognition of a series of contacts between Nilotic and Cushitic peoples, contacts evidenced in both the cultures and languages of the peoples involved.

But the Nilo-Hamitic viewpoint did historians the great disservice of making a unity of diversity. Only too often the Nilo-Hamites became in the eyes of their proponents a single people created in one era of history, a true amalgam of Nilotes and Hamites distinct from either Nilotes or Hamites alone. Moreover, the hypothesis, almost without exception, took the form that the Hamites were the creative and dominant force in the amalgam. The truth seems to be that influences flowed not only from the Cushites to the Nilotes, but in the opposite direction as well; that Cushitic influences were exerted in far greater quantity and in different ways on the Highland Nilotic peoples than on the Plains Nilotes; and that cultural influences, even ultimately deriving from Cushitic-speaking peoples on occasion, were borrowed by Nilotes from other Nilotic peoples, and not directly from Cushites at all.

While the Nilo-Hamitic hypothesis thus greatly oversimplified the history of Cushitic and Nilotic contacts, it also focused attention on the very prominent Galla and Somali and related eastern Cushitic peoples as the sources of the 'Hamitic' element in 'Nilo-Hamitic'. As a result it led attention away from the investigation of evidence for still other and wider contacts of the Highland and Plains Nilotic peoples. In particular, the extremely important place of Southern Cushites in the history of the Highland Nilotic group has gone entirely unrecognised.

A yet greater disability of the Nilo-Hamitic hypothesis was its integral participation in the still more ambitious oversimplification of African history, the Hamitic hypothesis. The fallacies and weaknesses of this viewpoint have previously been discussed in chapter 4. The term Nilo-Hamite has thus not been used here. Other designations for the Plains and Highland Nilotic peoples, such as 'Paranilote', which try to get around the Hamitic pitfall but still imply a special linguistic or historical community between the two groups, should similarly be avoided.

Historical evidence and migrational patterns

Both the preceding criticism of past approaches and much of the following re-evaluation of Cushitic and easterly Nilotic history in East Africa depend primarily on linguistic and cultural evidence. Archaeology

151

will eventually also play an important part in this sort of historical reconstruction, because it can far better define the locations of early cultures, describe their materials and economies, and date their beginnings, developments, and ends. But the effective correlation of cultures discovered by archaeologists with cultures revealed by language and social evidence will in many cases require a more detailed archaeological knowledge of East Africa's past than has yet been obtained. Nevertheless, some tentative correlations of this kind will be suggested. Oral tradition, of course, provides historical evidence for only the last few centuries, and written documents are of value for a yet much shorter period.

For most of the areas of East Africa and periods of history in which the easterly Nilotes and the Southern and Eastern Cushites figure, not only the investigation of archaeology, but also the collection of tradition and the analysis of linguistic and social evidence are just beginning. The present chapter cannot therefore be more itself than a beginning. Without a doubt, most of its statements will be greatly elaborated and expanded as knowledge grows, many will be amended, and others changed.

Three further considerations should be kept in mind in understanding the following discussions. The first is that migration is a common feature of human existence. People move because of lack of status in their own communities, because of the disruptions of war, and for numerous lesser reasons. They move as groups and as individuals. Migration which brings language or major culture changes is only a special case of a more general pattern. For every movement in East Africa that triggered change there must have been several occasions when migrants were quietly absorbed into pre-existing communities.

The second consideration is that migration is generally a very short-distance affair. People move from one village or valley to the next. The great Ngoni movements of the nineteenth century are notable only because they are such exceptions. More often than not the expansion of a people in East African history is best understood as the accumulation of many small movements of people over a period of generations.

The third point is that extermination or expulsion of a previous population by immigrant invaders is the rare exception, and interaction and assimilation of peoples the rule. If one says, 'The Q people spread south,' it must not be taken to mean that the previous inhabitants to the south disappeared in some fashion. Rather, certain of the Q people moved southward, interacted with the previous Z people and for some reason the Zs assimilated to the Qs and adopted the Q language. Assimilation occurs, not only because it is difficult to kill or drive away large numbers of people, but for the better reason that a 'tribe' or 'people' is a fluid grouping. It grows and changes by adoption and amalgamation, and declines by attrition and schism.

152

Early southern Cushitic history

The earliest Nilotic or Cushitic speaking settlers of East Africa were the Southern Cushites. From the distributions of later Southern Cushitic populations, the early Southern Cushitic territories in East Africa are best placed in Kenya; the extensive differences between modern Southern Cushitic languages suggests that this settlement dates from a very early period, perhaps three to four thousand years ago or even earlier. The Southern Cushites in East Africa were, from the first, agriculturalists. The ancestral Southern Cushitic community may have emphasised pastoral pursuits: the evidence of ancient Southern Cushitic vocabulary suggests that they herded goats and sheep in addition to cattle and that they probably both bled and milked their cattle for sustenance. But they were also cultivators, although indigenous African grains are the only crops that can as yet be attributed to them.

The culture thus described has notable similarities with the first archaeologically attested food producing communities of East Africa described by Dr Sutton in chapter 4. There seems to be no present reason for questioning his attribution of that culture to Cushitic speakers coming ultimately from Ethiopia. Dating, location, and type of material culture all agree with the solution that the bearers of the culture were the ancestral Southern Cushites.

The people who brought Southern Cushitic speech into East Africa formed no conquering, all-powerful horde, despite the profound economic advantage that their possession of agriculture gave them over the hunter-gatherers they settled among. Southern Cushites long coexisted with some hunter-gatherer groups, while at the same time many other descendants of earlier hunting populations joined Southern Cushitic speaking societies and adopted the subsistence practices of those societies. The ancestral Southern Cushitic community itself, as it developed and grew, very soon incorporated both descendants of the immigrant Cushites and descendants of the indigenous peoples. The proto-Southern Cushitic language became the language of the amalgam community, presumably because of the prestige attaching to the immigrants as introducers of revolutionary new subsistence techniques. In social practices the ancestral and later Southern Cushitic communities also maintained many of the customs brought in by the immigrants, for example, circumcision and clitoridectomy as the signs of passage from adolescence to adulthood. No doubt some of the customs in Southern Cushitic communities were, on the other hand, contributed by the former hunter-gatherer component, but this aspect of Southern Cushitic development has not yet received sufficient attention.

A number of hunter-gatherer peoples, in varying degrees and ways, did successfully resist full assimilation into Southern Cushitic societies.

153

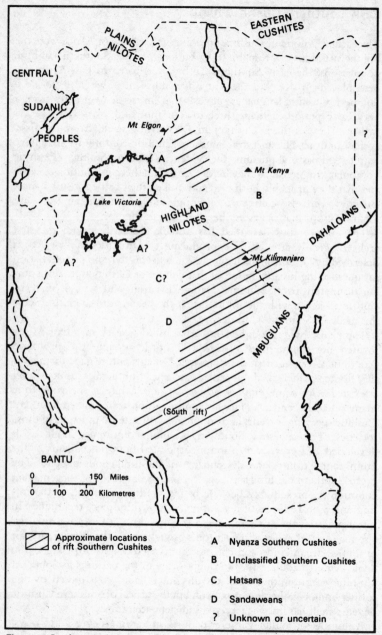

CENTRAL

SUDANIC

PEOPLES

PLAINS
NILOTES

EASTERN
CUSHITES

Mt Elgon

A

▲ Mt Kenya

B

Lake Victoria

HIGHLAND
NILOTES

DAHALOANS

A?

A?

▲ Mt Kilimanjaro

C?

D

MBUGUANS

(South rift)

BANTU

?

0   150   Miles
0   100   200   Kilometres

Approximate locations
of rift Southern Cushites

A   Nyanza Southern Cushites

B   Unclassified Southern Cushites

C   Hatsans

D   Sandaweans

?   Unknown or uncertain

Figure 16 Southern Cushites and neighbours just before Bantu expansion into East Africa

154

A few adopted Southern Cushitic languages, yet remained food gatherers in economy. The Dahalo in eastern Kenya and the Aramanik and Qwadza of north-central Tanzania are examples of Southern Cushitic speaking peoples who are today, or were until recently, hunter-gatherers. The ancestors of the Sandawe took an opposite course: they adopted agricultural techniques, but maintained their old language despite the centuries of strong Southern Cushitic influence attested to by the many Southern Cushitic loanwords in Sandawe. The nearby Hatsa even more strongly resisted Southern Cushitic pressure: they retained both their non-Southern Cushitic language and their old subsistence practices, even though they too have long lived near Southern Cushites.

As the Southern Cushitic speakers grew in numbers during the last two millenia B.C., both through natural increase and continuing assimilation of former hunter-gatherers, they expanded in territory, at the same time evolving into a number of successor communities. By about two thousand years ago, the heaviest concentration of Southern Cushites may have been about the Rift Valley areas in Kenya and northern Tanzania, but Southern Cushitic-speaking peoples could also be found scattered as widely as Lake Victoria and the Indian Ocean and from the Kenya highlands southward to central or south-central Tanzania (Figure 16). The most numerous and important Southern Cushites of the era spoke languages of the Rift branch of the Southern Cushitic language group and were spread over a vast area from central Kenya southward through Tanzania. Five of the seven Southern Cushitic languages still spoken today—Iraqw with its dialect Gorowa, Burungi, Alagwa, Qwadza, and Aramanik—belong to the Rift branch. To the east of Rift speaking communities, in the near interior of the East African coast, lived Cushites speaking languages of the Dahaloan and Mbuguan branches of the group. Dahalo, of coastal eastern Kenya, and Ma'a, spoken in Usambara, are each respectively the one remaining language of their branch. Other Southern Cushites, which we might collectively call 'Nyanza' Southern Cushites, lived west of the Rift peoples two thousand years ago, in parts of the Lake Victoria region. No languages descended from the ancient Nyanza Southern Cushitic languages are now spoken.

Southern Cushites and the Bantu

But the turn of the eras marked the high point of Southern Cushitic expansion. Other agricultural peoples had by the onset of the first millenium A.D. begun to push into eastern Africa, settling among their Southern Cushitic predecessors and competing with them for the best agricultural lands. In the centuries of social interaction that followed,

Southern Cushitic communities were successively absorbed into the immigrants' societies, the introduced Bantu and Nilotic languages replacing the Southern Cushitic languages, but the Southern Cushitic social and subsistence practices often deeply influencing the resultant restructuring of societies.

The set of contacts of widest impact on the incoming Bantu were with the southernmost rift Southern Cushites. The Bantu contacts with these South Rift people began with the first Bantu movements into East Africa—thus probably just about two thousand years ago—and they affected the ancestors in language of a majority of the Bantu of Kenya and Tanzania. On present evidence the region of initial interaction between the two groups of people is best placed somewhere in central or south-central Tanzania. The Southern Highlands, ecologically suitable in most parts both for the grain and cattle mixed farming of the Southern Cushites and for the partly planting agriculture posited for the Bantu immigrants, might well have been that region. In the course of the interactions, the South Rift peoples . . . came under pressure from a complex array of small Bantu-speaking communities moving in all along South Rift country, settling among and around the Southern Cushites.'[1] Some of the Bantu immigrants, for instance, those speaking the dialect ancestral to Kikuyu and Kamba, participated only briefly in the contacts with the South Rift communities; others, including those speaking dialects from which derive Hehe, Gogo, Nyamwezi, and other modern Bantu languages of south-central and western Tanzania, probably continued, sometimes for several centuries, to interact with and gradually absorb the remaining South Rift populations.

But South Rift peoples were only the first of the Southern Cushites to feel the pressure of Bantu expansion. The Bantu immigrants who had only briefly encountered South Rift groups spread on northward, to interact in northern Tanzania and in Kenya with other Southern Cushitic communities, many of them also Rift speaking, which variously inhabited the regions attractive to the immigrants. The early lacustrine Bantu—linguistic ancestors of such modern peoples as the Ganda, Nyoro, and Rwanda—although they did not have dealings with the South Rift peoples, nevertheless were notably influenced by some of the peoples we have called Nyanza Southern Cushites. Many of the Southern Cushites in northern East Africa were eventually drawn into Bantu speaking societies, but in Mbulu and Kondoa areas in Tanzania the old pattern of interaction between Southern Cushites and Bantu has continued down to the present.

The former Southern Cushitic populations of East Africa have contributed more than simply a sizeable proportion of the physical ancestry

[1] C. Ehret, *Ethiopians and East Africans*, chapter 2.

of modern Bantu speaking East Africans. Among subsistence practices, the bleeding of cattle, where it is found among the Bantu, is in most cases a probable legacy of the South Rift peoples or, among Bantu on the west of Lake Victoria, of the Nyanza Southern Cushites. Knowledge of milking may also have come to Bantu peoples through the mediation of Southern Cushites. Irrigation and manuring of fields, found in various parts of northern East Africa, probably was originally brought, too, by Southern Cushites. Social customs have been given little historical study so far, but at least the associated practices of circumcision and clitoridectomy among Kenya and Tanzania are in most instances likely bequests of Southern Cushites to their Bantu speaking descendants and successors.

The early highland Nilotes

While Bantu expansion was by stages constricting Southern Cushitic territory from the south in the first millenium A.D., Highland Nilotes (Southern Nilotes) at the same time were displacing Southern Cushites as the dominant peoples in Kenya and parts of central northern Tanzania. Bantu peoples were not without impact on Southern Cushites in Kenya and on the Highland Nilotes, even from the beginning of the millenium; but it was the Highland Nilotes who had the most pervasive influence on events in Kenya and northern Tanzania in the first thousand years of our era.

The Highland Nilotes form one of three groups into which the Nilotes can be divided on linguistic grounds. The other two are the River-Lake (or Western) Nilotes (see chapter 7) and the Plains (or Eastern) Nilotes. The people ancestral to all the Nilotes probably inhabited an area along the south-western fringe of the Ethiopian highlands near the regions of Lake Rudolf. Evidence of cultural and language contacts with other peoples requires a homeland in these regions, and present distributions of Nilotic languages fit in well with the postulation of such an origin. About the time the ancestral Southern Cushitic community was coming into being, the original Nilotic people were already differentiating into at least three successor communities, each speaking a dialect ancestral to one of the three modern branches of the Nilotic family.

These successor peoples probably for a while carried on much of the culture inherited from their Nilotic origins. They certainly kept cattle and may have both bled and milked them. They extracted lower incisor teeth of adolescents, perhaps as an initiatory rite, and they probably had some kind of linear age-set organisation. In this period Nilotic culture seems to have been a dominant influence along the edge of the

157

Ethiopian highlands. In particular, that influence was felt by early Eastern Cushitic peoples, who may have borrowed the idea of age-sets and habits of more intensive cattle keeping from Nilotes.

In later periods the histories of the three groups of Nilotic peoples began to diverge sharply. The River-Lake Nilotes spread west to the Nile River region and dropped out of immediate touch with events along the southern Ethiopian fringe—and thus out of the considerations of this chapter—even as the Eastern Cushitic peoples began to attain a new prominence in those events. Although the Plains Nilotes may have developed into a separate group nearer the Abyssinian Highlands than the River-Lake Nilotes, modern Plains cultures and languages do not suggest any direct or especially important contacts with Cushites during the early eras. But while these two groups had, if any, only limited contacts with Eastern Cushites, the early Highland Nilotic people seem to have come under exceptionally strong Cushitic influences: they adopted a Cushitic prohibition against eating fish and began to practise circumcision of youths and clitoridectomy of girls as the chief initiatory observances.

The Highland Nilotes, in addition, borrowed many words from an Eastern Cushitic language; some of these words occur even in portions of vocabulary where borrowings are normally rare. Together, the borrowed features indicate that the particularly Eastern Cushites who influenced the Highland Nilotes were more closely related to the Konso, Arbore, and their congener peoples in far southern Ethiopia than to such better-known Eastern Cushites as the Somali, Afar, Sidamo, or Galla. The simplest explanation is that these contacts occurred in the northern parts of East Africa near the Ethiopian highland fringes, before the spread of Highland Nilotic speakers southward into Kenya and prior to their encounter with Southern Cushites.

At some point also between the break-up of the ancestral Nilotic community and the Highland Nilotic move into East Africa proper, the Highland Nilotes reorganised their society around a cycling type of age-set system resembling those of their modern Kalenjin speaking descendants. Some of the nearby Eastern Cushites similarly developed cycling systems during much the same eras. Obviously one development influenced the other, but the direction of influence is not so obvious. The innovation may have been adopted by the Highland Nilotes under Eastern Cushitic influence, or it may have been borrowed by Cushites from Nilotes in the period before the Eastern Cushitic presence became a dominating one in Highland Nilotic affairs.

The highland Nilotic settlement in East Africa

The spread of Highland Nilotic peoples into central Kenya occurred probably sometime during the last millenium B.C. By the time of Bantu settlement along the south borders of Kenya, just about two thousand years ago, the forefront of the Highland Nilotic advance had carried into northern Tanzania, and Highland Nilotic communities were located from the south-eastern shores of Lake Victoria eastward through the Rift Valley country and perhaps beyond. Several of these communities have been absorbed over the last two millenia into other East African societies —the Highland Nilotes of the Lake Victoria plains, for instance, by Bantu peoples who settled that area—but one group of these Nilotes went on to attain even greater importance in the events of East African history. It is from this community or cluster of communities that all the remaining Highland Nilotic peoples of East Africa derive. We call this ancient people the proto-Highland Nilotes. The proto-Highland Nilotes both herded livestock—including cattle, sheep, goats, and donkeys—and cultivated the East African grains, sorghum and eleusine.

As the proto-Highland people incorporated former Rift Southern Cushitic speaking groups and grew in numbers and territory, they began to break up into several different communities, each carrying on the process of expansion and assimilation of other peoples begun by the ancestral proto-Highland Nilotes. By the second half of the first millenium three important descendant societies had developed—the pre-Kalenjin people located somewhere in west-central Kenya, the ancestors of the Dadog (Tatoga) to their south, and the Kenya-Kadam people on their north.

The first of these peoples, like earlier Highland Nilotic communities, expanded through the process of incorporation of former Rift Southern Cushites, in particular, those of western Kenya. By the end of the first millenium, westward expansion of the pre-Kalenjin had resulted in their assimilation of most of the Southern Cushites and had carried them into a much more complex situation of cultural interaction than one simply of contacts with Rift peoples. In this situation two centres of pre-Kalenjin population began to evolve. The more westerly group, the Kitoki Southern Nilotes, especially became involved in a complicated network of relations with the several Bantu communities settled in parts of what is today north and central Nyanza, as well as with the Nyanza Southern Cushites of the region and even one early Plains Nilotic people, which had settled along the west of Mt Elgon. The proto-Kalenjin, as descendants of the eastern pre-Kalenjin group, probably controlled parts of the Uasingishu Plains and, though influenced in some areas of agricultural knowledge by a Bantu people, operated largely on the eastern periphery of the complex ethnic situation of the Nyanza areas.

The different situations of the Kalenjin and the Kitoki highland Nilotes presaged much different futures. The Kalenjin, largely free of external pressures in the early second millenium, were in a position to gain a much wider importance in East African history, as we shall see. The Kitoki peoples had no such options. Caught up in the historical processes of central and north Nyanza, they gave ground linguistically, but not culturally, to the Bantu of the region. By 1800 few, if any, Kitoki Highland Nilotic speakers remained, and the advance of Bantu speech had similarly extinguished the Plains Nilotic and Southern Cushitic languages once spoken in the region. Yet the cultural contours defined by the Kitoki expansions almost a millenium before remained visible. To the south and west, nearer Lake Victoria, where Bantu settlement antedated the arrival of Highlands peoples, older Bantu norms prevailed; e.g. women tended to do all the regular agricultural work, and cultivation overshadowed stock-raising as a value as well as an activity. In the north, nearer Mt Elgon, where Kitoki Highland Nilotes once dominated, the Bantu speaking communities, in particular the Gishu and Bukusu, remained, in many aspects of culture, Highland Nilotes. Among other traits, they bled cattle, as most Luhyia to their south-west did not; they emphasised cattle in their value systems; they gave a share of agricultural work to men, as the Kalenjin do; and one people, the Bukusu, maintained the cycling age-set system of their Kitoki Highland Nilotic ancestors.[1]

While early pre-Kalenjin people were expanding their territory in the western highlands of Kenya, a parallel expansion of the related Kenya-Kadam people was taking place across the lower, drier country to the north. By early in the present millenium, the country of Kenya-Kadam speakers had come to extend from eastern Uganda, where they strongly influenced Nyangiyan peoples, eastward to Mt Kenya, where their most notable contacts were with the ancestors of the modern Yaaku (Mokokodo).

The third theatre of Highland Nilotic expansion in the latter first millenium A.D. was in northern Tanzania where, as early as 1000, Dagog speaking Highland Nilotes may have spread into northern and central Maasailand. Especially evident in early Dadog history is the continuing importance of the ancient pattern, begun with Southern Cushitic settlement, of interaction and coexistence between agriculturalists and hunter-gatherers. The Dadog case suggests the broader generalisation, that it has been possession of distinctive, even mutually exclusive, economic systems which has allowed coexistence of distinct peoples in the same territory. Not only did the Dadog coexist, like East Africans both before and since, with food gathering peoples—in this instance with the ancestors of the Aramanik, among others—but they also coexisted successfully with the ancestors of the Sonjo, a tradition

---

[1] A few of the far eastern Luhyia peoples also had cycling age-sets at the beginning of the twentieth century.

still carried on in the relations today of the Maasai and modern Sonjo in presumably the same areas of far northern Tanzania. The economic distinction between the Dadog and Sonjo was not between farming and hunting; rather the Dadog emphasised pastoral pursuits, while the ancestors of the Sonjo practised sedentary, irrigation agriculture in certain favourable locations within the broader territories of the pastoralists.

The rise of the Plains Nilotes

The histories of the Highland Nilotes and Southern Cushites since about A.D. 1000 up to the close of the eighteenth century were by no means simple unfoldings of trends already evident in the tenth or eleventh centuries. The Kitoki Southern Nilotes, as already described, were gradually absorbed into Bantu speaking societies, and areas still Southern Cushitic in speech continued to decrease in number and territory before the advance of Bantu and Highland Nilotes. Yet in one instance, among the west rift Southern Cushites of Mbulu and Kondoa areas, the Southern Cushitic role was enhanced by events of the present millenium. And although the Kalenjin maintained and even increased their importance in East African events, the Dadog were relegated to successively more restricted roles, and the Kenya-Kadam people, for their part, completely absorbed into expanding Plains Nilotic communities—by Maasai in the east and by Karamojong-Teso in the west. Plains Nilotes became, indeed, the major new factor in the history of the northern half of East Africa in the present millenium, and not only Highland Nilotes, but Bantu as well, had to turn major attention to the problems of dealing with this new force.

The Plains Nilotes divide into two branches, one consisting of the Bari dialects alone and the other, the Teso-Maasaian branch, consisting of the rest of the Plains Nilotic speakers. Only the latter set of peoples have contributed directly to development in Uganda, Kenya and Tanzania. The beginning of the rise of Plains Nilotes to an important role in East African history thus coincides with the break-up of the ancestral Teso-Maasaian community at some point in the first millenium A.D. Out of the split-up of this community three major sets of peoples arose, the Lotuko, the Karamojong-Teso, and the Maasaians. The Lotuko settled in the Sudan and thus, like the Bari, fall outside our direct concerns here; of the other two, the most wide-ranging and influential were Maasaian peoples.

The earliest Maasaian community interacted for a time with Eastern Cushites in the far north of East Africa. One social result was that the Maasai took up Eastern Cushitic prohibitions against eating game and

161

fowl. With this background the ancestral Maasaians began then to spread southward through Kenya, perhaps sometime in the range of a thousand years ago, settling at first to the east of the Rift Valley, possibly in parts of the country between Mt Kenya, Mt Kilimanjaro and the Taita Hills. There the early Maasaians began strongly to influence local Bantu populations, no doubt through the same sorts of processes which have continued into recent times—of trade with the Bantu and extensive intermarriage. An example of Maasaian influence is the prohibition among some of these Bantu against the eating of game and fowl, a prohibition which the Maasai themselves had earlier adopted from Eastern Cushites. And former Maasaian speakers probably constitute a significant element in the physical ancestry of both the Kikuyu and Chagga, among others.

Interaction between Bantu and the early Maasaians was not a oneway process, however. Bantu influence on the Maasaian communities is especially evident in loanwords in Maasaian agricultural vocabulary, and the specific sources of this influence were the ancestors of the Kikuyu-Kamba peoples. In some cases the borrowed words were for items known previously to the Kikuyu-Kamba Bantu but probably new to the Maasaians, e.g. the banana. But the Maasaian borrowing also of words for items with which they certainly had previous acquaintance, e.g. the name for the mortar for pounding grain, probably indicates major differences in values and practices between the two sets of societies. The early Maasaians had long known of cultivation, but they emphasised pastoralism in their own thinking and activity and so may have looked upon the Bantu as the bearers *par excellence* of agricultural knowledge and skills.

Equally important for the early Maasaian settlers in Kenya were their relations with Highland Nilotes. It is from Highland Nilotes, and at this early period in their settlement, that they borrowed the ideas of circumcision and clitoridectomy and many elements of their armament, such as their large oval-shaped shield. Yet these interactions were only the beginning of contacts which have continued between Highland and Plains Nilotes through the past thousand years. So often intertwined were the activities of the two groups of peoples during the period that this intertwining can be a serviceable theme for pulling their histories together in one account.

Plains and Highland Nilotes in the second millenium

In the central portions of southern Kenya and northern Tanzania, successive Kalenjin and Maasaian expansions must have greatly overshadowed other events during the present millenium. The proto-Kalenjin community during the first half of the millenium differentiated into several successor communities, the most important of which were the

Elgon, Pokot, Nandian, and south Kalenjin. Most of these successor peoples to the proto-Kalenjin experienced only moderate growth in territory during those centuries. The exception were the south Kalenjin who probably took on their separate existence in the Rift Valley country of far southern Kenya. Sometime before 1500 they embarked on an expansion which spread their Kalenjin dialect and their culture, in many respects identical with modern pastoral Maasai culture, across a territory reaching from Kenya as far south as the borders of modern Gogo country in Tanzania (Figure 17). In short, it must have been remarkably similar to the subsequent, better known Maasai expansion.

By perhaps 1600 the great South Kalenjin expansion was over, and the Maasai had already begun to move southward, imposing their language on descendants of the South Kalenjin even as the South Kalenjin had earlier imposed theirs on those Dadog and Southern Cushites who had preceded them in Maasailand. The Maasai began as only one of probably several Maasaian communities in existence in the first half of this millenium, but, through their expansions, gained for themselves a territory and an importance in the affairs of neighbouring peoples far out of proportion to their numbers. By the eighteenth century, the Maasai movements begun so few centuries before had already reached Gogo country. Former South Kalenjin people must have composed an important, probably even majority, element in the developing Maasai tribes, so numerous are the south Kalenjin loanwords in modern Maasai vocabulary.

Yet Maasai expansion was far more extensive than the earlier expansion of the South Kalenjin: where the latter people spread only southward into Tanzania, Maasai speakers advanced their territories north and north-eastwards as well. The movement of the Wuasinkishu Maasai onto the Uasingishu Plateau had by the eighteenth century split the Nandian speaking Kalenjin into eastern and western sets of peoples. Tuken, Mara-kwet, and Keyo communities developed to the east of the plains; and the Nandi and Kipsigis, out of the Nandian speaking groups to the west and south. Nandi history is illustrative of the Maasai impact. The Nandi seem to have grown from a nuclear settlement located in the early seventeenth century along the southern Nandi escarpment. They gradu-ally expanded northward by absorbing other Kalenjin groups into their community. Eventually the growth of the Nandi brought them into conflict with the Wuasinkishu, and from sometime in the eighteenth century on into the nineteenth century their major preoccupation became to cope with those militarily stronger eastern neighbours. The disparity in power between the Wuasinkishu Maasai and the various Nandian peoples is also evident in the geography of their respective settlements. The Maasai held the open plains, while the Nandian peoples controlled the more defensible hilly country on both sides of the plains.

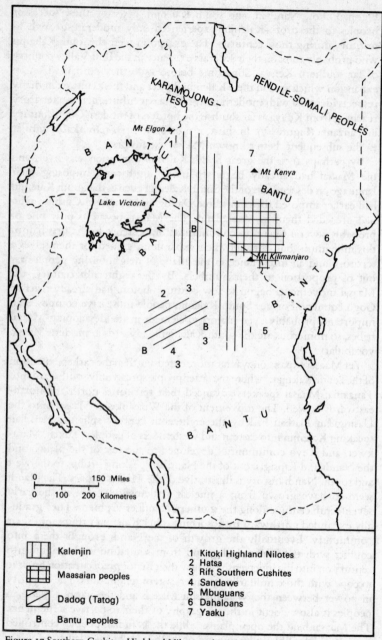

Figure 17 Southern Cushites, Highland Nilotes and neighbours c. A.D. 1500

Kalenjin

Maasaian peoples

Dadog (Tatog)

B   Bantu peoples

1 Kitoki Highland Nilotes
2 Hatsa
3 Rift Southern Cushites
4 Sandawe
5 Mbuguans
6 Dahaloans
7 Yaaku

North of the Kenya highlands, as far as Lake Rudolf, still other Maasai speaking tribes settled during the eras of Maasai expansion. The most northerly, the Samburu, fought and traded and intermarried with the Eastern Cushitic Galla and the Rendille east and north of them, and with Turkana and Pokot on their west. South of the Samburu, the early Laikipiak Maasai engaged in trade, as well as in more bellicose relations, with Bantu peoples of the Mt Kenya region. It was presumably these Maasai groups who replaced the Kenya-Kadam peoples from countries west and north of Mt Kenya, but otherwise Laikipiak and Samburu contacts with Highland Nilotes were few in comparison to those of the Wuasinkishu and the southern Maasai tribes.

The history of one other Highland Nilotic people, the Pokot, can also be viewed through the spectacles of conflict and interaction with Plains Nilotes. Alone among the Kalenjin, the Pokot assimilate in most outward cultural respects to the Karamojong-Teso peoples. Karamojong-Teso speakers have, at least for the last thousand years, lived in parts of northern Uganda, because the Plains Nilotic people who settled, as mentioned above, on the slopes of Mt Elgon by A.D. 1000 appear to have spoken an early form of the Karamojong-Teso language. As other early Karamojong-Teso speakers displaced the western Kenya-Kadam people, the developing Pokot community was brought into direct contact along the north of the western highlands with a Plains Nilotic people, perhaps by the middle of the present millenium; and these contacts inaugurated a process of gradual Pokot adoption of Karamojong-Teso traits and ideas which has continued to the present. Subsequent Pokot expansion northward at the expense of the Karamojong-Teso has only confirmed and extended this process of acculturation. Recent situations along the borders between Pokot and Karamojong-Teso peoples, and also the evidence of oral traditions, suggest that these relations, despite their very strong effects on Pokot social history, were very often unfriendly and characterised by periodic warfare.

While a great many of the Pokot might have been directly affected by their relations with Plains Nilotes, most Karamojong-Teso peoples, at least during the seventeenth and eighteenth centuries, concerned themselves with matters much further afield. In particular, oral tradition testifies to the beginning of a great and rapid expansion of Karamojong-Teso in those centuries. The spread of all the modern Karamojong-Teso peoples to their present locations stems from events of this period. The Teso seem to derive from a westward expansion of people out of the Kenya-Uganda border regions north of Mt Elgon into the area between Mt Nepak and Lake Bisina. Teso were established there by the beginning of the nineteenth century, and from this secondary homeland were later to spread southward into the larger territories they now inhabit.

But even as the original Teso speech area was being expanded westward toward Lake Bisina, the Karamojong were beginning a southward expansion which was to end with the complete assimilation of any Teso remaining in the east. The Jie and Dodos peoples to the north of the Karamojong seem, on the other hand, to derive from northward expansions from Karamojong areas. At about the same time as the other movements, the Turkana began to expand north-eastward, then later to the south-east, where, in the later 1700s, they apparently came into conflict with the Samburu. The Toposa of the far south-eastern Sudan also speak a Karamojong-Teso dialect and certainly owe their existence in part to people spreading from the same general region as the other groups, but these events occurred in the nineteenth century and are not properly the concern of this chapter.

Nor would these examples seem to exhaust the mobements of peoples traceable from the Uganda-Kenya border areas. In particular, one element in the formation of the Lwo speaking Lango was a people who originally spread westward from Karamoja. A very interesting question for future historical studies will be why so many movements of peoples should have emanated from one particular area within the space of only a century or two.

Nilotes, Bantu, and southern Cushites

To emphasise the interrelations between the histories of Plains and Highland Nilotes in East Africa during the past thousand years is not to deny the importance of other factors in those histories. Among the Plains Nilotes, both the Maasai and the Karamojong-Teso, as has been noted, operated in contexts where relations with highland peoples were not of immediate importance. And even Maasai tribes which did have important contacts with Highland Nilotes continued, like earlier Maasaian peoples, to maintain important trade and other relations with nearby Bantu groups. In general, these relations were markedly peaceful. The Maasai, as can be seen in their dealings with Kikuyu and Pare, valued the Bantu traders as providers of iron and iron implements; the Bantu on their side were anxious to obtain livestock and hides from the Maasai.

Kalenjin peoples, too, had important peaceful contacts with Bantu speakers. The Nandian communities continued in the present millenium to be influenced, like their proto-Kalenjin ancestors, by the agricultural knowledge of their western neighbours. Since 1500 both maize and tobacco have been introduced to their regions from the west, and there is evidence to suggest that earlier in the millenium they may even have adopted iron hoes and learned of banana cultivation from the Bantu of the eastern shores of Lake Victoria. In contradistinction to the Nandians, the Elgon Kalenjin were not notably influenced by Plains Nilotes at all, and so Bantu influences appear as not just one, but as the predominant external factor in Elgon history. To be sure, Wuasinkishu Maasai and Karamojong raids in the later eighteenth century may sometimes have made life uncomfortable for Kony and Sabiny peoples, but it was Bantu influence which led to such a basic change as the restructuring of society around local territorial clans, a Nyanza Bantu trait, rather than around the usual Kalenjin non-localised age-set organisation.

Nor did Plains Nilotes have a major role in Dadog social history in this millenium. In Maasailand in Tanzania, it was the South Kalenjin, a related Highland Nilotic people, who replaced the Dadog as the politically and culturally dominant people before 1500. The Maasai entered the region only after the effective eclipse of the Dadog. Other Dadog communities continued to exist to the west of Maasailand after the south Kalenjin expansion; Dadog expansions in the early centuries of the second millenium had carried them into the Mbulu and Singida areas and adjoining lands, where the Dadog found themselves in fully as complex a situation of interaction between peoples as the Kitoki Highland Nilotes had encountered in the Nyanza region. Bantu speakers, West Rift Southern Cushites, and Hatsa and Sandawe, descendants of the old hunter-gatherer peoples of East Africa, all lived within the small compass of that region. The Hatsa remained unassimilated food gatherers, but the Sandawe competed by adopting the agricultural knowledge of their neighbours, a process not yet datable, but one in which Rift Southern Cushitic influence seems, from linguistic evidence, to have been the primary stimulus. A strong Dadog influence is apparent, though, in Sandawe cattle herding vocabulary. Dadog expansion into the Mbulu and Singida areas came after the break-up of the ancestral west rift people into the early Iraqwan, Burungi, and Alagwa communities. Early Dadog dealings were almost exclusively with the Iraqwan people. After a period of initial Dadog dominance through most of Mbulu, the Iraqwan community began to expand, generally at Dadog expense, and this process has continued down to the present. The growth of the Bantu-speaking Nyaturu people in the last few centuries has similarly swallowed up former Dadog territory in Singida Area, so that the modern Dadog inhabit only a small part of their former territories.

As the eighteenth century came to an end, the most important and influential of the groups we have been discussing had become the Plains Nilotes. Their territories had come to extend from the northern borders of East Africa, south to central Tanzania. The Maasai were approaching the height of their power through central Kenya and northern Tanzania. They were arbiters of a vast stretch of East Africa's finest grazing lands, and trading partners, on a small scale, with a large number of neighbouring peoples. The related Karamojong-Teso peoples were still expanding across northern East Africa; though widely spread, their impact on their neighbours did not approach that of the Maasai tribes. Of the Highland Nilotes, the Kalenjin remained numerous and strong in the western highlands of Kenya, but the Dadog were a declining force in events in northern Tanzania. Only a few Southern Cushitic peoples remained, the most numerous of them inhabiting parts of Kondoa and Mbulu areas in Tanzania. One Southern Cushitic people, the Iraqw, were at that point, however, entering on a period of rapid expansion and population growth, a sharp reversal of the then current trend of Southern Cushitic interaction with their neighbours.

There remains only the small matter of defining the Eastern Cushitic role in East African history. The Hamitic viewpoint, of course, gave a very prominent position to Eastern Cushites, but this interpretation can not be sustained. As has been apparent, Eastern Cushites at several points impinged on East African developments; yet their settlements have been limited, apparently, to the fringes of East Africa, north and north-east of the Kenya highlands. The Eastern Cushitic influences on the evolution of Highland Nilotic society and on the early Maasaians can both best be seen as operating in the far north of East Africa. One relatively early Eastern Cushitic settlement, belonging to the first millenium A.D. or earlier—that of the Yaaku (Mokokodo)—reached at least to the north side of Mt Kenya. But they were not the same Eastern Cushites who influenced either the Highland Nilotes or the Maasaians; and, in any case, the agricultural Yaaku speakers were quickly absorbed into other East African societies, and only a hunter-gatherer people which adopted the language maintained it down to the present.

In the last thousand years other Eastern Cushitic populations have expanded into north-eastern parts of Kenya. The initial Somali and Rendille settlements date probably to the beginning of the millenium. Galla incursions into the region began much later. Their movement into East Africa was only one phase of much wider Galla expansions, beginning in the early 1500s, by the end of the century affecting the major part of the Ethiopian highlands, and in effect transforming the Galla from an insignificant tribe of the south-eastern edge of the highlands into one of the dominant Ethiopian peoples. In Kenya, the Galla Boran pushed first southward between the Rendille and Somali, then into the dry country on both sides of the Tana River. Here they particularly influenced the Bantu Pokomo, some of whose clans claim Boran origin and whose language contains many borrowings from the Galla language. The Galla reached their heights in the seventeenth and eighteenth centuries when their raids extended to the edge even of far north-eastern Tanzania. Since then their power has declined, especially before a resurgent Somali presence north of the Tana.

Further reading

The bibliography for this chapter can only be a very short one. Few articles and books deal specifically with the periods covered by the chapter, and fewer still are easily accessible to the general reader. Most of these few are concerned with only a certain series of events, namely those producing the 'Nilo-Hamites', and their viewpoints are generally hopelessly at odds with the views expressed here. The broader arguments, evidence, and methodologies on which the historical analyses of this chapter are based are delineated in the three works by the author which are listed below. In addition, an attempt has been made to put the reader on to some of the basic data used here for historical reconstruction. Besides the works by the author, several survey works have been noted, which summarise much of the available ethnographic material on the peoples whose histories are discussed in the chapter. Linguistic evidence for the conclusions reached can be found in two books by the author.

CERULLI, E. *Peoples of South-West Ethiopia and Its Borderland,* International African Institute, 1956.

EHRET, C. *Ethiopians and East Africans: The Problem of Contacts*, East African Publishing House, 1972.

EHRET, C. 'Linguistics as a Tool for Historians', *Hadith, 1,* Ed. B. A. Ogot, East African Publishing House, 1968.

EHRET, C. *Southern Nilotic History: Linguistic Approaches to the Study of the Past*, Northwestern Univesity Press, 1971.

GULLIVER, P. and P. H. *The Central Nilo-Hamites*, International African Institute, 1953.

HUNTINGFORD, G. W. B. *The Southern Nilo-Hamites*, International African Institute, 1953.

MURDOCK, G. P. *Africa: Its Peoples and Their Culture History,* McGraw-Hill Book Company, Inc., 1959 (chapters 24, 25, 42, 43).

9

The Western Bantu Peoples from A.D. 1300 to 1800

Gideon S. Were

As used here, the term 'the western Bantu' refers to the Bantu speaking communities of East Africa to the west of the rift valley. In Uganda this group comprises the Banyoro, Banyankole, Batoro, Baganda, Basoga, Banyole (Banyuli) and the Bagisu. Further east in western Kenya live the Abaluyia to the north of the Kavirondo Gulf and the Abagusii to the south of the gulf. Further south in mainland Tanzania the group is represented, among others, by the Bahaya, Bakuria, Wasukuma and Wanyamwezi.

Information relating to the early history of Bantu speaking peoples, especially their more remote origins and migrations into East Africa, will be found in chapter 4. The same chapter also deals with the all-important subject of the introduction of agriculture and of the more efficient iron tools which are always associated with the expansion of the early Bantu. The iron tools greatly facilitated the opening up of the thick forest and more extensive cultivation of the land than had been possible in the past. The cultivation of bananas, yams and, later, eleusine, millet and sorghum was another significant factor which facilitated the expansion and eventual settlement of Bantu speaking peoples in East Africa.

For the purposes of this chapter the significant point is that because the Bantu were basically cultivators by occupation, they tended to occupy the more fertile and well-watered land in the region. Another important point to note is that their pattern of settlement was considerably influenced by their mode of livelihood. In other words, unlike the nomadic hunters and gatherers and the more mobile pastoralists, the Bantu built more permanent homesteads, and early became a settled community. All this, coupled with the fact that food was relatively abundant, led to population growth in the settled areas. It should be added, however, that this is a broad generalisation; the actual picture tended to vary according to the local environment. This will become evident in due course.

To a large extent, the history of the western Bantu is still incomplete, despite the enormous amount of research already accomplished or still in progress. Even where research has been done, there are many important gaps: this is a long-term problem which no individual researchers can be expected to solve within a short time.

For purposes of illustration let us first examine the history of the famous but now defunct lake kingdoms of East Africa. It is customary to start the 'modern' history of these kingdoms with the period immediately preceding the coming of the Abachwezi. Very little is known or remembered about this remote period, and that little is so fragmentary that it does not make the historian's task lighter.

In Bunyoro and Ankole, the pre-Abachwezi period is actually associated with the time of creation. During this period, Ruhanga (the Creator) is said to have created the world and all that is in it. In Bunyoro in particular, this period of the gods and creation is associated with the reign of the Abatembuzi. Their dynasty was founded by Ruhanga and his brother Nkya from heaven and lasted for only four or five reigns. The order of succession was as follows. Ruhanga seems to have ruled with his brother Nkya. The latter was succeeded by his son, Kakama Twale, and he in turn by his son, Baba. Baba was succeeded by his son Ngonzaki, and he by his son, Isaza. Since they were gods, the Abatembuzi are said never to have died; they simply disappeared or went back to heaven.

There is no need to regard this mythical period and all its details literally. Rather we should look at it as an attempt by these particular peoples to explain their origins beyond the known or remembered past. Hence the references to gods and creation. This is a common characteristic in all societies; history and literature are full of such legends.

As we move from the remote and vague period of the dynasty of the Abatembuzi to that of the Abachwezi, the picture becomes a great deal clearer. Much has been said and written about the Abachwezi, their material culture and identity. Taking note of the relics of the culture of the Abachwezi and also of the oral traditions relating to them, some writers have hastily concluded that they were an offshoot of a Caucasoid people, perhaps the Egyptians. Others have jumped to the conclusion that these people must have been related to the Greeks. Another group holds the view that they are the descendants of 'Cushitic immigrants from southern Ethiopia'.

171

The main weakness of this 'Hamitic' approach is that it assumes that black Africans were incapable of evolving and developing a high degree of material culture or civilisation. Consequently, its exponents prefer to attribute any such cultural traits in black Africa to light-skinned people, the distant connections of the white race. They ignore the fact that it is not only possible for social and political institutions to be imported, but also to evolve locally, sometimes as a reaction to external influence. Adaptation is an essential ingredient of any culture, adopted or otherwise. The subject is dealt with at length in chapter 4.

Though we are not yet in a position to be precise about the identity of the Abachwezi and their original homeland, a few points are worth noting. First, as will be clear from chapters 3 and 4, a migration by Cushitic-speaking people into East Africa cannot be ruled out. What is being questioned is the extent of the cultural influence of such a people. Second, throughout Bunyoro, Ankole, Toro, Rwanda, Burundi, and the Bukoba District of mainland Tanzania, there are local traditions of a strange people variously called Bachwezi (Abachwezi), Batutsi, Bahima or Bahuma, and Bahinda. It is generally agreed in the region that the strangers were great pastoralists who kept long-horned cattle as distinct from the local short-horned humpless variety.

The immigrants are further said to have been eminent hunters and magicians. They wore cow-hide sandals and built grass houses. Legends suggest that they came from the north or north-east and settled in the country without any resistance by the local people. Unlike the Abatembuzi, the Abachwezi were not mythical. Their descendants can still be identified throughout the region especially in Bunyoro, Ankole, Rwanda, Burundi and Karagwe. Until recently they formed the ruling aristocracy in the last four.

According to tradition the Bachwezi dynasty was related to the Abatembuzi who preceded the former in the country. In actual fact some accounts suggest that the Abatembuzi were the advance party of the Bachwezi. At any rate the two do not appear to have been vastly different. They both possessed superhuman qualities—so the traditions claim.

Be that as it may, tradition asserts that long ago, the Bachwezi succeeded the Abatembuzi as the rulers of Bunyoro-Kitara, a kingdom at that time presumably a great deal bigger than it is today. Its centre was to the south of modern Bunyoro, in the downlands which include part of present-day Ankole, Toro, and part of Buganda and Karagwe. It is uncertain whether at that time this great empire was effectively governed as one administrative unit or was rather a congeries of semi-independent sister states. Nevertheless, tradition relates that Ndahura (Karubumbi), the founder of the Bachwezi dynasty, was the paternal grandson of Isaza, the last ruler of the Abatembuzi. He was succeeded by his son, Wamara, the last of the Bachwezi rulers. Altogether, the Bachwezi would appear to have been in the country for only a generation or two.

We know almost nothing about the indigenous peoples who became the subjects of the pastoral newcomers. It is generally agreed that they were Bantu and that they were primarily cultivators. Some of them, however, kept short-horned humpless cattle. They appear to have been organised on a clan basis, both socially and politically. Before the coming of the pastoral Bahima, Bunyoro is said to have been partly occupied by the Bantu Basita, Karagwe by the Bantu Banyambo, Rwanda by the pygmoid Batwa and Bantu Bahutu, and Ankole by the Bantu Bairu. It is quite obvious that there were many more communities but memory of them is now dim.

The Bachwezi seem to have been one of the last bands of the pastoral Bahima who entered Uganda from the north-east and appear to have brought in a better material culture than that of their predecessors. They are credited with the reorganisation of the Kitara empire after the departure of their Abatembuzi predecessors, and are associated with the introduction of barkcloth manufacture, coffee cultivation, iron working, earthwork fortifications, and reed palaces. To the Bachwezi is also attributed the introduction of a centralised monarchy and a hierarchy of officials both in the palace and in the provinces. As there is evidence to suggest that the pre-Bachwezi (or pre-Bahima) communities were organised on a clan basis, perhaps it is justifiable to associate the introduction of a centralised monarchy and larger political or administrative units with the Bahima. However, it is not certain whether they actually imported this institution into Uganda, although in Bukoba this was certainly the case. It seems quite probable that in western Uganda this political system evolved from the encounter of the pastoral immigrants and the indigenous communities. In that case, the system must have been significantly influenced by the native culture and the Bahima rituals which the Bahima introduced.

The Bachwezi left behind their regalia—ancient crowns, royal drums, spears, arrows, stools, etc., and also the institutions of slave artisans, palace women, and of administrative officials ruling small areas in the provinces and districts as the representatives of a centralised monarchy.

Archaeological evidence in western Uganda gives support to the belief that at one time there was an extensive pastoral society. A careful examination of relics at the important cultural sites at Bigo, Mubende, Kibengo, Kagogo, Kasonko and Ntusi revealed this valuable information. The principal features of this ancient culture are pottery forms consisting of spherical bowls, jars, shallow basins and footed dishes, decorated with roulette patterns. Another outstanding feature is large earthworks which seem to have been generally situated in undulating country, usually located by a river.

At Bigo, the largest of these cultural sites, there was a ditch system of over 6.5 miles [10 km]. As the ditch system is known to have included good grazing in the meadows of a Katonga tributary, the makers of the site at Bigo would seem to have intended it partly for defensive purposes and also to protect large herds of cattle. This is further proof that there was a pastoral state in the area. The pastoral Bachwezi, or a similar people, may, therefore, safely be associated with the Bigo culture.

An ancient enclosure bank at Bigo, which has been interpreted as a royal enclosure (*orirembo*) is similar to those which survived in Karagwe, Ankole and Rwanda till late in the nineteenth century. This, together with finds of large quantities of cattle bones, is a clear indication that Bigo was the capital of a pastoral society in western Uganda. In that case, the other territories, e.g. Ankole, Karagwe, and Rwanda must have been ruled by subordinate chiefs. However, the Bachwezi reign was short: they were in the country for only one or two generations. Oral tradition and archaeological evidence suggest that the Bachwezi culture flourished between about A.D. 1350 and 1500.

The impact of Lwo invasions—Bunyoro and Buganda

About the beginning of the sixteenth century or a little earlier, the Lwo migrated southwards from the south-east corner of the present Sudan Republic. In Bantu Bunyoro, the Nilotic immigrants adopted the local language; further north in modern Acholiland, Alurland, and the Lango country, they retained their native language and culture. In Bunyoro, the Nilotic invaders founded a new dynasty called the Babito. The local ruler was called Omukama or Mukama.

Traditional evidence in western Uganda, notably Bunyoro, suggests that the Babito came in peacefully. This occurred during the reign of Wamara, the second and last of the Bachwezi rulers. It is further suggested that Isingoma Mpuga Rukidi, the founder of the Babito dynasty, was the son of Kyomya, the half-brother of Ndahura, the founder of the Bachwezi dynasty. Rukidi is said to have come from a district vaguely called Bukedi, not necessarily the present Bukedi. It must, however, be added that the Bachwezi culture just described was superior to the much less sophisticated culture of the Lwo newcomers. Rukidi himself had to be trained in the Bachwezi rituals of kingship and other affairs of state by the local people. It does seem, therefore, that the Bachwezi were not related to the Lwo Babito, who must be regarded as invaders of the pastoral Bachwezi kingdom of Bunyoro-Kitara which was already in the process of disintegration.

The factors responsible for the disintegration of the once extensive pastoral state are not clear. Traditional evidence suggests that the Bachwezi voluntarily left the country because they were weary of constant strife, insubordination, and increasing misfortunes. The mysterious death of Bihogo, the darling cow of one of the princes, and the unfavourable interpretation of the incident by a soothsayer from Bukedi is said to have been the last straw. It is, however, quite probable that there were other factors. The Bachwezi power may have been undermined by natural calamities such as smallpox and cattle disease. To a pastoral community, like the Bachwezi, the latter would be particularly fatal. Local revolts and even civil war may further have weakened the central government. Whatever the case, the collapse of the Bachwezi state must have been accentuated by the contemporary Lwo invasion.

The coming of the Lwo had a tremendous impact on the history of this region. First, the disintegration of the Bachwezi state was completed. There now arose a number of separate states such as Bunyoro, Ankole, Buganda and Karagwe. The foundation of a Bahima (Abamuhima) state at Imanga (the nucleus of the later Kingdom of Wanga) which was dominated by the Bahima immigrants from western Uganda, may also be associated with these developments. The Nilotic newcomers founded a number of related dynasties in Uganda, of which the Babito of Bunyoro was the most important. Babito sub-dynasties were subsequently founded in Bukoli, Bugwere, Bulamogi and Bugabula in Busoga, and in Kiziba in the Bukoba District of Tanganyika. All this happened between nine and seventeen generations ago, around A.D. 1490 to 1733. A separate Babito dynasty was established in Toro in the nineteenth century. Apart from ritual connections, there is no reason to believe that these principalities were actually tributary to Bunyoro.

Further east in Buganda, similar developments were also taking place. Bunyoro accounts suggest that dynasties in Buganda and Bunyoro were founded respectively by Lwo twin brothers, Kimera and Rukidi. The Lwo origin of the former ruling dynasty of Buganda has been accepted by many writers. On the other hand, there is ample evidence to support the contrary theory that Kimera belonged to the Bachwezi and, therefore, to the pre-Lwo inhabitants of Bunyoro. The coming of Kimera and his followers to Buganda may have been caused by the appearance of the Lwo in Bunyoro.

At first, Buganda was a small state, presumably on the same scale as some of the principalities of Busoga. Busiro-Mawokota was probably the home of the earliest inhabitants, who seem to have been Bantu. The area of first occupation may have included present-day Kyadondo. By the eighteenth century, however, many more immigrants had arrived and the state gradually expanded as more settlers came in from Bunyoro,

175

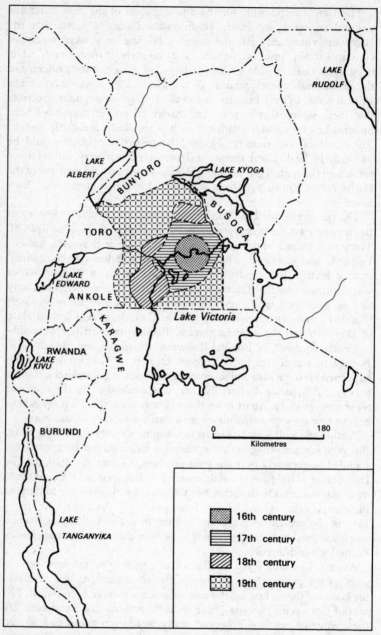

Figure 18 The growth of Buganda in the sixteenth to nineteenth centuries

176

the Mount Elgon direction and the Sese Islands. After Kabaka Junju's annexation of Buddu from Bunyoro in the eighteenth century, the local clans joined Baganda clans.

About thirteen or fourteen of the present clans claim to have come with Kintu, the Baganda hero who is credited with the centralisation of the state. He is said to have originally come from the Mount Elgon region via either Bunyoro or Bugisu, Budama and Busoga. On the other hand, six clans claim to have come with Kimera, the founder of the former Buganda dynasty.

Up till the middle of the seventeenth century, Bunyoro was powerful, aggressive, adventurous and successful in most of its expeditions against neighbouring communities. About this time, Buganda, Ankole, Rwanda, Karagwe and the principalities of Busoga were subjected to increasing harassment from Bunyoro. Indeed the Bunyoro raids were so common and devastating that only the most optimistic could have foreseen the decline of that state.

This state of affairs could not last for ever. The balance of power was upset during the closing years of the seventeenth century right through to the eighteenth and nineteenth centuries. During this period, Buganda emerged from her long period of obscurity into a new position of strength. By the close of the eighteenth century she had waged successful wars against Bunyoro and its neighbours and increased her territory by more than two hundred per cent, largely at the expense of Bunyoro.

Certainly by the nineteenth century, Buganda had grown so powerful that it was raiding all over the neighbourhood. In addition it absorbed Koki, Buddu, and Mawogola (Bwera), and most of the principalities of Busoga were tributary to it.

The explanation for Buganda's ascendancy is far from simple. For one thing, Bunyoro was a large country with many internal problems. Some of these problems were created by secessionist factions within the state and in its general sphere of influence. In other words, the rulers of Bunyoro were preoccupied with domestic problems at the very time when Buganda was growing bigger and more powerful. Secondly, Buganda was a small state and was, therefore, better able to impose rigid discipline and efficient, if ruthless, administration within its frontiers. Many other factors contributed to the ascendancy of Buganda by the nineteenth century. Some of these relate to the military reorganisation of the latter half of that century during the reigns of Suna and Mutesa I. However, the most important single factor was connected with the increasing power of the king or kabaka. This was largely accomplished through the creation of a strong royal bodyguard and the centralisation of the administration. In the latter case the royal power was augmented as now all government officials were under direct control of the king and his subordinates. The centralisation of the state was completed by

177

the subordination of district and sub-district chiefs, who had now to be appointed by the ruler. They could only remain in office during the king's pleasure. By the same token the original clans and their traditional heads were successfully suppressed. By the end of the eighteenth century, for example, seven of the ten county chiefs were appointive and only three were still hereditary.

It has been suggested that one reason why Buganda became powerful, extensive, and culturally and politically advanced was the fact that its staple food, the banana, is plentiful and does not require much labour. The result was that the Baganda had plenty of free time on their hands. And this in turn enabled them to be creative, e.g. to build good houses and canoes; to manufacture barkcloth; and to devise a highly bureaucratic system of government. This argument is not convincing and must therefore be rejected. There are many communities which subsist on the banana but which never accomplished what the Baganda did. If the Baganda built canoes it was because both their environment and military requirements as well as pressure from some of their island neighbours made it necessary to do so. The only valid part of the banana theory is that its steady supply and abundance enabled the population to grow. This was in turn made possible by the favourable climate, rainfall and fertile soil.

The Bahinda of Ankole and Karagwe

As already noted, Ankole was one of the small successor states to the defunct Bachwezi empire. Here the pastoral Bachwezi held their own. Under Ruhinda, son of Wamara, the last of the Bachwezi kings, Ankole maintained its independence. The dynasty of the Abahinda which flourished in Ankole until 1966 was founded by Ruhinda. This is further proof that the Bachwezi were a real people; they were not mythical though their history is surrounded with mystery and colourful legends.

As already pointed out Karagwe was one of the states ruled by the pastoral Bahinda. In fact traditional evidence suggests that Karagwe was part of the general sphere of influence of the Bachwezi, the progenitors of the Bahinda. But the situation is not as simple as all that. It is evident, according to the same traditions, that the effective occupation of Karagwe by the pastoral Bahinda occurred either towards the close of the fourteenth century or early in the next century. The invasion was led by Ruhinda, from Ankole, who deposed the local ruler, Nono. He built his capital at Bwehange.

Ruhinda is credited with a number of important achievements. First he extended and consolidated his empire and appointed his sons as rulers over the component states. They were answerable to him. Secondly, he built the new capital of Bwehange from where the country was governed. Thirdly, from his native Bunyoro and Ankole, Ruhinda brought the Bachwezi (Bahima) royal insignia, such as drums and spears, which were adopted by the new polity. His party also brought herds of the famous long-horned cattle of the Bahima. Altogether seven new subdynasties of the Bahinda were founded by Ruhinda's sons. They comprised Gisaka, Kyamtwara, Ihangiro, Buzinza, Busubi, Ukerewe and Nasa. Karagwe was the parent state.

It would, however, be wrong to jump to the conclusion that the first attempt to centralise the state was made by the Bahinda. On the contrary, long before the arrival of these pastoralists Karagwe had attained a large measure of centralisation. Originally Karagwe consisted of numerous small political units based on lineage and clan organisation. But in the course of time this gave way to larger political units. What finally emerged was a united and coherent political entity which was identical with the entire territory of Karagwe. The Basita became the dominant clan; they provided the rulers of the kingdom. Nono, who was ousted by Ruhinda, was the last such ruler.

This political and social transformation would have been virtually impossible but for a number of factors. First, the original Bantu population was greatly augmented by a continuous influx of immigrants from the north, notably Bunyoro, Ankole and Toro. The ancestors of many of these had left Karagwe sometime in the ninth or tenth century and gone to these northern territories. While there they mingled with the Bachwezi. All this happened long before the Bahindan invasion of Karagwe. Secondly, the increase in population resulted in the growth of villages.

To sustain the growing population agriculture and pastoralism combined to bring about a revolution in food production, i.e. the economy. More food could now be produced. Originally the Bantu cultivators had grown sorghum, millet, eleusine and yams. They used iron tools. The influx of new immigrants from Uganda with cattle and new crops and more iron tools was significant for economic growth and the agricultural revolution in particular. The economy was now based on pastoralism and agriculture. By the close of the fourteenth century, therefore, when the Bahinda invaded the country, Karagwe had gone through a successful economic, social and political transformation.

However, as a result of the highly complex developments which took place in Karagwe and Bukoba in general there developed significant common features in the history of this area and of the area to the north in Uganda. For example while some Banyambo (the predecessors of the Bahinda) claim that their ancestors came from Bunyoro, others assert that their people have always lived in Karagwe.

Many of the clans of the Bahaya (i.e. the inhabitants of Bukoba District) claim that their ancestors came from Bunyoro where the histories and traditions of such clans usually begin. Many of the clans would thus seem to be sub-clans (*mahiga*), of clans in Bunyoro. This may partly explain the close relationship of the Lunyoro and Luhaya languages. It also supports the theory that the Karagwe region of Tanzania was part of the wider cultural area of western Uganda. Banyankole sources in fact suggest that the territories south of the Kagera River were part of the domain of the Bahinda of Ankole even before Ruhinda transferred his headquarters there.

The immigrants from Bunyoro seem to have come in small family bands, each under his own leader. Apparently, they settled without much resistance as, apart from minor skirmishes, no major military encounter is reported. Before this immigration, the district was primarily agricultural although a few of the inhabitants kept short-horned humpless cattle. Thus from their native Bunyoro and Ankole, the pastoral immigrants brought with them their famous long-horned cattle and the institution of a centralised monarchy. However, the pastoral Bahinda allowed the existing clan and sub-clan organisation to continue at the local level. Their major administrative reorganisation entailed the regrouping of the independent clans together into bigger administrative units, the chiefdoms. There were eight such chiefdoms — Kianja, Bukara, Kiamtwara, Kiziba, Bugabo, Ihangiro, Misenyi, and Karagwe.

The Bahinda would seem to have been accepted as rulers because of their mental and physical qualities. Being unbiased judges and arbitrators, they were welcome and preferred to their predecessors. Furthermore, the Bahinda newcomers were rich in the all-important commodity of cattle with which they could reward and assist their subjects. And the fact that people believed in their divine origin (see the Abatembuzi and Bachwezi above) and associated them with the supreme deities of the Bahaya world of gods was of no less significance.

On Ruhinda's death the seven principalities became independent. Like Ankole they were characterised by two classes, the pastoralists and the agriculturists. Little is known about the period after Ruhinda's death beyond the collapse of the empire. In the case of Karagwe, its history was uneventful for almost three centuries following Ruhinda's death. This big gap may one day be filled as more information comes to light.

The situation becomes a little clearer towards the end of the eighteenth century. About that time the famous Wanyamwezi and Basumbwa traders made their first known appearance in the country. This was an important development, for the country was now linked with the main trading area including the east coast. The main impact of trade with the coast was not felt until the nineteenth century which falls outside the present study. In brief outside traders exchanged their beads, chinaware and iron coils for local commodities such as ivory and iron products. In the course of the nineteenth century Karagwe greatly benefited from the expanding trade between the east coast of mainland Tanzania and Buganda.

Another important development towards the close of the eighteenth century concerns the Banyoro invasion. This was during the reign of the child Ntare IV. His mother fled with him across the Kagera to Buha leaving his brother Luzenga to act as regent. The Banyoro overran the country, killed Luzenga and ruled Karagwe for about six years. Later, however, after the Banyoro had been greatly weakened by disease, Ntare came back. It is believed that with the help of magic, the young ruler drove the Banyoro out of the country. This earned him the name of Kiit'Abanyoro, 'slayer of Banyoro'.

One final point about the lake kingdoms. The origins of their political institutions are still obscure. As already noted, it may well be that they evolved as a result of the interaction of local and external influences, most likely as a result of the coming of certain immigrants. It is also possible that they evolved locally; there was nothing to stop that happening. Whatever the case, the impact of local forces cannot be underestimated. For one thing, favourable climatic conditions as well as the suitability of the soil for agriculture made the region productive in respect of food. This in turn influenced and sustained the growth of large populations. Being a settled people, the local inhabitants early built permanent homesteads; continuity and adaptation were major factors in the resulting culture.

However, the culture of these people, particularly their political institutions, need not necessarily be viewed from this restricted angle. It is well known that for centuries past the region experienced a series of complex migrational waves. The impact of such a tremendous phenomenon cannot be underrated. Neither can one under-estimate the initiative and genius of the local people themselves and their rulers. In this regard the role of necessity must be emphasised; it is the mother of all inventions and even adaptation. It could influence the nature and extent of military, social and political organisation. The interaction of all or some of these factors could have given rise to the relatively sophisticated material culture of the region.

Wanyamwezi and Wasukuma

Further south and south-east live the Wanyamwezi and Wasukuma. In general they seem to belong to the same group as the Bantu of western

181

Uganda and the lake region of mainland Tanzania. Though our knowledge of the Wanyamwezi has considerably improved in the last two years, the data on the Wasukuma remains basically the same. The little evidence that is available suggests that the lake area of Usukuma (the country of the Wasukuma) was previously occupied by the pastoral Bahima. It is not clear whether they were preceded in the district by any other people though this was most likely the case. If so, the ethnic identity of their predecessors has yet to be established. What the traditions are emphatic about is that the Wasukuma advanced northwards from the south. On arrival in the lake area of the country they encountered the pastoral Bahima whom they subsequently drove out.

In the opening paragraphs of this chapter it was noted that the environment played a significant role in the nature of human occupation and settlement among the western Bantu. The Wanyamwezi are a case in point. Because their country is fairly flat it was generally easy for people to move around. Secondly a considerable part of the country is suitable for cultivation and grazing, but on the whole, the soil is not fertile enough to withstand intensive cultivation. As such it could not indefinitely support large numbers of people using simple agricultural techniques. The result was that people tended to move from one area of settlement to another. Again instead of congregating in one large district, they built small settlements. As the population gradually increased, people moved out into new territories which were easily reached and brought under cultivation.

It is not clear yet when the country was first settled. What is evident is that the first Bantu settlers arrived many centuries ago. Since they lived around big rivers such as Igombe, Malgarasi and Ugalla, it is reasonable to suppose that they were fishermen as well as cultivators.

The result of all this was that the Wanyamwezi lived in numerous small independent groups. Whatever cultural traits they may have had in common (as a result, largely, of the free and easy movement of people), the various Wanyamwezi social and political units had no single group name. There was no single political authority to which they were subordinate. In this regard it is worth noting that their present name of Wanyamwezi was given to the first traders from their country to visit the coast. They came from the west, the country where, to the coastal people, the new moon was always first seen. The first such traders had reached the east coast by 1800.

Though they did not form a united community, the Wanyamwezi chiefdoms shared many cultural traits in common. By 1800 their country was traversed by a complex network of internal trade routes. These brought people into close social contact. Trade became particularly important in the nineteenth century when copper, ivory and slaves became profitable commodities in trade with the east coast. This

182

topic lies outside the limits of the present chapter. However, long before 1800 the Wanyamwezi had established important trade links within their own politically fragmentary society as well as with their neighbours. Among the commodities traded in by 1800, when Wanyamwezi traders reached the east coast, were salt (from Uvinza), iron products, e.g. hoes and spears from Usangi and Mhunze, livestock, grain, and metal wire, which was also used as currency particularly after the establishment of links with the east coast.

Another important common feature among the Wanyamwezi chiefdoms was the fact that they were ruled by chiefs called *ntemi* (singular). The royal drums figured prominently on the list of the royal regalia. Though in the past this has led some authors into associating the origins of these chiefdoms with the lake kingdoms, there is no concrete evidence to support such a theory. The nature of their country and the pattern of settlement seems to have favoured the evolution of small political units. The use of the drum as a symbol of royalty could have either originated locally or been borrowed from outside or evolved as a result of the interaction of local and external influences. The lake area is one possible source but by no means the only one. Moreover, these chiefdoms were small and lacked the cohesion of the lake kingdoms. In addition local traditions suggest that the ruling dynasties had diverse origins. For example, those in western Unyamwezi (Galagansa) were founded by immigrants from Rwanda during the seventeenth century. It is not clear whether they were Bahima or Batutsi. The dynasties of Uyui and Usagari in central Unyamwezi were founded by people from the east coast, perhaps Uzaramo or Usagara. The dynasty of Unyanyembe was founded by immigrants from Ngulu farther south. In contrast, there is ample proof that the Ha, the Vinza and the Jiji of north-western Tanzania as well as the Fipa and certain Nyamwezi chiefdoms along Lake Tanganyika were influenced by the political system of the lake kingdoms. Traditions point to an immigration in the general area during the eighteenth and nineteenth centuries; the migrants came from Burundi. In the case of the Fipa the first such rulers arrived between 1675 and 1725, coming from the south-west.

Finally, the ntemi had both administrative and priestly powers. The well-being of his people, country, crops and animals depended on his personal health. When he fell sick the chiefdom was supposed to suffer in one way or another. He was assisted by a hierarchy of subordinates— priests, councillors, headmen, etc. The office of the ntemi was not hereditary. Thus though the Wanyamwezi and related peoples had no corporate past before the nineteenth century, they shared common political institutions and cultural traits.

Bagisu and Basoga

The history of the eastern half of the region is largely that of the origins and migrational movements of the ancestors of the local communities, and their development as cultural and political units. Included in this group are the Basoga, Bagisu, Abaluyia and the Abagusii.

The more closely we examine the past of these peoples, the more we become convinced that, between about nine and twenty generations ago, therefore around A.D. 1382 to 1706, this whole region experienced tremendous migrational movements, particularly affecting the present Eastern Province of Uganda, and as a result of which eastern Uganda and neighbouring western Kenya were peopled by the great majority of their present occupants. For the sake of clarity, the history of each community will be analysed separately.

To the north-east of Lake Victoria in the Mount Elgon region of Uganda live the Bagisu. They are closely related to the Babukusu, the northernmost section of the Abaluyia. So far, relatively little is known about their history. Nevertheless, traditional evidence strongly suggests that between A.D. 1517 and 1652, the first settlers had arrived in Bugisu. Earlier, they would appear to have been driven from the Uasingishu Plateau to the east of Mount Elgon by the Nandi, Maasai, Turkana, and perhaps the Abyssinians. Nothing is known about their country of origin, but some traditions suggest that their forefathers moved into the Uasingishu Plateau from the direction of Abyssinia.

The immigrants were probably preceded in the country by other people about whom we now know nothing. Their predecessors may have been Bantu, probably akin to the present Banyole (Banyuli) and Bagwere to the south-west. The newcomers would, therefore, seem to have abandoned their native speech and culture and adopted the local ones. Whichever the case, modern Bugisu must have been peopled from different territories, particularly the neighbouring districts. Eventually, the Bagisu expanded from the foothills of Mount Elgon into the surrounding plains, presumably more recently in the peaceful period of British rule. Their southward and westward expansion had earlier been hindered by the hostile Teso.

Like the Bagisu, the Basoga who live to their south-west are a mixed community whose ancestors came from different territories. Some of them later moved into western Kenya where their descendants still live. We shall come back to this later.

Traditional evidence suggests that the first settlers arrived in the country long before the advent of the legendary Kintu of the Bagisu, Basoga and Baganda traditions. By far the oldest and best known of these early settlers of whom we have any information is the lineage of Kibwika of the Reedbuck clan. Kibwika's lineage has been in the country for about

Figure 19 Western Bantu territories

185

thirty to thirty-five generations, a very long time indeed. He and his colleagues first settled at Bukonge where many of their descendants still live. Further evidence indicates that at about the same time that this was happening Buyaga and other islands were occupied by members of the Reedbuck clan who were in some way related to Kibwika's line. It was about this time, too, that people with various bird totems settled in the north-east corner of the lake, Kyaggwe and most probably in south Busoga proper.

Sometime later other members of the Reedbuck clan came to south Busoga. Their journey was rather intricate. Starting from Bugaya island (which was also settled by members of the Pangolin totem) they travelled eastwards by canoe as far as Nsumba (Sumba) Island to the north-east. They then reversed and moved on to Bugoto about 3 miles [5 km] from the lake-shore. This happened about twenty to thirty generations ago. The group finally split up; one section moved north-westwards to Byanirwa where they were subsequently joined by other members of the Reedbuck, this time from Buganda. The second group appears to have stayed behind in the neighbourhood of Bugoto.

Thus by about twenty generations ago, between A.D. 1382 and 1409, south Busoga including the neighbouring islands was already settled by the earliest immigrants. Among them were the ancestors of Nanyumba's people, Banyole, who lived on the lakeshore areas of modern Bukoli. These early settlers were joined sometime later by others from the Mount Elgon area. They were led by either the famous Kintu or Mukama who eventually crossed over into Bunyoro. Some of their descendants live in the south-west and north-east of Busoga.

In due course, more people came from the neighbouring territories of Budama, western Kenya, Kigulu (Sigulu) Island in the Kavirondo Gulf, and Bugwere. By this time too the Lwo had also arrived in Bukoli and the northern districts of Busoga on their way from the southern Sudan. All this happened between about thirteen and fifteen generations ago, between 1517 and 1598. The great majority of the Lwo later crossed over into western Kenya. By about twelve generations ago, A.D. 1598 to 1625, more settlers had arrived, this time from Bunyoro; many of them settled in Bugabula and Bulamogi.

Thus by about nine generations ago, A.D. 1679 to 1706, Busoga was already peopled from different territories. Among the settlers in the southern districts were the ancestors of some of the major clans of the Abaluyia. Notable among these are the Abashitsetse of Wanga, Abafo-foyo in Marachi, Abaguri of Bukhayo, and the Abakhekhe of Samia locations. On the other hand, as has been noted, some of the immigrants came from Bugishu, the immediate homeland of the Babukusu. It is therefore evident that between about nine and twenty generations ago, 1382 to 1706, modern Busoga and Bugishu as also Buluyia in western Kenya were partly settled by people of the same stock.

As already noted, as a result of the establishment of the Lwo Babito dynasty in Bunyoro, a number of related sub-dynasties were founded in Busoga. They ruled in Bukoli, Bugwere, Bulamogi, Bukono, Bugabula, and Bugweri. Whereas the first two were contemporary with the Babito dynasty of Bunyoro, the rest were founded between about 1598 and 1733. At first they were virtually independent and formed separate alliances from those of the Banyoro.

By the nineteenth century there were about fifteen such principalities, most of them very small. In the northern district where there were Banyoro migrants, the Baisengobi (Bushbuck) clan provided the rulers for seven of the northern and eastern principalities. Much of the north was under Bunyoro domination in the nineteenth century. In fact, by 1862 when Speke visited Bunyoro, the north was paying tribute to the *mukama* (ruler) of Bunyoro. On the other hand, the south seems to have been ruled by dynasties of either an eastern or a Lake Victoria islands origin. The southern principalities were generally smaller than the northern ones.

The Abaluyia and Abagusii

About the same time (i.e. A.D. 1382 to 1706) that the Bantu of eastern Uganda were settling there, similar developments were taking place further east in Buluyia. The Abaluyia also are a hybrid community founded by people of different origins and cultures. The earliest settlers in the northern half of Buluyia were of Kalenjin origin. By the beginning of the seventeenth century, the ancestors of the Kalenjin had migrated from their original homes and settled on Mount Elgon.

Some time later, the migrants staged a second dispersal which ultimately gave rise to the present Kalenjin septs—the Nandi, Kipsigis, Tugen, Suk, Marakwet and Elgeyo. Those who remained behind in the Elgon area became the ancestors of the present Kony, Bongomek and Bok or Sebeyi of the same district. They still retain their original language and culture. On the other hand, a few of them were completely Bantuised. They include the present Abatachoni, Abashieni of South Marama, and Abamulembo, Abanashieni and Abatobe of Wanga. Thus by about A.D. 1598 to 1625, northern Buluyia was already inhabited by people of Kalenjin origin. On the other hand, the south was largely unoccupied except for isolated Bantu communities in four of the locations. Traditional evidence suggests that many of the clans of the Abaluyia were founded by people from a country vaguely called *Misri* (Egypt). The only district which fits the description is the Lake Rudolf area. They subsequently settled in eastern Uganda.

The period between about eight and twelve generations ago, A.D.

187

1598 to 1733, saw large scale immigration from the Bantu areas of eastern Uganda and Buganda. The ancestors of the majority of the present occupants of the locations of Tiriki, Wanga, Bukhayo, Samia, Marama, and Bunyore, parts of Kabras, Butsotso, Maragoli and Marachi arrived about this time. By about ten generations ago, A.D. 1652 to 1679, the migration from southern Busoga, Bunyole, and parts of southern Bugishu was virtually over. Some of the migrants settled in central Nyanza from where they moved further north on the appearance of the Luo. The migration from eastern Uganda seems to have been caused by dynastic and domestic disputes, overcrowding, tsetse flies and sleeping sickness, and the desire for a better country.

Between about eleven and thirteen generations ago, A.D. 1571 to 1652, a small column of Maasai or Nandi came from the eastern direction and settled in Idakho. They were later Bantuised and lost their original language and culture. Their descendants (variously called Abashimuli, Abamuli, Abashisa and Abashirotsa) today live in Idakho, Kisa, Bunyore, Gem and Tiriki locations. Some of the Abamani and Abakhobole of Gem and Kisa belong to this group. By about eight generations ago, 1706 to 1733, the southern half of the country had been settled. Some of the immigrants came from Ankole (e.g. Abamuyima of Wanga) and the Mount Elgon area (i.e. those of Kalenjin origin). A few others, especially in the Port Victoria area, were of Luo origin. The earliest immigrants arrived between about 1463 and 1625.

As already seen, by the beginning of the seventeenth century, the ancestors of the Bagisu, Bamasaba and Babukusu had settled in Bugisu and the Tororo district. They were living as a single united community. However, between about six and eight generations ago, A.D. 1706 to 1787, the Teso invaded their settlements in eastern Uganda and dispersed them. The majority of them moved farther north and joined their kinsmen in modern Bugisu. Others scattered all over western Kenya—Samia, Bunyala, Marachi, Bukhayo, Isukha and Buholo. A few others went to Ebwayi, Amukura hill and to Bukusu hill. Nevertheless, it was not until four or six generations ago, around 1760 to 1841, that the Teso greatly increased in proportion (they were joined by others from Kumi and Soroti), expanded into the border territories of Amukura and Ebwayi, and forced the great majority of the Babukusu into their present settlements in Buluyia.

It was also due to the Teso invasion that the ancestors of the Abanyala (Navakholo) left their homes in Buyemba (then occupied by the Bagisu, Babukusu, etc.) and settled in presentday Bunyala (Navakholo). Some of the Abanyala are of Maasai origin. Thus by the second half of the nineteenth century, the long process of immigration into Buluyia was virtually complete.

About this time too, the present country of the Abagusii and related peoples to the south of the Kavirondo Gulf was being settled. According to linguistic evidence, the Abagusii have their closest affinities with the Abalogoli section of the Abaluyia, the Bakuria (Batende), and the Kikuyu. However, some of these relationships are not supported by traditional or other evidence.

In general the early history of the Abagusii before their arrival in their present country is still far from clear. So far one can only rely on the traditions of the Abagusii themselves and those of the Abaluyia for this early phase. Yet these sources do not agree on a number of important points. Abaluyia sources suggest that the ancestors of the Abagusii and the Abalogoli section of the Abaluyia moved together from southern Uganda. This was after the supposed migration from Misri. From southern Uganda they entered the lake and travelled by canoe as far as Rusinga Island. Here they separated, one group going northwards across the gulf while the second moved farther south across the gulf. These became the ancestors of the Abalogoli and Abagusii respectively.

According to Abagusii traditions, however, their ancestors were originally related to the Kuria, Abalogoli, Abasuba, Kikuyu, Meru, etc. It is further evident that the ancestors of the Abagusii came from a country called Misri. They are said to have moved southwards to Mount Elgon where a dispersal took place. This gave rise to the various ethnic groups already mentioned plus the Baganda and Basoga.

From Mount Elgon the ancestors of the Abagusii, Kuria, Abasuba, and Abalogoli moved down the Nzoia River valley. By about the beginning of the sixteenth century they had arrived on the eastern shores of Lake Victoria. They subsequently moved eastwards and settled at Goye in Yimbo. Later still, after the coming of the Luo, the Abagusii and Abalogoli moved to the shores of Lake Gangu in Alego and thence to Sakwa, Asembo, Seme and Kisumu.

As a result of severe famine and plague there was a further migration, this time from Kisumu. The ancestors of the Abagusii therefore left Kisumu for the Kano Plains in search of food and better country. They were probably there around 1640–1755 though an advance group seems to have reached the area around 1436–1571. They later spread out and occupied their present country. Meanwhile the ancestors of the Abalogoli had stayed behind in Kisumu when their colleagues went to the Kano Plains. They subsequently migrated to Seme from where they moved to their present settlements in Buluyia.

Some time between about 1790 and 1820, the Abagusii sections of Kitutu, South Mugirango, Wanjari, Bassi, and Majoge fled to the north of the Kavirondo Gulf under separate leaders. The flight was presumably caused by mounting pressure from their Maasai neighbours. After about thirty years, they all recrossed the gulf, again individually. As a result of these movements, intermarriage, and the arrival of new immigrants of diverse origins such as the Maasai, Kipsigis and the Luo, the people became very much mixed. Furthermore, in the first half of the eighteenth century, more settlers arrived from southern Buganda and Busoga and settled on Mfangano and Rusinga Islands. Later, however, they moved to Gwassi on the mainland where they became the ancestors of some of the Abasuba community.

Western Bantu religious beliefs and political organisation

Although religion played an important role in the day-to-day life of the western Bantu peoples, it was generally at the family level. This form of religion, which has been called ancestor worship, is still active to this day in many areas. The whole basis of this religion was a strong belief in the continuity of human life—life after death. It was this belief which gave rise to the idea that though a man might die physically, he would, all the same, continue to protect and care for his family, relatives and even friends. The deceased thus became the guardian angel of the living, particularly of the family. He was supposed to see to their welfare and to protect them against the evil actions and intentions of their enemies. Such enemies, or supposed evil-doers, might themselves be dead or alive.

The very fact that the dead could still protect or harm the living necessitated the latter's taking appropriate measures. They resorted to sacrifices of all sorts and for diverse purposes. In many areas each clan or village had a leading sacrificial priest. Similarly, each family had an elder who performed sacrificial duties at the family level. Periodically sacrifices were offered to good spirits as a gesture of gratitude and an expression of goodwill. In contrast, evil spirits were usually expiated, again through sacrifices. The latter was particularly the case where the people concerned had a reason to believe that their calamity, misfortune, or ill health was the work of the evil spirit of a particular person. Again, the good spirit of one of the ancestors might be appealed to for intercession should some evils spirits be suspected of malicious and harmful intentions or acts.

It would, however, appear that the ancestral spirits were primarily regarded as influential and authoritative agents or media. In other words, despite their supposed ability to give help or harm, their powers were actually limited. For, throughout this whole region, there was a vague belief in the power of the omnipotent creator who was in complete control of all life and the elements. The sun, the moon, a river, a mountain, or even a hill might personify such a being. Again, throughout the region, there was a general belief in minor gods—the god of the river, the god of the lake, etc. However, all these gods were vague, remote and impersonal, unlike the guardian spirits of the ancestors. Ancestor

190

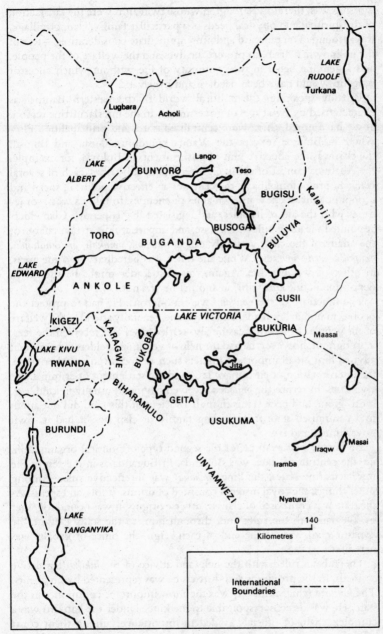

Figure 20 Western Bantu peoples and their neighbours

191

worship was, therefore, a religion whose twin aims were the satisfaction of the spiritual and physical needs of a particular family, clan, or village. It was founded on practical and more immediate considerations—fear of the unknown, a desire to protect the lives and the welfare of the people, and a genuine belief in the continuity of life without which ancestor worship would have been needless and irrelevant.

Broadly speaking, the political world of the western Bantu was characterised by two types of government. In the interlacustrine region, as we have noted, there were centralised states and principalities. Elsewhere in Buluyia (except the Wanga kingdom), Gusii, and Bugisu, the clan was the effective unit of government. In Buluyia, for example, the Abaluyia consist of about eighteen major sub-tribes, each of several clans. In pre-colonial days, the clan was an effective political, social and economic unit: it chose its own allies or enemies, fought its wars, sometimes with the aid of its allies, and legislated for its people. Clan elders appointed a leading influential, wise, and impartial elder to take charge of the affairs of the clan, variously called *omwami, omukali, omukhulundu, omukasa, weng'oma,* etc. While the office was hereditary in some areas, in others it was elective. Again, this clan leader might be subject to deposition in one area while in another he was not.

The functions of the *omwami* were numerous. He had to protect the people, maintain law, order and peace, and generally attend to the welfare of his people. In many areas he also settled cases and received the fees. Throughout, however, he had the help of a council of elders. The council advised him on all important matters such as land disputes, inheritance, the interpretation of customary law, and the settlement of criminal and civil cases. In return the *omwami* received payment, usually in kind, e.g. meat, grain, and beer. Thus though a society of this kind did not attain to a centralised state transcending family or clan ties, it had its own government and laws.

By far the best example of the second type of political organisation, i.e. the centralised state, was Buganda. In Buganda as in the rest of the interlacustrine states, the king (*kabaka*) was an effective ruler. Among other things, the royal insignia consisted of drums, stools, and spears. As the state was composed of clans of diverse origins, it was bound together by allegiance to the ruler and, through him, to the state. Despite the dynastic civil wars at the end of each reign, the office of kabaka was hereditary.

The kabaka ruled with the help and advice of the *lukiko* (legislative council). In the provinces and districts he was represented by his agents. The *katikiro* (chief minister) was the most important commoner in the state. He was directly responsible to the king. Under the katikiro was a complex chain of officials graded in importance, among them court officials, county chiefs, county agents, court servants, pages and messengers. By the close of the eighteenth century the majority of the county chiefs and agents were appointive rather than hereditary. This was a source of great strength and influence to the monarchy for the ruler had virtual control over the appointment and dismissal of leading servants.

Unlike the first category of political organisation, the centralised states were generally much bigger. This does not apply to several principalities of Busoga, some of which equalled the clan in size. Due to the size of the centralised states which necessitated an efficient machinery of government, the kingdom had to be subdivided into counties and sub-counties. This was particularly the case with Buganda. The counties and sub-counties were directly ruled by appointed chiefs and the entire kingdom legislated for by a common lukiko. The administration which resulted from this complex organisation was highly efficient, if rather ruthless and autocratic.

Further reading

ROSCOE, J. *The Northern Bantu,* Cambridge, 1915.

ROSCOE, J. *The Bagesu*, Cambridge, 1924.

ROSCOE, J. *The Baganda*, London, 1911.

ROSCOE, J. *The Bakitara*, Cambridge, 1923.

BEATTIE, J. *Bunyoro, An African Kingdom*, Oxford, 1960.

DUNBAR, A. R. *A History of Bunyoro—Kitara*, Oxford, 1965.

MORRIS, H. F. *A History of Ankole*, Nairobi, 1962.

CORY, H. *Historia ya Wilaya Bukoba (History of the Bukoba District),* Mwanza.

CORY, H. *The Ntemi, Traditional Rites of a Sukuma Chief in Tanganyika,* London, 1951.

LUBOGO, Y. K. *A History of Busoga*, Kampala, 1960.

RICHARDS, A. I. (Ed.), *East African Chiefs*, London, 1960.

FALLERS, L. A. *Bantu Bureaucracy*, Cambridge, 1956.

LA FONTAINE, J. S. *The Gisu of Uganda*, Ethnographic Survey of Africa, East Central Africa, Part X, London, 1959.

ROBERTSON, D. W. *The Historical Considerations Contributing to the Soga System of Land Tenure,* Kampala, 1940.

BARKER, E. E. *A Short History of Nyanza*, Nairobi, 1958.

WHITELEY, W. H. *The Tense System of the Gusii*, East African Linguistic Studies, IV, 1960.

MAYER, P. *The Lineage Principle in Gusii Society*, London, 1949.

WAGNER, G. *The Bantu of North Kavirondo*, London, 1949.

OSOGO, J. *A History of the Baluyia*, Oxford, 1966.

GOLDTHORPE, J. E. and WILSON, F. B. *Tribal Maps of East Africa and Zanzibar*, Kampala, 1960.

WERE, G. S. *A History of the Abaluyia of Western Kenya c. 1500–1930*, Nairobi, 1967.

WERE, G. S. *Western Kenya Historical Texts*, Nairobi, 1967.

WERE, G. S. and WILSON, D. A. *East Africa through a Thousand Years*, London, 1968.

10

The Eastern Bantu Peoples

Isaria N. Kimambo

The aim of this chapter is to reconstruct the history of the eastern Bantu peoples to the beginning of the nineteenth century. In doing this we have to rely on scattered evidence, coming from linguistic, archaeological and oral information. Unfortunately, for the eastern Bantu group, very little linguistic and archaeological evidence is available. The bulk of our information has to come from oral tradition collected at different periods. For some groups even oral information is nonexistent, and where it does exist it is not always reliable since not all the recorders followed up-to-date scientific research methods. Apart from the Pare, Shambaa, Kamba and Kikuyu who have recently been studied, for the rest of the members of the group we have to rely on scattered evidence, most of which is of dubious quality.

The term 'Eastern Bantu' is here used linguistically to refer to the Bantu speaking peoples inhabiting the region between the highland area stretching from north-eastern Tanzania to the Kenya highlands and the coast. They comprise such ethnic and linguistic subgroups as the Kikuyu, Embu, Meru, Kamba, Chagga, Pare, Taita, Shambaa, Nyika, Pokomo and Bajun. The history of their settlement in the area has already been discussed in chapter four. From that discussion it is clear that the region was inhabited by Bantu speaking peoples since the early Iron Age period in the first millennium A.D. From traditions of migration held by these peoples, however, it is also clear that population movements continued in this area throughout most of the second millennium A.D., thus overshadowing the main historical development in the region. It is no wonder that the historical literature available concentrates so much on migrations. In this particular region the geographical features encouraged such movements, not only as a process of expansion into empty spaces but also as a means of survival during droughts by moving from the drier *nyika* (dry grassland) plain to the wetter highlands. For reasons of clarity, it is proposed to discuss briefly some of the settlement issues again in this chapter before concentrating on the historical developments of the group prior to the beginning of the nineteenth century. The chapter is therefore divided into four sections: settlement; migration myths; interaction with non–Bantu speakers; and developments to about A.D. 1800. Naturally the main emphasis will be put on the last section.

1 Settlement

Chapter four has established the general framework of Bantu expansion. In the case of the Eastern Bantu speaking peoples a south–north direction of expansion is demonstrated by the available linguistic, documentary and archaeological evidence. First of all, Malcolm Guthrie's linguistic studies have proposed a Bantu dispersal area around the Katanga woodlands from which quick expansion in elliptical form took place to the east and west as evidenced by the prevalence of a high percentage of common Bantu roots in Kikongo (on the west coast) and Kiswahili on the east coast. The varying percentage of these common roots has been used to indicate the direction of expansion from the dispersal centre. For the Eastern Bantu group, however, our linguistic information is too meagre to continue Guthrie's scheme from the base-line. Yet, if we accept the principle established by the scheme itself, it is possible to continue the northward expansion by using other evidence.

For the Eastern Bantu group we are lucky to have some documentary evidence which, when combined with other evidence, helps to indicate that there was an arm of Bantu expansion around the coast. The first well-known document about the history of the east coast is the Greek sailor's guide of the first or second century A.D. known as the *Periplus of the Erythrean Sea*. It speaks about the existence of people on the coast who traded with sailors across the Indian Ocean. Most writers have categorically dismissed this as a reference to Bantu speaking peoples simply because there was no mention of colour. It is argued that the first reference to black people appears in Ptolemy's *Geography* (a compilation of the fourth century A.D.), which speaks about the existence of 'man-eating Ethiopians' on the east coast. Thereafter Arab geographers continue to mention black people and it is assumed that by the tenth century A.D. the Bantu speaking peoples had expanded as far north as the

Somalia coast. When the existing documentary evidence is combined with the archaeological information just beginning to come to light, there is no reason why the reference in the *Periplus* could not have applied to Bantu speaking peoples. Certainly, it can be argued that nothing can be based on the mere fact that the skin colour of the people referred to in the sailor's guide is not mentioned. It is therefore important to examine briefly the archaeological evidence recently made available through the efforts of the British Institute of History and Archaeology in East Africa.

Archaeological evidence for the Bantu Iron Age has seemingly agreed very well with the general linguistic proposal. The distribution of channel-dimple-based pots from the Zambezi to Lake Victoria with radiocarbon dates varying from the beginning of the first millennium A.D. has generally supported the theory of the south–north expansion of Bantu speaking peoples. For the Eastern Bantu group, however, almost no radiocarbon dates existed until recently. The work of R. C. Soper has revealed an Iron Age Bantu culture (known as Kwale culture) extending from the hinterland of Mombasa to the Pare Mountains, and with radiocarbon dates ranging from the third to the ninth century A.D. More recent reconnaissance work by Knut Odner has indicated that the Kwale wares extend to North Pare as well as Kilimanjaro.

When all this evidence is put together, it logically indicates the possibility of Bantu speaking peoples expanding quickly not only along the east coast but also along the highland areas immediately bordering the dry plain. Most likely the Pangani river valley was the earliest channel into the highland region. When this is borne in mind, one can clearly see why it has been so difficult to reconcile the archaeological evidence with the traditional evidence whether recorded or oral.

2 Migration myths

One of the most difficult problems of Eastern Bantu history centres on the interrelationship between the known traditions of migration. This problem is further complicated by the existence of the famous Shungwaya tradition which seems to have coloured most of what has been written on the subject. Shungwaya has been understood by historians as a mythical dispersal centre to be located at some place on the Somalia coast, probably around the present Port Durnford. The name has appeared on maps since the sixteenth century, at first as a town and later as a general area. Arab geographers have referred to well organised societies in the coast region. Al Mas'udi, for example, wrote in the tenth century describing black people who had a divine king, believed in one God, but also worshipped ancestral spirits and totems.

Unfortunately no organised states have remained on the coast to be identified with Al Mas'udi's accounts. The establishment of Muslim sultanates, such as Kilwa, Mombasa, Malindi, etc., belongs to a different tradition, and we must assume that if Bantu states of the nature described by Arab travellers existed they later disappeared. This is still a puzzling assumption since there is no clear evidence that the tradition of a state system has been retained in the region. States do occur among the Shambaa, Pare and Chagga, but their formation can be traced to more recent events of political, economic and social mobilisation within these societies.

What has remained is the migration tradition connected with Shungwaya. Most coastal groups (Nyika, Pokomo, Bajun) do have traditions of having migrated from a place called Shungwaya. Taking this as a general dispersal area, historians have tended to view this mythical place as the northmost extremity of Bantu territory. This would mean that the Bantu speaking people expanded quickly along the east coast up to the Somalia coast. They formed strong societies there, but because of pressure of other societies (including the Somali and Galla), they later migrated southwards to form the existing societies on the coast and in the interior. It is this kind of general interpretation which has made certain writers connect the Shungwaya myth with all the Eastern Bantu peoples.

It is now clear that this interpretation is not quite correct. First of all, it is unlikely that there is a single dispersal area for all the eastern Bantu peoples. We have seen how archaeological evidence demonstrates settlement in the highland region much earlier than is claimed for Shungwaya. What is already known about migration into Pare, Kamba and Kikuyu areas indicates a continuous movement of people which cannot be limited to a single period or place. The migration pattern agrees well with the environment which naturally demands constant movements from dry areas to greener ones during dry spells. Secondly, the Shungwaya migration story is not shared by all eastern Bantu peoples as it was assumed. It is definitely a common story among the coastal group. In the interior the name is not mentioned by any group. Among the Meru there exists a tradition of migration from an area near 'the great water' where they had lived under the rule of a 'fair-skinned' people. On the basis of the Meru tradition it was assumed that all the members of the highland groups must be connected with the Shungwaya dispersal.

From what we have already said, one can assume that the existing traditions of migration for the Eastern Bantu peoples cannot be taken to represent movement of a whole ethnic group. The present societies have been built up through a gradual process of intermingling of people from different places. Although certain groups of people may have direct connection with the Shungwaya tradition, we can conclude that the migration myth symbolises this history of continuous movement which has clearly had tremendous effect on the formation and organisation of the societies comprising the Eastern Bantu speaking peoples as a whole.

3 Interaction with non-Bantu speakers

The story of intermingling of population covers non-Bantu speakers as well. In chapters three and four it has been indicated that East Africa was inhabited by hunting, gathering and agricultural peoples long before the coming of the Bantu speakers. Archaeological evidence for pre-Bantu communities in East Africa is generally not lacking. In chapter eight Christopher Ehret has reconstructed the history of their interaction with Bantu and Nilotic speaking peoples. The historical linguistic studies of Ehret are especially significant for the Eastern Bantu speakers since they almost entirely inhabit territory formerly occupied by the earlier agricultural communities identified as 'Southern Cushitic speaking peoples'. Some Southern Cushitic communities still exist among Eastern Bantu speakers, although their strength is diminishing fast through the process of Bantuisation. Others have completely disappeared and their presence can only be identified through the presence of loanwords among the existing Bantu population.

Among the existing Southern Cushitic speaking peoples, the most important group comprises the Mbuguan speaking people who, for the past five hundred years or so, have been a declining force among the Eastern Bantu speakers of north-eastern Tanzania. Their absorption by the Pare can clearly be identified in Pare traditions, and some of them still exist as seperate clans, though speaking the Pare language. In Usambara several thousand Mbuguan speakers still exist and their recognisably Southern Cushitic language has been very much modified due to intensive Bantu influences. The study of loanwords among the Shambaa and Zigua has suggested that the territory of original contact between the Mbuguan and Eastern Bantu groups was probably in the present Zigua country, although more recent traditions of Mbugu movements into Pare and Usambara from the Maasai steppe make the dating more difficult. Most likely these traditions refer to movements of some of the ancestors of the Mbuguan speakers who were already in the Pangani region.

Other existing Southern Cushitic speaking people further west are known as the Rift group. Their interaction with the Eastern Bantu (with the exception of the Sonjo) is still rather unclear since some of the groups have been completely absorbed and their existence has to be detected from loanwords remaining in the Bantu dialects. The most interesting case is that of the appearance of loanwords in the Taita language, suggesting the existence of a separate subgroup of Rift Southern Cushitic speakers on the Taita Hills. Further north linguistic evidence of contacts between Southern Cushitic speakers and Eastern Bantu has been pointed out. The interaction between the Dahalo and coastal Bantu probably of the Nyika group is easier to detect since the Dahalo were mainly hunters and are indebted to the Bantu speakers for words dealing with cultivation.

In the Mount Kenya region the linguistic evidence available is also of great historical importance since it suggests interaction between Bantu speakers and Southern Cushitic communities as early as the first millennium A.D. The earliest contacts were probably with the Yaaku speakers, while loanwords among the Kikuyu suggest some interaction with Southern Cushitic speakers later than the Yaaku: this would indicate that Southern Cushitic speaking people remained as separate communities in the eastern highlands into the present millennium. The later contact with the Kikuyu group is largely corroborated in their traditional history, as recorded by Godfrey Muriuki, which tells of Kikuyu interaction with the Athi and Gumba during the process of expansion into their present land.

This survey of interaction between Eastern Bantu and Southern Cushitic speaking peoples indicates that the present Bantu population in this area was built up through a long history of intermingling of peoples of different tongues. A more detailed study of the cultures of these people will indicate how this interaction helped in building societies with complex cultures by blending cultural traits of diverse communities. Even with the little knowledge we have of this interaction, some scholars attribute the existence of Southern Cushitic traits found among the Bantu speakers to this interaction. Such traits include circumcision, linear age-set systems, irrigation and possibly the idea of milking and bleeding cattle. If this assumption is correct, then the eastern Bantu speaking peoples have come under heavier Cushitic influence than any other Bantu group.

4 Developments to about 1800 A.D.

In chapters three and four the process of forming settled societies by iron-using agricultural peoples has been discussed. In this section we are dealing with discernible features of development within the eastern Bantu speakers after the settlement period, despite the fact that by A.D. 1800 most of these societies were still expanding into new areas in the territories they occupy today. As already pointed out, the structure and culture of these societies were affected by the non Bantu speakers

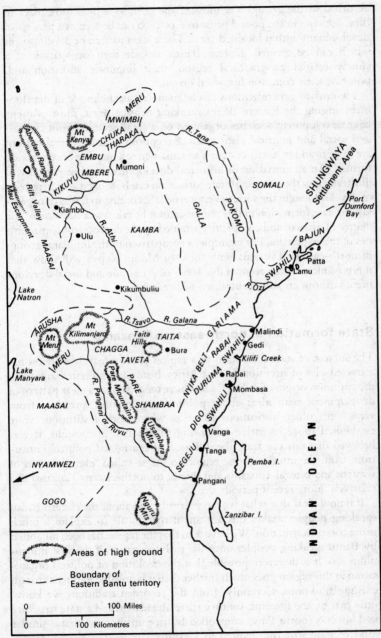

Figure 21 Eastern Bantu territory c. 1800

absorbed in the group. Yet most of the changes which took place in these societies in the period prior to A.D. 1800 can be seen as a process of development within localised areas. There is no pattern of development which can be termed 'Eastern Bantu' despite their occupation of a closely related geographical region, their linguistic affiliation and, possibly, their common historical origin.

Two major generalisations can be made about the mode of development among the Eastern Bantu speaking peoples. First, most of them have development societies organised on a small scale without centralised social and political institutions. Exceptions to this general pattern are to be found in north-eastern Tanzania where a number of states were formed. An examination of historical developments in this region will illustrate how the process of state formation can be looked at as a strategy of development in the societies concerned. Secondly, in terms of organisation, state formation in this region cannot be taken as a measure of the degree of growth and complexity attained by the component communities of these societies. For example, a comparison of the highland groups of north-eastern Tanzania with those of Mount Kenya will show that it is possible to reach comparable levels of economic and social development without creating centralised institutions.

State formation in north-eastern Tanzania

The subject of state formation in a region predominantly stateless has attracted a lot of attention. In East Africa, historians interested in tracing the common origin of political ideas have tended to see a clear pattern of development with ideas about political organisation spreading from areas with older institutions to areas where such institutions were established more recently. According to this line of thought, it was believed that one can trace the diffusion of centralised political institutions from the interlacustrine region to the so-called 'ntemi' region of western and central Tanzania and thence to north-eastern Tanzania in a relatively more recent period.

It is now clear that what we have already said about the eastern Bantu speaking peoples makes this argument too simple to explain a much more complex situation. We have seen that the region has been inhabited by Bantu speaking peoples since the early centuries of the first millennium A.D. It is therefore possible that the evolution of political organisation in this region goes much further than it is possible to trace through existing traditions. Certainly, from the recorded traditions we know only that by the fifteenth century there already existed a state structure in Ugweno (north Pare) controlled by ironsmiths, and that a similar kind of state structure existed in Usambara when the Kilindi family appeared on the scene in the eighteenth century. It is, however, beyond the capability of the existing traditions to tell us how long these states had existed when new changes were introduced.

From identifiable developments since the sixteenth century, it is possible to establish certain facts. First, there are several ruling families in Pare and Kilimanjaro with varying traditions of origin but none of them has a clear connection with the imagined common route of political ideas. For example, the four ruling families of rainmakers in south Pare all trace their origin to the Taita Hills and established their authority over other groups in the region some time in the seventeenth century. Similarly there are ruling families in Kilimanjaro with traditions of migration from the Taita, Kamba, Maasai, Shambaa, etc. Secondly, there is the point of evolution of political structures illustrated by the Gweno state in north Pare. About the beginning of the sixteenth century the loosely organised state, controlled by the iron smelting clan called Shana, underwent a drastic transformation which was introduced by one of the oldest clans existing within the Gweno society.

Briefly, this is what happened: the Shana ruler had traditionally appointed his chief minister from the Suya who were among the four major clans forming the Gweno society about the end of the fifteenth century. Most Gweno traditions indicate that the population was expanding over the north Pare plateau and that the existing institutions were becoming inadequate to solve the problems of the expanding community. Eventually the Suya decided to take over the political machinery through a bloody coup which killed a large number of the Shana. However, the main transformation was brought about by a Suya ruler known as Mranga who initiated a process of centralisation based on control of all institutions connected with initiation. Through this method it was possible for the Suya to control the whole of the north Pare Plateau and establish a Gweno kingdom which survived well into the nineteenth century. The Gweno example is of great historical significance since it challenges the idea that stimulus for change has to come from the outside.

The third point centres on the role of diffusion. Here the case of Usambara offers a good illustration. In the eighteenth century a group of people is said to have moved from the Nguru Mountains northwards, crossing the Pangani river to the Usambara Mountains. This event is dramatically told by the well-known Kilindi tradition centred on the hero known as Mbegha. From what is known it is difficult to ascertain whether or not Mbegha came from an organised state. Nevertheless, the direction of his migration has been taken as a link between the 'ntemi area' and the north-eastern region. Certainly this can be described as a case of diffusion of ideas brought about by the coming of a new group of people into an existing society. But the role of the new group has to be seen as that of stimulating change in a society where change was needed. In Ugweno such a change had taken place two centuries earlier through a stimulus which came from within. In Usambara change was stimulated by the tensions created by the arrival of the Kilindi group. The centralisation effected in Usambara since the second half of the eighteenth century was as thorough and effective as that introduced in Ugweno two centuries earlier. Another point to be noted is that in this region we have many examples of such stimuli of new groups, e.g. the rainmakers of south Pare, and the ruling families of Kilimanjaro already mentioned.

It is interesting to note that while Kilindi rule in Usambara brought about significant political reorganisation, the customs of the Shambaa remained unaffected. Steven Feierman's recent studies among the Shambaa have indicated that the Kilindi tended to adopt the customs they found in the country rather than introduce new ones. By doing so they were able to control the main rituals in much the same way as the Suya had done in Ugweno. But the main weapon of centralisation used by the Kilindi was that of spreading their kin to all parts of the region. Mbegha is said to have initiated the process of centralisation by taking at least one wife from each major clan; sons of these marriages were sent to administer their respective provinces. Mbegha's son, Bughe created a large council and a bureaucracy made up of commoners. Kilindi district rulers had to be represented at the court by non-Kilindi, thus keeping a check on the members of the royal clan. Bughe ruled near the end of the eighteenth century. His son Shebughe (or Kinyashi) built up a military force and started the process of expansion towards the coast, the task which was to be accomplished by his son, the famous Kimweri ye Nyumbai, whose story belongs to the nineteenth century.

In terms of the development of societies, therefore, the region inhabited by the Shambaa, Pare and Chagga was undergoing important changes in the period between the sixteenth and eighteenth centuries. A number of states appeared: the Gweno state built by Mranga had expanded to cover the whole of north Pare; the Kilindi state of Usambara had covered the whole Usambara region and by 1800 was already expanding into the plains to the Zigua country and towards the coast. In south Pare a number of smaller states had been formed and in Kilimanjaro as many as thirty small states had been established on different ridges. By 1800 a number of Kilimanjaro rulers were beginning to compete for domination of several ridges, though without success.

This political development went hand in hand with social and economic developments about which, unfortunately, very little is known. It is known, for example, that it was during this period that the Mbugu expanded into Pare and Shambaa territory and that in the former they were completely absorbed while the process of absorption is still going on in Usambara. The social and economic consequences of this contact are still to be determined. Secondly, we know that the expansion of Maasai speaking people into the Pangani river valley dates to this period. Certainly social and economic contacts between the Pare, Shambaa, Chagga and Maasai communities are well known in the traditions of these people and can be dated to the middle of the eighteenth century. With stronger political entities, border markets in which Maasai could exchange livestock for iron products (especially from Pare and Kilimanjaro) were encouraged. Some kind of regional trade also seems to have developed in this area. The salt trade from two important sources (the plain between Pare and Kilimanjaro and the western Usambara Plain) was shared by the whole region. Iron was the most important item of regional trade and, since the Pare dominated the sources of iron ore, their neighbours had to turn to them for this essential product. This was to become even more prominent in the nineteenth century when political competition in Kilimanjaro made patronage for iron smelting necessary. Regional exchange for livestock products was also known between the Pare and the Shambaa, and between the latter and their coastal neighbours.

One puzzling phenomenon in this region is the lack of control of long distance trade with the coast by those who were in control of the centralised political entities. Perhaps this can be explained by the fact that all these states were established on the mountains away from the natural route provided by the Pangani river valley. Rulers established on the mountains found it difficult to control the trade routes which were developed by coastal traders who were venturing as far inland as Kilimanjaro by 1800. In the nineteenth century a number of individuals from this region were to learn how to take advantage of the new economic opportunities by establishing residences on the plains along the trade routes. This in turn increased competition for political power in the region, thus weakening the existing states.

The highland regions of Kenya and the nyika plains

Despite the lack of centralised political institutions in the rest of the eastern Bantu territory, the society maintained the same kind of stability by adopting different methods of organisation. Kinship ties combined with territorial allegiances played an important part. But, above all, age-grade and age-set groupings were extremely significant. As we have already seen, the age-set system, shared by almost all the eastern Bantu speakers, was inherited from the Cushitic speaking predecessors in the region. Where centralised authority developed (as in north-eastern Tanzania), the political role of age-grouping institutions tended to be

205

weaker. In the Kenya highlands, for example, where environmental conditions favoured the same kind of economy as in Kilimanjaro, age-set institutions tended to play a prominent role, providing an orderly territorial organisation within the geographical boundaries of ridges. In this case the ridge organisation resembled the chiefdom organisation in Kilimanjaro, except that the Kikuyuland ridges tended to be smaller units. The age-set system with its authority system spread through various age-groups and their councils, tended to develop a territorial political and social organisation with corporate responsibility and leaders without personified authority.

The similarity between the Kikuyu system and that of north-eastern Tanzania is clear. For, while the descent group was the primary factor governing social relationships, the age-set system provided a way of ranking individuals on the basis of which all major duties in society were performed, e.g. military, police and judicial services. As we move out of the highlands, we encounter different environments with less stable economies. The whole region sloping from the highlands towards the coast (loosely known as the nyika) has experienced constant movement of population because of its semi-arid condition with periodic occurrences of drought and famine. In this region the age system becomes even less significant. Descent groups combined with residential affiliations formed the main political and social units. Authority tended to centre on the councils of elders based on these small units. Occasionally, however, age-sets provided a means of uniting a larger segment of the ethnic group, especially in defence. There is also some evidence that, among the Kamba, an age system may have provided the basis of organisation in long distance trade.

Like north-eastern Tanzania, the eastern Bantu area of the Kenya highlands and the nyika had, by 1800, developed considerable inter-group contacts. Some of these were on a hostile level. For example, Maasai-Kikuyu contacts since the late eighteenth century were not always peaceful; nor were Galla contacts with the eastern Bantu since their expansion into northern Kenya began in the sixteenth century. Nevertheless, there were many peaceful interactions among these groups with mutual social and economic interdependence. For example, the Kikuyu supplied agricultural foodstuffs to the Maasai, and iron to the Embu and the Kamba, and obtained livestock to augment their herds. Similarly, the Pokomo supplied agricultural produce to the Galla in exchange for ivory; to the Swahili speaking peoples near them for axes and hoes; and to the Boni hunters for bows and arrows. Throughout the eastern Bantu region markets in which exchanges took place were found. Some of these were more formal than others; some were situated within villages and others just outside in order to facilitate exchange with neighbouring groups. Even in periods of hostility, economic exchange was made possible through organisations mutually respected by the parties involved. Rabai, near Mombasa, came to be known in the nineteenth century as one of the most famous open markets where various groups—the Kamba, Taita, Swahili, Dahalo, Sanye, Nyika and Galla—'met to exchange their goods. The Swahili communities on the coast are also known to have provided markets for the surrounding peoples, although this system has often wrongly been described as tribute simply because it was believed that the surrounding groups were expected to provide foodstuffs for the Swahili towns.

It was through this system of exchange that there developed a regional trading network very similar to those developed in western-central and southern Tanzania. Here the principal controllers of the trade were the Kamba. Until recently their fame had mainly been connected with long distance trade in the nineteenth century. Yet, recent research has indicated that the Kamba had controlled a fairly wide network of trade well before the beginning of the nineteenth century. They are known to have monopolised the livestock trade on the coast as far south as Digo country and as early as the beginning of the eighteenth century. At least two important Kamba communities absorbed among the Pare are likely to have settled there before the beginning of the eighteenth century. All this indicates that the tendency of the Kamba to venture far away from their country was not a nineteenth century phenomenon.

Prior to the rise of long distance trade in ivory (and later slaves), therefore, the Kamba played a prominent role in an important network of regional trade, and it was through this network that they were able to control long distance trade in the nineteenth century. This regional trade network depended mainly on foodstuffs, poisons for arrows, livestock and possibly some iron implements. From known traditions, this trade may have been carried on in a region ranging from the Kikuyu in the north and the Embu and Tharaka in the west, to the Rabai, Giriama and Digo in the south.

Conclusion

This chapter has attempted to reconstruct the history of the Eastern Bantu speaking peoples to about A.D. 1800. As it emerges, the story is uneven and, therefore, much more research is needed before the gaps can be filled. Nevertheless, this synthesis does indicate the value of putting together what is already known in order to obtain an overall picture. Thus, though uneven, the picture emerging from this story emphasises three points hitherto blurred in the existing literature. Firstly, it indicates that it is impossible to give a coherent history of the Eastern Bantu speaking peoples by focusing on migration stories of individual ethnic groups. In this sense the so-called 'Shungwaya epic' has become a symbol of the continuous history of the intermingling of peoples. Secondly, it emphasises the cultural similarities existing among the group as a whole, despite its big size and dialectal diversity. Some of these similarities stem from the process of intermingling of population, of non-Bantu and Bantu speakers. Thirdly, the evolution of institutions within these societies is viewed as a strategy of development. In this case the environmental condition of the region as a whole falls within a rational range in which the existing cultural elements can be utilised to build institutions of varying scales of participation.

Further reading

EHRET, C. *Ethiopians and East Africans*, East African Publishing House, Nairobi, 1971.

FEIERMAN, S. 'The Shambaa Kingdom: A History', Ph.D. dissertation for Northwestern University, Evanston, Illinois, 1970.

FORBES-MUNRO, J. 'Migrations of the Bantu-speaking peoples of the Eastern Kenya Highlands: A Reappraisal', *Journal of African History*, *VIII*, 1967.

GREENBERG, J. H. *Studies in African Linguistic Classification*, New Haven, 1955.

GUTHRIE, M. 'Some Developments in the Prehistory of the Bantu Languages', *Journal of African History*, *III*, 1962.

KIMAMBO, I. N. *A Political History of the Pare of Tanzania, 1500–1900*, East African Publishing House, Nairobi, 1969.

KIMAMBO, I. N. and TEMU, A. (Eds) *A History of Tanzania*, East African Publishing House, Nairobi, 1969.

LAMBERT, H. E. Systems of Land Tenure in the Kikuyu Land Unit, Part I: *History of the Tribal Occupation of the Land*, Cape Town, 1950.

LINDBLOM, G. *The Akamba in British East Africa*, Uppsala, 1920.

MURIUKI, G. 'A History of the Kikuyu to 1900', Ph.D. thesis for University of London, 1969. (Shortly to be published.)

OLIVER, R. 'The Problem of the Bantu expansion', *Journal of African History*, *VII*, 1966.

PRINS, A. H. J. *The Coastal Tribes of the North-Eastern Bantu*, Ethnographic Survey of Africa, London, 1952.

ROBERTS, A. *Tanzania before 1900*, East African Publishing House, Nairobi, 1968.

SABERWAL, S. C. *The Traditional Political System of the Embu of Central Kenya*, East African Publishing House, Nairobi, 1970.

SABERWAL, S. C. 'Historical Notes on the Embu of Central Kenya', *Journal of African History, VIII*, 1967.

SOPER, R. C. 'Iron Age Sites in North-Eastern Tanzania', *Azania, II*, 1967.

STAHL, K. M. *History of the Chagga People of Kilimanjaro*, London, 1964.

11

The Arab Impact

Norman R. Bennett

By the latter part of the eighteenth century the peoples of the East
African interior had developed political organisations that made it
possible for Arabs[1] to travel inland with profit in search of the two
commodities of the interior—ivory and slaves—that could survive the
heavy costs of transportation to the coast. The initial stimulus for this
movement came from Africans of the interior, especially the Nyamwezi,
Bisa, Yao and Kamba, who opened trade routes that Arabs later
followed. As early as the mid-eighteenth century, there are reports of
trade goods reaching distant Buganda, probably through African
traders, and by the beginning of the nineteenth century, a regular trade
carried on by Africans with the coast was on in full force. Three general
routes of penetration developed as the century went on. On the southern
Tanzanian coast, centring on such ports as Kilwa Kivinje, Mkindani,
and Lindi, trade routes crossed the sparsely populated southern region of
Tanzania, the areas inhabited by such peoples as the Makonde, Makua,
and Yao, to reach the more populated, and thus more profitable, area
around and beyond Lake Nyasa. By the middle of the nineteenth
century, the trade along this route was primarily in slaves, with the Yao
playing a major role in securing them. There was little lasting Arab
impact along these trading routes, however, since the Arabs founded
their principal bases outside present-day Tanzania.

The principal penetration route for the coastal traders began opposite

[1] The term 'Arab' in this chapter is used for both Arabs and the Afro-Arabs of East Africa.

Zanzibar, from such ports as Bagamoyo and Sadani, and passed through the areas of many peoples—the Zaramo, Kami, Sagara, Luguru and Gogo, among others—before reaching the land of the Nyamwezi. From there the traders followed routes to Ujiji and across Lake Tanganyika into the Congo, to Karagwe and northwards to Buganda and beyond, and to the south-west to the area north and west of Lake Nyasa. Some slave raiding and trading did occur throughout these regions, especially in the earlier years of the nineteenth century, but the main concern of traders was the securing of ivory.

The third general route of penetration began on the northern Tanzanian and southern Kenyan coasts, from such ports as Pangani, Tanga, and Mombasa. Various roads led to the Chagga around Mount Kilimanjaro, and beyond through the territory of the Maasai to the eastern shores of Lake Victoria. Other routes led north from Kilimanjaro passing the fringes of Kikuyu territory, eventually reaching even the distant regions around Lakes Baringo and Rudolf. There was no strong Arab impact throughout this region. The coastal traders did come to dominate the use of the routes and to displace the earlier successful Kamba traders but they did not found any major Arab centres. The caravans, because of the dangers present, did not attract the leading coastal traders. Rather they were made up of cooperative groups of traders, each with moderate amounts of capital to invest in trade goods. After leaving the Kilimanjaro region the caravans tended to proceed to minor centres along the route from which smaller groups could leave the caravan to search for the limited amounts of available ivory. Very little slave raiding went on since the goodwill, or at least the toleration, of local African groups— such as the Maasai, Nandi, and Kikuyu—was necessary, because of the harsh nature of the land through which the traders passed, for the survival of the caravans. And it was virtually impossible to recruit new porters to replace men lost in battle. There were exceptions to this general pattern, however, since some traders did join in raids in the Kavirondo region, inhabited by the Luo and Luyia, especially with the Wanga Luyia. Thus although there developed a steady trade in the exchange of cloth, wire, beads, and some firearms for ivory (it was estimated that about twenty per cent of the ivory coming to the coast came from this route), the African predominance ensured that no strong coastal influence would flourish.

In all areas the nature of the Arab impact directly reflected the realities of African political power and of African control over the supplies of food and water necessary to long-distance traders. The Arabs did have a certain superiority because of their possession of firearms, but this advantage was not absolute. They, with their African followers, were not numerous, and given the often primitive nature of their firearms and the lack of training of the men who used them, they had

211

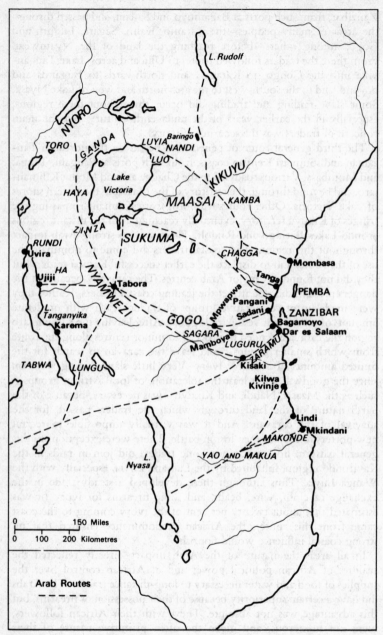

Figure 22 The Arab impact in East Africa

little chance in the long run of success in battle against a well-organised and resolute African society. The main concern of the traders was naturally a profitable trade and thus outright conflict had to be avoided unless there was no doubt of an Arab victory which would contribute to their aims.

The Arabs of Unyanyembe

One way to study the Arab impact is to examine the nature of the contact between the coastal visitors and selected African groups along the routes of penetration. The Nyamwezi are one of the most important African peoples for this type of examination. In the early years of the nineteenth century most of the trade along the important central routes was carried on by Nyamwezi caravans. Groups of Nyamwezi, after the planting season, would organise to visit the coast. As they neared the trading settlements, agents of Indian firms based in Zanzibar would attempt to induce them to trade at a particular port. The whole resulting process of bargaining was a long one, and one that had to change as the demand in Zanzibar for ivory and slaves increased.

Under the able leadership of Said bin Sultan, ruler of Zanzibar and Muscat from 1804 to 1856, began developments from the late 1820s that ensured the island port city a pre-eminence that endured until the days of European rule. Said bin Sultan developed the clove industry of Zanzibar and Pemba, thus making the import of slaves for working the crop a constant necessity. He also made contacts with Indian, American, and European traders who bought the products of his island and of the interior. With these regular trade channels established it was essential to regularise the penetration of the interior to ensure a constant movement of slaves and ivory into Zanzibar.

The Nyamwezi and other Africans could not ensure this regularity and thus a more systematic penetration of the interior began, stimulated by Said bin Sultan with the vital aid of other Arabs and of Indian merchants residing in Zanzibar. The Indians quickly became the most important individuals in this process. Said bin Sultan left the principal direction of his economic affairs to an Indian official, the Customs Master of Zanzibar, who, for the payment of a yearly sum, had virtual control over the economic life of the island. The Customs Master, with the collaboration of the Indian community, advanced to caravan leaders the funds which made their inland ventures possible. The risks being great, the Indians charged heavily for these advances. Despite the failure of many individual caravans, profits were ensured by very high rates of interest, in addition to the equally high prices charged by the Indians for the merchandise and porters which they supplied for the caravans.

213

The impetus to an ever-deeper inland penetration came as the ivory producing regions near the coast were denuded of elephants to supply the ever-demanding markets of Asia, America, and Europe. With this penetration a need developed for Arab centres along the central routes to serve as collection points for ivory and slaves, and as provisioning depots for the increasing number of caravans. An early centre was founded at Zungomero (near present-day Kisaki) in the territory of the Khutu, but bases farther inland were soon required.

The principal Arab settlement of East Africa developed among the Nyamwezi who continued to be the chief providers of caravan porters, and who also continued to send their own caravans to the coast. The Nyamwezi were divided into many independent chiefdoms—there were thirty one in 1959—which were often at odds with each other. This lack of political unity, plus ever-present political quarrels over succession to the office of ruler, or *ntemi*, allowed the Arabs to maintain an influential presence among some of the Nyamwezi until the European conquest. The Arabs first established a camp at Msene to the west of Tabora, but Tabora itself, then a mid-point in the Unyanyembe chiefdom, eventually became their main centre.

On the road to Unyanyembe, caravans leaving the coast were able to obtain provisions and water, often from small stations established by Arabs, as they passed through the territories of such peoples as the Zaramo, Sagara, and Luguru. The Gogo provided the first significant difficulty to the traders. Their territory lacked easily available resources for travellers and the Gogo, although not politically united, were a strong people who could prove a major hindrance because of their power to cut off supplies. Gogo prices for these essentials were often high but the Arabs generally accepted them from necessity. However, despite their long years of contact with the Arabs, the Gogo were never significantly influenced by their coastal visitors. Once past the Gogo, the traders entered Nyamwezi territory, a prosperous agricultural region, where they could secure provisions and replacement porters.

The Nyamwezi of Unyanyembe were fully aware of the benefits of trade to be gained from an Arab settlement, and recognised the potential political and military support the Arabs could offer against rival Nyamwezi states. Thus an Arab establishment was not opposed; marriages soon occurred between the daughters of Nyamwezi leaders and important Arabs to help insure a permanent alliance. Unyanyembe had Arab, and Indian, resident agents from the early 1820s. These coastal men were without any significant control from the authorities in Zanzibar, and in their small community, which varied in size as traders and their followers arrived and left, direction for settling disputes and other problems gravitated into the hands of leaders accepted by the consent of the trading community. The African population had little direct contact with most of these visitors except for the needs of trade. The Nyamwezi lived in scattered clusters—what we now call Tabora was a series of these clusters. The Arabs had their own area of residence where their efforts were concentrated and, in distinction from Muslim traders in many other parts of Africa, they showed little inclination to spread their religion. They did not, of course, discourage those Africans who wished to accept Islam, but their main concern was clearly concentrated on business affairs.

But the growing needs of the Zanzibar market led to an effort from Zanzibar for a greater control of the Arabs in the interior. In the 1860s the Indian Customs Master appointed an agent, Said bin Salim—a former companion of Burton and Speke—as head of the Tabora community. He was given little means to enforce his will but the need for most Arabs to return to the coast at one time or another inevitably gave Said bin Salim a position of some strength.

The permanent Arab establishment inevitably led to their continuous involvement in the political life of the Nyamwezi of Unyanyembe. It has been suggested that, previous to the death of the Unyanyembe chief Ifundikira in the late 1850s, an agreement between Arabs and Nyamwezi was concluded whereby the Africans freed the Arab traders from taxes on their trade. The return to the Nyamwezi was the benefit of an Arab establishment in their centre rather than in one of the rival Nyamwezi chiefdoms. But when Ifundikira was succeeded by Msabila (or Mnywa Sere) the power the Arabs could exercise became apparent. Msabila was challenged for the rule by a half-brother, Mkasiwa (or Kiyungi). The father of the later famous Tippu Tip, Muhammad bin Juma, who had married a daughter of Ifundikira, intervened to rout Mkasiwa. Stable political rule was of course vital to the Arabs because of their trading needs.

Despite this Arab support, Msabila, dissatisfied with his share of the profits of trade through Unyanyembe, increased the Nyamwezi share, a policy that was accepted for a time but which eventually turned the Arabs against him. The Arabs then joined with Mkasiwa and drove Msabila from his capital. Mkasiwa became *ntemi* but, being a man of weak character who clearly owed his position to the Arabs, remained their puppet throughout his career.

The change of rule led to difficulties. The result demonstrated the limitations of Arab strength when faced with a determined African military challenge. Msabila, until killed fighting the Arabs in 1865, was able to rally enough Nyamwezi to his side to carry on a war against Mkasiwa and his protectors. This war seriously affected Arab trade and no doubt was one of the principal reasons for the appointment of Said bin Salim as the representative of Zanzibar in Unyanyembe.

The Arab impact on the Nyamwezi

The Arabs soon found that their support of Mkasiwa would not in itself secure them a position of unquestioned dominance among the Nyamwezi. Mirambo, originally ruler of the small nearby Nyamwezi state of Uyowa, came forward to contest the predominant position of the Unyanyembe Nyamwezi with the Arabs after 1871. The Arabs maintained their support of Mkasiwa, and despite victories in battle by Mirambo that interrupted Arab trade, they gave no serious thought to supporting any other Nyamwezi but those of Unyanyembe. The war convincingly demonstrated the fundamental weaknesses of the Arabs of central Tanzania. They were a community geared to trade, loosely directed by a leader, Said bin Salim, whose purpose was not to win battles but to settle the problems that arose within the Arab community. Arab trade, however, supplied firearms to dynamic African leaders such as Mirambo and helped to make him an enemy they could not control. And the Arabs in the face of such a threat would not show a united front. Without powerful centralised control some Arabs continued to trade with Mirambo during the hostilities. An additional proof of Arab weakness was demonstrated when Sayyid Barghash of Zanzibar attempted to end the losses to his trading revenues by despatching a large force to Unyanyembe in 1873. The new army proved itself useless since the Arabs resident at Unyanyembe resented this outside intrusion and by quarrels over the leadership of the force blocked all military action.

During the course of the struggle with Mirambo, Mkasiwa died (in 1876); he was succeeded by his son, Isike, who had Arab backing. There were rivals for the chieftainship as usual, with Isike gaining his office only through Arab military strength. Isike—threatened both by his defeated rivals and by Mirambo—offers a good example of how an African ruler could deal with a potentially dangerous Arab resident community. Isike appeared in two widely different roles—one in the earlier and one in the later years of his rule. European visitors at first described him as a generally worthless individual who was merely a puppet in the hands of his Arab masters. But later in his career Isike was known as a fierce and resolute leader of his people and a determined enemy of both Arab and European. Since the change in character occurred when the Arabs became of little use to Isike, it is apparent that the Nyamwezi leader was playing a waiting game. Isike gave the Arabs the obedience they required in return for their support against his enemies, dropping this distasteful role when it no longer suited his interests.

The fact that Isike could maintain such attitudes illustrates the limited nature of the Arab impact among the Nyamwezi, the people of the interior with the most intimate contact with Arabs. The Arabs always remained a foreign group at Unyanyembe. They lived in their own centres, surrounded by their followers, while the Nyamwezi remained apart in their own clusters. Isike, like most Nyamwezi rulers—Mirambo was a great exception—generally did not leave his own residence, his *ikulu*; he was not a leader of warriors and he did not participate in campaigns as did Mirambo. Thus, except when specific Arab demands required his presence, Isike could remain supreme in his own Nyamwezi sphere where he acted as a traditional ruler. Both Isike and his people profited from the general prosperity the Arabs stimulated in Unyanyembe and by the supplies of gunpowder and muskets that alliance with the Arabs brought. In view of the potentially dangerous situation that could at any time threaten Isike through a combination of his Nyamwezi dynastic rivals and the Arabs, Isike's apparent subservience to the Arabs is understandable.

The most important individual to Isike was the forceful Arab raider and trader, Abdulla bin Nasibu. When Isike came to power Said bin Salim still held office as the leading Arab of Unyanyembe, but the dissensions caused by the unsuccessful war against Mirambo led to the expelling of Said bin Salim by a faction grouped around Abdulla bin Nasibu. Isike's Nyamwezi carried out the actual expulsion for the Arabs. Said bin Salim was held to be close to Mirambo, Isike's rival, while Abdulla bin Nasibu was a strong opponent of Mirambo. Therefore the expulsion was not the act of an Arab puppet but rather that of an interested ruler.

Abdulla bin Nasibu was in many ways typical of the leading Arab figures of the interior; he resembled the far more important Tippu Tip who rose through war to a prominent position in the Congo. Abdulla bin Nasibu originally came from the coastal region. He gained his reputation by successful raiding campaigns among the Zaramo and Sagara and from his generous distribution of booty to those who served under him. He had enough power of his own to keep the Arabs of Unyanyembe in order, and with the able aid of his brother, Shaykh bin Nasibu, Abdulla bin Nasibu soon became the most powerful Arab yet resident among the Nyamwezi.

In face of this Arab leader, Isike had to be all the more openly subservient, especially since Mirambo and other rivals remained actively plotting against him. This situation must cause reconsideration of such interpretations as that made recently by Trimingham in his *Islam in East Africa* (p. 24) where he asserts that the Arabs of the interior existed on the 'sufferance' of the local population. If the local population had been united behind a ruler, this might have been true, but in this case it was Isike who maintained his rule on 'sufferance'. Trimingham also feels that the Arabs feared involvement in local quarrels since this might hinder trade, but in Unyanyembe the Arabs involved themselves in a manner that ensured their local ascendancy; by giving vital support to Isike, the Arabs were assured of local dominance and thus of control of trade.

A secure local base was essential for Arab control of trade and was not necessarily antagonistic to African interests. An example of how African and Arab interests could coincide came in 1881 when a French trader, Emile Segère, attempted to establish a centre in Unyanyembe for the purchase of ivory. Segère naturally antagonised the Arabs since he challenged their control of the ivory market; he at the same time roused the opposition of Isike by sending, or at least planning to send, gunpowder to Mirambo. Thus Isike and the Arabs combined to force Segère to flee Unyanyembe to save his life. To outsiders then reporting on Isike he was again acting as a puppet supporting Arab interests whereas he had to act to ensure that Mirambo did not become too strong.

The Segère affair had major repercussions for the Arab community and fo the Nyamwezi. On his enforced return to Zanzibar, Segère protested to Sayyid Barghash and the French consul about his treatment. As a consequence, although there were other matters involved, Abdulla bin Nasibu was recalled to Zanzibar in the latter part of 1881. There he was imprisoned; he later died, allegedly through poison administered on Barghash's orders. Abdulla bin Nasibu's brother, Shaykh bin Nasibu, had carried on as governor in Unyanyembe but he died in 1882, also supposedly from poison administered by an agent of Barghash. The Arab community never recovered from this double loss. No replacement was sent from Zanzibar for the Nasibus because, said Sayyid Barghash, he feared any new agent would fail to carry out orders and thus cause trouble with the increasing number of European visitors to central Tanzania. The remaining Arabs in Unyanyembe proved incapable of nominating a successor and there was consequent degeneration into factional strife.

Isike was placed in a dangerous situation with this loss of firm Arab support against his rivals and, had he been a mere puppet, would have been driven from power. Instead, Isike reacted successfully to make himself the undisputed ruler of Unyanyembe, and even to expand his influence over many of the neighbouring Nyamwezi states. Finally, the death of Mirambo in 1884 cleared Isike's way of all obstacles. The Arabs now, lacking effective leadership, had to suffer his exactions upon their trade and the high costs he charged for recruiting porters. This situation remained essentially unchanged until Isike met his death fighting the German invaders in 1893.

Thus the Arab influence in their most important inland East African base was very tenuous. Drawn there by trade, a small group of Arabs settled and proceeded to run their own affairs with little control from Zanzibar. They were sufficient in number to make them an important factor in the fluid power struggle within that Nyamwezi state. With able leadership the Arabs could and did profit from this situation, as did the Nyamwezi who allied with them. But with their main concern limited to commercial ends, the Arabs really had little influence upon the life and future of the Nyamwezi. New ideas and techniques were no doubt introduced along with trade goods from the coast. This process, however, would have gone on without the Arabs, although in a slower fashion, since the Nyamwezi kept their role as the main caravan men of East Africa throughout the nineteenth century.

The Arabs of Ujiji

Arab traders had pushed beyond Unyanyembe to reach Lake Tanganyika before 1830. Here an important Arab settlement developed at the port town of Ujiji in Bujiji, one of the six independent chiefdoms of the Ha people. Bujiji stretched along Lake Tanganyika's shores from the Luiche River to the frontiers of Burundi, with an inland extent of about 20 miles [32 km]. Only those Ha living around Ujiji, usually called the Jiji, had commercial relations with the Arabs; the Ha to the east remained isolated, with a reputation for unfriendliness to visitors—to Stanley, the explorer, they were 'the most extortionate tribute-takers in Africa'.

The Jiji shared in this reputation, but the area around Ujiji was an important one to the Arabs. Ujiji had a useful harbour, and the nearby region provided the necessary agricultural resources for a permanent trading base. And, despite their reputation, the Jiji proved willing to receive resident Arab merchants and to give them the security necessary for their operations. The political organisation of Ha states centred around the chiefs, called the *abami*, whose subordinate chiefs, the *abatware banini* (singular, *umutware munini*), administered their districts in the name of their superior. Ujiji port was included in the districts of Ugoy and Kawele, each ruled by a separate umutware munini. The abami had little military strength and generally left the details of government to subordinates who were often the hereditary rulers of their districts. They collected revenues, forwarding part to their abami after securing a share of their own. This loose system gave the necessary stability for the establishment of a community of coast merchants.

When the Arabs reached Lake Tanganyika in search of ivory they needed a port for the penetration of the territory to the west and south-west of the lake. Ujiji filled this need. By the 1840s the lake had been crossed; by the 1860s reports from Zanzibar indicated that the great bulk of the ivory reaching the island came by the route from Ujiji through Unyanyembe to the coast. Our first clear information about the role of Ujiji dates from the late 1850s when European visitors reported a small and unhealthy settlement with only a few Arabs present. Its principal use was as an outlying base for the Unyanyembe traders who sent caravans there to pick up ivory and to return to the Arab centre among the Nyamwezi as soon as possible.

Ujiji soon became more important due to its strategic location and to the rise to power of an important Arab, Mwinyi Kheri. He originally came from the coast opposite Zanzibar, probably arriving in the Lake Tanganyika region in the 1840s. Mwinyi Kheri became head of the Arab community by 1872 due to his long years in the country and the wealth and influence gained thereby. He also had firearms enough for his followers, a significant asset since reports indicate that the Ujiji Arabs were able to prevent the Jiji from acquiring these weapons as had the Nyamwezi. But the real source of Mwinyi Kheri's power came rather from the relationships which he worked out with the rulers of Ujiji. The chief lived inland and never visited Ujiji; he was satisfied with an Arab settlement because it drew trade to his chiefdom and allowed him to profit from visiting caravans. Thus left alone, Mwinyi Kheri easily controlled the abatware banini of Kawele and Ugoy, who also profited from the visiting traders, and he sealed this system by his marriage to one of the daughters of an umutware munini.

Thus again Arabs and Africans came together in a manner that brought the greatest mutual benefit to both. Since the local African power structure was different from that of the Nyamwezi, a different arrangement resulted. At Unyanyembe the Arabs gained their aims by using their power in the intergroup struggles of a potentially powerful people; at Ujiji Arab aims were gained by a virtual incorporation into the Ha political structure. Mwinyi Kheri took advantage of the Ha organisation to become in reality a part of the Ha state. Since the Ujiji Arabs lived in an outlying and consequently weaker section of an African state, their position was stronger than the Arabs of Unyanyembe living at the capital. The political and commercial arrangement was in many ways the most satisfactory worked out between Arab and African in East Central Africa. The Arabs received a secure base, with ample provisions for passing caravans; the Ha received duties on these operations and were left virtually in control of all aspects of their daily life. There was little of the friction here that was common between Arab and Nyamwezi in Unyanyembe. An indication of the established Arab position at Ujiji is the fact that once when a new chief of Bujiji had to be chosen, an Arab supervised the election of the ruler.

Prosperity came to Ujiji; it became a busy market town for all the peoples of the Lake Tanganyika region through two types of commercial activity. The Arab rush into the Congo, dating from the late 1860s, gave the Ujiji Arab and African residents the chance to profit from selling needed supplies. The resident Arabs left the Congo ivory traffic to other Arabs and, under the direction of Mwinyi Kheri, used Ujiji as the main base for their expeditions after slaves and ivory along the regions bordering Lake Tanganyika. Areas of especial concern were those of the politically weak Lungu and Tabwa (or Marungu) on the southern and eastern shores of the lake, and the well-organised Rundi to the north. The profits were no doubt less than those gained by other Arabs in raiding the peoples of the Congo, but they were sufficient for Mwinyi Kheri and his followers.

The Ujiji Arab settlement gave no formal recognition during its formative years to the authorities in Zanzibar. The Ujiji Arabs were on their own, a fact that did not greatly concern Zanzibar since the trade of the lake eventually found its way to the coast. In this situation of isolation, Arab and African at Ujiji usually managed to settle their disputes in peace. For minor differences between individuals of each group, the aggrieved parties went either to Mwinyi Kheri or to the umutware munini. For major difficulties, the Jiji and Arab elders met jointly and made a settlement to prevent any disruption of the course of trade.

Mwinyi Kheri's position in Ujiji was so secure that he could devote much of his time to activities in the northern regions of the lake, where he was one of the pioneer Arab visitors. This region was a very difficult one for the Arabs. The state of Burundi was a powerful African entity, despite its frequent internal difficulties, and the Rundi opposed allowing Arab traders into their country. The Arabs had to content themselves with bases at the port town of Uzige and in nearby Uvira. Mwinyi Kheri recognised the Rundi strength and generally remained content with this sphere of operations. Later Arab leaders, notably Muhammad bin Khalfan (or Rumaliza) went beyond Mwinyi Kheri's cautious policies but their forces were decisively defeated when they attempted to move inland.

Mwinyi Kheri came formally into the Zanzibar orbit in 1881 when, due to difficulties stemming from the increasing European visitors, he finally recognised Sayyid Barghash's authority and hoisted the flag of Zanzibar. The recognition did nothing to alter the realities of the local power system and Mwinyi Kheri remained the effective head of the Ujiji community until his death in 1885.

In Ujiji therefore a very stable and mutually profitable relationship grew between Arab and African. The Arabs, by a careful policy, entered into the loose political fabric of the Ha state of Bujiji and both sides were satisfied with the result. Many other Africans of the Lake Tanganyika region suffered from Arab raids, but not the Jiji who remained allies of the Arabs.

The Arabs in Buganda

In distinction to the establishment of a balance of interests between Arab and African in Ujiji, or to the Arab involvement in the politics of the Nyamwezi, was the relationship of the Arabs to the powerful and united state of the Ganda. Arab traders moving northwards from Unyanyembe reached Buganda in the 1840s where the *kabaka*, Suna, welcomed them. Not many Arabs, however, had made this long trip by the 1860s and no large Arab trading centre developed on this route. The Arabs followed a route that took them through many small Nyamwezi and Sukuma chiefdoms, through the troublesome Zinza, and then through the several Haya states to the west of Lake Victoria. The southern regions of the lake shore were relatively little visited, as African internal instability provided unsatisfactory conditions for an Arab centre. Thus there was a late development of a regular dhow traffic across Lake Victoria to replace the long overland trip. One minor centre flourished for a time to the west of the lake, among the Haya of Karagwe, during the period when Rumanika ruled. The disorder following his death in 1878 ensured the ruin of this settlement.

Suna of Buganda died in 1856, and his successor Mutesa I, after some delay, allowed the return of Arab traders who had been prohibited from visiting Buganda for some years. The Egyptian authorities were then trying to extend their control southwards, and Mutesa particularly sought firearms and ammunition from the Zanzibari visitors. Slaves and ivory were, as usual, what the Arabs traded for, but the trade was carried on entirely under conditions imposed by the Ganda. Arab traders entered the Ganda state only with the permission of the kabaka's officials. The Arabs sent gifts of considerable value to the kabaka to ensure their reception, and were conducted to the Ganda capital where they remained until the terms of the kabaka's trade were arranged. Only when this royal trade—in which the kabaka had a monopoly of the firearms sold—was completed could the Arabs exchange their remaining merchandise with other Ganda.

The slaves and ivory traded to the Arabs were gathered by the Ganda through raids on their neighbours, or from tribute paid them, and the Arab traders were confined to the process of bargaining in the capital. They were also prevented from proceeding beyond Buganda, especially to the Nyoro rivals of the Ganda. This was ensured in the 1880s by the Ganda domination of the Karagwe, Zinza, and Toro territories that led to Bunyoro. A few Arab traders reached the Nyoro during the reign of Kabarega (about 1870 to 1899), but they never developed an important position there. Despite the restrictions imposed by the Ganda, this 'wholesale trade', as Stanley described it, was a profitable one for the Arabs, important enough to lead the ruler of Zanzibar to send an official representative to Buganda in 1869.

Even with the inequality of power between the small Arab community and the Ganda state, the Arabs had a greater measure of success in conversions to Islam than in any other East African area. Efforts were made to spread Islam from the early years of contact, especially by the Arab, Ahmed bin Ibrahim, who first arrived in Buganda in 1844. Islam had not been accepted by significant numbers of Ganda by the time of the arrival of Christian missionaries in the late 1870s, but some success had been achieved. Mosques were built in the 1860s, while Mutesa observed the rituals of Ramadan from 1867 to 1877 and also followed the Muslim calendar. Islam did not secure a similar success in any other state of this region, and even in Buganda the Muslim gains did not prove decisive. The representatives of the superior technical cultures of Europe soon achieved greater success, perhaps aided by the work already accomplished by the Muslim visitors. The resulting problems will be discussed below.

Arabs, Africans, and Europeans

Into the balance of interests between Arab and African came European intruders. The early explorers had little impact; the Arabs usually welcomed them, sold them needed goods, and then let them go on their way. The first significant intruders were missionaries. There was little missionary endeavour in East Africa until the 1870s when the exploits of Livingstone and others stimulated a new movement and most of the Arab centres soon had missionary visitors.

The British Church Missionary Society (CMS) organised a mission party for Karagwe or Buganda in 1876. Stations along the route inland were planned to support the venture; one location chosen was Mpwapwa in Ugogo. Mpwapwa was located on the main caravan route to Unyanyembe, and although it did not have a major Arab settlement, Mpwapwa nevertheless was a vital provisioning place for Arab traders entering or leaving Ugogo. The Africans at Mpwapwa gave permission in 1876 for a CMS settlement, and the principal resident Arab caused no undue difficulties. But once the settlement was organised the missionaries raised problems by acting against the slave trade. Slaves escaping from passing caravans were given asylum by the missionaries, who refused to return refugees who wished to remain. The Arabs could have reacted by using force, but no doubt fearing the inevitable difficulties that would face them in Zanzibar if coercion was used, they accepted the situation with bad grace. The Arabs, to solve the problem, rerouted their caravans to bypass the mission, an expedient that avoided serious difficulties in the period before the European occupation of East Africa.

Another British group, the London Missionary Society (LMS), in

1878 reached Ujiji where they were welcomed by the Africans, but not by the Arab community. The Arabs were fully aware of the dangers the European missionaries might cause to the Arab relationship with the Ha, but again managed to avoid outright hostilities. Delaying tactics were used to prevent an effective settlement in order to avoid a major crisis. Mwinyi Kheri's Arabs left the missionaries free to proselytise; at the same time Arab influence was strong enough to ensure that no special ties were formed with the Ha power structure. The LMS, frustrated, finally left Ujiji in 1883.

The White Fathers, a French Roman Catholic group, arrived in East Africa in 1878 to found interior missions. One party of White Fathers came to Ujiji in 1879 where they very quickly observed that Arab influence would be a lasting hindrance to their work. But the Frenchmen saw the need to act with the Arabs, and, with the cooperation of Mwinyi Kheri, they attempted operations on the shores of Burundi. There, one White Fathers' mission was destroyed by Africans, following a quarrel over slaves purchased by the missionaries from slave traders. Some have blamed the resulting missionary deaths on the Arabs, but there appears no foundation for the charge. Mwinyi Kheri had nothing to gain from involvement in an action countering his policy of peaceful containment of the Europeans resident in his territories. In most later instances he aided the White Fathers—often at a price—to found stations on the lake shores.

The White Fathers in 1881 also set up a station in Unyanyembe. Their main concern was a school for the education of African boys. They attempted little local conversion, and both Isike and the Arabs tolerated the newcomers. The mission was forced out of Unyanyembe in 1889, but this was due to the exactions of Isike and not to the Arabs.

European missionaries in Tanzania were joined by representatives of the International African Association (IAA), a society founded in 1876 through the efforts of Leopold II of Belgium as part of his policy to secure a foothold in Africa. The IAA planned to establish what it called centres of civilisation; they would serve as places for supplying European travellers and for pacifying the neighbouring regions. This mainly Belgian organisation set up depots at Unyanyembe and at Karema on Lake Tanganyika. In general, the Arabs aided the IAA in East Africa and the IAA's representatives at Unyanyembe lived at peace with the Arabs throughout the station's existence (1879–81). The French and Germans also sent expeditions under the auspices of the IAA, the French with an establishment in Usagara and the Germans among the Nyamwezi of Ugunda. Neither group had significant problems with the Arabs.

But if missionaries and IAA members were left alone by the Arabs since they did not greatly upset the Arab-African balance, one other class of European was not left in peace. European traders began to come inland from the early 1870s. We have already commented on the fate of

224

the trader Segère at Unyanyembe, driven away for trying to interfere with the Arab-controlled ivory market. German traders, attempting to succeed where Segère had failed, opened in 1885 and 1886 a trading station in Unyanyembe where the Arabs and Africans did all possible to block the Europeans' business. When this did not entirely succeed, one of the Germans was killed by an Arab. This ended European inland trading ventures in the days before European occupation, except for the Irish trader, Charles Stokes, who succeeded by allying himself with the Nyamwezi of Usongo and by staying clear of Arab-dominated centres.

The Arab reaction to European non-governmental intruders amply demonstrates the nature of the Arab presence in East Africa. These Europeans were in the long run devoted to the ending of the slave trade, but as long as they took no direct measures the Arabs were content to leave them in peace. Conversion efforts were of little concern to the Arabs, and the spreading of Christianity would not be an issue causing friction. But when Europeans became commercial rivals, the Arabs had to react. European competition could displace the Arab traders, and thus threats and even violence were used to protect their established commercial positions.

This generally tolerant attitude changed with European attempts to assert political control in East Africa. A German society was given a charter for the area behind the northern Tanzanian coast in 1885, a control that was later extended to most of present-day Tanzania by an Anglo-German treaty of 1886. The Germans claimed that the Arab government in Zanzibar had no rights to the interior. They justified this by asserting that the Arabs had merely commercial and not political centres, a claim that was essentially true. The only inland Zanzibari garrison was at Mamboya, near Mpwapwa, which had been occupied since 1880. Mamboya was not a significant base, however, and Sayyid Barghash secured no recognition of political control from it.

Barghash did try to increase his control on the coast and in the interior in the face of German claims, but the threat of German force put an end to his efforts in August 1885. But this resolution had little effect in the interior where we have seen that it was a local Arab-African agreement that ruled affairs, and not any decision of the Arab ruler of Zanzibar.

German mismanagement on the Tanzanian coast led to war (1888–90) ending the Arab power there. The German victory, however, had sealed the fate of the Arabs of the interior, since the outlets for Arab trade to the Indian Ocean ports were in German hands, while at roughly the same time the authorities of the Congo Independent State were turning the ivory trade of the Congo towards the Atlantic and away from the Ujiji route. Many of the important Arabs therefore left inland East Africa, either for the East African coast, or more commonly, for the Arab-dominated regions of the eastern Congo which remained independent of

Congo Independent State control until the defeat of the Arabs (1892–4).

The Germans moved inland in 1890, signing agreements with the small Arab settlements on the route to Unyanyembe with little difficulty because of the overwhelming German military might. The Arabs of Unyanyembe readily accepted a treaty, actually welcoming the Germans because of the heavy exactions of Isike. Most of the Unyanyembe Arabs remained loyal German allies in the forthcoming hostilities against Isike.

The situation at Ujiji was different. Muhammad bin Khalfan had succeeded Mwinyi Kheri and had attempted to extend Arab control over all the coasts of Lake Tanganyika. Most of his raiding, however, went on in areas of the present-day Congo and not in Tanzania, thus allowing the Jiji to continue profiting from the Arab presence. The Germans, too busy elsewhere to do anything significant about this Arab centre, did not occupy Ujiji until 1896. By this time Muhammad bin Khalfan had been defeated by forces of the Congo Independent State during the 1892–4 Arab war and had fled to Zanzibar. The once powerful Arab community melted away following this defeat of Rumaliza and the Germans found in 1896 only a very few Arabs, who were fully disposed to recognise their new rulers' authority.

The Arabs of Buganda lost power in a very different way. There the successful conversion efforts of Muslims and Christians led to the rise of a class of young men who were no longer willing to accept the values of traditional Ganda society. Faced with threats from the kabaka, Mwanga, the Muslim and Christian groups combined in 1888 to depose him. This cooperation did not long endure, and soon the Muslim Ganda, aided by the few remaining Arab traders, expelled their Christian rivals. This success lasted only a short time. The Christian Ganda rallied to defeat the Muslim forces; in the hostilities the Arab community of Buganda was completely broken. The Ganda Muslims would later gain a place in a Buganda under British control, one in which the Arabs would have no role.

Conclusion

The story was much the same in other areas of East Africa. The Arabs of the interior usually did not oppose the European invaders because they had little hope of victory. They could not count on African support since their local agreements had been marriages of convenience, usually limited to largely commercial aims. The Arab penetration of East Africa had been a movement of individuals, supported and stimulated by the Arab ruler of Zanzibar and his Indian officials, which led to the creation of numerous trading centres throughout East Africa. In these communities, organised by the resident Arabs and little influenced from Zanzibar, the Arabs had come to terms in one way or another with their African neighbours. Where slave-raiding occurred, the areas of Arab establishment were left alone, while their African allies usually joined in the raiding to make Arab victories possible. Only among the Ganda had successful Muslim conversion taken place, but with little hope of long run success due to the even more successful efforts of Christian missionaries; without conversion there was little hope of really gaining African loyalty and support. The Africans were willing to accept the profits of the trade the Arabs stimulated, but accepted little else.

Thus when the Europeans arrived the Africans did not support the Arabs. Those who resisted were defeated and the fragile Arab community of the interior, little over a half-century in age, crumbled. What influences remained after this defeat? The Arabs had helped to open the interior by developing the routes initiated by Africans which later became the main avenues of commerce for the new European colonies. Perhaps their most important contribution to East Africa, and especially to Tanzania, was the spread of the Swahili language to the farthest corners of East Africa. As a whole, however, these few beneficial influences appear small when contrasted to the devastation that the Arabs and their African allies brought to the many regions affected by the slave trade and its aftermath of famine and disease.

The Arabs had built a domination that outwardly appeared powerful to nineteenth-century observers, but there were no germs for successful development within it. They remained a small and often alien group, using their successful commercial position to keep Africans, who were inherently more powerful, had they been united, under Arab influence. When the Europeans interfered with this influence, Arab weakness soon became apparent and their domination quickly passed away.

Further reading

BENNETT, N. R. (Ed.), *Leadership in East Africa. Six Political Biographies*, Boston University Press, Boston, 1968.

BENNETT, N. R. *Mirambo of Tanzania*, Oxford University Press, New York, 1971.

BENNETT, N. R. *Studies in East African History*, Boston University Press, Boston, 1963.

GEE, T. W. 'A Century of Mohammadan Influence in Buganda, 1852–1951', *Uganda Journal*, XXII, 1958, (pp. 139–150).

GRAY, J. 'Ahmed bin Ibrahim—The First Arab to Reach Buganda', *Uganda Journal*, II, 1947, (pp. 80–97).

GRAY, J. 'Trading Expeditions from the Coast to Lakes Tanganyika and Victoria before 1857', *Tanganyika Notes and Records*, IL, 1957, (pp. 226–246).

HARRIES, L. (Ed.) *Swahili Prose Texts*, Oxford University Press, London and Nairobi, 1965.

KABEYA, J. B. *Mtemi Mirambo*, East African Literature Bureau, Nairobi, Dar es Salaam, and Kampala, 1966.

LEWIS, I. M. (Ed.) *Islam in Tropical Africa*, Published for the International African Institute, Oxford University Press, London, 1966.

KATUMBA, A. and WELBOURN, F. B. 'Muslim Martyrs of Buganda', *Uganda Journal*, XXVIII, 1964, (pp. 151–163).

TRIMINGHAM, J. S. *Islam in East Africa*, Clarendon Press, Oxford, 1964.

(Tippu Tip), *Maisha ya Hamed bin Muhammed el Murjebi yaani Tippu Tip*, Supplement to the East African Swahili Committee Journals, XXVIII, 2 (July 1958) and XXIX, 1 (Jan. 1959).

12

The Nineteenth Century: Prelude to Colonialism

Edward A. Alpers

East Africa at the beginning of the nineteenth century

By 1800 East Africa was poised on the brink of a new era. Until then there had been only limited contacts between the coast and the interior. These were most intensive along the trade routes running from Lake Nyasa to the Kilwa coast, which were dominated by the Yao of northern Mozambique. By the last quarter of the eighteenth century a few adventurous Swahili had also traded inland along these routes. Besides the Yao, the people who were most affected by these contacts were the Tumbuka and the Ngonde of northern Malawi. But in central Tanzania the Nyamwezi probably began to journey to the coast opposite Zanzibar to trade only from about 1800. In the previous chapter we saw that a sprinkling of foreign trade goods had already reached the royal court of Buganda by the late decades of that century, but direct trade links between the coast and Uganda remained limited for about another sixty years. To the north, finally, although Mombasa's most lucrative trade was conducted with the Miji Kenda peoples of its own immediate hinterland, by the late 1700s the Miji Kenda were trading farther afield with the Kamba and, less certainly, with the Chagga of Vunjo.

New ideas and influences did not, however, enter only from the coast. Nyamwezi and Fipa traders frequented the court of the eastern Lunda paramount chief, Mwata Kazembe, on the Luapula River in Zambia, while the numerous peoples of the corridor between Lakes Nyasa and Tanganyika were regularly absorbing immigrants, and their ideas of political organisation, from north-eastern Zambia. But these contacts with peoples living outside the modern borders of the three East African

229

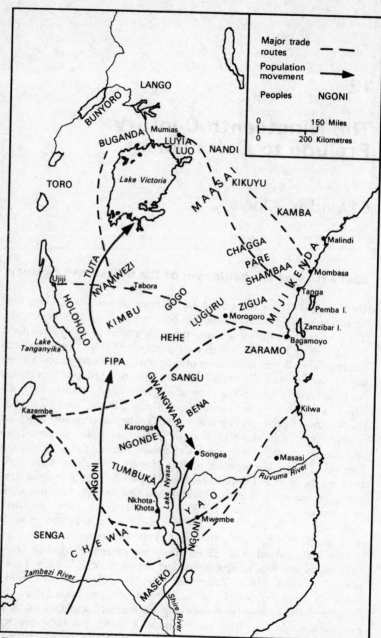

Figure 23 Prelude to colonialism

230

territories were minimal. Their importance cannot be compared to the political and social changes which had been brought about in the north-west by the Nilotic migrations over the previous three centuries. East Africa was certainly not stagnant: changes were taking place within many societies; people were still moving into the agriculturally less attractive areas of central and south-eastern Tanzania; Luo and Maasai influences, among others, were still being assimilated by their neighbours. Except in the immediate coastal hinterland of Tanzania and on Zanzibar and Pemba Islands, where the evil effects of the slave trade were already taking their toll, this internal process of change continued largely undisturbed until the early 1840s. At that time two separate invasions of East Africa began to take place. From the coast entered the Arabs, about whose impact we have just read. From the interior of southern Africa came the Ngoni.

The Ngoni invasion of southern Tanzania

On 19 November 1835, a day remembered in tradition for the occurrence of an eclipse of the sun, the great Ngoni chief Zwangendaba led his people north across the Zambezi River. The Ngoni traced their origin back to South Africa, where they had been one of the Nguni speaking peoples of northern Zululand. In about 1820 they had fled from their homeland to escape the rising power of Shaka Zulu. During the next fifteen years Zwangendaba's army wandered through southern Mozambique and further inland before turning towards the middle Zambezi. After fording the river, the Ngoni continued their relentless march northwards through Malawi and Zambia until they reached the Fipa plateau in the early 1840s.

Over the years, many different people had been assimilated into the Ngoni nation—Thonga from Mozambique, Shona from Zimbabwe, Senga, Chewa, and Tumbuka from north of the Zambezi. Zwangendaba's success in capturing so many non-Nguni speakers, who actually outnumbered the true Ngoni, and in fully integrating them into the Ngoni social and political system may be traced to his adoption of the revolutionary Zulu military techniques designed by Shaka. These innovations included the substitution of a short, stabbing spear for the traditional long, throwing spear. The new weapon was employed by warriors who were protected by massive cow-hide shields which left only a man's face exposed to the enemy. The warriors fought in organised age-regiments and their usual deployment in battle was in the shape of a bull's horns, the idea being to encircle the enemy and then to crush him. These regiments were maintained for long periods so that there was always a standing army ready for battle. Men who were captured from other tribes took their place in these regiments, while women and children fell to the married Ngoni men. There was practically no stigma attached to being from a conquered people, and a man of ability could quickly rise to a position of importance.

Zwangendaba's peculiar genius was the ability to keep his nation united, but on his death in about 1848, factionalism triumphed. Eventually, the nation split into five kingdoms, only two of which were established in Tanzania, while the others took root in Malawi and Zambia. The first Tanzanian group to break away from the main Ngoni body struck north from Ufipa. These Ngoni became known as the Tuta. Raiding all the while, they encountered the Holoholo living on the eastern shores of Lake Tanganyika. But the Holoholo successfully repelled the Tuta, having profited by their experience of an earlier defeat at the hands of the Ngoni in the Holoholo homeland to the southwest of the lake. Many Holoholo had fled east across the lake, settled in Tanzania, and adopted the impressive Ngoni military methods. Thus when the Tuta attacked them some years later, the Holoholo were able to pay them in kind. Here we have the first of several important Tanzanian examples of people who cast aside their traditional means of defence and took up Ngoni military tactics to preserve themselves from falling victim to the Ngoni. The Holoholo are a good example of a society which adopted radical new techniques in order to preserve its basis, indeed its very existence.

Recovering from this temporary setback, during the 1850s the Tuta harassed the Nyamwezi and upset the Arab trade route between Tabora and Ujiji. They eventually settled north-west of Tabora and raided as far as the southern shores of Lake Victoria. Many Nyamwezi were captured, the most important of whom was Mirambo, who later incorporated refugees from Tuta raids when organising his own forces, called *rugaruga*, against the Arabs. Clearly, the Tuta were an important element in unsettling a vast area of central Tanzania, but they also contributed to its stability by enabling Mirambo to build up a stronger Nyamwezi chiefdom than otherwise might have been possible.

This same contradictory pattern recurs in southern Tanzania, where the Ngoni were a much more important factor than the Tuta in Unyamwezi. This second Tanzanian Ngoni group, the Gwangara, was led east from Ufipa to Songea by Zulu-Gama. But there they found yet another Ngoni kingdom already established, the Maseko Ngoni, who had never been a part of Zwangendaba's nation. They had come from southern Mozambique, and had crossed the Zambezi nearer to its confluence with the Shire River than had Zwangendaba, continuing their march to the east of Lake Nyasa until they reached Songea, probably early in the 1840s. Led by Maputo, the Maseko Ngoni were more powerful than the Gwangara, but various intrigues weakened their superiority and in about 1860 the Maseko were driven back across the Ruvuma River, eventually to settle in south-western Malawi. It was not too long, however, before old rivalries split the always precarious Gwangara union into a northern and a southern kingdom.

From their centres in Songea, the Gwangara raided extensively throughout the area between Lake Nyasa and the coast, right until the imposition of German colonial rule. Southern Tanzania lived in constant fear of raids by the Songea Ngoni, who were always eager to build up their numbers by incorporating captives into their society. Furthermore, unprincipled bands of brigands, usually known as *maviti* or *mafiti*, mimicked the external trappings of the Ngoni and terrorised the neighbourhoods in which they operated. These robber bands were considerably more destructive than the Ngoni; not being concerned with building a stable society in which their captives became members, they were more interested in gaining immediate profit from raids and usually sold captives into slavery. The Ngoni chiefs were not above dealing with slavers on occasion, but in general this was not the point of their expeditions.

In some very important cases, however, the Ngoni example provoked a constructive response in southern Tanzania, just as it had for the Holoholo. This was so in Usangu, bordering Ufipa on the east, which had been badly ravaged by the Ngoni in the 1840s. During this period Mwahawangu, one of the many small Sangu chiefs, had withdrawn north-east to Uhehe. Returning after Zwangendaba's death, Mwahawangu conquered the other Sangu chiefdoms and created a united Sangu state. He was succeeded in about 1860 by his grandson, Merere, who dominated much of the southern highlands from his base at Utengule into the early 1870s. Thereafter, the Sangu were overshadowed by the Hehe, whose fifteen or more independent chiefdoms had been united under the leadership of Munyigumba during the previous two decades. Instrumental in Hehe unification was the adoption of Ngoni-influenced military regiments, weaponry, and field tactics which they borrowed indirectly from the Sangu. A crushing defeat of the Bena, who had also only recently begun to unite, was delivered by the Hehe in about 1874-5; and Merere lost most of Usangu to Munyigumba in 1877. Not surprisingly, the Hehe soon came to blows with the Gwangara. Wars were fought in 1878 and 1881, but as no clear victory was won by either side a truce was concluded by the great Mkwawa, who had succeeded his father Munyigumba as chief in 1879. Together with the Songea Ngoni, the Hehe remained the most powerful state in southern Tanzania until effective German rule was established in the interior.

Munyigumba and Mkwawa are prime examples of the new and innovative leadership that marks so much of the history of nineteenth-century East Africa. Each was alert to the many newly available military techniques upon which a much more substantial and personal source of political power could be established. Each sought to aggrandise his position even further by raiding his neighbours to acquire wealth which was not otherwise obtainable in Uhehe itself. The leadership which each developed during the second half of the century was marked by the construction of a loose administrative system in which loyalty to the paramount chief became the most important vehicle of political and social integration. And although trading was not so significant an element in the creation of the Hehe state as it was elsewhere in East Africa, each apparently maintained a monopoly over such trade as was carried on with coastal caravans on the borders of Uhehe, while Mkwawa pursued an aggressive policy of raiding caravans for plunder during the 1880s. Mkwawa's opposition to the Germans was a natural outgrowth of this policy.

It is clear that the Ngoni invasion was a major factor in shaping the history of southern East Africa. Was it, as Professor Omer-Cooper suggests, 'a terrible disaster for the peoples of East Central Africa'? Or was it, as Professor Oliver writes, 'a kind of inoculation against what was to follow', against the Arab invasion and the worst atrocities of the slave trade? Within the dominions of the various Ngoni and Ngoni-inspired kingdoms, life was relatively secure, whereas the raids carried on by the Ngoni and by Ngoni-influenced bands of renegades exposed many defenceless peoples to the depredations of the slave traders. In view of the slave trade, we can see that the forcible integration of many weaker peoples into the Ngoni kingdoms was ultimately to the advantage of those weaker peoples. But it is more difficult to show that the Ngoni invasion paved the way for the slave trade and made it worse than it would have been if there had been no Ngoni invasion. For the period of the Ngoni and maviti raids did not come before the height of the slave trade, but coincided with it.

The slave trade and the international economy

Important as it is to consider the slave trade separately as a major factor influencing the course of East African history during the nineteenth century, it is essential to recognise at the outset that the slave trade was but one aspect of a much more pervasive system of international trade which was ever drawing East Africa into the world market in a distinctly subordinate role. In its degradation of human life the slave trade had a much more disastrous personal and moral impact on East African society than did the economically more important and stable ivory trade. But to the extent that East Africans diverted their energies from the development of their own economies for their own purposes to the supply of

234

raw materials in exchange for foreign manufactured goods at unfavourable terms of trade, there were no significant differences between the trade in slaves and ivory. In each instance the peoples of East Africa were being drawn into the world economy in accordance with someone else's economic goals, be they Arab, Asian, or European.

This is not to argue that East Africans took no part in the development of international trade on the ground in East Africa. Indeed, it was mainly they who seized the initiative in establishing trade relations with the coast, and in many situations at the local level it was they who determined both the conditions and terms of trade. These trading opportunities were the springboard for the rise of a whole new generation of aggressive and imaginative East African leaders—irrespective of whether the trade was primarily in ivory or slaves—who established their personal rules over large economic, political, and social units for which there was no historical precedent.

Although slaves had been taken from East Africa for many centuries, the slave trade was not really very important until after the middle of the eighteenth century. Only with the growth of a plantation economy on the French-dominated islands of Mauritius and Réunion, far to the east of Madagascar, was there a steady call for large numbers of slaves from East Africa. The French slavers favoured the Mozambique coast, but the high death rate of labourers on the rapidly expanding sugar plantations produced an insatiable demand that sent them looking for new sources of supply. Soon they were dealing in human lives at Kilwa and Zanzibar. At about the same time, there was a parallel growth in the Omani Arab demand for slaves, who were largely supplied by the Kilwa market. From the very beginning, then, the slave trade was focussed on the southern interior of East Africa, and it remained so throughout the nineteenth century. By about 1810 at least six thousand slaves, and perhaps as many as ten thousand were being sold annually at Kilwa and Zanzibar town to the Arabs and the French. Thereafter the Arab slave trade became increasingly dominant, while the French colonial demand for slaves very slowly subsided in the face of British and metropolitan pressure to abolish both the trade and the institution of slavery.

In the following decade the pace of the Arab trade grew slowly, but it shot up from the late 1820s, as Sayyid Said bin Sultan of Muscat began to take a more active interest in his East African domain and to encourage his Arab subjects to settle in Zanzibar and Pemba. Many of these Arab settlers established plantations for growing cloves, which had been introduced in about 1818, and copra, on a considerable scale. Consequently, for the first time there was a big internal demand for slaves on both Zanzibar and Pemba. In 1839 a British observer estimated that some forty to forty-five thousand slaves were sold annually in the Zanzibar market. Only about half of these people seem to have supplied the largely Arab demand abroad, while the remainder were purchased by Arab plantation owners on the two islands. In the 1860s a contemporary estimate suggests that as many as seventy thousand souls may have been sold each year in the Zanzibar slave market. These figures are very general, and may well be exaggerated, but they give some idea of the scale of the slave trade in East Africa during the mid-nineteenth century. As the result of an Anglo-Zanzibar treaty signed in 1873 and two proclamations issued by Seyyid Bargash bin Said of Zanzibar in 1876, the export slave trade from the mainland of East Africa was rapidly reduced to a trickle. But this did not signal the end of slaving within East Africa. Rather, slaving actually increased; and the suppression of the export slave trade inadvertently encouraged a final period of unprecedented outrage, during which the value of human life was pitiably cheapened.

Although it was the Arabs and the French who had created and sustained the demand for slaves, and who thus bore the ultimate responsibility for the East African slave trade, it cannot be argued that they were equally accountable for its operation in the interior. The French never were involved in this aspect of the trade; the Arabs clearly were, but the exact role which they played inland varied according to the area in which they operated. We have already noted that the principal source of slaves was the southern interior, in particular the Kilwa hinterland and the Lake Nyasa region. Here, except for isolated pockets like Nkhota-Khota and Karonga, in Malawi, the Arabs were never in control of the trade, but were generally the clients of powerful Yao chiefs. The commercial and political base of these Yao chiefs was simply too strong to be challenged by the Arabs who moved inland from Kilwa. Writing in 1866, Livingstone noted that 'the caravan leaders from Kilwa arrive at a Waiyau village, show the goods they have brought, are treated liberally by the elders, and told to wait and enjoy themselves, slaves enough to purchase all will be procured: then a foray is made . . .' Side by side with this sort of activity, the Yao chiefs continued to send large caravans of slaves and ivory to the coast on their own account.

Outstanding among these Yao chiefs were Mataka I Nyambi, Makanjila I Mpaliwalingwa, and Mtalika I Litete. Their backgrounds had little in common: Nyambi began as the ambitious nephew of a chiefly family and Litete as a commoner, while Mpaliwalingwa was not even of Yao origin, but a Chewa interloper. Yet each one of them shared a combination of enormous energy, ambition, and the right political and economic skills needed to take full advantage of the opportunities of the age. Their towns became bustling centres of population far larger than any previously known in that part of East Africa. At first they competed severely against each other for control of the southern trade route to Kilwa, but by about 1880 their successors realised that their long range interests dictated a greater need for cooperation than for

236

competition. By that time all three were attempting to deal more efficiently with their coastal trading partners and with the Sultan of Zanzibar by encouraging the development of literacy in Arabic script. Clearly they were seeking to modernise their societies in terms of their experience as trading chiefs in nineteenth-century East Africa. But the changed conditions of the twentieth century imposed a false conservatism on men who had been among the most 'progressive' in the nineteenth, while their commitment to the slave trade was to make the Yao chiefs strong opponents to the imposition of colonial rule.

Central Tanzania also witnessed the emergence of new political and economic leadership. One such leader was Mirambo, who created a personal empire in response to the challenge posed to Nyamwezi society by the Arabs of Tabora. An equally successful trader and a more effective state-builder was another Nyamwezi chief, Nyungu-ya-Mawe. Nyungu was a dissident member of the ruling dynasty of Unyanyembe and, like Mirambo, a staunch opponent of the Arabs of Tabora. He fled south into Ukimbu and in a remarkably short time established himself as a military and trading chief of impressive stature. With the aid of his rugaruga he quickly subdued the traditional Kimbu chiefs and created an efficient system of political and economic administration through his loyal *vatwale*, who were appointed by him as governors over large regions of Ukimbu which had formerly been subject to a great many small-scale ritual authorities. In return for their loyalty, by contrast, Mirambo had left the traditional chiefs whose lands he conquered in authority; Nyungu rejected such a policy as being inefficient and insecure. At his death in 1884 Nyungu's solution proved itself in the smooth transfer of power to his daughter, Mgalula, while Mirambo's domain was totally dissipated when he died in the same year. Nevertheless, when Mgalula's niece Msavira was confronted by the Germans in 1895, she had to agree to the enforced dismantling of Nyungu's creation, so that even the efforts of his particular administrative genius did not survive the century.

Further to the east, another good example of intrusive, non-traditional leadership which was typical of nineteenth-century East Africa is provided by the rise of the Zigua adventurer, Kisabengo. His progression from an ambitious, but unimportant, young man to the *simba mwene*, or lion-king, of a predominantly Luguru chiefdom was based upon his alliance with Zanzibari traders who supplied him with guns in exchange for his promise of future cooperation in trade. With a handful of followers he established himself as chief over the vicinity of modern Morogoro Town, where he had built a thickly walled town with assistance from artisans from Zanzibar. Kisabengo introduced a number of new crops at Morogoro and provided water for the mushrooming population of his town by diverting the waters of a nearby small river, a solution to one of the problems of rapid nineteenth century urban growth in the interior of East Africa which was also practised at Mataka's town of Mwembe. Raiding extensively in the plains around Morogoro, Kisabengo extended his authority over a large portion of eastern Tanzania. Although his successors did not command the same wide obedience, they nevertheless succeeded in preserving the integrity of his chiefdom into the colonial era.

A slightly different situation with respect to the impact of the slave and ivory trades in the interior obtained in north-eastern Tanzania. Here Arab and Swahili traders came into contact with three well established political systems among the Shambaa, Pare, and Chagga. Perhaps the most important trading partner whom they encountered in this region was Kimweri ye Nyumbai, the greatest of the Kilindi kings of the Shambaa. From his traditional capital at Vugha in the Usambara Mountains, Kimweri sought to take advantage of the new opportunities offered by trading with the coastal caravaneers as a means of augmenting his already extensive political authority. But in the long run he was unable to maintain the vitality of the Shambaa political system, as his adventuresome and less tradition-bound son, Semboja, left Usambara to establish himself independently as chief of a new, multi-ethnic caravan town, called Mazinde, in the Pangani valley. After Kimweri's death in 1869, Semboja became the most important power in Usambara. Semboja never actually became king, however, preferring instead to install his son as king at Vugha, while he remained in force at Mazinde. Semboja, then, was very much of a piece with the other new trading chiefs in nineteenth-century East Africa, but in the context of Shambaa history his triumph marks a particularly acute political revolution.

In Upare the same process of attempting to turn the new trading opportunities to local advantage took place, but with different results. In South Pare the pre-existing political system was characterized by many small-scale chiefdoms, as in Unyamwezi. Here, however, there was no great process of personal empire-building, but a more modest one of political consolidation. In North Pare, by contrast, there was already a long established centralised state in existence in Ugweno. But the highland centre of Ugweno power was located far from the main trade route in the plains below. Struggling to overcome this geographical disadvantage, while at the same time attempting to keep pace with the unavoidable changes being effected by the development of the caravan trade, Ugweno produced a leader, Ghendewa, who diligently sought to maintain control over the rapidly changing historical environment.

Ghendewa built up the traditional military strength of Ugweno and marshalled the resources of the country more effectively than ever before. Lacking firearms, however, he had to forge an alliance with the equally ambitious Chagga chief of Moshi, Rindi, in order to assert his control over the new trade in ivory and slaves. In the end he made the mistake of inviting Rindi to enter his country to assist in putting down some rebellious elements in his southern districts. Before long Rindi's forces invaded Ugweno itself and Ghendewa was killed in battle. Upon his death all vestiges of Ugweno's former unity were destroyed as several competing chiefs struggled ineffectively to carve out their own spheres of influence.

Not all traditional leadership failed in this attempt to adapt to the extension of the international economy into the interior of East Africa during the nineteenth century. Among the Chagga of Mount Kiliman-jaro, the advent of traders from the coast fitted conveniently into the pattern of pre-existing inter-chiefdom rivalries. The most powerful and extensive Chagga chiefdom was that of Kibosho, which reached its peak under Mangi Sina in about 1870. Sina actively encouraged Arab traders to come to his fortress at Maua, for he profited by their trade in ivory. Sina was supreme in the 1880s, but to the east, Mangi Rindi of Moshi had been bidding to eclipse Kibosho since he took power in about 1860. Temporarily dispossessed by Sina's father, Rindi returned to power by enlisting Arusha military assistance, then concentrated on enticing the Arabs to make their mountain headquarters at Moshi. Rindi's diplomatic game was aimed at the destruction of Kibosho and he ultimately turned to the Germans to achieve his aims. This style of Chagga chiefly politics persisted into the colonial era.

Another figure who saw that it could be to his advantage to ally himself with these new outside forces was Nabongo Shiundu of the Wanga, the most important Luyia sub-tribe. The Luyia, like their neighbours the Luo, were a loosely organised people; but unlike the Luo they had a tradition of kingship in the Wanga chiefship, which had reached its zenith in the previous century. During his reign, however, Shiundu was so hard pressed to maintain Wanga sovereignty that he sought outside military assistance. He first turned to the Uasingishu Maasai who had settled in Wanga after they were driven from their homeland in the 1870s. Soon he was attracting Arab traders to his town so that he could receive a steady supply of arms and ammunition. Shiundu's success was only partial, but his tactics were continued after his death in the early 1880s by his famous son, Mumia, whose triumph was based on his early alliance with the British, who were seen to be just another means to the same end of re-establishing Wanga supremacy among the Luyia.

A final variation on the impact of the international economy on East African societies in the nineteenth century can be seen in the case of the Kamba. The Kamba were the northern counterparts of the Yao and the Nyamwezi. Sending forth hunting and trading colonies from the dry highlands which they inhabited between Kikuyuland and the coast, they constructed a vast trading network in the north-eastern interior.

Responding to the demand for ivory at the coast, which had initially been transmitted to them by the Nyika, Kamba trading superiority was at its height in the 1850s; but in the following decade they began to lose their markets to Arab traders. By the 1880s the Kamba route had become an Arab route. Nevertheless, they continued to trade with the Arabs at markets in their own country. Indeed, their trade and influence was on the upswing when the British came on the scene, and their early relations with the British were dominated by this revival of their involvement in the international ivory trade.

Two features mark the Kamba off from the other trading peoples of East Africa. First, because of their egalitarian political organisation they were less involved in trading and acquiring slaves than were most of their contemporaries. Yet even the Kamba were drawn into slave raiding towards the end of the century, an indication both of their weakened position in the ivory trade and of their continued dependence on the international economy. Second, for the same reason they never developed trading chiefs. But they did produce a number of outstanding individuals whose careers in every other respect paralleled those of men like Mirambo, Nyungu, Mataka, and Kisabengo. The most famous and powerful of these new men was Kivoi, who became an undisputed leader of a section of his people in Kitui. He commanded a large personal following, including a significant number of slaves, and traded the length and breadth of what is today eastern Kenya.

But despite the creative genius which leaders like Kivoi displayed, it cannot be argued that the trading chiefs of the nineteenth century established viable institutions for dealing with the new historical circumstances of the twentieth century. The trading empires of Kivoi and Mirambo did not survive their own lifetimes, while that of Nyungu did not last the century. Neither could Semboja provide a durable foundation for meeting the challenges of colonialism for the Shambaa. As for the Yao, although their chiefdoms endured successfully, we have already seen how the experience of the nineteenth century distorted their ability to re-adjust to the radically altered situation under colonialism. On the other hand, Kisabengo's successors as chiefs of Morogoro were able to make this difficult transition, despite the fact that Kisabengo was the most obvious creature of his times. In this context, however, the example of Kisabengo stands as an exceptional instance of continuity of this sort of nineteenth century leadership in East Africa. Continuities there were, but these operated at a different level of social experience and focused most significantly on the patterns of dealing with foreigners which East Africans developed during the nineteenth century, patterns which directly shaped their responses to the imposition of colonial rule.

Internalised changes in the north-central interior

Beyond the reach of the Ngoni invasion and much less affected by the international economy than the rest of East Africa, the experience of most of the peoples of the north-central interior was considerably different in that comparatively, less consideration had to be given to dealing directly with foreigners and indirectly with influences emanating from the coast. External contacts came later and were both less widespread and less intensive here. Many of the more important peoples of the region remained aloof from, or were actually hostile to, traders coming from the coast. Three peoples in this category were the Kikuyu, Maasai, and Nandi.

Despite the ever-present threat and the occasional reality of conflict with the pastoral Maasai, the Kikuyu had been trading peacefully in a wide variety of local goods with their Nilotic speaking neighbours on the forest fringe for many years. From about the 1840s they also began to trade with the Kamba. Yet while they were willing to continue this business with the coastal operators in the second half of the century, they resolutely refused to permit the Arabs to enter their homeland. Kikuyuland was prosperous, and a regular market system enabled goods to circulate freely within it. Eventually they were forced into an increasingly hostile attitude to these strangers as the result of continued abuses against their hospitality. When the first Europeans came along they, too, were regarded with considerable suspicion, an apprehension which was soon borne out by their actions. Anxious to preserve their internal prosperity and seeing little need for either the services or the material goods of the Europeans, the Kikuyu opposed their relentless advance, despite a sudden weakening of the entire structure of their society resulting from a disastrous sequence of natural calamities spanning the last five years of the century.

As for the Maasai, by 1800 they had already seen their greatest days of power. Expansion during the nineteenth century was minimal, and a precarious state of balance was struck with their neighbours. Thus thwarted, the Maasai turned their aggressiveness inward. The struggle for grazing rights and chronic cattle raiding now took place among themselves in a long series of civil wars. The basic division of these Maasai wars was between the pastoral (*il-Maasai*) and the agricultural (*il-oikop*) Maasai. Within the pastoral grouping there was also a struggle for leadership waged by the Purko sub-tribe. On another level, there was the rivalry for the largest personal following between the various priestly rain-makers (*il-oibonok*) who increasingly came to exercise secular power among the Maasai. Of these the most outstanding were the Purko il-oibonok Supet, who died in about 1866, and his son Mbatian, who was unrivalled by 1884. Despite the civil wars, however, the Maasai were still masters of the plains. Indeed, the triumph of the pastoral Maasai paved the way for the penetration of coastal caravans into the north-central interior during the last decades of the century. But, in the waning years of the pre-colonial era, a rapid succession of epidemic diseases, affecting both the Maasai and their cattle, made their dominance even more precarious than it had ever been before. As a result the Maasai found it more prudent to accommodate the incoming British than to oppose them.

In contrast to the declining fortunes of the Maasai was the rise of the Nandi, which itself owes much to the successful transformation of the uninfluential ritual office of the *orkoiyot* by an immigrant Uasingishu *ol-oiboni* named Barsabotwo. With the example of Supet before him, Barsabotwo was able to reshape the orkoiyot-ship into a powerful institution for uniting the segmentary Nandi. Faced with several external threats, the Nandi were very much in need of a leader like Barsabotwo, who advised them on all matters of warfare. As Nandi success in war increased, so did Barsabotwo's voice in the affairs of his adopted people. In time he was able to demand a share of the spoils of war and to impose his authority over the sectional councils by means of a system of consultants to each council as his personal representatives. Before he died in the 1860s his blessing was essential for making war, for opening the male circumcision ceremonies, for transferring power from one age-grade to another, and for making the annual offerings. Although there was no immediate successor to Barsabotwo's unrivalled position of authority among the Nandi for over a decade , the way for their seizure of power between the Rift Valley and Lake Victoria in the 1870s was paved by the crushing defeat of the Uasingishu by an alliance of pastoral Maasai. In the 1880s the orkoiyot Kimnyolei arap Turugat claimed undisputed power until he sanctioned a series of unsuccessful raids and was assassinated. But when in the next decade Kimnyolei's ominous prophecy of the impending conquest of the Nandi by white people was seen to have some substance, the stock of the orkoiyot-ship rose accordingly and provided the focus for Nandi resistance to the imposition of colonial rule. Among both the Nandi and the Maasai, then, as also among the Hehe, it is possible to see that the development of new leadership in the nineteenth century was not entirely dependent upon the stimulus of coming to grips with foreign trade.

Uganda and the European advance

The key to Uganda lay in the kingdom of Buganda, both from its bitter rivalry with the kingdom of Bunyoro and from the peculiar composition of Ganda society. In Chapter 9 we saw how Buganda grew from a small sub-kingdom of Bunyoro until, by the beginning of the nineteenth century, it was more powerful and aggressive than Bunyoro. The struggle against Bunyoro dominated all external policies of Buganda in the second half of the nineteenth century. Within Ganda society, allegiances of the people both as clansmen and as chief's clients was owed to the *kabaka*, who stood at the top of the hierarchies of the clan heads (*bataka*) and the territorial chiefs (*bakungu*). This factor, plus progressive centralisation and bureaucratisation, which meant that all chiefs were appointed by the kabaka, enabled the kabaka personally to dominate the kingdom of Buganda. But the office demanded a ruthless and skilful politician who could eliminate his rivals and then balance all the competing forces within the system. Kabaka Suna, who reigned until 1856, and his son Mutesa, who ruled until 1884, both possessed these qualities.

During the first half of the century Buganda had little to fear from Bunyoro, whose weakness was highlighted by the loss of Toro to a royal usurper in the 1830s. Kabaka Suna was relatively free to cultivate his commercial relations with the Arab traders coming from Tabora. Under *Mukama* Kamurasi, however, Bunyoro experienced a notable revival. Kamurasi gained the throne through an alliance with the Lango, and then successfully beat off a Ganda attack. He also extended Bunyoro's trading connections so that he was not only competing with Buganda for the Zanzibar trade to the south, but was also dealing with Arab traders from Khartoum. For six years after he became kabaka, Mutesa was too preoccupied with disposing of his rivals to stand in the way of Bunyoro's revival. By the time he felt reasonably secure on his throne, Bunyoro was already a serious threat to Ganda domination of the region around the lakes. Kamurasi died in 1869, but his successor as Mukama, Kabarega, immediately proved to be a leader of even greater stature. Meanwhile both sides were busy equipping themselves with firearms. Mutesa sought closer ties with Zanzibar, and the assurance of a steady supply of muskets to supplement the traditionally armed Ganda raiding parties, which brought in the trade goods which Buganda did not produce itself. Kabarega organised new military regiments, equipped with firearms, and employed men from Khartoum to help lead them. Into this explosive situation came the first agent of foreign imperialism in Uganda.

Sir Samuel Baker entered Bunyoro in April 1872 as the representative of Egypt. Kabarega's main concern was to prevent a rival claimant to the mukama-ship, Rionga, from following his lead in getting military aid from the Sudanese. Baker's demand that Bunyoro become an Egyptian protectorate as the price for assisting Kabarega against Rionga destroyed any chance of cooperation between Egypt and Bunyoro. When Baker threw his support behind Rionga, he was driven out of

243

Bunyoro by Kabarega's army. As Baker's successor, General Charles Gordon focused Egyptian efforts on Buganda. Had Mutesa felt that he could join forces with Egypt to crush Bunyoro without sacrificing Buganda's independence, he undoubtedly would have done so. But he, too, saw that this was impossible, and Gordon described him in 1875 as 'fearing Egypt immensely and capable of anything to avoid annexation'. Mutesa even held an Egyptian column hostage at his capital for some months in 1876, but the men were released unharmed. Gordon recognised Buganda's independence, and in 1880 Egypt retired permanently from northern Uganda. While the balance of power between Bunyoro and Buganda was unchanged by this Egyptian interlude, their bitter hostility was further aggravated. Moreover, the aftermath of Egypt's imperial ambitions in northern Uganda was very costly to Bunyoro, whose open clash with Baker permanently stamped her as being hostile to the advances of 'civilised' nations. This liability was eventually made worse by the fact that the European doorway to Uganda was through Buganda, so that the British came to see Bunyoro through the eyes of the Ganda hierarchy, that is, as an implacable enemy. The consequences were to be a dominant issue in Uganda politics right through the colonial period and into independence.

Meanwhile, within Buganda itself the basis of even more fundamental twentieth century issues was being laid. Alert to the possibility of foreign threats to Buganda's sovereignty, Mutesa was nevertheless willing to tolerate outsiders in his kingdom so long as he felt that they could be useful to him and remained within his control. The position of the Arabs in Buganda is a case in point.[1] So it was that Christian missionaries of the Anglican Church Missionary Society were tolerated on their arrival at his capital of Rubaga in June 1877. The conditions for missionary work were unique in Buganda, and the results were to be unique as well. Early missionary efforts elsewhere in East Africa were thwarted wherever they were directed at integral societies. The only successes were being registered among the detribalised freed slave communities at Rabai, Bagamoyo, Masasi, and particularly at Zanzibar. Three factors made Ganda society unusually receptive to missionary ideas, both Christian and Muslim. First, Ganda thinking was characterised by what Professor Low calls a 'forward-looking approach' which made them very receptive to any new and promising ideas. Second, Buganda was an open society in which ability and loyalty to the kabaka could earn one a high position in the power structure. Ambitious young men were eager to acquire new skills, both secular and religious, which would help them on their way. Third, Mutesa was very much concerned to establish centralised religious authority over Buganda which was equal to the

[1] See chapter 11.

244

unique secular supremacy which the kabaka already exercised. His fascination first with Islam and later with Christianity is best understood in the light of his search for a viable source of religious authority which the kabaka could employ against the still vital traditional gods, who were associated with the centrifugal forces of the bataka.

In 1879 the Anglicans were joined at Rubaga by the French Catholic White Fathers. Their differences with the CMS were as apparent as those between Christianity and Islam. Bewildered, Mutesa practised his old art of playing one off against the other in the religious discussions which were held at court. But Mutesa's indecision concerning which one of these creeds was right for Buganda was a critical abdication of leadership and aggravated the growing confusion and conflicts which were developing in Ganda society. Working among the pages who were attached to Mutesa's court, both the CMS and the White Fathers soon won small but dedicated congregations. By 1884 each faith had over one hundred converts. It was to be of unrivalled significance for the later history of Uganda that these young men were taken from the lower ranks of the Ganda political hierarchy. When Mutesa died in October 1884, to be succeeded by his erratic son, Mwanga, the foundations had already been laid for the 'Christian Revolution' in Buganda.

Mwanga's accession marked the end of a political era in Buganda. Less capable than either Suna or Mutesa, and beset by unprecedented external and internal forces, he failed from the beginning to re-establish the tradition of strong royal leadership. Unwilling to eliminate potential rival claimants and unable to secure the loyalty of the bakungu who had served his father, Mwanga initially sought and gained support from the ambitious young men of the court. Mwanga probably believed that by placing these men in powerful positions he would forever secure their loyalty to him. But the bakungu were not prepared to let a generation of upstarts, led by an insecure youth, deprive them of the leadership to which they aspired as Mutesa's lieutenants. Each group strove to gain Mwanga's confidence in the first years of his reign, but the kabaka was too uncertain of his own position to choose irrevocably. Such a critical situation could not endure for long and in 1888 the crisis erupted into violence which persisted, off and on, until Mwanga's deportation by the British in 1899.

This conflict is often called the 'Christian Revolution' in Buganda because many of the victorious party of young men were Christian converts. In fact, the young men's party also numbered among its ranks both Muslim converts and Ganda religious traditionalists. For this struggle was not about religious matters, but political power. In it the Ganda young men were the victors; the old generation of bakungu and Mwanga, now reduced to a figurehead, were the vanquished. Moreover, this was not merely a political coup involving conflicting personalities and generations, but a genuine revolution, as it brought with it a complete subordination of the kabaka-ship to the chiefly hierarchy. This is not to suggest that new religious ideologies were not a significant factor in late nineteenth-century Buganda. Indeed, immediately following the young men's victory of 1889 religious factionalism disrupted their united front. Pitting Christian against Muslim, and then Protestant against Catholic, these religious parties were not, however, primarily disputing religious doctrine, but the question of which one of them would hold the upper hand in the new political order. The intervention of Protestant Great Britain and the declaration of a British Protectorate in 1893 assured the Protestant party of victory. Led by Apolo Kagwa, who from 1890 to 1926 was *katikiro*, or Prime Minister, it was they who profited most from the Uganda (Buganda) Agreement of 1900, the effects of which dominated the history of both Buganda and the Uganda Protectorate throughout the era of colonial rule. Only after the political issue was settled did the real 'Christian Revolution', involving conversion of practically the entire society, take place.

Conclusion

The nineteenth century was one of momentous change in East Africa. The key to this revolution was the growth of contacts with the outside world, and the way in which different East African peoples responded to this process. During the century a number of factors contributed to bring about rapid change, foremost among them being the Ngoni invasion, the expansion of the international economy and of the slave trade in particular, and the coming of European missionaries.

We must not forget, however, that the internal workings of the many East African societies were at least as important in defining their reactions to these external forces as was the nature of these new forces themselves. In other words, these outside influences were not simply acting upon a passive population, but were calling forth a very positive response from the people with whom they came in contact. In some cases, this response led to the formation of new political units. In others, it led to the adoption of new military techniques, or to basic changes within a particular society.

Finally, we must remember that there were important independent changes taking place within many East African societies in the nineteenth century, and that there were some groups who remained notably isolated from many of the more outstanding external factors which were coming into play. These circumstances, as well as those resulting from interaction with the invaders of East Africa, were vitally important in preparing East Africans for the harsh realities of colonial rule.

Further reading

OLIVER, R. and MATHEW, G. (Eds) *History of East Africa, I,* Clarendon Press, Oxford, 1963. (The relevant parts of Oliver's chapter, and the chapters by A. Smith and D. A. Low are essential reading for the nineteenth century.)

OMER-COOPER, J. D. *The Zulu Aftermath: A Nineteenth-Century Revolution in Bantu Africa,* Longman, London, 1966. (Especially chapters 1, 2, 5, 12. The most accessible account of the rise of the Zulu and the Ngoni invasions.)

ALPERS, E. A. *The East African Slave Trade,* The Historical Association of Tanzania, Paper No. 3. East African Publishing House, Nairobi, 1967. (A more detailed look at the slave trade.)

ROBERTS, A. D. *Tanzania before 1900: Seven Area Histories,* Published for the Historical Association of Tanzania by the East African Publishing House, Nairobi, 1968. (An important collection of essays based on both archival and field research. This chapter draws particularly upon the essays by Steven Feierman, Isaria Kimambo, Alison Redmayne, Andrew Roberts, and Aylward Shorter.)

GRAY, R. and BIRMINGHAM, D. *Pre-Colonial African Trade: Essays on Trade in Central and Eastern Africa before 1900,* Oxford University Press, London, 1970. (The chapters by Roberts on the Nyamwezi and John Lamphear on the Kamba are the best studies available.)

KIMAMBO, I. N. and TEMU, A. J. (Eds) *A History of Tanzania,* Published for the Historical Association of Tanzania by the East African Publishing House, Nairobi, 1969. (The chapters by Alpers and Roberts deal with the rise and impact of the caravan trade.)

ALPERS, E. A. 'Trade, State, and Society among the Yao in the Nineteenth Century', *Journal of African History,* X, 3, 1969, (pp. 405–420). (Explores the relationship between Yao involvement in international trade and the changes in Yao society during the nineteenth century.)

SHORTER, AYLWARD *Nyungu-ya-Mawe: Leadership in nineteenth century Tanzania,* Historical Association of Tanzania Paper No. 7 East African Publishing House, Nairobi, 1969. (An exciting and authoritative interpretation of Nyungu's remarkable career.)

STAHL, K. 'Outline of Chagga History', *Tanganyika Notes and Records,* *LXIV,* Dar es Salaam, 1965, pp.35–49. (A brief, clear account of the style of Chagga chiefly politics.)

BENNETT, N. R. *Mirambo of Tanzania, 1840?–1884,* Oxford University Press, New York, 1971. (A full-scale biography of Mirambo, with particular emphasis on his relations with the Arabs and the Europeans.)

OSOGO, J. *Nabongo Mumia of the Baluyia*, East African Literature Bureau, Nairobi, Dar es Salaam, and Kampala, 1966. (A popular biography tracing Mumia's career as chief of the Wanga.)

MURIUKI, G. Kikuyu Reaction to Traders and British Administration, 1850–1904, *Hadith 1*, Proceedings of the annual conference of the Historical Association of Kenya 1967, Ed. by B. A. Ogot, Published for the Historical Association of Kenya by the East African Publishing House, Nairobi, 1968, (pp. 101–118). (The first fruit of Dr. Muriuki's major study of pre-colonial Kikuyu history.)

OLIVER, R. *The Missionary Factor in East Africa* (2nd edition), Longman, London, 1965. (The standard history of missionary activity in East Africa.)

LOW, D. A. 'Converts and Martyrs in Buganda', in C. G. Baëta (Ed.) *Christianity in Tropical Africa*, Published for the International African Institute by the Oxford University Press, London, 1968, (pp. 150–163). (A brilliant introduction to the religious history of late nineteenth century Buganda.)

KIWANUKA, M. S. M. *Muteesa of Uganda*, East African Literature Bureau, Nairobi, Dar es Salaam, and Kampala, 1967. (A compelling study of Mutesa's reign as Kabaka of Buganda and his place in the history of Uganda.)

DUNBAR, A. R. *Omukama Chwa II Kabarega*, East African Literature Bureau, Nairobi, Dar es Salaam, and Kampala, 1965. (A popular biography tracing Kabarega's career as king of Bunyoro.)

TARIKH, *III*, 2, The Peoples of Uganda in the 19th Century, Longman, London, 1970.

13

Kenya Under the British, 1895 to 1963

Bethwell A. Ogot

Kenya as a Consular District, July 1895 to April 1905

The declaration on 1 July 1895 of a protectorate over the small area between Mombasa and the Rift Valley came as a by-product of British involvement and activities in Zanzibar and Uganda. To the British Government, the East Africa Protectorate, to give it its official name, appeared in itself to be of little economic or strategic significance. But since Zanzibar and the coast formed a necessary base for British operations in East Africa and in the Indian Ocean complex, the protectorate, a kind of Zanzibar backyard, had to be made safe. In the same way, the security of the East Africa Protectorate was regarded by the British as an essential part of the major strategic consideration for retaining control of Uganda and the Nile Valley.

The protectorate was to be administered from Zanzibar by career diplomats. Indeed, the first Commissioner of the East Africa Protectorate, Mr (later Sir) A. H. Hardinge, was also Agent and Consul-General in Zanzibar. This system of dual responsibility continued until 1904, when, because of changed circumstances which we shall examine later, Sir Donald Stewart was appointed only to the position of Commissioner and Commander-in-Chief of the East Africa Protectorate.

This dual responsibility had other implications in the administrative field. Britain deliberately maintained the fiction which was already operating in Zanzibar, that the new protectorate would exercise an important degree of control over its internal affairs. The British officials would be consuls supervising a local administration. The commissioner had, therefore, to be a diplomat and the affairs of the protectorate had to be conducted through the Foreign Office. Such arrangements usually operate only between two sovereign states. And even in the case of Zanzibar, Britain soon gave up the pretence, transferred the control over Zanzibar affairs from the Foreign Office to the Colonial Office, and replaced the position of Consul-General with that of Resident.

In the East Africa Protectorate, the consular theory of administration was even more meaningless. Hardinge had inherited no definite system of administration from the Imperial British East Africa Company which had been trying to administer and develop the British sphere since 1888. With a capital of just under £250,000, its affairs being mismanaged, and the cost of military actions, especially in Uganda, soaring higher and higher, the company was obviously unlikely to prove equal to such a pioneering enterprise.

When, therefore, the Foreign Office took over the running of this area in 1895, a system of administration had still to be worked out. It is true that the company had succeeded in establishing its presence at the coast and in Buganda, as well as along the caravan route linking these two areas. But this did not produce an administrative system, nor was there any proper machinery of government. And to attempt to administer the East Africa Protectorate, which at that time was nothing but a geographical expression, on the basis of the consular theory, was really to attempt the impossible.

Hardinge's first task was to establish British overrule. He soon discovered that the local people were opposed to any form of foreign rule, and were prepared to fight for their rights.

In February 1895, four months before Hardinge was appointed, a serious rebellion had broken out at Takaungu, the northern headquarters of the Mazrui dynasty, over a disputed succession. On the death of Salim-bin-Hamis el-Mazrui, his son Rashid was selected by the IBEA Company's representative at Malindi, K. Macdougall, to succeed him. There was another claimant, a younger Mbaruk, who according to Muslim law, had a better right to the governorship, but as he was not well disposed towards the British, his claim was disregarded. He thereupon withdrew to the elder Mbaruk's camp at Gonjoro and threatened armed resistance.

While affairs were thus unsettled, the rule of the company came to an end. The 1895 treaty which transferred the 10-mile wide coastal strip to the British in return for an annual fee and interest to the Sultan of £16,500 was unacceptable to the coast peoples—The Twelve Tribes, the Mijikenda and the Arabs—who had recognised neither the Sultan of Zanzibar's overlordship nor the company's rule. They had expected the territory to revert to them on the expiry of the company's lease. But when it was learnt that the British Government would take over from the company, the people decided to resist such foreign rule.

250

The result was the so-called 'Mazrui rebellion'. It was neither confined to the Mazrui family, nor was it restricted to the Arabs. The Twelve Tribes, led by the Hamisi Kombo and Mwinjaka; the Mijikenda people, especially the Giriama under their leader Ngonyo; and the inhabitants of most of the coast towns from Kipini in the north to Vanga in the south, actively participated in the resistance movement. The resisters successfully attacked Freretown and Malindi. The Foreign Office could no longer leave matters to the Commissioner, because British prestige was at stake. Troops were sent from India to aid Hardinge's local force in crushing the resistance. Mbaruk and his followers escaped to German East Africa. There was thus a general opposition to the imposition of British rule at the coast, and it took over nine months of active fighting to establish political control of the area. The coastal strip was declared a protectorate, and an Arab sub-imperialism was re-established by the British to administer the area. This rule by the Omani Arabs in the service of the British was operative up to 1963, and hence much of the history of the coast during the colonial period is the story of the struggle of the other coast peoples—the Twelve Tribes and the Mijikenda— against these agents of British imperialism.

Further north in Jubaland, the Ogaden Somali refused to recognise British overrule. And despite their defeat by protectorate forces, again aided by Indian troops, in the middle of 1898, government control was never really established in the area up to 1925, when Jubaland was ceded to Italy.

As far as the interior was concerned, the major concern of the Foreign Office between 1895 and 1901 was not so much the establishment of effective control over the different peoples, or the evolution of a suitable administrative system: their main interest was the construction of the Uganda Railway. For strategic and economic reasons, it was desirable for the line to be built with the utmost speed, and this could only be done if peace was maintained with the surrounding peoples. Peace could not have been maintained if the government had tried to extend its authority beyond the vicinity of the proposed railway line. Nor would it have been politic to employ outsiders such as the Arab or Swahili people (who were used extensively in German East Africa) in this delicate task of enlisting the support of the local people for railway construction. Hardinge was therefore forced to fall back on the only people who had some experience in dealing with the local people—the former servants of the Imperial British East Africa Company. He particularly relied on John Ainsworth, the sub-commissioner at Machakos; Francis Hall, who had been working at Kikuyu since 1893; and C. W. Hobley, who arrived at Mumias in Nyanza in February 1895 as a sub-commissioner. Apart from their peace-keeping responsibilities, their main duty was to recruit local labour and to find food for the railway parties. Railway construction had thus to precede the establishment of political control. As far as administration was concerned, few officers, as a former colonial civil servant, A. T. Matson, has written, found 'time to organise their districts, to get to know the people, their customs and languages, or to extend the area of effective jurisdiction.'

The completion of the construction of the railway in 1901 brought many problems in its wake: Indian traders, who had been moving inland as the railway progressed, were now established at several key points between Mombasa and Kisumu. The other group of newcomers whose numbers steadily increased after 1901 were the Europeans, comprising adventurers, traders, missionaries and settlers. Neither the Indians nor the Europeans were content with operating within the administered districts: many of them pressed on into the uncontrolled areas. Since the government was responsible for their safety, the jurisdictions of several administrators had to be extended every now and then to include all the areas in which the newcomers were operating. Instead of being regarded simply as a 'barren country' through which one had, of necessity, to pass on the way to Uganda, the protectorate was beginning to acquire a character of its own. In the words of Sir Charles Eliot, Commissioner and Consul-General of the East Africa Protectorate (1900 to 1904), the country had 'unconsciously grown from a Consular District into a Colony'.

The new Commissioner not only wanted to introduce a Crown Colony type of administration, which he argued would be more suitable; he also insisted that new sources of revenue must be found to make the railway pay. In particular, he recommended the introduction of a hut tax—already introduced in Uganda and German East Africa—and colonisation of the highlands of Kenya by Europeans. The Africans so far had remained passive spectators, and had tended to regard the European administrators in the same way as they had looked upon the Swahili and Arab traders, viz., as temporary birds of passage. Indeed, with the Foreign Office policy of non-involvement, nothing had so far happened to make the Africans think otherwise. But the implementation of Eliot's recommendations, which were accepted by the Foreign Office, was soon to awaken the African to the fact that the European had come to stay—and to stay as a ruler.

The emergence of the East Africa Protectorate as a distinctive territory was further hastened by the decision of the Foreign Office on 5 March 1902, to transfer the Eastern Province of Uganda to it. Not only was a large area added to the protectorate, but much of this land was suitable for European settlement. And this had been one of the motivating factors in the Foreign Office decision. Moreover, the former Eastern Province of Uganda included one of the most densely populated regions in East Africa, and this meant that by a stroke of a pen, the African population in the protectorate was more than doubled. Could the enlarged protectorate continue to be governed from Zanzibar by career diplomats?

The answer to this question was obviously in the negative. Eliot therefore set about to create a more suitable type of administration. He also wanted the headquarters of the protectorate moved from Mombasa to the more central new town of Nairobi. His immediate problem was that most of the African peoples had never accepted European rule. To obtain their acquiescence, it became necessary for the Government, between 1900 and 1908, to organise a series of military expeditions against recalcitrant Africans: expeditions against the Nandi in 1901, 1905 and 1906; against the Embu in 1904 and 1906; against the Gusii in 1904 and 1908; against the Kipsigis in 1905; and against the Bakusu and Kabras in 1907. And even in those areas to which no military expeditions were sent, force was used in the majority of cases to establish British rule. But as we shall see below, force alone would not have succeeded so quickly, if it were not for some fundamental social, economic and political changes which were already taking place among most societies in Kenya, and which facilitated the take-over.

Developments which were to take place later during the colonial period, as well as their nature and significance, can be understood only if studied against the background of the dynamism of African societies.

Kenya as a Settlement Colony, 1905 to 1923

European settlers had been arriving in the country since 1896. But it was during the period when Charles Eliot was Commissioner that the first official encouragement was given to white settlement. From about 1904 settlers began to arrive from South Africa. This was the first of several government-sponsored European settlement schemes that were to be a marked feature of Kenya history. They were soon followed by other immigrants from Britain, Australia, New Zealand and Canada who, on the whole, brought more capital than their predecessors.

The new colonists were inspired by a dream. Since most of Asia, America and Africa was already explored, the highlands of Kenya appeared to be the only suitable area left for European colonisation. Kenya was to be the last of the typically British settlements established overseas, after the U.S.A., Australia, Canada, New Zealand and South Africa. To quote the words of one of these early colonists, 'the goal of this generation is the establishment in East Africa of a new, loyal, white dominion, securely founded in the principles of British tradition and western civilisation.' It was assumed by Eliot and the settler leaders that this settlement was being carried out in a vacuum, and that their duty was to create an entirely new society and polity.

Any attempt to turn this European dream into a reality was bound to run into several difficulties. To begin with, in Kenya, unlike in other settlement colonies, colonisation in terms of the settlement of a white community was preceded by the establishment of a form of Crown Colony government. In all other countries, the pioneer settlers had preceded the establishment of any government. Moreover, almost for the first time in the British Empire, the Crown Colony system which had been specially designed for the government of so-called 'backward races' was now extended, from April 1905 when the protectorate was transferred from the Foreign to the Colonial Office, to include not only the Africans and Asians but comparatively well-educated and politically articulate Europeans. It was an interesting constitutional experiment, but one which was fraught with difficulties right from the beginning. The Colonists' Association was soon formed to demand 'the ancient liberties' of every British person. And although the settlers were still very few, the British Government yielded to their pressure and agreed in 1906 to introduce a Legislative Council.

The system could not function smoothly. The most politically dominant element in the protectorate was given the maximum chance for criticism and no opportunity for exercising responsibility, while the other communities were denied the same opportunity. The result was that politics among the Europeans assumed an unreal and irresponsible character, with much agitation and acrimony. European politics soon set a pattern first for Indian and later for African politics.

The other point which had not been taken into consideration was that Europeans who felt superior to the Africans were unlikely to agree to do manual work in a country inhabited largely by Africans. The natural role of most of them working on the land, they felt, should be that of supervisors of African labour. Conscious of their status they hoped that a poor white residuum would not appear, as had happened in South Africa. A class of poor whites, they feared, would pave the way to miscegenation, which in return would result in a debasement of racial standards. When many undesirable and penniless European characters swarmed into Nairobi from South Africa, the government quickly dealt with them under the Distressed British Subjects' Act. If they failed to satisfy the court as to their financial resources or past record, they were committed to prison at Fort Jesus in Mombasa for six months, followed by deportation to Bombay. This policy is perhaps responsible for there being very little miscegenation in Kenya, compared with South Africa, for instance. There is no separate population of 'coloureds' in Kenya. What is important, however, is that the policy of relying on black labour in what was intended to be a 'white man's country' was bound to pose difficult racial problems.

But the most serious challenge to the concept of a settlement colony came from the Indians in Kenya. They, too, had a dream. Their influence, which for over fifty years had been strong at the coast, with the building of the Uganda Railway extended up-country. Large numbers of coolies (as many as 13 000 were employed in December 1898) were brought in from India to build the line. Indian traders, as we have already seen, followed in the wake of the railway, pioneering retail trade inland. Indian troops were called in every now and then to help with the suppression of revolts. Much of the legislation in the infant protectorate was based on Indian precedents and the currency was Indian rupees and annas. So by 1905 there was already a strong Indian influence in the territory.

Even with settlement, it was not clear initially whether this was not going to be a joint enterprise between the Europeans and the Indians. Sir Harry Johnston, when he was Special Commissioner for Uganda, had stated that 'East Africa is, and should be, from every point of view, the America of the Hindu.' But he also conceded that the Kenya highlands were 'admirably suited for a white man's country.' Eliot, at least up to 1902, was prepared to encourage both Indian and European settlement, but increased pressure from the European pioneer settlers forced him to the conclusion that the Kenya highlands must be reserved for the white colonists only.

It should, however, be emphasised that the Indians in Kenya were not the helpless and innocent victims of British imperialism, as many writers would want us to believe. Benarsidas Chaturvedi, a leader of the Greater India Movement, wrote in one of his letters of the Indian dream:

'If there is any man in India who has got a true perception of this vision and who has worked incessantly for its realisation it is Mr Andrews and none else. In fact he has been living in Greater India for the last fourteen years and his mind has wandered from Borobuder, the famous temple of Java, the Yava Dwip of Greater India of ancient times to the Khoja Jamat Khana—the great mosque in Nairobi. He realises that India had her cultural colonies in the distant past and she may have them again in the near future. Mr Andrew's Greater India will not belong to an Imperial system. It will be definitely cultural. . . What Mr Andrews sees in his imagination and what we cannot see is the Greater India of A.D. 2000. The fact is that many of our leaders have not been abroad. It is said that some of our Indian Sadhus in olden times had a sort of miraculous power by which they could fly away to any part of the world. I wish some Sadhu like that could send a good number of our leaders to the colonies in the twinkling of an eye. Let them be sent to Mombasa or Dar-es-Salaam. Let them see that Mombasa is just like any town of Gujerat. Sir John Kirk, the British Agent at Zanzibar used to refer to East Africa as India's America. Let some of our leaders see this America. A fine walk by the seaside at Dar-es-Salaam or a view of the Indian Ocean from Mr Yusuf Ali's bungalow on the seaside at Tanga will give them an idea of the infinite possibilities of India—an idea which cannot be given by hundreds of books or articles.'

This was not just the dream of a fanatic. In Kenya itself, Mr A. M. Jeevanjee, one of the Indian leaders, said in 1910: 'I would go so far as to advocate the annexation of this African territory (Kenya) to the Indian Empire, with Provincial Government under the Indian Viceroy. Let it be opened to us, and in a very few years it will be a second India'. In 1921, the *East African Chronicle*, which was at that time the official organ of the Indian Congress in Kenya, published an article visualising the future when Kenya would be Indian-administered, and drawing a parallel between such a position and that of South Africa administered by Dutchmen. The Aga Khan himself, in an addendum to Gokhale's political statement, suggested that East Africa be set aside for Indian colonisation.

At the root of the so-called 'Indian question' in Kenya was a clash between two dreams, the solution to which had wider imperial implications. Was Kenya to be European or Indian? And was development to be based on European of Indian foundations? In Canada and Australia, the white settlers had already reserved the right to decide what class of non-Europeans, if any, would be permitted to settle in their countries. In South Africa, too, restrictive measures against the Indians were already operating, making the Indian a mere sojourner. The strength and virility of the British Empire was seen to reside in its homogeneous European stock. Was Kenya prepared to undermine the empire by allowing racial admixture?

The European settlers were determined to resist such a policy. They demanded an increasing measure of self-government for themselves, in order to deal with 'the Indian menace'. They got the Colonial Office to reserve the highlands, on the pretext of administrative convenience, for European settlement. Racial segregation was introduced in towns. They wanted an end put to Indian immigration. The Indians, in their turn, demanded complete political and electoral equality.

It is in this wider context of a clash between two rival civilisations that the decision to transfer the headquarters of the East African Protectorate from Mombasa to Nairobi in 1907 must be considered. Established in 1896 as a transport depot, Nairobi replaced Mombasa as the headquarters of the Uganda Railway in July 1899. Mombasa, on the other hand, had had a long and distinguished history and was the centre of a long-established Swahili culture. It would have been contradictory for the protectorate government, which was bent on creating a new society based on British values, to have used Mombasa, with its oriental background, as a base. Whereas in Tanzania the coastal Swahili cul-

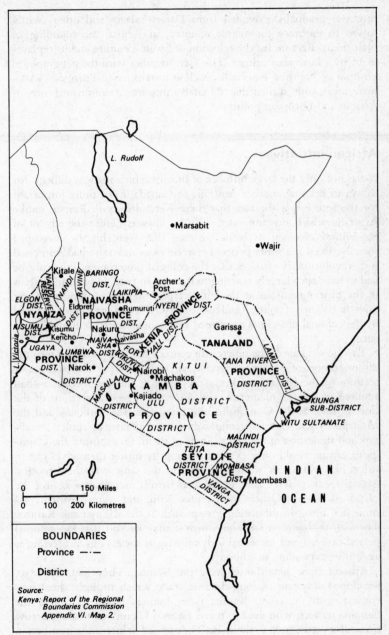

Figure 24 Kenya: Administrative boundaries as at 1909

ture was gradually extended from Dar-es-Salaam and other coastal towns to embrace the whole country, in Kenya, the founding of Nairobi in effect meant the rejection of Swahili culture and its replacement by a European culture. This fact, together with the geographical position of Nairobi, especially its close proximity to European settlement areas, soon turned this old safari camp into a dominant centre of African and European politics.

African initiatives

It was not only the large number of Indians which made it difficult for Kenya to become another Australia or Canada. Even more important for the future was the fact that there were already in Kenya, unlike Australia which was inhabited only by hunters before the advent of the white colonists, dynamic societies that were highly developed socially. Even the short period between 1850 and 1895 had witnessed such revolutionary changes that the colonial government can truly be said to have been largely reacting to these up to 1920. Indeed, an analysis of the power relations at the time of partition shows how in many cases the balance of political and economic power in Kenya (often checked by the colonial phase) has continued as if uninterrupted with independence.

The second half of the nineteenth century had, for example, seen the disintegration of Maasai society. Civil wars between the two major sections of the Maasai-speakers—the Il-oikop and the Il-Maasai—had resulted in the fragmentation and dispersal of several sections of the Iloikop such as the Uasingishu, the Loogolala, the Laikipiak and the Moitanik. These scattered groups were further afflicted by cholera, small-pox and rinderpest in the 1890s. Some of them, for example, the Uasin-gishu group, could only eke out a living by hiring themselves out to rulers like Mumia in western Kenya. In the same way these rootless Maasai speakers were later to enlist as British mercenaries against the Nandi in 1905–6. Others took refuge with, and were eventually as-similiated into, neighbouring groups such as the Kikuyu and Kamba. There is, therefore, a sense in which it may be said that the colonial period revived and recreated a dying Maasai society, by protecting it against its expanding neighbours.

Among these neighbours were the Kamba. They had, by 1830, developed a system of long-distance trade which brought them into contact with the coast. Kamba ivory hunters began to follow the Giriama traders, who used to travel far into Ukambani to trade arrow poison for cattle, back to the coast. They settled in increasing numbers in the southern Giriama district of Weruni. By 1850 they dominated the ivory trade, not so much displacing the Giriama as supplementing their rather modest trade with new sources from Mount Kenya and beyond.

At the coast dramatic changes occurred among the Mijikenda (literally 'Nine towns' or 'Nine *kayas*') in the last quarter of the nineteenth century. A series of terrible famines and epidemics forced these pastoralists to abandon their kayas completely and drove them further afield. By 1900 they had filled out the lowlands between their kayas, cleared all the virgin forest in the district, and a large group was moving towards the coastal lowlands. At the same time permanent crops were being introduced that changed the pattern of shifting cultivation. The cultivation of coconut palms spread inland from the coast, first to Digo and then progressing slowly north to Rabai and Kaloleni in the 1930s and these were followed by other permanent tree-crops, citrus fruits and cashew nuts.

With expansion and the new crops came increased contacts among the Mijikenda themselves and with others. Specialised regional trade networks grew of a highly personalised and ritual nature. These specialised networks involved contiguous peoples trading selected required goods—ironwares, poison, palm wine, cattle—but a series of famines and epidemics of the 1880s and 1890s prompted the growth of a new form of trade as people entered into cash trade with the coast in order to obtain food. The Jibana tapped copal and rubber while others increasingly planted coconuts for copra as well as wine. These new products pulled the Mijikenda into the wider world market as they responded to the increasing demands in Europe for oils and other raw materials.

But while the Mijikenda were expanding towards the coast, the Arabs and the Swahili of the coast began to expand into the interior, staking out large coastal plantations utilising the abundant cheap slave labour which had resulted from the bans on the export of slaves, in response to the same world market demands. This brought them increasingly into conflict with the Mijikenda moving coastwards and the resultant land disputes and ten-mile strip controversy have continued to this day. During famines many people were adopted by wealthy families, and the majority of these were often fully integrated into the clan and lineage of their protector. The influence of the kaya as a central institution thus waned among the Mijikenda.

In central Kenya, the period was characterised by the southern expansion of the Kikuyu into Kiambu. And as G. W. T. Hodges has said in his stimulating chapter in *Hadith III*, this expansion 'gave the Kikuyu the control of the area which was to become the hub of Kenya, with the future European capital of Nairobi embedded in its eastern flank, and astride the vital lines of communication. . . . All this, followed by the land alienations in South Kiambu, was to give the Kikuyu an enormous advantage over the other peoples of Kenya in all the techniques of the Europeans and Asians: trade, commodities, the beginnings of education at Kikuyu and Kabete and above all, political negotiation.' In fact, what colonisation did was temporarily to halt Kikuyu expansion into the Rift Valley, except as squatters, for about sixty years. Thus the bitter Kikuyu land politics during the colonial period can only be understood against this background of the expanding frontier.

Further west, we see the emergence of the Nandi as a strong, well-knit military power during this period. This centralisation was achieved under the unifying personality of the *orkoiyot*, their ritual and political leader. The office was the result of the Nandi adaptation of the Maasai institution of the *oloiboni* in the 1860s, a fact which emphasises the high degree of cultural borrowing that took place among the different peoples in the pre-colonial days.

Around Lake Victoria, the small semi-nomadic Luo group had evolved by 1900 into a strong settled community, practising a mixed economy. And although they were among the last groups to arrive, they had by the beginning of this century established themselves as the dominant ethnic group in the lake region of Kenya. Many alien groups took refuge in Luo society and were adopted and assimilated into Luo lineages.

The British administrators were, therefore, imposing their rule on African societies that were changing fast. Movements of people either through migration or trade which were already a marked feature of the period were to be intensified, under different circumstances, during the colonial period. But, on the other hand, at the level of the mass of the people opportunities for movement and absorption into other language groups were to be greatly restricted by the colonial concepts of tribalism which aimed at preserving the 'tribe' as an administrative and political unit by discouraging inter-tribal mobility. Also, most of the economic initiatives which, as we have seen, were being taken by different African societies during the last two decades of the nineteenth century, were killed by the imposition of alien rule. The economy was soon to be geared towards serving the interests of the European settlers.

The establishment of British administration

The major problem facing the British administrators in Kenya before 1914 was the establishment of a sound system of administration. There was no reference model such as the Kiganda system to export to the rest of the country. And since the British were committed to the idea of governing 'native peoples' through chiefs, the problem became that of establishing the institution of the chief in the largely chiefless societies of

Kenya. Moreover, this difficult experiment was to be carried out by young, often inexperienced, semi-educated and overworked colonial administrators. Sir Charles Eliot wrote: 'In theory their chief duties are to collect revenue and administer justice. In practice a young man of between twenty-five and thirty often finds himself in sole charge of a district as large as several English counties, and in a position which partly resembles that of an emperor and partly that of a general servant.'

Moreover, the type of administrator who was sent out to Kenya in the early days, with the exception of the former servants of the IBEA Co., was on the whole below standard. As Col. Meinertzhagen has recorded in his *Kenya Diary* (1902–6):

'Few of (the administrators) have had any education, and many of them do not pretend to be members of the educated class. One can neither read nor write. This is not surprising when one realises that no examination is required to enter the local Civil Service. Sir Clement Hill, who recently visited the Colony on behalf of the Foreign Office, remarked that "so long as Civil Servants were enlisted from the gutter" we could not expect a high standard of administration. When such men are given unlimited power over uneducated and simple-minded natives it is not extraordinary that they should abuse their powers, suffer from megalomania and regard themselves as little tin gods.'

With such an undermanned public service, the British colonial government was anxious to enlist the support of any person with a semblance of authority. On the other hand, many of the traditional rulers such as Mumia in western Kenya, Lenana in the Rift Valley and Wang'ombe in central Kenya needed the military support of the 'little tin gods' to survive. It was, therefore, to the mutual benefit of both parties to collaborate in the administration of the colony. In such situations the chieftainship was frequently used to continue, through the colonial apparatus, disputes that antedated the colonial period.

But just as the colonial service had attracted adventurous young men from Britain, it also provided opportunities for local young men with initiative. In fact, the majority of Kenyan chiefs up to 1920 fall into this category. Their authority had no traditional basis, and most of them were selected because they had been effective caravan leaders or labour recruiters or simply because they spoke Swahili. The authority of these local 'little tin gods' was rejected both by the elders, who regarded them as upstarts and by the younger generation for whom they soon symbolised colonial oppression and exploitation. The migration of young men from rural areas to urban or settled areas, as we shall later see, can partly be explained as an attempt to escape from the ruthless administration of these upstarts. Kinyanjui in Kiambu and Karuri Gakure in Murang'a are often regarded as typical examples of such colonial chiefs. Many of these chiefs became wealthy and wielded considerable political power. The

261

political and social structure of African societies was thus being transformed through the institution of chieftainship. And consequently the struggle for political power among Africans during the colonial period centred around this institution. Indeed many of the 'revolutionaries' who attacked colonial chiefs did so not because they were opposed to the institution as such, but because they themselves had not been appointed chiefs.

New opportunities for personal advancement were also provided by the Christian missionaries, who by 1906 had already established fifty-eight mission stations, concentrated largely on the Coast, Central and Nyanza Provinces. Most of these stations were established in the rural areas and they soon attracted young men whose prospects in traditional societies were dim. For example, most of the converts at Kikuyu Mission Station were the *ahoi*, the landless people, who were being created as a result of land alienation to the European settlers. In the same way, the first children in the interior of Kenya to go to school were twenty-two Maasai children from Kaputie who were sent by the administrator Francis Hall to the East Africa Scottish Mission at Kibwezi in 1894. Their parents had flocked to Fort Smith as refugees who were running away from the ravages of the epidemics and famines of the 1890s. These mission stations produced a second category of political upstarts whose claim to authority was based on education. They were the people who were to lead the first revolutionary movements in Kenya in the 1920s.

But it was not long before some of the new Christian adherents were able to distinguish between Christianity and Westernism. They were willing to accept the new faith, but on their own terms, and without accepting the white man's ways or his rule. The most outstanding example of the first Christian rebels in Kenya was John Owalo, who had started as a Roman Catholic, then joined the Scottish Mission at Kikuyu, and later the CMS at Maseno. In 1907, he claimed that he had received a direct call from God to start his own religion. Yahweh had told Owalo in the Third Heaven, 'I am now sending you to be my messenger and the bearer of my sharp sword. I shall require you to raise it high. He who hears your message and understands it, let him hold fast to it. He who refuses shall be left alone.'

The CMS Missionaries at Maseno attempted to suppress his rebellious spirit, but after much investigation, the P.C. of Nyanza (Ainsworth) authorised him to start his own religion, since his teaching was not subversive to good order and morality. So in 1910 John Owalo founded the first Independent Church in Kenya, the Nomia Luo Mission ('the Luo Mission that was given to me'). He proclaimed himself a prophet and arguing like a Unitarian, denied the divinity of Christ while accepting that he was a prophet and son of God. And according to his revelations, which today constitute the creed of the Nomiya Luo Mission, Owalo is supposed to have stayed in heaven with many angels. We read:

'It is a beautiful place; and all the Nations of the earth wanted to enter in, but the Angels closed the gate. When all the Nations of the earth had gathered at the gate of heaven, the Angels let the Jews in first, and the Jews were followed in by the Arabs. After them went in John Owalo, the Angel Gabriel and the Angel Rafael, all three entering together. The White races attempted to enter in after them, but the Angels closed the gate on their face and chased the white men away, kicking them.'

We read further on in the same Section V of the creed that the Indians and the Goans were also chased away.

Within the next few years, he had over 10,000 followers, had built his own primary schools (the first African independent schools in Kenya) and was demanding representation on local councils and a secondary school free from 'undue missionary influence'.

While the movement led by John Owalo represented a determination on the part of Christian Africans to control their own churches and schools and to have the right to accept or reject the white man's teachings, two other contemporary movements, the movement led by Siotune and Kiamba in Ukambani (1911–1913), and the cult of Mumbo which affected most of the Luo and Gusii areas from 1913, presented much more radical programmes whose advocates preached complete rejection of everything European and a return to the African way of life.

Leadership in Kamba society had been shared by three main groups—the *atumia* (elders), the *athiani* (warleaders) and the *andu awe* (medicine men). With the establishment of British administration in Ukambani, the first two groups were rendered ineffectual. But the medicine men had not been and could not be superseded by the colonial chiefs. In traditional society, the medicine men had been the leaders of the *kilumi*, the dance for the exorcism of evil spirits in which the participants were mostly women. Between 1911 and 1913 *kilumi* dancing in Machakos and Kitui was used effectively as a channel for expressing opposition to the colonial government. During these dances, an evil spirit known as *mwiitu wa Ngai* (girl of God), assumed the form of an unmarried girl and preached anti-government and anti-European messages.

At the beginning of 1911, the only leader of this *Ngai ngoma*: (God dance) was a widow, Siotune wa Kathuke. Later in the year she was joined by Kiamba, and between them they soon had an extraordinary domination over the people. The Kamba were ordered not to agree to work as porters or to pay the Hut and Poll Tax. Kiamba told the people that he intended to remove all the Europeans from Kenya. He formed a small army of women and mounted a guard and sentries on his village.

The colonial government moved troops into Ukambani, arrested Siotune and Kiamba and deported them to Kismayu. Other leaders of the moment were similarly deported.

The second radical movement was the cult of Mumbo, which started in Alego location of central Nyanza in 1913. A certain Onyango Dunde claimed to have been swallowed by a sea-serpent from Lake Victoria, which after a short interval had spat him out unhurt. The serpent then proceeded to address Onyango in the following words:

'I am the God Mumbo whose two homes are in the Sun and in the Lake. I have chosen you to be my mouth-piece. Go out and tell all Africans . . . that from henceforth I am their God. Those whom I choose personally and also those who acknowledge me will live forever in plenty . . . The Christian religion is rotten and so is its practice of making its believers wear clothes. My followers must let their hair grow never cutting it. Their clothes shall be the skins of goats and cattle and they must never wash. All Europeans are your enemies, but the time is shortly coming when they will all disappear from our country.'

From Alego, Mumboism quickly spread to neighbouring locations, and thence across Lake Victoria into south Nyanza, including Gusii district. And between 1914 and 1918 the movement gained such momentum that the colonial government had to take drastic steps to suppress it, especially as the period coincided with the First World War which was being fought only a few miles away in German East Africa. But although active steps were taken in 1919 against the Mumboites, their leaders being exiled to Lamu, the movement continued to be a powerful protest movement, especially in south Nyanza and among the Gusii, until it was proscribed together with other African political groups in 1940.

The history of African nationalism in Kenya must, therefore, be traced back to these early protest movements.

The First World War 1914 to 1918

As the researches of G. W. T. Hodges on the Carrier Corps in the East African Campaign of 1914–1918 have shown, the First World War provided a shattering experience for the peoples of East and Central Africa. From Kenya alone over 10,000 soldiers and about 195,000 military labourers were involved. The Africans also provided slaughter cattle and other forms of food. In 1916 the Hut and Poll Tax was increased in order to meet the high cost of fighting what was regarded by all Africans as a foreign war. The groups most affected were the Kikuyu, Luo and Kamba.

Of the 195 000 African porters employed during the war, over 50 000 died. This high mortality rate was due to the poor treatment they received during the campaign. As Sir Philip Mitchell, a volunteer in the war, has written, 'Of the porters a large number died on service, a larger number than that service justified, for, though there were exceptions, the feeding and care of the porters and protection against excessive loads were seldom of an adequate standard.'

The collective wartime experience of the Africans and Europeans was to prove of great significance during the post-war period. The European and African soldiers ate, washed, slept and fought together. The African soldier soon discovered the weaknesses and the strength of the European, who up to that time had been regarded by the majority of Africans as a superman. In fact, the warrant and non-commissioned African officers were instructing European volunteers in the technique of modern warfare. It was becoming evident that the European did not know everything. The returning porters and soldiers spread the new views of the white man; and much of the self-confidence and assertiveness that the Africans in Kenya displayed in the 1920s had a lot to do with this new knowledge. 'The experiences of the years from 1914 to 1918', Dr H. R. A. Philip, who was a medical doctor in Kenya, has recorded in his book of reminiscences called *A New Day in Kenya* (1936), 'were such as to effectively awaken the Kenya native from the sleep of the centuries.'

In summary, therefore, as a result of the experiences of the First World War, the Africans became more aware of themselves as a distinct racial group; they discovered the weaknesses and heterogeneity of the white men and, even more crucial, they learnt the importance of organised resistance. It is not without significance that several African political leaders in the 1920s and 1930s, including Jonathan Okwirri, first president of the Young Kavirondo Association, and Joseph Kangethe, later president of the Kikuyu Central Association, had either fought or served in the Carrier Corps in German East Africa.

The post-war period 1918 to 1923

By 1918, the African was restless. He had fears about his future which were soon confirmed by the actions of the government. During the war years, the settlers had cleverly exploited the weakness of the British Government to obtain several concessions aimed at consolidating their power against both the Indians and the Africans. In 1915 the Colonial Office accepted the settlers' demand for greater security of land tenure by extending leases of land from 99 to 999 years. In the following year, the Europeans' demand for direct representation in the Legislative Council was accepted in principle. After the war, the policy of the paramountcy of European interests was intensified by Major-General Sir Edward Northey, the new Governor, who himself had led the Allied forces against the Germans in Nyasaland. He nominated two Europeans to the Executive Council, issued the notorious Northey Circulars on labour recruitment to assist the European settlers, introduced a Soldier Settlement Scheme with a view to doubling the European population, and alienated a further 12 810 square kilometres in the highlands. Most significant, the country, now renamed Kenya, was formally annexed and declared a Crown Colony. It appeared that Kenya might, after all, become another South Africa.

Perhaps no other problem illustrates the colonised status of the African in Kenya better than the post-war labour policy. As we have already seen, African societies had their own forms of production and livelihood. Instead of developing these forms, the colonial government introduced labour policies which forced the Africans to go out for paid employment. Such policies fostered the attitude that employment could only be found away from home, on European plantations and in towns, where one received wages. A herdsman became a farm labourer and a fisherman became a domestic servant.

But initially the response of the African to this kind of economic argument was negative. Hence, severe measures had to be taken by the government, prompted by the European settlers, to obtain the African labour from their homes. Even in 1918–19 when there were widespread famine and several outbreaks of smallpox and other killing diseases throughout Kenya, the government was less concerned with improving food production in the rural areas than with recruiting labourers for the European farms. According to Ainsworth, at least 155 000 people died from famine in 1918. Many others died from smallpox and other diseases. But the Europeans had returned to their farms at the end of 1918, and therefore labour had to be recruited.

During the war, each European farmer had been allocated a location and he could therefore recruit directly through a chief. Such a system, though liked by the settlers, had become very unpopular with the Africans, as district reports testify. For example, the District Commissioner for Fort Hall writing in 1918, said, 'I would go as far to say that 75 per cent of the able-bodied population plus a large number of boys and women work more or less regularly with one master returning from time to time to their reserves to rest and cultivate. At any rate the labour recruiter has little or no chance in the reserve. He is viewed with suspicion by all and sundry, he is known to sell the people (in their own words) and is generally thoroughly unpopular.'

In another report, this time from Kisumu, we read that 'the conditions regarding recruiting of Labour in Kisumu are chaotic. The old slave trade could not have been worse than this present-day recruiting. Briefly, the recruiting agents bring in porters, some fall sick, some die by the way. Those sick on arrival are turned loose by the recruiters in Kisumu and left to starve.'

266

At Kisii, a European trader, Richard Gethin, formed a recruiting company with two other Europeans. He tells us in his memoirs that labour was 'forced out by the chiefs for the new farms and government departments . . . . the chiefs were frequently handed out cases of whisky and brandy for so many recruits produced. On arrival at Kisii they (were) placed in a hut under strong guard and in the morning those who had not escaped were tied together and sent to Kisumu by road.'

These contemporary records speak for themselves in the picture of degradation they portray.

No debate took place on the merits of African production as opposed to European plantations as had occurred in Tanganyika, for example. Instead, the Governor, General Northey and his chief lieutenant, Ainsworth, justified coercion of labour within the framework of the civilising mission. Cooperation had to be taught to 'unproductive idle natives'. To achieve this, several ordinances were passed: the Native Authority Ordinance, Amendment (1920), the Native Registration Ordinance, Amendment (1920), the Masters and Servants Ordinance Amendment (1919), and the Residents Labourers Ordinance (1918) and its Amendment (1920). Taxation was also increased to achieve the same objective.

The Native Authority Ordinance of 1912 was amended in 1920 to give powers to headmen and chiefs to recruit labour for public works. Under this amendment any man could be recruited to work for a period of up to sixty days in any one year, unless he had been fully occupied in some other occupation (which meant wage labour and not work on his farm) for three out of the previous twelve months. Those who could not produce evidence of having been so employed were given the choice of either doing sixty days' work in a public department or finding a private employer—the aim being to try and meet the serious shortage of labour on settler farms.

The Native Registration Ordinance of 1915, amended in 1920 introduced the obnoxious *kipande* system. Though passed in 1915, it had not been put into effect until after it was amended in 1920. Its purpose was to catch deserters, men who ran away from an employer. Each working man over the age of sixteen was to be fingerprinted so that he could be identified whenever he came out of the reserves. The operative clause in the amendment was contained in Section 14(1) and it read: 'Any magistrate, Justice of the Peace, employer or his agent on his farm or premises, or his agent, Registration officers or any other person authorised thereto by the Governor, may at any time demand from any native the production of the metal case issued to him under the Ordinance. Refusal to produce the metal case. . . shall be an offence.' The amendment thus curtailed personal freedom considerably. It also made desertion a criminal offence. And although Ainsworth had tried to curb the excesses of certain employers by introducing a Labour Inspectorate of about five through an amendment to the Master and Servants Ordinance, the kipande system remained one of the major grievances of the Africans until it was abolished after the Second World War.

Another measure introduced at this time intended to stimulate wage labour was the Residents Natives Ordinance to regulate 'the residence of Native families on farms and on areas not included in the native reserves.' The purpose of the law was to encourage 'natives to emigrate from the reserves and become labour tenants on European farms.' In short, the law introduced the squatter system which has persisted right up to the post-independence era.

In central Kenya and in Nyanza Province the new law merely legalised a process that had been going on since about 1907. Most of the new squatters were escaping from oppression in the reserves, where the chiefs were undoubtedly resorting to undesirable methods of keeping up the labour supply. Consequently, there was a growing feeling of discontent among the rural populations. On the other hand, the chiefs were disciplined through the levying of fines if they failed to provide adequate labour or if they failed to control dancing and drinking, regarded as signs of laziness, in their area. The chiefs retaliated by imposing fines on the people, to recoup themselves. Thus life in rural Kenya was deteriorating into a life of servitude for the majority of the inhabitants.

Nor did the chiefs or their retainers spare women and children. They provided cheap labour for European farms and public works.

Harry Thuku has described how women were recruited thus: 'A settler who wanted labour for his farm would write to the D.C. . . . The D.C. sent a letter to a chief or headman to supply such and such a number, and the chief in turn had his tribal retainers to carry out this business. They would simply go to people's houses—very often where there were beautiful women and daughters—and point out which were to come to work. Sometimes they had to work a distance from home, and the number of girls who got pregnant in this way was very great.'

The labour laws of 1918–1920 resulted in widespread discontent in the rural areas. It was this discontent in the rural areas which produced the radical political movements of 1921. The masses were being oppressed politically and economically and many of them decided to migrate to European farms to avoid further harassment. The movement from the Luo, Kamba and Kikuyu areas had begun before the First World War. For example, by 1915 the majority of labourers at the coast consisted of people from these areas. The silent protest was, however, greatest among the Kikuyu. By 1919 they had reached Kipsigis District, where they were welcomed as squatters by the local farmers. In October 1920, Kikuyu squatters were said to be settling on European farms 'right down the line from Lumbwa to Nairobi'.

268

Besides the oppressive labour laws, African wages were reduced by a third and direct taxation was increased to sixteen shillings a head. Kenya had become a 'white man's country'.

The rise of the new leadership among the Africans

Both the African and Indian communities reacted sharply to these discriminatory and oppressive policies. In order to protect their interests, the Africans formed their first political organisations almost simultaneously in Nyanza and Nairobi. It is important to note that both the Young Kavirondo Association, founded in 1921 by the former students of Maseno School such as the Rev Simeon Nyende, the Rev Ezekiel Apindi, Reuben Omulo, Jonathan Okwirri, Mathayo Otieno, Benjamin Owuor and Joel Owino, and the East African Association (known since 7 June 1921 as the Young Kikuyu Association in imitation of the Young Baganda Association), established in Nairobi on 10 July, 1921 by Harry Thuku and other Kikuyu and Kamba Muslims such as Mwalimu Hamisi, Abdulla Tairara bin Assuman and Mohamed Sheikh, were transtribal organisations. The former was dominated by the Luo and Luyia and operated in a rural environment, while the latter, though urban, was dominated by the Kikuyu. Harry Thuku, in particular, emphasised through action and in his speeches and writing the importance of inter-tribal unity. Present at the foundation meeting of the East African Association were, for example, Maasai representatives such as Molonket ole Sempele, Ndongongo ole Rimisek, T. Maitei ole Mootian and Haikoko, the chauffeur of Mr Jeevanjee; Kamba delegates: Ali Kironjo (Kilonzo), James Mwanthi, and Mohamed Sheikh; a few Luo delegates, for example, Samuel Okoth and a certain Abednego, as well as a few representatives from Nandi. 'What all of us wanted,' Harry Thuku has written, 'was to show people that we were all one family and that there was no difference between all the tribes of Kenya.'

This mass leadership was a new phenomenon in African societies and its rise at this time can be ascribed to the acquisition of western education and culture. The new leaders, in fact, represented the first generation of educated Africans. They were dissatisfied both with the traditional life and with the colonial practices, and they were determined to challenge both. The colonial authorities tended to view them as detribalised malcontents and therefore no attempt was made at this time to fit them into the political structure of the Colony. Because of this lack of sympathy, the young African leaders tended to ally themselves with Asians, who also constituted another group of the underprivileged. Harry Thuku's friendship with influential Asians such as Mangal Dass, M. A. Desai, Jeevanjee, Shams-ud-deen and Suleiman Virjee, can only be understood in this wider colonial context.

269

It was the fear of this alliance, as B. E. Kipkorir has shown in his important study of the *Alliance High School and The Origins of the Kenya African Elite 1926–1962*, which led the leaders of the Protestant Alliance to found the Alliance High School. The African-Asian Alliance, according to the missionaries, was inimical to the future of both the missionary and African interests. A new type of education which would create an African leadership independent of Asian control was necessary. In other words, the missionaries believed that future African leaders needed more and better education if they were to be independent of the Asians, and their only hope was that the new type of education would be controlled by the missionaries and not the government. And from this time onwards there was to be a struggle, described by J. Anderson in his book *The Struggle for the School*, between the missions and the government for the control of African societies centred on the control of schools. But the Africans, while demanding the establishment of more schools for their children, were increasingly insisting that they themselves should control their education.

'The first group of radical African political leadership was emasculated through this policy,' Dr Kipkorir has concluded. 'A new leadership, much more pliable, was to be created through a new system of education.'

The European-Indian struggle for the control of Kenya

The Indian opposition to European rule took the form of demanding equality of treatment for the two immigrant communities. They opposed the policies of residential and land segregation, and of restricting Indian immigration. They demanded direct and adequate representation on the Legislative Council, based on a common roll. They argued, with much justice, that separate representation would perpetuate and intensify racial antagonism. In these demands, they were supported by the Indian Government.

The Europeans defended their segregationist policies on the ground that neither the Indian nor any other section of the community—since they were not members of the ruling race—'have the same status or can claim the same rights as appertain to British colonists in a British Colony such as Kenya'. 'To grant the Indian more representation than is sufficient adequately to meet his own interests,' one of the settlers wrote, 'would automatically put the direction of the affairs of the colony into the hands of two antagonistic cultures.' They also added that the promotion of oriental influences would be detrimental to African interests. In this last contention, they were supported by the Church in Kenya and in Britain. If their requests were not granted, they warned, they would take the law into their own hands.

It was this European-Indian struggle for the possession of Kenya that constituted the so-called 'Indian question'. To solve it, a special conference was called in London by the then Colonial Secretary, the Duke of Devonshire, in 1923. Both Europeans and Indians were represented, and each tried to win sympathy by invoking the principle of safeguarding the interests of the only group that was not represented, the Africans.

The resulting White Paper satisfied neither of the protagonists. The European demand for self-government was rejected; the policies of residential segregation in townships and immigration restriction were to be abandoned; but the policy of land reservation in the Highlands was to continue. The Indians, on the other hand, were granted five representatives only in the Legislative Council, these to be elected on a communal roll. Thus the colonial government made it clear that Kenya would be surrendered neither to the Indians nor to the European settlers. It was to remain a responsibility of the Imperial Government, which would hold it in trust for its inhabitants. In the famous words of the White Paper: 'Primarily, Kenya is an African territory; and His Majesty's Government think it necessary to record their considered opinion that the interests of the African natives must be paramount, and that if, and when, those interests of the immigrant races should conflict the former should prevail. Obviously, the interests of other communities, European, Indian or Arab must be severally safeguarded . . . But in the administration of Kenya His Majesty's Government regard themselves as exercising a trust on behalf of the African population, and they are unable to delegate or share this trust, the object of which may be defined as the protection and advancement of the native races.'

In trying to solve one form of racial conflict, the White Paper in effect created a more serious form in proclaiming the policy of 'the paramountcy of native interests'.

The age of separate development, 1923 to 1952

The major challenge facing Kenya during this period was the future of its tri-racial population, European, Indian and African. Had one community to advance at the expense of the others? Were the Indians to be squeezed out by the other two groups? Or could Kenya develop an harmonious amalgam where each community would be complementary to its fellows and all three could render their appropriate contribution to the well-being of the social whole? These are some of the basic questions that policy-makers had to bear in mind constantly.

The theory of separate development was a logical sequel to the policy of land reservation on racial and tribal lines. As early as 1905, the imperial government had recognised the principle of 'reserves for natives', and in

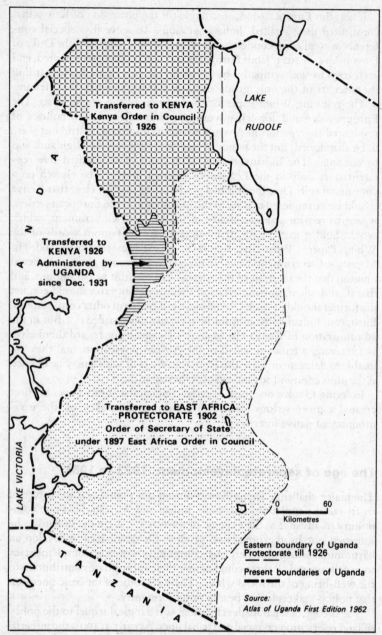

Figure 25 The evolution of the western boundary of Kenya

the following year, five of these were created. But since it was still possible for land in the Reserves to be alienated, the Africans naturally felt apprehensive over their land. Although the Crown Lands Ordinance of 1915 gave statutory recognition to 'native' Reserves, it also increased the feeling of insecurity and unrest among the Africans by turning them into tenants-at-will of the Crown, who could be dispossessed at any time. In order to allay this feeling of insecurity, the government finally agreed in October 1926 to delimit the reserves. The boundaries of twenty-three of them were gazetted, and they could be alienated only by the local government with the consent of the Secretary of State for the Colonies.

But it was evident that in many areas, the land set aside would not be adequate for the future needs of the Africans. Indeed, several of these reserves were already over-populated. The population density in Kiambu, for instance, was about 154 to the square km in 1919; in Nyeri and Fort Hall, it was about 72 per square km; in central Nyanza about 63; and in Bunyore location in north Nyanza, it had reached 386. On the other hand, the average European farmer occupied about 200 hectares of land in 1925 and in the whole of the 'White Highlands' only 9 per cent of occupied land was under cultivation. Thus even as early as 1926, the reserves were already inadequate; and with the increase in African population, the position was bound to deteriorate.

Furthermore, the discovery of gold in western Kenya in 1931 soon demonstrated to the African the futility of placing faith in legislation which could easily be altered by a body on which they were not represented. The Native Lands Trust Ordinance of 1930 was hurriedly amended in 1932 in order to exclude from the Reserves the land containing minerals. To the question of the inadequacy of the 'native' Reserves was thus added the problem of their security. Land was still a major political and radial issue in Kenya.

In April 1932, the Secretary of State for the Colonies appointed a Commission to investigate certain matters concerning land problems in Kenya. In particular, the Commission was:

'(a) To consider the needs of the native population, present and prospective, with respect to land, whether to be held on tribal or individual tenure . . .

 (b) To define the area, generally known as the Highland, within which persons of European descent are to have a privileged position in accordance with the White Paper of 1923.'

The chairman of the Commission was Sir W. Morris Carter, and its report was published in May 1934.

Undoubtedly, the report gave great satisfaction to the European settlers; 414 398 square km of good land were to be reserved exclusively and permanently for the European settlers. In 1939 the boundaries of the White Highlands were gazetted. Also, the Reserves, which were left

273

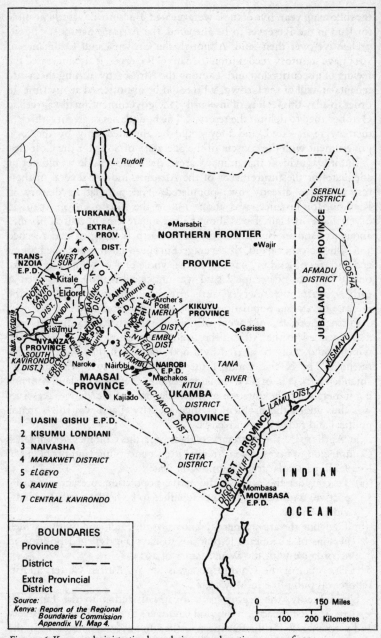

Figure 26 Kenya: administrative boundaries—proclamation no. 54 of 1924

substantially as they were before 1934, were to cease to be designated as Crown Land, and were to be known as Native Lands. In other words, the Commission's recommendations, which were accepted by the British Government, implied that Kenya was to be partitioned into two racial blocs, African and European. In the African sector, all economic, social and political developments were to be conducted on tribal lines. Racialism and tribalism thus became institutionalised.

What did the British and colonial Governments have in mind in advocating the policy of separate territorial development? Were they thinking of transferring political power to Africans in their areas? Or was it rather to be what has been called 'the policy of racial separation and guardianship of white over the natives'? A brief review of the facts would show that it was the latter.

The 1923 White Paper had declared that Kenya was primarily an African country. This declaration posed the question: Was Kenya to be developed largely by the Africans? The European settlers were already demanding that white settlement must be the economic backbone of the colony. On the other hand, West African countries and Uganda were being developed by the Africans themselves under the guidance of a small number of government officials and a small number of traders and companies. At the other extreme, there was the case of South Africa, where the African had been deprived of the bulk of the land and had by force of circumstances been driven to become largely a wage earner in mining or on European land. Which of these policies was to apply in Kenya?

It was argued that neither alternative suited Kenya. Instead, the 'dual policy', that is, complementary development of non-native and native production, was recommended. Mr L. S. Amery, when Colonial Secretary, defined the dual policy as 'a policy which recognises our trusteeship both to the native population—whom we had found on the spot and whom it was our duty to bring forward and develop in every possible way—but also our trusteeship to humanity at large for the fullest development of those territories and towards those in particular of our own race who had undertaken the task of helping forward that development'. This was tantamount to a rejection of the 1923 paramountcy policy.

Lord Delamere, the Kenya European leader, contended that the corollary to the dual policy must be separate development. And the latter, according to him, was 'based on a perfectly rational desire to protect a civilised standard of living from an economic competitor on a lower grade of life'.

Although in theory both African and non-African production were to be encouraged, in actual fact only European production was promoted in Kenya. A prospective European farmer had adequate provision made for training and he could obtain low interest loans from the Land Bank and direct grants for the purchase of capital farming equipment. Additional aid to European farmers was provided by government-sponsored agricultural research, maize and wheat subsidies, government-sponsored marketing schemes and transport facilities.

It is worth noting that Uganda's exports in 1934, for instance, amounted to £3¾ million, while the Kenyan exports amounted to less than £2 million. It is also worth remarking that of Uganda's exports more than £3 million came from African agriculture, mainly cotton, while in Kenya not more than £300 000 worth of exports came from African production, and more than half of these from the export of hides. Would it not have paid Kenya from a purely business point of view to concentrate on stimulating African production for export? And even if the government was committed to the dual policy, it would still have paid the country to accept the consequences of such a policy with the promotion of balanced development both African and European. But this did not happen.

The racial approach which we have noticed in the economic field also applied to the provision of social services. Medical services, education and even sports were organised on strict racial lines, with the Europeans always getting the best services, the Indians the second best and the Africans having to do with whatever was left over. In 1938, for example, an Education Department memorandum said the aim of European education was 'to provide a good general education for all children who do not attend private schools between the ages of six and sixteen years'. The aim of Indian education was 'to provide an eight years' course of primary education—for all children of six years of age and over'. In the case of the Africans, the memorandum reiterated the policy first enunciated by the Colonial Secretary in a Command Paper in 1925, which said that 'the first task of (African) education is to raise the standard alike of character and efficiency of the bulk of the people, but provision must also be made for the training of those who are required to fill posts in the administrative and technical services, as well as those who as chiefs will occupy positions of exceptional trust and responsibility'. The emphasis in African education on producing clerks and other junior officials for the colonial administration is evident.

The same memorandum estimated that only about 12⅓ per cent of African children of school age were receiving any education at all. Of this number, 96 983 were in sub-elementary and elementary schools, 3 059 in primary, and 176 in junior secondary schools. There was no African attending a college or a university. Thus by 1938 only the fringe of the problem of African education had been touched. By contrast there were already several well-established and well-equipped secondary schools for Europeans and every year a number of students from these schools went to British universities on government bursaries.

Such discrimination might have been defensible if the Europeans were willing to tax themselves in order to pay for these expensive social services. The fact is that, although most of these services were provided from the central government funds, the Europeans were throughout this period very reluctant to tax themselves. If we take education again, we find that in the case of Africans the Local Native Councils paid for much of this education levying special education rates to run elementary schools and to subsidise primary schools. This was necessary because they received very little in direct grants from central funds. Successive annual reports show that the amount spent on education from central funds per head of the African population fell between 1932 (the first year in which Arab figures were separated from African) and 1936:

1932	64 cents	1935	50 cents
1933	50 cents	1936	44 cents
1934	50 cents		

For Europeans, the figures for 1929 and 1930 were 852 and 800 shillings respectively.

Looking at the budgets of the local authorities, through which most of the social services were provided, it is evident that whereas the Local Native Councils rapidly and willingly assumed major finanical responsibilities, the European District Councils rapidly became, in the words of a Commissioner for Local Government, 'little more than agents for the expenditure of government funds'. In 1945, for instance, 97 per cent of all European District Council Revenue came from government and military grants, while of the Local Native Council revenue only one-seventh came from the government and one-third came from rates on the people.

Nor was it true, as many Europeans contended, that most of the central funds came from non-African sources. The principal source of central government revenue was taxation. Between 1925 and 1936, for example, taxation accounted for between 71 and 77 per cent of the net revenue. The two principal items of taxation were Customs Import Duties and African Hut and Poll Tax, which between them accounted for over 70 per cent of the total yield of taxation. The yield from the two items from 1925 to 1936 was as follows:

	Customs Import Duties	African Hut and Poll Tax
1925	£679 727	£537 478
1926	£741 374	£558 044
1927	£830 550	£570 783

	Customs Import Duties	African Hut and Poll Tax
1928	£915 282	£564 405
1929	£949 725	£539 641
1930	£815 286	£591 424
1931	£698 584	£530 877
1932	£597 262	£515 277
1933	£581 770	£557 791
1934	£611 606	£514 480
1935	£690 380	£502 302
1936	£775 010	£537 219

On top of direct taxation, it should be remembered that the African paid indirect taxation, which must have increased as he became more familiar with and dependent upon imported goods. It is therefore evident that the African community was not only paying more taxation in proportion to their resources than the other communities in Kenya, but also that much of the revenue derived from them was being diverted to non-African services.

This was in fact the conclusion of Lord Moyne, who made an exhaustive examination of the financial situation of Kenya in 1932. He found, for instance, that since 1926 the Local Native Councils had voted £33 381 for the provision of school buildings to make up for the insufficiency of government grants, 'although accommodation on a very generous scale has quite properly been found entirely from Central funds for the school buildings of the European and Indian communities'. He also noticed similar anomalies in the case of road, medical and agricultural grants. 'On examining the general structure of these Colonial services,' he concluded, 'and the proportion of cost due to the provision of such convenience as motor roads, municipal services, comparing also the services in settled areas with those provided in neighbouring areas where European interests are less dominant, I have formed the opinion that in the development of the undivided or colonial services in Kenya the prevailing bias has been towards the convenience of a civilisation in which the native so far shares little of direct advantages.'

The theory of separate development faced its greatest challenge in the political field. It was generally assumed that for many generations the European element must have a major influence in the direction of the government and that the proper line for African political advance was in local government. The African, in other words, was to be restricted to local and tribal politics. But the system of local government itself had to conform with the theory of separate development. Consequently, three different types emerged, one for the European settled areas, one for the African Reserves and one for the urban areas.

Apart from the District Road Boards, there were no proper local government bodies in the 'White Highlands' until 1929. Before that date, in 1926, Sir Edward Grigg had appointed a Commission of Inquiry under Mr Justice Feetham, a former Town Clerk of Johannesburg and a member of the 1915 South African Local Government Commission 'to make recommendations as to the establishment or extension of Local Government' in the settled areas and the municipalities.

The Commission's report endorsed the view that local government in Kenya should be developed along racial lines. It recommended that seven European District Councils should be established. Only six councils (Nakuru, Uasin Gishu, Nairobi, Kisumu-Londiani, Naivasha and Trans-Nzoia) were established in 1929 to 1930, after the passing of the Local Government (District Councils) Ordinance in 1928. The seventh, the Aberdare District Council, was set up much later in January 1939.

As local authorities they were a dismal failure. Although empowered under the law to impose rates, they did not do so except for a specific purpose, such as a hospital. Up to 1945 they failed to provide social services for over half a million Africans who lived in the settled areas. As the Europeans gradually lost political power at the centre after 1952, they fell back on these councils, which became a kind of political citadel.

The development of local government in the towns was also bedevilled by the theory of separate development. Apart from the Swahili towns at the coast, urbanism was a new phenomenon in Kenya and was a direct consequence of European settlement and Indian commercial activities. Africans might work in the new towns but they were not expected to live in them. The planning and development of all Kenya's towns during this period was based on the assumption that the African workers in the towns were sojourners who could be housed in periurban shanty settlements. Urban local government was therefore controlled by the European.

Nairobi, for example, which had been declared a township in 1903 and became a municipality on 15 July 1919, was largely controlled by a European-dominated council which had been instituted in 1928. In a council of twenty, the Indians had seven representatives and the rest were Europeans. Although Africans were in the majority in the town, they had no direct voice in the affairs of the Nairobi Council until 1946. The result was a proliferation of tribal welfare associations, especially in the 1930s. Since there was little hope of obtaining reasonable social services from the council, the Africans turned to self-help schemes organised on a tribal basis. In 1936, for example, the Commissioner for Local Government said in his annual report that 'Native Associations based on districts are increasing and are, on the whole, well-organised and useful.' These associations were also the channels for the expression

279

of African opinion, and they were to prove useful during the post-1945 period in the mobilisation of nationalist forces.

Because of the long history of Mombasa and the high degree of racial admixture that had taken place, the bitterness which characterised the politics of Nairobi was lacking. Otherwise, the pattern here as in other Kenya towns such as Nakuru, Kisumu, Eldoret, Kitale, Nyeri, Nanyuki and Thika, was similar to that of Nairobi. In all these towns, there were definite segregationist policies in planning residential areas.

The age of progress, 1923 to 1940

Considering the colonial period and looking at developments in the African areas, it is evident that the age of separate development over-lapped with the age of progress. The political upheavals of 1921–22 caused the Government to review its policy of political control. It was now obvious that the 'mission boys' were an important threat to the system of native authority. In an effort to contain the leaders of the young associations, the colonial government decided to establish the Local Native Councils in 1925, where the District Commissioners, the chiefs and the elders could sit together with the radical and young leaders of the associations. They were to enable so-called responsible Africans to express their views constructively and to participate in the development of their areas. They were also intended to kill any trans-tribal associations, since all communication with the Government was to be sent through the District Commissioners, who were the ex-officio presidents of these councils. In the words of the 1924 Native Affairs Department Report, 'the Councils ... should go far towards countering any mischievous tendencies which might develop in native political societies, for representations made to government by the latter would in the ordinary course be referred to the former in the first instance.'

African politicians, on the other hand, saw in the new councils a useful forum for ventilating their grievances. They were also keen to use these councils for the improvement of their areas and individual members. Political organisations such as the Kavirondo Taxpayers' and Welfare Association and the Kikuyu Central Association enthusi-astically sponsored candidates for these councils, at least initially.

This desire for progress reflected in the enlightened policies of these councils was part of a general awakening on the part of many Africans in Kenya at this time to the advantages of having western education and culture. Self-improvement based on the acquisition of western education and economic power became the goal of the new leaders. The failure of the 1921–22 movements had convinced them that the European could only be fought successfully with his own tools—

280

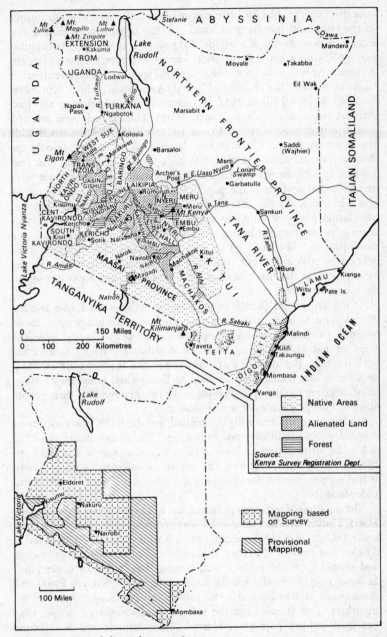

Figure 27 Native and alienated areas 1938

Within the map:

ABYSSINIA

UGANDA

EXTENSION FROM UGANDA

NORTHERN FRONTIER PROVINCE

ITALIAN SOMALILAND

Mt Zulia
Mt Mogillo
Mt Lubur
Mt Zingote
Kakuma

L. Stefanie

R. Dawa
Mandera

Lake Rudolf

Moyale
Takabba

Eil Wak

Lodwar

Napao Pass
Turkana
Ngabotok

Marsabit

Saddi (Wajhier)

WEST SUK
Kolosia
Kitale
Marakwet
Barsaloi
Merti
Lorian Swamp

Mt Elgon

TRANS NZOIA

NORTH KAVI-RONDO

UASIN GISHU
Archer's Post
R.E. Uaso Nyiro
Garbatulla

Kisumu

CENT KAVIRONDO

Kericho

SOUTH KAVIRONDO

Kisii

KERICHO
Sotik

LAIKIPIA
Rumuruti

NYERI

MERU
Meru

R. Tana
Sankuri

TANA RIVER

Naivasha
EMBU
Embu

KIAMBU
KIMBU

Nairobi

MAASAI
Narok

PROVINCE

Magadi

KITUI

Machakos
Kitui

MACHAKOS
R. Athi
Bura

LAMU
Kianga

Witu
Pate Is.

TANGANYIKA TERRITORY

Natron

Mt Kilimanjaro

R. Sabaki

DIGO
KILIFI

Malindi
Kilifi
Takaungu

TEITA
Taveta

Mombasa

INDIAN OCEAN

Vanga

Lake Victoria Nyanza

R. Amala

0   150 Miles
0 100   200 Kilometres

Native Areas

Alienated Land

Forest

Source:
Kenya Survey Registration Dept.

Lake Rudolf

Eldoret

Kisumu

Nakuru

Nairobi

Lake Victoria

Mombasa

100 Miles

Mapping based on Survey

Provisional Mapping

education and wealth. An examination of the activities and programmes of the two most important African political organisations during the inter-war period—the Kavirondo Taxpayers' and Welfare Association and the Kikuyu Central Association—reveal that even they were largely welfare organisations concerned with the personal improvement of their members. The Kikuyu Central Association which had been founded in Fort Hall in 1924 as a successor organisation to the East African Association, whose leader, Harry Thuku, had been arrested and deported to Kismayu in March 1922, was largely concerned with the appointment of a 'paramount learned chief', decent burials for Africans, sanitary inspection of their huts, the setting up of at least one hospital in each district and the building of more schools for their boys and girls. An analysis of the pages of *Muigwithania* (the 'Mediator' or the 'Conciliator'), the official organ of the KCA, reveals that the association put most emphasis on development. Sentences like 'Let us learn good farming, tailoring, grinding maize flour', 'Let us keep our houses clean', 'We must go to school and build more schools, since schools are the only light' appeared in practically every issue of the newspaper. As the first editor of *Muigwithania*, Jomo Kenyatta wrote in one of the issues:

'If Kikuyu people (which in this context includes the Embu and the Meru) want to be an important tribe, they must be industrious, trust-worthy, patient, happy and cooperate as Europeans do. An educated tribe or nation defeats an uneducated tribe or nation. You better swallow that. Remember that other tribes like the Baganda are busy in farming and taking their children to Europe and when they return, they are going to take up high posts in the country and help their people since in Europe people are well educated.'

Bildad Kaggia has recently contended that the KCA was a society of selected people with no mass following. 'The main objectives of the KCA,' he writes, 'were to demand fairer treatment for the Kikuyu from the British and to negotiate the return of alienated Kikuyu lands. It had no programme for changing the *status quo* or even for attaining independence.'

The question of self-improvement was to cause a major split between Harry Thuku, who had returned from detention in December 1930, and other leaders of KCA, especially Jesse Kariuki and Joseph Kangethe. Thuku had insisted that they should 'stop being full-time politicians and should combine politics with having their farms or other jobs'. In April 1935, he finally left the KCA to found the Kikuyu Provincial Association in which he tried to implement his theory. Most of the members were farmers and the rest were self-employed people who practised politics part-time. Harry Thuku himself was a full-time large-scale farmer and only a part-time politician.

As Dr Kipkorir's study has shown, most of the key positions were occupied by the 'improved', progressive Africans during the inter-war period. The majority of the present-day Kenya élite is rooted in these families, and their values and inspirations have not altered very much. The Aworis and the Ngairas of western Kenya, the Mwendwas of Ukambani, the Njiris, Waiyakis and Koinanges of Central Province and the Boits of Nandi are products of the age of improvement.

This marked the second phase of collaboration, a kind of alliance for progress between the colonial paternalists and the black collaborators, which was extended to the intermediate as well as to the bottom cadres in the new order. Much of the credit for any improvement to the status of the African during the colonial period should go to these progressive collaborators.

Towards a crisis, 1940 to 1952

Just as the First World War had precipitated a political crisis in Kenya, so did the Second World War. With the imminent threat of Italian invasion from Somaliland, a total ban was placed on African political activity. Political organisations which had emerged in the 1930s in different parts of the country—the Ukamba Members Association, the Taita Hills Association, the North Kavirondo Central Association— as well as the old Kikuyu Central Association were proscribed, and their leaders detained at Kapenguria.

The Europeans were again quick to exploit a war situation to consolidate their position. Their influence on the Executive Council and on the various committees and statutory boards increased enormously. Forced labour for Africans was introduced on European farms. In March 1943 some 16 000 conscripted Africans were in employment. Of these, about three-quarters were employed on private undertakings. When questions were asked as to how coffee and tea plantations came to be considered 'essential undertakings' for which labour might be conscripted, the Secretary of State replied that:

'The main object in declaring these two important industries in Kenya to be essential undertakings was in order that they might be maintained in operation on a scale which would enable the Colony to play its part in meeting the food supply requirements of the United Nations, including those of the large numbers of refugees and prisoners in East Africa.'

For this conscript labour a minimum wage of eight to ten shillings was laid down, or nine to twelve shillings for long periods of service.

In June 1943 the Agricultural Production and Settlement Board was divided into two sections, an Agricultural Production Section to carry on the work of organising agricultural production in the war effort and a Settlement Section 'to encourage and plan for increased white settlement in the Colony'. The membership of this Settlement Section consisted of Major Cavendish-Bentinck as chairman, two officials and fourteen European 'unofficial residents'.

At the end of the war, Sir Philip Mitchell introduced a 'membership' system which meant that the European unofficial members of the Executive Council could now be given portfolios. And the first to be given to European settlers (Agriculture and Local Government, to Cavendish-Bentinck and C. E. Mortimer respectively) were those which affected the Africans most intimately.

The failure of self-improvement as a political goal

The new political gains by the Europeans were being acquired in a radically changed environment. The new African leaders—most of them the products of the new education policy initiated in 1926—were beginning to realise that the policy of self-improvement was not enough. Even the few of them who had attained high economic and educational standards were still looked down upon by the Europeans. The result was a widespread disillusionment and bitterness among the new leaders such as Eliud Mathu, James Gichuru, B. A. Ohanga, W. W. Awori, J. D. Otiende, F. W. Odede and Tom Mbotela.

Mathu's background and aspirations may be regarded as typical of the new leadership that was emerging in the 1940s. He was born at Riruta in Kiambu in 1910. His father was a medicine man and his mother a Christian. He attended Protestant mission schools in Kenya, first at Riruta and later at the Church of Scotland Mission at Kikuyu and at Alliance High School. He then went to Fort Hare University in South Africa and thence to Balliol College, Oxford, where he obtained a diploma in education. As a result of this training he, like many of his colleagues, came to believe in a rational and constitutional approach to problems. The new leaders who had successfully acquired western culture now felt that they were the living proof—if any were needed—that the African could be civilised and could successfully compete with the white man in the acquisition of western education. So they demanded not less but more western culture for the Africans. As Mathu stated in the Legislative Council on 21 February 1952:

'If there is a capacity for the African to absorb the new institutions from Britain and if the African absorbed the British way of life, why take it gradually? I submit that an African has absorbed it, he has absorbed more than any other people I know in the world in 50 years . . . It has taken 2 000 years to bring the British people to the standard they are now in many ways. Now for goodness sake do not tell us it will take 2 000 years.'

284

The new leaders had thus adopted western values and standards of living, and these standards became the measure of their achievement, with white men acting as their reference group.

On his return from England, Mathu, like most other educated Africans, became a teacher. He began his career at his old school, Alliance High School, and in 1934 while there he founded the first Kenya African Teachers' Union. In 1943, he resigned from his post and went to Dagoreti High School as principal. On 5 October 1944, he was nominated as the first African unofficial member of the Legislative Council, a position he was to occupy until 1957, when he was defeated in the first direct African elections.

The decision to nominate an African to the Legislative Council had been made in an effort to channel the emergent voice of African nationalism toward a support of the administration. All African political organisations, with the exception of the Kavirondo Taxpayers' and Welfare Association and the Kikuyu Provincial Association, had been proscribed in 1940. In order to control the new leaders, it was necessary to do what the government had done in 1925, that is, to give an opportunity for so-called moderate African voice to be heard. According to the system introduced by Governor Henry Moore, each Local Native Council had to recommend three names to the Governor, who had to choose one person to represent all Africans. In 1947 a second African, B. Apolo Ohanga was appointed in the same way to replace L. J. Beecher, Bishop of Mombasa, who, with Mathu, had represented African interests. In the following year, the number of African members (all nominated and unofficial) was raised to four, while the Europeans had eleven elected members. In 1952 the African unofficial representation was increased to six, and Mathu was appointed to the Executive Council.

On the nomination of Mathu to the Legislative Council, as the sole African, there was felt a need to found a colony-wide organisation to give him support. A meeting was convened in October which led to the founding of the Kenya African Union—'the first sustained effort of the Africans to create a congress organisation to cover the Africans of the whole colony and . . . an important landmark in the political evolution of the Africans in Kenya', to use the words of F. D. Corfield. The founding members who met in Thuku's shop in Nairobi included the following people: Mathu, Gichuru, Otiende, Jonathan Njoroge, John Kebaso, Henry Mwaniki, Francis Khamisi, Kamau Njoroge, Albert Awino, S. Otieno Josiah, J. Jeremiah, E. K. Binns, Simeon Mulandi, Ambrose Ofafa, Mucohi Gikonyo, S. B. Kackoyo and Harry Thuku, who was elected the Union's first President.

The aims and objects of the organisation were (i) to unite the African people toward an African nation and (ii) to foster the social, economic, and political interests of the Africans. Political independence in the foreseeable future was not considered as a practical goal. Despite the KAU's nationalist aims, its character was clearly reformist. Any changes were to be carried out from within and through the existing institutions of government.

But in spite of such a moderate programme, the colonial government felt uneasy about the KAU and in November, on the advice of the Governor, its name was altered to the Kenya African Study Union (KASU), which implied that its chief purpose was to instruct the people on public affairs, as a kind of debating society.

The emergence of radical politics

Although Harry Thuku was a respectable father-figure, he was also the president of the Kikuyu Provincial Association, which required all its members to pledge loyalty to the British Crown and to the established government. They were 'bound to do nothing which is not constitutional according to the British traditions or do anything which is calculated to disturb the peace, good order and Government'. Any political organisation he led was not likely, therefore, to fight seriously for the liberation of the country from colonial rule.

At the first delegates' conference in 1945 he was replaced by James Gichuru, who immediately began a transformation of the organisation from a government-sanctioned study union to a political party. In February 1946 this change was announced by dropping the 'study' from the title of the organisation which became once more the KAU. In the same year Jomo Kenyatta returned from Britain, and in June of the following year he took over from Gichuru as KAU president.

As we have already seen, KASU was formed by a few educated Africans in and around Nairobi to advise Mathu on various problems affecting the lives of Africans. These educated Africans largely operated as individuals and had no mass following. The age of the 'party boss' in Kenya politics had not yet arrived. Under the leadership of Kenyatta (1947–52) the party rapidly developed into a mass political movement, whose membership was opened to the workers, the uneducated and ex-soldiers.

A growing friction soon developed within the organisation between the moderates and the radicals. The moderates, who were led by Mathu and Tom Mbotela, believed in effecting changes through constitutional means. They used rational arguments with the colonial power and appealed to their followers to adopt a rational and peaceful approach to their problems. Tom Mbotela's decision to translate Tom Paine's *The Rights of Man* into Kiswahili, for instance, was symptomatic of this attitude. They therefore opposed certain methods advocated by the

286

militants. For example, in March 1950, they dissociated KAU from the boycott that was planned by Fred Kubai and his East African Trades Union Congress of the civic celebrations to be held during the visit of the Duke of Gloucester in connection with the elevation of Nairobi to the status of a city.

The moderates and the militants also differed on the question of the tribal composition of the Executive Committee and the relationship between the organisation and the Asians. The radical element of the KAU was growing rapidly, and most of its members were Kikuyu. As a result there developed a Kikuyu domination of the Executive Committee. W. W. W. Awori, a Legislative Council representative from western Kenya, for instance, resigned as editor of the organisation's newspaper, *Sauti ya Mwafrika* (Voice of the African) in protest against this domination. Mathu and Mbotela argued that the organisation's leadership had to remain multi-tribal.

This conflict reached its climax in 1951. The Nairobi branch of the KAU had been captured by the radicals in June of that year. The officials, consisting of F. Kubai (chairman), B. M. Kaggia (general secretary) and Paul Ngei (assistant secretary), were demanding that a delegates' conference be convened with the express purpose of getting rid of the moderate elements from the party executive. As Kaggia has explained in his *Autobiography*, they were particularly keen to get rid of Mbotela by abolishing the post of vice-president of the party (a tactic which was later to be used by the moderates in KANU to get rid of Odinga, Kaggia and other radicals from the party in 1966).

But the plans of the radicals were frustrated by Kenyatta, who insisted that they must not turn KAU into a Kikuyu union. The secretary-general of the party, he suggested, should come from Nyanza and other parts of the country should also be represented on the Executive Committee. Hence, J. D. Otiende was elected secretary-general, with P. J. Ngei as his assistant; and Mr H. Nangurai, from Narok, was elected treasurer.

The radicals, including Kenyatta, were also co-operating with the East African Indian Congress arguing that the Afro-Asian alliance would strengthen the African case against the imperialists. The moderates, led by Mathu, opposed this. They argued that the Indians were as guilty as the Europeans of exploiting the African and therefore any political alliance with them, however expedient, was wrong in principle.

But by this time the radicals, who were demanding complete liberation, had taken over the movement, and the small original group of educated gentlemen who still remained in KAU had to toe the line. But the majority of educated Africans in the country supported the moderates, and it is therefore not surprising that they did not participate in the 'Mau Mau' uprising.

Mau Mau revolt

No detailed historical study of the uprising has yet been undertaken. But there are, however, several theories which have been advanced by various writers to account for the origin of the movement. The colonial historians have tended to accept the conspiracy theory of history, which views Mau Mau as a conspiracy hatched out by a few power-hungry individuals, most of them Kikuyu. L. S. B. Leakey and Bishop Carey have interpreted Mau Mau as a religious movement. Still others, including Waruhiu Itote ('General China'), Rosberg and Nottingham and J. M. Kariuki, have, surprisingly, accepted Corfield's interpretation that 'Mau Mau . . . was the . . . manifestation of a . . . nationalistic revolutionary movement . . . the *evolutionary* child of . . . the Kikuyu Association.' They regard Mau Mau as a nationalist movement which aimed at political independence. Kaggia has recently joined this group. He defines Mau Mau as an 'organisation formed by KAU militants who had lost faith in constitutional methods of fighting for independence'. There is also the economic interpretation which maintains that Mau Mau broke out as a result of the misery, want and poverty of the oppressed Africans, especially the Kikuyu. A New Zealand historian, M. P. K. Sorrenson, has argued in his book, *Land Reform in the Kikuyu Country*, that Mau Mau was in fact a civil war in Kikuyuland between the 'haves' and the 'have-nots'. He points out, for example, 'that Mau Mau activists were to a considerable extent landless or the owners of small areas of land', while 'the active loyalists were, on the whole, from "the landed and wealthy classes".' Sorrenson's theory ties in with the explanation given by D. L. Barnett and Karari Njama in *Mau Mau from Within* as well as by Oginga Odinga in *Not Yet Uhuru*, that Mau Mau was 'a peasants' revolt', caused by agrarian grievances.

In our attempts to provide a more convincing interpretation of the causes of this important movement, it may be beneficial to adopt the approach of George Rude in his study of *The Crowd in the French Revolution*. We need a more detailed study of the 'people' or the 'heroes' who participated in the Mau Mau revolt than the current superficial distinction between the literate and the illiterate participants or the forest fighters and the detainees.

Mau Mau is likely to be explained if we accept that there were, in effect, several revolutions taking place simultaneously. For example, there was the rise of the petty bourgeois—the products of 'the improvement associations' of the 1920s and 1930s—who wanted more political power and more wealth, but in a colonial situation which safeguarded their interests. There was also the emerging élite symbolised by people like Mathu, who wanted power in an independent Kenya at some future date. Furthermore, there was the peasant's revolution represented by the forest fighters and the workers' revolution championed by the trade unionists.

The 'Mau Mau crowd' should therefore be broken down into different categories. Each category had distinctive characteristics, needs and wants, although they all formed a united front in the revolution. Each section of the 'crowd' had its own grievances and did not simply ally with 'the emerging bourgeois'. We should therefore study the size of each group, its grievances and the development of events within each section. The fact that it is now common to talk about 'the revolution betrayed', to borrow the title of one of Trotsky's books on the Russian Revolution, suggests that the aspirations of some sections of the 'crowd' have not been fulfilled.

Already a useful start has been made by Kaggia in his attempt to explain the relationship between KAU and Mau Mau. He maintains vehemently that Mau Mau leaders like himself simply hid under the umbrella of KAU, whose leaders, including the president, knew nothing of Mau Mau. The only links between the two executive committees (KAU Executive and Mau Mau Central Committee) were Kaggia and Kubai.

The period of reconciliation, 1952 to 1963

The declaration of the state of emergency in 1952 meant, in effect, that the policy of separate development had failed. It also meant that the British policy of devolving responsibility upon the people in the colony, i.e. upon the colonial officials and the settlers, had failed. An alternative policy had to be found.

The years between 1952 and 1960 are therefore crucial for a proper understanding of post-independence Kenya. A new Kenya society had to be built. But one cannot build a new society on injustice. There was a long heritage of discrimination to contend with and there was the bitterness engendered by the Mau Mau rebellion. Was reconciliation between the races possible?

In working out the new policy, it was necessary for the Colonial Office to play a more dominant role than would have been the case otherwise. In the eyes of the Africans, the colonial government had been discredited, and there was little hope that any agreement could be worked out. Initiative therefore reverted to the Colonial Secretary. In 1954, 1957 and 1960, successive Secretaries of State for the Colonies promulgated new constitutions for Kenya (the Lyttleton, the Lennox-Boyd and the Macleod constitutions). All three were multi-racial in form. Britain, in deference to the wishes of the white settlers, maintained that parliamentary democracy could not work in the plural societies of Kenya, Tanganyika, and central Africa, if civilised standards were to be kept. 'Multi-racialism' or 'partnership' was therefore evolved as the system of government suitable for these areas.

To the Africans, accepting the policy of 'multi-racialism' meant accepting the injustices of the past. They wanted the government to open up the chances of a decent life for their people. This meant land redistribution, expansion of African education, making available job opportunities for Africans, etc. In short, the African leaders demanded that their people be given a chance to attain equality. To achieve this, 'non-racial' rather than 'multi-racial' policies were necessary.

What is important to remember is that the shock of 'Mau Mau' had created the right atmosphere in that the imperial power was now willing to talk with the African leaders. In the course of these dialogues, power shifted from the Europeans to the Africans. The first African Minister, Mr B. A. Ohanga, was appointed in 1954. And in the 1960 constitution the majority of Ministers were African.

But it would be misleading to give the impression that after 1952 everything else simply followed. With the political leaders of the Africans detained, with the failure of the policy of 'association' and with the Emergency continuing, the Africans had to find a way of continuing the struggle under these difficult situations. Bitter constitutional battles were fought in Kenya and London. And the fact that the Africans were, by 1960, victorious says much for the dedication and tactics of their leaders during these eight difficult years.

African political parties, which had been prohibited since 1953, were again allowed except in the Central Province in mid-1955. But they could be formed only on a district basis; and the government declared that such district organisations would later be allowed to join together in some form of loose organisation. In December, this policy was challenged by Mr C. M. G. Argwings-Kodhek, the first African lawyer in Kenya. He formed in Nairobi a body called the Kenya African National Congress, which declared that the government's policy of limiting associations to the district level would encourage tribal feeling and prevent the development of any national sense. The government refused to register it, and Kodhek had to content himself with a Nairobi Congress.

The only body which could speak for the Africans across the colony was the Kenya Federation of Labour. Under the youthful though vigorous leadership of its general secretary, Mr T. J. Mboya, the federation operated to a large extent as a political movement. Its impact was soon felt throughout the country. In February 1956 the government threatened to proscribe the KFL if it did not stop its political activities. Indeed, the federation was saved only by the intervention on its behalf with the Kenya Government of the British Trades Union Congress.

Political activities in Kenya were given a new fillip by the first African election, on a limited franchise, which took place in March 1957. Seven Africans were elected to the Legislative Council. In October of the same year, the Lennox-Boyd constitution added to the Africans six more seats, thus bringing them to parity with the elected Europeans. The new constitution also gave them a second Ministry. In order to introduce a multi-racial sense of representation, provision was made in the new constitution for specially elected seats to be chosen by members of the Legislative Council. The African elected members accepted the increased seats but rejected the idea of specially elected members. They also refused the ministerial posts. 'Multi-racialism' as a policy was completely unacceptable to the Africans.

In 1959, another serious attempt was made to sell the concept of 'multi-racialism' to the Africans. The initiative this time came from one of the European leaders, Mr (later Sir) Michael Blundell. He published a policy statement in July in which he argued for the ending of all racial barriers. With the encouragement of the Kenya Government, Blundell resigned from his post as Minister of Agriculture to lead a new multi-racial pressure group—the New Kenya Group. At first he was supported only by specially elected Africans and Asians. But he soon gained adherents from among the moderates of the African elected members. Thus strengthened, Blundell formed a multi-racial party, the Kenya National Party. It appeared that the policy of 'multi-racialism' was at last succeeding, especially since the majority of the African elected members had joined Blundell's party.

The opponents of 'multi-racialism' were not disheartened. In the Legislative Council they formed the Kenya Independence Movement, with Oginga Odinga as president and Tom Mboya as secretary. They declared that the membership of their movement would consist thenceforth only of Africans. The battle between African nationalism and settlerdom was about to begin.

Several important changes precipitated the clash. In October 1959, the Kenya Government, in a desperate attempt to assist Blundell's party, declared the objective of the removal of all racial barriers, including that to entry on to land in the Highlands. Immediately the settlers were up in arms. They condemned Blundell and other Europeans with similar views as traitors. In Britain a new Colonial Secretary, Ian Macleod, announced that the Emergency would end, and that a constitutional conference would take place the following year.

In the following year at the Lancaster House Conference in London, the battle between the forces of African nationalism and those of European settlerdom was fought. The Africans emerged victorious. The Kenya Europeans regarded this settlement as a major betrayal of their work in the country over sixty years. Under their old leader of the

1930s and 1940s, Cavendish-Bentinck, they gathered together in the Kenya Coalition in what proved to be a last-ditch rearguard action.

With independence in sight, the Africans had now to agree among themselves on the kind of society they wished to see established. Here differences soon emerged, resulting in the formation of two political parties, the Kenya African National Union (KANU) destined to be led by Kenyatta, and the Kenya African Democratic Party (KADU) led by Mr. Ronald Ngala. The latter claimed to represent the so-called minority tribes; and even the efforts of Kenyatta after his release in August 1961 failed to give them the assurance they sought.

KADU's fears for the future soon led them to call for the establishment of regional governments (*majimbo*), and the protection of their interests through a federal constitution. They declared that a unitary state on the Westminster model which KANU favoured would place too much power in the hands of the majority party.

This was the question which was debated at the last Lancaster House Constitutional Conference from February to April 1962. In the end Mr Maudling, the Colonial Secretary, had to impose a compromise. There was to be a strong central government, but with federal provision for regional governments. Provision was also made for an Upper Chamber (the Senate). On 12 December 1963, Kenya achieved her independence with one of the most complicated constitutions in the world. But the question which KADU raised in 1962 remains unanswered—although KADU is no more: What is the best way of protecting minorities in an independent Kenya?

Conclusion

In this chapter we have been concerned with showing the multi-racial origins of Kenya. We have indicated how most of the economic and social institutions were originally designed to cater for the needs of the different races. Although there was a general awareness from 1952 that different institutions were needed to build the new Kenya, much of the energy was devoted to political reforms. There was insufficient time in which to evolve economic and social structures appropriate to political independence. The result was that when Kenya attained her independence many of the old racialist institutions still existed. The problem of creating a society based on authentic African values was therefore likely to be difficult.

Further reading

MUNGEAM, G. H. *British Rule in Kenya, 1895–1912*, Clarendon Press, Oxford, 1966.

BENNETT, G. *Kenya, A Political History*, Oxford University Press, London, 1963.

OGOT, B. A. 'British Administration in the Central Nyanza District of Kenya, 1900–1960', *Journal of African History*, IV, 2, 1963, (pp. 249–74).

DILLEY, M. R. *British Policy in Kenya Colony*, Thomas Nelson and Sons, New York, 1937.

GHAI, D. P. (Ed.) *Portrait of a Minority: Asians in East Africa*, Oxford University Press, Nairobi, 1965.

ROSBERG, C. G. and NOTTINGHAM, J. *The Myth of 'Mau Mau' Nationalism in Kenya*, East African Publishing House, Nairobi, 1967.

HARLOW, V. and CHILVER, E. M. (Eds) *History of East Africa, 2*, Clarendon Press, 1965.

BENNETT, G. and ROSBERG, C. G. *The Kenyatta Election: Kenya 1960–1961*, Oxford University Press, London, 1961.

WELBOURN, F. B. *East African Rebels*, S.C.M. Press, London, 1961.

WELBOURN, F. B. and OGOT, B. A. *A Place to Feel at Home: A Study of Two Independent Churches in Western Kenya*, Oxford University Press, London, 1966.

HOWARTH, A. *Kenyatta—A Photographic Biography*, East African Publishing House, Nairobi, 1967.

MBOYA, T. J. *Freedom and After*, André Deutsch, London, 1963.

KENYATTA, J. *Suffering Without Bitterness*, East African Publishing House, Nairobi, 1968.

SORRENSON, M. P. K. *Origins of European Settlement in Kenya*, Oxford University Press, Nairobi, 1968.

THUKU, H. *An Autobiography*, Oxford University Press, Nairobi, 1970.

BARNETT, D. L. and NJAMA, K. *Mau Mau from Within*, MacGibbon and Kee, London, 1966.

SORRENSON, M. P. K. *Land Reform in Kikuyu Country*, Oxford University Press, London and Nairobi, 1967.

ODINGA, O. *Not Yet Uhuru*, Heinemann, London, 1967.

GHAI, Y. P. and MCAUSLAN, J. P. W. B., *Public Law and Political Change in Kenya*, Oxford University Press, Nairobi and London, 1970.

SINGH, M. *History of Kenya's Trade Union Movement to 1952*, East African Publishing House, Nairobi, 1969.

KAGGIA, B. *An Autobiography*, East African Publishing House, Nairobi, 1971.

KIPKORIR, B. E. The Alliance High School and the Origins of the Kenya African Élite 1926–1962, Ph.D. thesis, Cambridge, 1969.

ANDERSON, J. *The Struggle for the School*, Longman, London, 1970.

ITOTE, W. *'Mau Mau' General*, East African Publishing House, Nairobi, 1967.

OGOT, B. A. (Ed.), *Hadith I* (1967), II (1970), III (1971), East African Publishing House, Nairobi.

LONSDALE, J. M. *The Political History of Western Kenya* (forthcoming).

LONSDALE, J. M. and OGOT, B. A. *The African Voice in Kenya* (forthcoming).

14

Tanzania Under German and British Rule

John Iliffe

German invasion and African resistance, 1884–98

Great changes took place in East Africa during the nineteenth century, especially in the south, which was to become Tanzania. Some areas were devastated by slave raiding and Ngoni warfare, but elsewhere some African societies began to adapt themselves to long-distance trade and European penetration. At the same time, greater changes were happening in Europe as a result of the industrial revolution. Throughout the world, Europe's new economic and military power forced other peoples either to reorganise themselves or to suffer defeat and colonial rule. In Asia, Japan escaped colonial rule and carried out its own industrial revolution. East Africa, by contrast, was partitioned into European colonies. This happened for three main reasons: the ambitions of individual Europeans, the responses of African societies to European pressure, and the hopes and fears of European governments.

The southern part of East Africa came under German rule between 1884 and 1898. Before 1884, German interest in this area was limited. The idea of conquest came from an individual, Carl Peters. He visited East Africa late in 1884 to obtain 'treaties' over land on which Germans could settle. When he returned to Germany in 1885, his government declared a protectorate over the area inland of Sadani in which he had travelled. The German government did this for two reasons. First, it was quarrelling with Britain, and wanted to use its East African claims as part of the quarrel. Second, it was ignorant of East Africa and feared that unless it took part in the scramble for Africa other European countries might gain some unknown advantages.

Peters organised the German East African Company to rule his protectorate. In 1888 he forced the Sultan of Zanzibar to grant him the right to govern the coast. The German Government helped Peters, but did not want the responsibility itself. Nevertheless, when the coastal peoples resisted in 1888, the Government had to intervene.

The Germans called this resistance 'the Arab revolt', a rebellion of slave traders frightened of losing their economic position. This was partly true, but the movement was also a popular resistance by the coastal peoples to foreign rule, just as they had resisted Portuguese and Arabs before. The resistance began in Pangani in August 1888 and quickly spread along the whole coast. Although it had no central organisation, two main leaders emerged. One was an Arab settler near Pangani, Abushiri bin Salim, an enemy of the Sultan. 'He was brave as a lion,' wrote a Swahili poet, 'and intolerant of oppression; where there was trouble, he would be in it.' The other leader was Bwana Heri, the ruler of Sadani, who had never accepted the Sultan's control.

The company was driven out of all the coastal towns except Bagamoyo and Dar es Salaam. The German government was forced to send troops, led by Major Wissmann, who arrived in May 1889. Within two months, he had captured the northern towns. The resistance began to collapse. The Arab aristocrats made peace with the Germans. Abushiri was betrayed in December 1889. 'At the beginning of the rising,' he told his captors, 'we all swore on the Koran not to rest until we had driven the Germans out. All the others have broken their word. I am the only one who has remained true to that oath until today.' He was hanged in Pangani. Bwana Heri submitted in April 1890, and the southern coast was occupied soon afterwards. The Arabs who had made peace became German agents in the coastal towns. On 1 January 1891, the German government replaced the company as ruler of German East Africa.

African resistance had forced the German government to replace the company. It is wrong to think that the European occupation of East Africa was easy, that the Europeans had complete military superiority, that Africans could not influence what happened. The Germans had little money and few troops—never more than three thousand to control an African population of six or seven million (including Rwanda and Burundi). This had two consequences. First, the German occupation was very gradual. Second, the Germans needed African allies. Because the peoples of German East Africa were not united, such allies existed. Some African peoples negotiated with the Germans, while others resisted violently. To understand this, one must realise that the objects of both were the same: to retain as much power and independence as possible.

The warlords were among those who resisted. Machemba, the Yao ruler of the Makonde Plateau, defeated several German expeditions until he was overcome in 1899. 'I have listened to your words,' he had written to Wissmann, 'but can find no reason why I should obey you—I would rather die first. . . . I am Sultan here in my land. You are Sultan there in your's. . . . I will not come to you, and if you are strong enough, then come and fetch me.' In Tabora, the chief of Unyanyembe, Isike, fought the Germans when they tried to gain control of the town and trade route. In January 1893 the Germans stormed his fortress. Isike blew himself up in his powder magazine.

The most famous resistance was that of the Hehe under their great warrior chief Mkwawa. The Hehe first tried to come to terms with the Germans, but Mkwawa refused to visit the coast. Hehe warriors cut the trade route from Bagamoyo to Tabora, and in 1891 the Germans sent a military expedition to Uhehe, with orders to make peace. Mkwawa wanted to remain free, but hoped to succeed by negotiation. He sent men to offer presents and make an agreement, but the Germans thought these men were coming to fight, and killed them. Mkwawa then ordered an ambush, in which 290 German troops were killed. For three years Mkwawa remained independent, but on 30 October 1894, a very large German force captured his capital at Kalenga. The chief escaped, and for four years he fought a guerilla war. Finally, sick and alone save for two young pages, Mkwawa was found by a German patrol. He shot himself as it approached his camp. With his death in June 1898, the period of occupation and resistance ended. The Germans built powerful forts at strategic points throughout the country. In 1898 they began to demand taxes. A new period of administration was beginning.

Yet occupation had taken fourteen years. For those who had resisted, there remained a proud memory which they were to preserve throughout the next sixty years of European rule. Those who had allied with the Germans gained more immediate advantages. Often their power and territory were increased. Mkwawa's rival, Merere of the Sangu, regained his homeland. On Kilimanjaro, Marealle of Marangu, a skilful and ruthless politician, made use of the Germans to become the most powerful chief on the mountain. In Buhaya, power passed to Kahigi of Kianja, who cleverly used the Germans against his rivals. By 1898, through alliances which the Germans had been forced to make, the balance of power in parts of German East Africa had been altered to the advantage of those who understood the possibilities opened up by European rule.

German administration and the Maji Maji rebellion, 1898 to 1914

By 1898, the main pattern of German administration was established. At its head was the governor, at first usually a soldier. The colony was divided into districts. Their numbers changed, but by 1914 there were twenty-two. Communications were so bad that almost everything was left to the District Officer (*Bezirksamtmann*). He commanded a small police force or a company of one to two hundred African troops. He collected taxes, appointed and dismissed African chiefs and agents, judged cases, and administered punishments. Often he ruled with a strong and ruthless hand. Yet the government's power was limited, for it lacked staff and money. On the coast and in areas of European settlement, the administration was quite strong. Elsewhere, two German officers and a hundred troops might face a million Africans. This weakness had several consequences. The Germans feared African risings, and suppressed the slightest discontent with great brutality. In normal times, the district officer relied greatly on his African allies. Clever men like Marealle and Kahigi could use the Germans to strengthen their own power. Writing of the Chagga, Mrs K. M. Stahl describes the many intrigues by which Marealle persuaded the Germans to defeat his enemies, until he too became the victim of a similar intrigue. The Germans preferred to employ existing chiefs as their agents. Where there were none, they appointed an *akida* to collect taxes and try cases.

Because administration was expensive, the German rulers emphasised economic development. They tried three methods: they started plantations of tropical crops, employing many African labourers; they assisted Europeans to farm in the highlands; and they encouraged or forced Africans to grow cash crops in order to pay taxes. German experiments were concentrated along the River Pangani and in the highland areas of Usambara, Kilimanjaro, and Meru. A railway inland from Tanga, begun in 1891, reached Mombo in 1905 and Moshi in 1911. Between 1904 and 1914, a second railway was built from Dar es Salaam to Kigoma. The first plantations grew coffee in Usambara, but the soil was poor and they failed. By 1905 the main crop was sisal. Later, from 1908 to 1912, German planters made large profits from rubber, until the market collapsed. Yet most German administrators preferred to encourage individual European farmers, because plantation labour was scarce, and because they wanted their colony to be a 'white man's country' like Rhodesia or Kenya. Large-scale settlement began in Usambara in 1898, Meru in 1905, and Kilimanjaro in 1907. Most of the land was taken from the Maasai, some from other peoples. The settlers grew coffee and rubber, but very few were successful. Their main problem was shortage of labour, for they paid low wages. Labourers were recruited from long distances, especially from Unyamwezi. Much deceit and brutality was used. Often the chiefs in the settlement areas were forced to supply labourers. By 1913, there were 5 336 Europeans in German East Africa, of whom 882 were adult male settlers. They dominated the Governor's Council, formed in 1904 as the equivalent of a legislative council. Few Tanzanians now realise how nearly their country came under settler control. Only the expulsion of the Germans after the First World War prevented it.

African cash crop agriculture began in several ways. Coffee, for example, was introduced to Kilimanjaro by missionaries and spread by African catechists. In Buhaya, coffee was a traditional crop, and was first exported in 1898. Cotton was introduced into Usukuma by a European settler, and became popular about 1911. In 1902 the Governor decided that cotton should be grown in the south of the colony. He ordered that every headman must establish a cotton plot, where all his people would come to work. When the cotton was sold, the workers, headman, and marketing organisation would each receive one third of the profits. By 1905 this system operated in all the coastal districts south of Dar es Salaam, and also in Morogoro and Kilosa.

The cotton scheme brought great hardship. The land chosen was unsuitable and the crops poor. The work was badly organised and brutally controlled. Virtually no profits were made. Zaramo workers refused the 35 cents they were each offered for the first year's work. In July 1905, the workers resolved to fight. On the night of 31 July, the Matumbi drove their hated akida and all other foreigners from their hills. The Maji Maji rebellion had begun. It spread first throughout the cotton area around the middle and lower Rufiji River, then to Uluguru, the Mahenge Plateau, and the Lukuledi and Kilombero Valleys. On 30 August, several thousand men of the Ngindo and Mbunga tribes, armed only with spears, tried to assault Mahenge fort, to drag away the machine-guns with their bare hands. They failed, with terrible casualties, and this was perhaps the turning-point. Early in September the Ngoni joined the rising, but already its first momentum was lost. By November the Germans had regained control of the Southern Highlands. The rebel area was now divided. In the west, the Germans encircled and destroyed the hard core of Ngoni and Bena leaders. In the east, the Ngindo, among others, fought a long guerilla war until their leader, the elephant hunter Abdalla Mapanda, was shot in January 1907. Then came famine. 'I have never seen such scarcity,' a young woman wrote from Masasi. 'I have seen famine, but not one causing people to die. But in this famine many are dying, some are unable to do any work at all, they have no strength, their food consists of insects from the woods.' In war and famine, seventy-five thousand Africans are thought to have died.

Maji Maji was important in three ways. First, it was an attempt to find a new method of regaining independence. Tribal resistance had been defeated because the weapons used were inadequate and the resistance was disunited. Maji Maji tried to overcome the strength of European weapons and unite people without regard for their tribes. For this it used religion. Every Maji Maji fighter 'drank' the water—

normally it was sprinkled on him. This protected him from bullets and committed him to war and brotherhood: *hiyo ni alama ya unamaji*, an applicant was told, 'this is a sign of comradeship.' The water was first distributed by a prophet named Kinjikitile, who lived at Ngarambe near the Rufiji river. Later his messengers carried the water to the people throughout southern Tanzania. Maji Maji was different from tribal resistance. The Germans called it 'a revolt of the people.'

Yet Maji Maji failed either to regain independence or to preserve the unity in which it had begun. A mass movement needs strong organisation, and the religious organisation of Maji Maji was not strong enough. As German military pressure increased, the movement broke up into its tribal sections. When the Ngoni joined, for example, they fought alone, and were defeated alone.

Perhaps the third point is the most important. After Maji Maji, Africans sought different methods to regain independence. Yet the spirit of protest had been demonstrated, and it remained until independence. Fifty years later, President Nyerere declared: 'They rose in a great rebellion . . . in response to a natural call, a call of the spirit, ringing in the hearts of all men, and of all times, educated or uneducated, to rebel against foreign domination. It is important to bear this in mind . . . in order to understand the nature of a nationalist movement like mine. Its function is not to create the spirit of rebellion but to articulate it and show it a new technique.'

The British in Zanzibar and the 'Arab Revolution', 1890 to 1934

Zanzibar became a British protectorate in November 1890. Unlike German East Africa, this was no sudden European invasion led by a private adventurer. During the nineteenth century, the Sultan had become dependent on British support, while by submitting to British demands concerning the slave trade he lost the support of his subjects. When threatened by the Germans in the late 1880s, he was forced to seek British protection.

Britain hoped to preserve the sultanate while suppressing slavery. The Sultan was told that Britain would control Zanzibar's foreign relations, while merely 'exercising a friendly influence' in her internal affairs, which would remain under Arab control. But late nineteenth century Europeans were not content with 'influence' when they detected inefficiency and injustice. In August 1891 the British Consul declared the Sultan's government 'an embodiment of all the worst and most barbarous characteristics of a primitive Arab despotism.' He seized its finances and appointed European officials to control the government departments. In 1896 the British navy bombarded the Sultan's palace and a British candidate was placed on the throne. The independence of Sayyid Said's dynasty was broken.

In Buganda, at this date, historians write of a 'Christian Revolution'. They mean that the kabaka's power passed to Christian chiefs. Through their privileged position in education, land-holding, and administration, these great families became an aristocracy which dominated Buganda until independence. A similar process took place in Zanzibar—an 'Arab Revolution'. Although the British broke the Sultan's personal power, they wanted Arabs to rule Zanzibar and their new administration needed trained civil servants. Arabs received special educational opportunities and the more important civil service positions. The personal rule of the sultan was replaced by that of an educated Arab aristocracy.

While the Arab aristocrats controlled the administration, their economic position was weakened through the abolition of slavery. Anxious to preserve the Arab position, British officials made the 1897 Emancipation Decree as favourable to the slave owners as possible. The slave had to claim his freedom in court. The slave owner (but not the slave) was compensated—an Arab Association was formed soon after 1900 to ensure this. Since there was little free land, the slave usually became a squatter on an Arab estate, paying rent in labour. Nevertheless, the blow to Arab economic power was serious. Many landowners were already in debt, and throughout this period the price of cloves was low. As in Buganda, the aristocracy gained administrative power while losing the economic strength to support it.

For the Africans, emancipation scarcely fulfilled its promise. 'Let us rejoice and give thanks,' a missionary newspaper had proclaimed, 'for men are not objects, and all children of Adam are of the same origin, even the foolish and the weak have their dignity. . . . Everyone has his rights, his property, his wife, his dignity, and must not be maltreated without cause. Africa too will have its day.' For Zanzibar Africans, that day did not come immediately. Yet new opportunities were opening. The career of Sheikh Abeid Karume demonstrates this. Born in 1905, he received three years education, and became a sailor at the age of fifteen. By 1930 he had travelled very widely and was already experienced in organising his comrades. He was later to become a leader of the African Association, an organisation formed in Zanzibar in 1934 to protect the rights of educated Africans. It was the first expression of an African political consciousness. For Zanzibar Africans, the age of improvement had opened.

The age of improvement, 1907–37

The violence of Maji Maji had failed as a method of regaining independence. New techniques were needed. Between the period of armed resistance and that of mass nationalism, there was throughout colonial Africa an age of improvement, when Africans concentrated on improving their positions, to face their European rulers on more equal terms. They emphasised education, economic development, and political advance in local government. The characteristic man of this period was the educated clerk, teacher, or pastor. The characteristic organisation was the welfare association in which these new men combined together to improve themselves. Improvement often meant westernisation. 'To the African mind,' said one, 'to imitate Europeans is civilisation.' It is difficult to understand such men, but in their quiet, earnest way they made an important contribution to Tanzanian history.

The first recognisable group were the akidas appointed after Maji Maji. They were educated in government schools on the coast. Following the German government inland, young coast men staffed the administration and the schools throughout the country. When the British defeated the Germans in 1916 and renamed the colony Tanganyika, a second group emerged. Many had been educated by the UMCA at Kiungani school in Zanzibar, where they received a literary education in English which, after 1918, secured them the best jobs in the new civil service. The outstanding member of this group was Martin Kayamba.

In his career and beliefs, Kayamba was characteristic of the age of improvement. His father was a schoolteacher in Zanzibar, where Kayamba was born in 1891. He was educated at Kiungani from 1902 to 1905. After travelling as a clerk and trader in Kenya and Uganda, and being imprisoned by the Germans, Kayamba was appointed chief clerk of Tanga District Office. Later he travelled twice to Europe and obtained the highest post open to an African in the civil service. While in Tanga, Kayamba founded the Tanganyika Territory African Civil Service Association, in March 1922. The association later moved to Dar es Salaam, where in 1928 or 1929 some of its members took part in the foundation of the Tanganyika African Association, from which, twenty-five years later, TANU was to be formed. Thus there is a link between TTACSA and later nationalism, but the association itself, of course, was no mass nationalist movement. It was a club for clerks and teachers, with newspapers and a football team, encouraged by the government. Historically, however, TTACSA was important. It linked these educated men with members of Tanga's coastal society. Kayamba later remembered a visitor to the club who 'was very pleased to see something at last had been done which he never thought he would see, and that was Christians and Mohammedans, Africans and Arabs joining together as members of the association, and all being very friendly.' Further, Kayamba and his group were perhaps the first Tanganyikans to think of their country as a unit, as a future independent state. For Kayamba, political development required self-improvement, and improvement required unity. 'I firmly believe,' he wrote, 'that Africans will never progress well unless they realise the necessity for unity.' Yet this progress would give special advantages to a privileged minority. 'Martin Kayamba,' wrote an African newspaper when he died in 1939, 'will be . . . remembered as the selfish African who rose to the highest rank . . . without being of any use to his race . . . . He never bothered about his African brothers.' Kayamba and his circle were not political leaders. They neither represented their people nor demanded independence. But they created an organisation, a central tradition, wider than the tribe, which later provided one foundation for Tanganyikan nationalism.

Similar changes were happening in the rural areas of Tanganyika. New men were emerging from the mission schools, anxious that their tribes should progress, willing to challenge the chiefs whom European administrators supported. These men founded tribal unions in many parts of Tanganyika. The earliest was the Bukoba Bahaya Union.

The first Haya with modern education included men who visited Buganda in the 1890s, became Christians, learned to read, and returned to Buhaya to found their own church long before Protestant missionaries arrived. Education spread quickly in Buhaya, especially in the northern chiefdom, Kiziba. Two members of the Ziba aristocracy, Fransisko Lwamgira and Klemens Kiiza, proved the ablest men of their generation. The story of how they came to oppose each other shows what was happening in Tanganyika during the age of improvement. Before 1914, Lwamgira was secretary to the German officer in Bukoba. Kiiza worked for both the government and the missionaries. After the war, Lwamgira retained his post, while Kiiza became a trader. In 1925, the British introduced the system of government called indirect rule into Tanganyika. They intended that African tribes should be administered by their own chiefs and elders, under British supervision. They hoped this would encourage political and economic development, without leading to 'detribalisation' or nationalist politics. Indirect rule caused conflict within the tribes between the privileged chiefs and their unprivileged subjects. This happened in Buhaya. Lwamgira was privileged: he became Secretary General to the Council of Chiefs. Kiiza, however, was not. In 1924 he helped to found the Bukoba Bahaya Union, 'for the establishment of an institution for the development of our country and for the seeking of a system for the simple way to civilisation to our mutual advantage.' The union became the centre of opposition to the chiefs' privileges. It demanded an educated paramount chief to replace them. At first it had no mass support, but when Kiiza began his own coffee-hulling plant he tried to organise the Haya farmers into a Native Growers' Association. Then in 1936 the chiefs issued orders controlling methods of growing coffee, to prevent disease.

The farmers resisted these rules. 'We do not need,' they wrote, 'to be taught how to grow coffee or banana trees or to stop from growing anything in our shambas or our soil.' In one village Lwamgira, the chiefs' agent, was stoned. Kiiza, by contrast, was blamed by the government for the unrest. The Native Growers' Association collapsed.

This is a complicated but important story. Apart from Kayamba and his circle, this was a period of local politics. Kiiza was not demanding national independence. He wanted power in Buhaya, power to bring progress to Buhaya, power to destroy the chiefs' privileges. For long he lacked popular support. Then his commercial interests led him to organise the farmers. When the government interfered with their agriculture and the farmers resisted, Kiiza briefly led a popular political movement.

Maji Maji had been a mass movement, but had lacked skilled leadership. During the next thirty years, potential leaders were educated, but they lacked mass support. By 1937, this situation was changing. Under government pressure, the people were coming back into politics. The problem now was to unite leaders and followers into an organised movement.

The origins of Tanganyikan nationalism, 1937–54

Nationalism has meant different things in different parts of the world. In East Africa, mass nationalism had three characteristics. First, it aimed to control the political centre of the country, the Legislative Council. Second, the nationalist leaders tried to do this by mobilising mass support and by expressing popular demands. Third, they intended to use their central power and mass support to unite all the people of the country into a single nation, in which the only test of full membership would be citizenship—not race, not religion, not political belief. In most parts of colonial Africa, and certainly in Tanganyika, such movements gained independence. But such movements were not bound to come into existence, nor need they have won independence. Colonies can gain independence in other ways. In South American countries in the early nineteenth century, independence was won, not by mass nationalist movements, but by unrepresentative minorities. Early in the twentieth century, Ireland won independence from Britain, not by a mass nationalist movement (a method which had failed) but through a terrorist campaign by a few thousand trained fighters. In South Africa, mass nationalism has so far proved a most ineffective technique to win African freedom. Nationalism was not inevitable in Tanganyika, nor was it inevitably successful. So the historian must explain why a mass nationalist movement came into existence, and why it won independence.

By the late 1930s, Tanganyikans had experience of three types of political action, none of which was nationalist. The political tradition of TTACSA and TAA aimed at the Legislative Council, but had no mass support. Tribal politicians like Kiiza rarely had mass support, and were concerned with tribal rather than national issues. Popular resistance, expressed in Maji Maji or in opposition to agricultural regulations, certainly had mass support, but did not seek control of the Legislative Council. None of these was a nationalist movement, but they were the elements from which a nationalist movement was eventually created. When the three types of politics came together, on 7 July 1954, Tanganyikan nationalism was born. Between 1937 and 1954, the three types of politics gradually became interconnected.

This was not just the work of educated leaders. The biggest changes took place in the rural areas, for here the people became involved in politics. As in Buhaya in 1937, the people acted because the government interfered with their agricultural methods. In the great world economic depression of 1929 the prices of tropical crops fell sharply. The government urged the people to grow more crops in order to maintain their incomes, but growing more crops accelerated the exhaustion of the land. The government began to make regulations concerning soil conservation, forcing the people to build terraces, to limit the numbers of their cattle, and do many things which needed much time and work. Sometimes the regulations seemed foolish. Increasingly, the people resisted. The Shambaa of Mlalo, for example, resisted as early as 1946. The most famous incident came later, in 1955, when the government tried to make the Luguru terrace their hillsides, although crops were better where the land was not terraced. In Uluguru there was serious violence. By the 1950s, Tanganyika's farmers were more ready to resist than they had been since 1905.

The farmers were also better organised, for tribal politics had changed greatly. The output of crops, and the wealth of the country, was rapidly increasing. For example, in 1945 Tanganyika produced 7 512 long tons [7 632 tonnes] of raw cotton; in 1952, 14 109 long tons [14 332 tonnes]; in 1960, 34 241 long tons [34 789 tonnes]. In 1945, coffee exports earned £896 000; in 1950, £3 471 000; in 1955, £6 905 000. This prosperity led to the growth of the cooperative movement. In 1945 there were seventy-nine registered cooperative societies. By 1952 the number had risen to 474. The greatest advance was still to come—the creation between 1950 and 1955 of the Victoria Federation of Co-operative Unions in Usukuma. The cooperatives were of great political importance. Tanganyika's farmers were at last brought together by modern organisations which were not dominated by the chiefs. The cooperative organisers often became local leaders of a new type, progressive and with real mass support. For example, between 1950 and 1953 a new group of political leaders emerged in Lake Province, including Paul Bomani, S. A. Kandoro, S. A. Maswanya and I. M. Bhoke Munanka. At this time, Mwanza was the centre of radical politics for the whole of Tanganyika. These new leaders were different from Kiiza's generation. They were not interested in tribal independence. They were concerned with bigger things, with the government's agricultural and marketing policies, with decisions made in Dar es Salaam. Whether they liked it or not, their local interests forced them to enter national politics, to become the most important men in the nationalist movement. They had practical organisational experience and mass local support from farmers who were increasingly discontented. If they could unite with each other, they could be immensely powerful.

Throughout East Africa, men like these became nationalist leaders. Yet only in Tanganyika was there a single and united nationalist movement. There were several reasons for this. Tanganyika had no dominant tribe and no deep linguistic division. Most important, Tanganyika alone had a central, non-tribal political tradition. When Kenyan or Ugandan politicians moved from local to national politics, they made tribal alliances among themselves. In Tanganyika they joined an existing central political organisation, TAA. This is shown clearly by the Meru Lands Case of 1951. In that year, the government moved three thousand Meru from their land and replaced them with Europeans. The Meru naturally resisted. They tried three successive methods. First, they formed the Meru Citizens' Union, Freemen, one of whose leaders was Kirilo Japhet, the secretary of the Arusha branch of TAA. They tried to oppose the government as a tribe. When that failed, they appealed to the United Nations, but the British ignored its resolutions. Finally, the Meru turned to national politics. 'Government,' wrote Kirilo Japhet in 1953, 'wants badly to hear the last of our Lands Case, but I have been asked by Mr Kandoro and Mr Nyerere of the Tanganyika African Association to go on safari and tell the whole country about the Meru eviction and my adventures in the United Nations. The eviction woke our Meru people up to the indignity of being ruled without our consent by foreigners. Now we are going to wake up all Tanganyika!' This shows how a local political leader, with mass support, came into contact with the central TAA organisation, with its national outlook. When local support and central organisation joined, nationalism began.

TAA had also changed. Previously it had been 'tea-party politics', a club for clerks and teachers. After 1945 it gained new strength and militancy from two directions. First, its branches were infected by the new radicalism of local politics. Through these branches, it had been in touch with tribal politicians throughout the 1930s. Now the branches began to demand greater action from the centre—early in the 1950s, the particularly radical Mwanza leaders demanded that TAA headquarters be moved there. Second, leadership was taken over by Makerere-trained intellectuals in Dar es Salaam, first by Vedast Kyaruzi in 1950, then by Julius Nyerere in April 1953. On his return from Britain in 1952, Nyerere insisted that TAA could be the nucleus of a mass nationalist movement. Meeting in October 1953, this new TAA leadership decided to reorganise the association and to model it on Nkrumah's Convention People's Party.

Seventeen delegates approved this transformation of TAA into TANU at a meeting on 7 July 1954 in Dar es Salaam. They represented the three political traditions from which TANU originated. The new intellectuals were represented by Nyerere himself and by Joseph Kasella Bantu. Kandoro was the delegate of radical Mwanza's leadership. Kirilo Japhet represented the mass politics of the Meru Citizens' Union. The traditions had come together, leaders and people had met — the nucleus of a mass movement existed.

The triumph of TANU, 1954–61

The problem was now to expand the movement, to hold it together, and to use it to regain lost independence. Maji Maji had failed partly because it neither expanded sufficiently nor remained united. 'Freedom and unity' was a slogan of the new movement.

TANU spread quickly, for three main reasons. First, its message was simple. 'National freedom, *uhuru*, was an uncomplicated principle,' President Nyerere has written, 'and it needed no justification to the audiences of the first few TANU speakers. All that was required was an explanation of its relevance to their lives, and some reasonable assurance that it could be obtained through the methods proposed by TANU.' Second, the movement made use of the existing TAA branches. 'During the last ten months . . .,' Nyerere said in March 1955, 'we have tried to organise ourselves. The branches of the former African Association became automatically branches of the Tanganyika National African Union, and they are scattered all over the country.' Third, throughout Tanganyika there was already conflict between the people and their rulers. The people felt the need for action; TANU had only to adapt itself to each local situation, either by taking over an existing popular movement or by organising the people against privilege.

In Buhaya, opposition to the government, to the chiefs and to agricultural rules had been continuous since the 1920s. It was led by several political bodies with similar leadership: the Bukoba Bahaya Union, the Kianja Labour Association, and the Bukoba branch of TAA. In 1953 the chiefs ordered that all banana trees must be felled after the crop had been picked, to prevent disease. As in 1937, the people opposed this

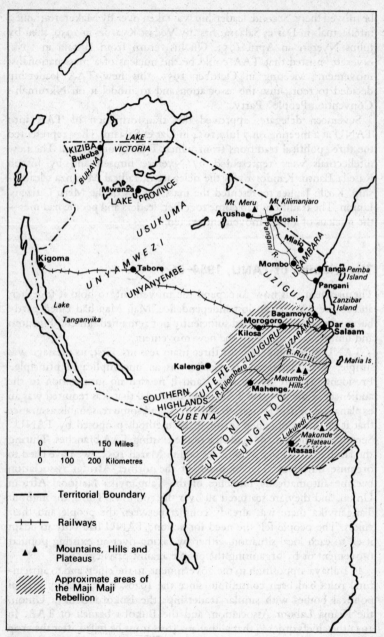

Figure 28 Tanzania

order. Their leader was Ali Migeyo. The police dispersed one of his meetings and he was imprisoned. In 1954 Mwanza was becoming the local headquarters of TANU. Ali Migeyo's colleagues consulted the Mwanza leaders. They returned as TANU members and eventually took over the members and organisation of the TAA branch. Buhaya's local politics became part of a national movement.

Elsewhere, the transition from local to national politics was more complicated, and needed a new organisation. Kilimanjaro was an example. There the government's land and agricultural policies caused unrest. In 1946 divisional chiefs (*waitori*) were appointed but soon became unpopular. The Kilimanjaro Union opposed them and sought to unite the Chagga in the face of new threats. In 1952 it secured the election of Thomas Marealle as paramount chief. Under this leadership, the Chagga experienced real economic and educational progress, but gradually Marealle became unpopular. He was opposed by TANU and its local ally the Chagga Democratic Party. Marealle was voted out in 1960. Thus in Kilimanjaro, in contrast to Buhaya, TANU established itself through opposition to the political leaders of the early 1950s.

By such means, TANU rapidly dominated local politics throughout the country. By late 1957, nearly 200 000 members held TANU cards. Now the main problem was not expansion but organisation and unity. 'My movement has reached a critical step,' wrote Nyerere in December 1957. 'We have virtually the whole country behind us . . . Mass support is no longer our immediate problem. The problem as I see it now is one of minute organisation.' During 1958 the whole party was reorganised. At the same time, unity was kept by concentrating all the movement's attention on freedom, without defining the exact nature of that freedom, for its followers might have disagreed about the definition and the movement might have divided. The most dangerous threats to unity were religion and race. In September 1959 the All Muslim National Union of Tanganyika urged that Tanganyika should not become independent until Muslims had greater educational opportunities, but the organisation was denounced by Muslim leaders. A more dangerous threat, at first, was the African National Congress, which was formed when TANU's annual conference at Tabora in January 1958 decided to take part in elections later that year, under a multi-racial constitution with a limited electorate. ANC was a racialist party which lacked popular following. The majority even of those who disagreed with TANU policy on this issue remained inside the national movement.

At first TANU's strategy was to attack the British through the United Nations. As the movement grew, this became unnecessary. The real battlefield was inside Tanganyika. TANU's power was its mass support. It had to prove to the British that it could make it impossible for them to rule except by armed force, and that TANU could replace

309

the British and rule effectively. By the late 1950s, Britain had ceased to be a major world power. Mau Mau and other colonial rebellions had proved that it was almost impossible—and certainly uneconomic—to suppress nationalism by force. Britain's problem was to hand over political power while retaining her economic interests. The mass nationalist party seemed to be an acceptable successor, for it was disciplined, popular, progressive, and led by the ablest men available. In other circumstances, constitutional mass nationalism might have been wholly ineffective to regain independence, but in the circumstances of the late 1950s it was the perfect technique.

TANU first persuaded the United Nations mission which visited Tanganyika in 1954 to accept it as 'a national movement'. With this recognition, Nyerere visited the United Nations in 1955 and 1956 and won international support. By this date TANU was opposed by the government-sponsored, multi-racial United Tanganyika Party. This opposition strengthened and disciplined the movement. TANU was fortunate that until 1958 its victory was not certain, for in African countries like Uganda, where African rule was certain from an early date, the national movement fragmented. The crucial event in TANU's campaign was its victory in the 1958–9 election. After long argument, the British and the party agreed that five TANU representatives should become ministers in June 1959. Following a further electoral triumph, responsible government was achieved in September 1960. At midnight on 9 December 1961, the people of Tanganyika regained their independence.

Zanzibar: background to the revolution, 1934–63

Zanzibar's modern history must centre on the revolution of 11 and 12 January 1964, in which the Afro-Shirazi Party leaders gained power and began major changes in Zanzibar's economic and social structure. Its origins go back to the 'Arab Revolution' of the 1890s. After 1945, this group of educated Arabs tried to create a mass political movement to replace the British. They hoped to gain control before the African population became politically conscious. They also believed they were best qualified to create a modern Islamic state. This attempt by a minority to use nationalist techniques to preserve its privileged position can be compared to that of the Ganda leaders at the same date.

In 1948–9 an Arab journalist, Seif Hamoud, revived the Arab Association to demand a ministerial system of government. Between 1949 and 1956 a number of political organisations were formed. Another journalist, Ali Muhsin, united these groups as the Zanzibar Nationalist Party in 1956. A Constitutional Commissioner who visited Zanzibar in 1956 recommended that elections for six seats in the Legislative Council should take place in 1957. This proposal found the African and Shirazi peoples unprepared. The African Association of 1934 had never been an effective political body, and in 1938 a Shirazi Association, based on Pemba, had broken away from it. The African and Shirazi leaders first opposed the idea of elections, but on 5 February 1957, they reunited to form the Afro-Shirazi Union (later the Afro-Shirazi Party). Of the six seats contested in 1957, ASP won three, two were won by independents from Pemba who later joined ASP, and one by the Muslim League. ZNP failed to win a single seat. The five ASP representatives remained a minority in the Legislative Council.

Between 1957 and 1961, three major changes took place. First, hostility between the parties grew. Afro-Shirazi boycotted Arab commerce. Arab landowners evicted Afro-Shirazi squatters. Second, the Pemba Shirazi leaders broke away in 1959 to form the Zanzibar and Pemba People's Party. Third, Ali Muhsin and the other Arab leaders reorganised ZNP on TANU lines, with a youth wing, social services and all the techniques of mass nationalism. By 1961, ZNP's organisation was balanced against ASP's natural appeal.

The election of January 1961 produced deadlock. Of the twenty-two seats, ASP won ten, ZNP nine, and ZPPP's three successful candidates split so that each side had eleven representatives. Amid growing unrest, another election was held in June. ZNP and ZPPP formed an alliance. The British added another constituency, in an area dominated by ZNP. The ZNP/ZPPP alliance won thirteen seats against ASP's ten, although ASP polled a majority of the votes. ASP claimed that the election had been corrupt. Tragically, it had been violent. Sixty-eight people were killed.

The final election before independence, held in June 1963, confirmed the 1961 results. Although ASP again received a majority of votes, it won only thirteen seats against its rivals' eighteen. In December 1963 Zanzibar became independent under a ZNP/ZPPP government. The revolution took place a month later.

Here it is necessary to ask why Zanzibar politics led to violent revolution while Tanganyikan politics did not. Historians have suggested three explanations, based on different ideas of nationalism.

Some historians believe that the main object of a nationalist movement was to unite all the citizens of a country, whatever their race. They feel that nationalism failed to do this in Zanzibar, so that the revolution was chiefly a racial conflict. 'The essential characteristic of Zanzibar nationalism,' it has been said, 'has been its failure to unify Zanzibaris.' Yet many nationalists were not concerned solely with unity: they also sought economic justice, which did not exist in Zanzibar under Arab rule.

311

Other historians believe that a nationalist movement was the political expression of a nation, of a large group of people similar in race, language, religion, and culture. These historians claim that the revolution was the triumph of the African nation in Zanzibar, that it was a 'nationalist revolution'. The revolution, writes one, was 'essentially nationalist in character though given the trappings of a socialist or class revolution'. Revolution was necessary because 'imperial domination gave place to a traditional type of reactionary rule, the sole beneficiaries . . . being a small rich class of Arabs.' Yet ZNP was not simply 'a small rich class of Arabs'. Further, the revolution had not only the appearance but the reality of a socialist revolution.

Perhaps the third explanation is more satisfactory. To be successful, a nationalist movement must bring economic justice to the mass of the people, since this was one of the reasons why the people joined it. Privileged political leaders might win independence, but for their followers that independence was not complete unless it led on to economic justice. From this viewpoint, the Zanzibar Revolution was the climax of a nationalist movement in which ZNP represented the privileged (especially the landed) and ASP the unprivileged and landless. Whereas in Zanzibar the conditions for economic justice were created by violence, in Tanganyika they were sought by the more difficult but more humane method of urgent persuasion.

Further reading

KIMAMBO, I. N. and TEMU, A. J. (Eds) *A History of Tanzania*, East African Publishing House, Nairobi, 1969. (The most up-to-date history of the country.)

ROBINSON, R. and GALLAGHER, J. 'The Partition of Africa', in F. H. Hinsley (Ed) *The New Cambridge Modern History*, *XI*, Cambridge University Press, 1962. (The best brief account of the scramble.)

RANGER, T. O. 'African Reactions to the Imposition of Colonial Rule in East and Central Africa', in L. H. Gann and P. Duignan (Eds) *Colonialism in Africa 1870–1960*, I, Cambridge University Press, 1969. (For the part played by Africans in the process of European occupation, and for the organisation and consequences of the resistance.)

KIERAN, J. A. 'Abushiri and the Germans', in B.A. Ogot (Ed) *Hadith 2*, East African Publishing House, Nairobi, 1970. (For the coastal resistance of 1888–90.)

REDMAYNE, A. H. 'Mkwawa and the Hehe Wars', *Journal of African History*, IX: 3, 1968 (pp. 409–36). (For Mkwawa's resistance to the Germans.)

GWASSA, G. C. K. and ILIFFE, J. *Records of the Maji Maji Rising, Part I*, East African Publishing House, Nairobi, 1968. (Documents illustrating the history of the rising.)

MAPUNDA, O. B. and MPANGARA, G. P. *The Maji Maji War in Ungoni*, East African Publishing House, Nairobi, 1969. (A detailed study of the war in one area.)

ILIFFE, J. *Agricultural Change in Modern Tanganyika: an outline history*, East African Publishing House, Nairobi, 1971. (A brief account of economic change, mainly in the colonial period.)

STAHL, K. M. *History of the Chagga People of Kilimanjaro*, Mouton, The Hague, 1964. (Good on the early colonial period, weak after 1918.)

KAYAMBA, H. M. T. 'The Story of Martin Kayamba . . . written by himself', in M. Perham (Ed) *Ten Africans*, Faber and Faber, London, 1936. (Kayamba's autobiography, from which quotations in this chapter are taken.)

LONSDALE, J. M. 'The Emergence of African Nations', in T. O. Ranger (Ed) *Emerging Themes of African History*, East African Publishing House, Nairobi, 1968. (The ideas about nationalism used in this chapter.)

MAGUIRE, G. A. *Toward 'Uhuru' in Tanzania*, Cambridge University Press, Nairobi, 1970. (The most detailed history of TANU, especially in Sukumaland.)

MUTAHABA, G. R. *Portrait of a Nationalist: the Life of Ali Migeyo*, East African Publishing House, Nairobi, 1969. (A biography of a nationalist leader.)

NYERERE, J. K. *Freedom and Unity*, Oxford University Press, London, 1966. (President Nyerere's most important writings and speeches from 1952 to 1965.)

LOFCHIE, M. F. *Zanzibar: Background to Revolution*, Princeton University Press, 1965. (The most detailed account of Zanzibar politics.)

OKELLO, J. *Revolution in Zanzibar*, East African Publishing House, Nairobi, 1967. (A personal account by one of the leaders.)

15

Uganda Under the British

M. S. M. Kiwanuka

By the stroke of the pen which signed the Anglo-German Agreement of 1890, the area north of Lake Victoria, which later came to be known as Uganda, became a British sphere of influence. And by Royal Charter, the Imperial British East Africa Company (IBEA) was authorised to trade as well as to administer this area. The man associated with the rule of the company in Uganda was Captain Lugard. Though primarily in the pay of the IBEA, he worked hard to further British colonial interests. The company remained responsible for this area until after the troubles in Buganda when the struggle for power and influence led Catholics, Moslems and Protestants to massacre each other. These troubles and other responsibilities in the East Africa Protectorate (modern Kenya) increased administrative costs enormously and led the IBEA to invite the British Government to assume responsibility. The IBEA like other chartered companies elsewhere had done its job, namely of preparing the ground for its home government to take over. Hence in 1893 the company's flag was replaced by the Union Jack, and soon afterwards an agreement or treaty was made between Kabaka Mwanga II of Buganda and Sir Gerald Portal, the first official representative of the British government.

The Portal Agreement of 1893 invalidated all previous agreements which Kabaka Mwanga had signed. He and his subjects put themselves under British protection, without asking themselves what they were being protected from. The agreement contained many articles and included provision for the assessment and collection of taxes as a responsibility of the new regime. Slave trade was prohibited and the Baganda were thenceforth bound by 'all and every' international act to which Great Britain might be a party! The Portal Agreement which was only provisional was confirmed in 1894 by another agreement signed by Colonel Colville and Kabaka Mwanga and incorporating similar provisions.

The extension of British rule and the reaction of African rulers

British rule in Uganda spread by force of arms, though, in some areas, military conquest was disguised by a series of agreements. Buganda was to be the centre from which the British octopus spread its tentacles to other parts of Uganda. During Lugard's short stay, he had marched westwards and reinstated Kasagama, the *Omukama* of Toro who had fled to Buganda when Kabarega, the Omukama of Bunyoro, attempted to reconquer Bunyoro's rebellious state. Lugard clashed with Kabarega as did his successors. In the process of fighting against Kabarega, the British extended their rule to the west and north-west. Meanwhile, British rule had also been extended to the east and north. As early as 1894 Captain Grant had already established himself in Busoga, and towards the end of the century, Kakungulu, a Muganda veteran general of the religious wars, crossed Lake Kyoga with a large following of his fellow Baganda. These started 'conquering' the regions of Teso and Lango, and eastern Uganda was brought under British rule by the Baganda agents. By the outbreak of the First World War in 1914, British rule had been established over modern Uganda, though there was no regular administration in Karamoja before 1919.

In 1900 another and more detailed agreement was made between the leading Baganda chiefs and the British representative, Sir Harry Johnston.[1] One of its chief aims was to define the position of Buganda in Uganda, by which it was ranked as a province. We cannot go into all its provisions, but some of the most important ones were in connection with the system of land tenure and the position of the kabaka and the chiefs. Politically, the agreement reduced the personal rule of the kabaka. Henceforth he had to be assisted by his chiefs and the lukiko. Since the kabaka at the time was a minor, this provision was actually put into practice. The kabaka, in fact, became a nominee of the British for he could retain his throne only so long as the colonial regime thought that he was cooperating fully with them. From the economic and social points of view, the new system of land tenure created a kind of perma-

---

[1] This, traditionally known as the Uganda Agreement, is referred to below as the Buganda Agreement.

nent aristocracy which had not existed before. The introduction of the private system of land ownership is believed to have led to the relative economic prosperity of Buganda as compared to that of other parts of Uganda. Similar but modified agreements were signed in 1900 with the kingdom of Toro, and with the kingdom of Ankole in 1904, but no agreement was made with Bunyoro until 1933. Thus the kingdoms, with the exception of Bunyoro, came to be known as the agreement states and it was owing to these agreements, particularly those made with Buganda, that Uganda owed its status as a protectorate.

Nearly everywhere in Uganda, colonial rule had been established by force, either directly by the arms of the British or by those of their agents, the Baganda. And everywhere this alien rule was resisted, with disastrous consequences for the resisters. The most notable were Kabarega, the Omukama of Bunyoro, and Mwanga, the Kabaka of Buganda. As enemies of imperialism, they had to be smashed. Kabarega resisted for nearly ten years, but in 1899 he was deposed and deported, dying in exile in 1923. Although Kabaka Mwanga had originally signed agreements with the British, he finally decided to fight rather than submit to the humiliation of foreign rule. He met with the same fate as Kabarega and died in exile in 1901. In the Ankole area, the King of Igara committed suicide and his neighbour the King of Kajara fled to Tanganyika. The King of Buhweju was killed by British bullets. In Busoga, cooperation was secured by the threat of deposition and deportation. In Teso, Lango and Acholi, alien rule was equally resisted, culminating in the last district in the Lamogi rebellion of 1912.

But perhaps the greatest threat to colonial rule in Uganda was not from African rulers or resisters, but from the Sudanese troops. Since Lugard first arrived in Uganda at the beginning of the 1890s, Sudanese troops had been gathered by the colonial powers and strategically located. In Uganda as well as in the British East African protectorate, they were Britain's men of action. Lugard used them in Buganda in 1892 to crush the Catholics and they were later used to smash the resistance of Mwanga and Kabarega. They fought in the Nandi country and in various parts of the rift valley. All this activity inevitably strained these troops. Underpaid, and with pay in arrears, when called upon to engage in further activities which would have taken them from western Kenya to the eastern borders of the Congo, some companies refused to move any further. A number of regiments mutinied and marched to Busoga. In subsequent fighting, casualties included several British officers. The mutineers held out for about a year, and it was not until Indian soldiers had arrived from the coast and sufficient forces mustered from Buganda that the mutinous soldiers were finally defeated. With the smashing of the African resisters and of the Sudanese mutiny, British rule in Uganda was established with no further challenges.

The beginning of administration

When the British took over Uganda, they had no clear plans of how to administer the country. But they found in Buganda the traditional system of a kabaka heading a hierarchy of chiefs. Though similar administrative structures existed in other kingdoms, the kiganda system had acquired a degree of efficiency which was unsurpassed in the whole of the lake region of East Africa. The system impressed the British, and as British rule in Uganda was extended by the Baganda, who generally provided the first chiefs, it was introduced to nearly all other parts of the protectorate, with varying degrees of success. The Baganda agents, in introducing the kiganda model, were the backbone of the new administration, and everywhere formed the first beginnings of local government. But perhaps to emphasise their role as agents, as soon as the ground had been prepared the British stepped in. Thus in 1901 Kakungulu was replaced and conveniently sent to Busoga where he became the first President and laid the foundation of the office of the *kyabazinga* (paramount ruler). Practically everywhere, the role of the Baganda as agents of British imperialism provoked reactions which led to violent clashes. Hence between 1902 and 1911 Baganda agents were gradually withdrawn from north-eastern Uganda, though they stayed longer in the administration of the east and west.

The traditional view of colonial rule in Uganda is that in the south the British adopted an indirect system of government. This administrative system endeavoured to vest power in the traditional sources of authority. Thus in areas where there were known traditional chiefs, the British used these to carry out their orders and functions. The degree to which the system was applied differed from area to area and from period to period. Thus in Buganda, where British administrative authority derived from the Buganda Agreement of 1900, the system was believed to be more indirect than elsewhere in the protectorate. Similarly the power of the chief everywhere was far greater before 1930 than after. In northern and eastern Uganda where there were no large centralised states or traditional rulers whose authority was recognised by many followers, a system of direct rule was adopted. In such areas, the British would appoint a chief even though he had no traditional or hereditary claim to office. It ought to be stressed, however, that the system of indirect rule was as old as mankind itself. Neither was it invented by the British nor were they the only colonial power which adopted such a system when it suited them. However, in actual practise, there was little difference between the so-called 'indirectly' administered areas and those which were directly administered. Kings and chiefs, whether traditional or not, were all nominees of the colonial power which would make or unmake them at will.

The protectorate administration was headed by the governor, under whom were provincial and district commissioners. These were assisted by county, *gombolola* (sub-county) and a large number of minor chiefs. It was on such a structure that the local government of Uganda was based. There were local councils which were modelled on the Buganda Lukiko, and their main function was to carry out local administration and to provide a forum for local politics. These councils, however, were unfortunately inefficient, and the men who sat in them were sometimes more interested in preserving their own positions than in efficient administration. After the First World War, the central government felt the need to introduce some kind of legislative council (referred to below as the Legco). The establishment of such a body was first proposed in 1919 and it was instituted two years later. It was to consist of the Governor, the Chief Secretary, the Attorney General and the Chief Medical Officer. These formed the official side of the council. The unofficial side consisted of two Europeans from the business community of Kampala. The Governor and his three assistants made up the Executive Council. One Indian had been nominated to sit on the unofficial side, but the Indian community had protested about under-representation. Their appeal was cold-shouldered by the Governor and the Colonial Secretary and as a result they boycotted the Council when it first assembled in 1921. The Africans, who were the majority and who grew the crops upon which the country's wealth depended, were not represented. Their interests were to be taken care of by the Europeans and Indians, though the latter continued their boycott until the new Governor, Sir William Gowers, persuaded them to end it. Hence in 1926, Mr C. J. Amin accepted the Governor's invitation and became an unofficial member of the council. Meanwhile, the government side had been enlarged by the addition of the Directors of Agriculture and Education.

The Legco obviously was shamelessly racial in composition, representing first the Europeans and second the Indians. Even the unofficial members of the council hardly showed interest in African representation. The attitude of the Uganda Indians in this differed from that of their counterparts in Kenya. It may be argued that the Africans did not show much interest in the new council. The Baganda, who might have taken the lead, regarded the Legco as an alien institution. They had their own lukiko (council) and as long as the new body did not affect the agreement of 1900, it could carry on without them. Nevertheless, even if Africans had shown interest at this time, the colonial government would, no doubt, have carried on regardless of their views. The Legco thus continued as a small exclusive body, catering primarily for the Europeans and Indians and only remotely for the African. It was not until 1945 that three African members, one from each province excluding Buganda, were appointed.

318

At first sight it seems paradoxical that such a policy should be pursued by a government which publicly declared that Uganda was to develop primarily as an African country. This 'primarily African' policy was applied only where it suited British interests. Nevertheless, its implications in other aspects were important. First of all, there was no large scale alienation of land to non-Africans such as that which had taken place in Kenya. Hence there could be only a small European settler community in Uganda, though both Lugard and Johnston had wished Europeans to settle in Uganda as they did in Kenya. Perhaps the most important aspect of this government policy was the decision that the economic development of Uganda would depend on peasant agriculture. Unlike Kenya, the Africans were thus encouraged to grow cash crops such as coffee and cotton which quickly became the mainstay of Uganda's economy. Two European civil servants ought to be remembered for blocking the ambitions of the European planters who were keen to grab the land and introduce plantation agriculture: Mr Simpson, who was the Director of Agriculture from 1915 to 1929, and Mr F. Spire, who was the Provincial Commissioner in the then Eastern Province. Their persistent support of peasant agriculture often provoked bitter opposition from their fellow Europeans. In Buganda, the greatest stumbling block against the would-be settlers was the Buganda Agreement of 1900 which made conditions under which land could be alienated to non-Africans too complicated.

Cotton as a commercial crop was introduced in 1904 by Mr Borup of the Uganda Company, first in Buganda and then in other parts of the protectorate. By 1910, cotton had already replaced ivory, hides and chillies as the leading export commodity. For a long time, cotton remained the dominant crop, and by 1930 cotton acreage was 304 000 [123 029 ha]. It was not until the 1950s that cotton was replaced by coffee as the leading export crop, but even then it occupied more cultivated land than any other export crop. Uganda is still the leading cotton exporter in East Africa and it must be remembered that it was upon cotton that Uganda's agricultural economy was built. The Eastern Province has always been the leading cotton area, followed by Buganda. But from the mid-1950s, the Baganda concentrated more on growing coffee. Coffee had been growing in many parts of Uganda before the colonial era, but not as a commercial crop. Other commercial crops such as sugar-cane and tea, which cover extensive acreages in eastern Buganda and Busoga, are grown mainly by Indians, though tea has been introduced in the western region.

Cotton Production 1906 to 1964 (thousands of bales of 400 lbs [180 kg] of lint)[1].

	Uganda	Buganda	E. Region	N. Region	W. Region
1905–6	I				
1910–11	12				
1915–16	22	6	14	2	
1920–1	81	23	46	10	2
1925–6	180	58	93	25	4
1930–1	190	62	94	30	4
1935–6	316	141	135	33	7
1940–1	365		not available		
1945–6	227	127	72	20	8
1950–1	346	139	154	41	11
1955–6	364	120	170	60	14
1960–1	371	71	185	60	14
1963–4	379	53	201	107	18

The development of peasant agriculture has had two important sociological and economic consequences. First, instead of becoming wage earners, the vast majority of Uganda Africans stayed on the land, which even today employs over eighty per cent of the country's population; the farm provided the African with cash income and it remained his source of security. Second, the urban population of Uganda has consequently always been largely non-African. The fact that the majority of the people stayed on the land occasioned a shortage of labour, particularly on the plantations of non-Africans. Thus, until recently, a large proportion of the labour force was non-Ugandan, coming mainly from Burundi, Rwanda and Kenya. Even in industries such as the East African Railways the labour force was largely Kenyan, from the Nyanza region. From a financial point of view, the Uganda African was generally better off than his counterpart in Kenya and Tanzania, for he shared, though in a very small way, in the economic development of the country. With the money they obtained, the African farmers were able to educate their children.

Trade and commerce

Although Uganda developed as a primarily African country, the bulk of trade and business remained in the hands of non-Africans. The job of the African was to grow the crops which were bought at prices

[1] *Source:* A. O'Connor, *Economic Geography of East Africa*, Bell, London, 1966.

320

fixed by the government. Price-fixing was usually the result of the influence upon the government of Indian and European traders. Thus the price of cotton paid to the African farmer was sometimes so low that the African lost interest and the acreage decreased considerably. Thus, although by 1918 the total export revenue, mainly from cotton, had reached £1 200 000, less than half went into the pockets of the Africans who produced over eighty per cent of the crop. It was also extremely difficult for the Africans to become middlemen. When in 1920 a development commission was appointed to promote the commercial and industrial development of the country it was singularly hostile to the advancement of Africans in every field, not only economic but also educational and political. Non-African associations of ginners and buyers were formed with the avowed aim of keeping prices low. The Buganda Lukiko protested and appealed to the government to protect the growers, but the government quietly connived at the activities of the Indian and European speculators. It was not until African opposition mounted that a commission of inquiry was appointed to look into the cotton industry. Although the commission's report mildly criticised the low prices paid to the growers, it was almost openly on the side of the buyers and ginners. The lukiko opposed the report and again appealed to the government to discourage the Buyers and Ginners' Association from paying low prices to African growers. In Busoga, several counties sent petitions to the Provincial Commissioner protesting against controlled marketing which enabled syndicates of Indian buyers to lower the prices. Discontent was widely spread throughout Uganda, even though Africans in other areas were not articulate enough to voice it. Despite these protests, the government, whose declared policy was to develop Uganda primarily as an African country, did little to break the Indian and European monopoly of middle men. Africans were denied an opportunity to enter the ginning industry with the excuse that they were 'entirely ignorant of the ginning system'. When Africans attempted to form buyers' associations, hostility was shown from all non-African quarters including the government. When the associations failed, the government gaily pointed out that the Africans had attempted to run before they had learnt to walk. But as one economic historian has pointed out, there were very few opportunities for the African to learn to walk.[1]

Adequate transport is the key to economic progress. History and geography had determined the joint development of the railway system of East Africa, and being inland, Uganda had a special interest in the maintenance of an efficient railway link with the coast and so with world markets. Even trade between Kenya and Tanganyika depended not only

[1] See C. Ehrlich, *Oxford History of East Africa*, 2, pp. 395–475.

on lake shipping but also on the railway system. Thus the completion of the 'Uganda Railway' as far as Kisumu in 1902, was a landmark. Not only did it reduce transport costs, but it provided Uganda with a quick link with the outside world. By 1912, the line between Jinja and Namasagali was completed, just when the cotton crop was expanding in the eastern region. Internally, railway development took the form of constructing branch lines to bring traffic from the production centres into the main lines of communication. A line was extended from Tororo to Soroti and in 1948 an extension was made through western Uganda to the copper-mining area of Kasese. In 1961, the Bukonte-Jinja cut-off was completed; further developments are taking place in the north where the Tororo-Soroti line reached Lira in 1962 and Gulu a year later. Railway transport has always been greatly supplemented by water and road. Like the railways, Lake Victoria has always been a major link between Uganda, Kenya and Tanzania. The 'Uganda Railway' originally terminated at Kisumu, and thus the main link between Uganda and the outside world was through Lake Victoria. Internally, Lake Kyoga and the short navigable stretch on the River Nile have always provided excellent waterways. But the increasing efficiency of motor transport must involve a decline in inland water transport. A road system radiating from Kampala, the commercial capital, to other trading centres, was the key to the agricultural development of the country. This was recognised from a very early period of colonial rule, and to facilitate the expansion of cotton growing a programme of road construction was adopted. Today, Uganda possesses one of the best road systems in Africa.

Educational development

It is sometimes assumed that education in Africa began with the coming of the Europeans. This mistaken belief springs from the assumption that the western type of education is the only system of education. Every community, in fact, has its own system of education and values. Among Africans, it was usual for young people to attend meetings of elders and listen to discussions and even to disputes. The elders would also tell the history of their ancestors, and in this way the young people learnt the history, the laws and customs of their own societies, and appreciated their values. This was one kind of education. The western type of education in Uganda was introduced by the Christian missionaries as an essential part of the process of conversion to Christianity. Inevitably therefore the first schools were Christian schools and were for the sons of chiefs. In the early period missionary efforts were concentrated primarily in Buganda and development outside came slowly. The first secondary boarding school was opened by the Mill Hill Fathers at Namilyango in

1902 and it became the prototype for other schools such as Buddo, Kisubi, Gayaza and others. The last school was for girls. The curriculum which was designed for potential leaders was mainly academic, with heavy emphasis on grammar and reading of English books, geography and mathematics. Technical schools were also opened.

During the first twenty years of the protectorate, the central government was mainly concerned with establishing a stable administration, spending little time and effort or money on social services. The principal result of this government neglect in financing education was that non-Christians were generally neglected in educational development. Hence for many years the education of the Moslems lagged behind. It was not until the 1920s that the government took an interest in the development of education. In 1925, a Department of Education was formed, and the next fifteen years were characterised by a gradual but steady expansion of schools; the government also began to subsidise the voluntary agencies which ran the schools. By the end of the Second World War there had been marked expansion in the number of schools and in expenditure. For instance, immediately after the first war, government allocation for education was £1 250. By 1950, the total estimated expenditure was £75 000 and in 1960 £5 million were spent on education.

From the very beginning, education in Uganda had developed along racial as well as religious lines. There were separate schools for Africans, Indians and Europeans. Among the Africans there were separate schools for Catholics, Moslems and Protestants; religious divisions existed also among the Asians. In order to bring an end to this chaotic state of affairs, the government announced in 1957 its intention to integrate the educational system. And since that date the government has steadily plodded along the road of integration. During the same period, another decision regarding the development of junior and senior secondary education was taken. The rapid expansion of primary education in the early 1950s made it necessary to slow the pace of development in the primary category in order to expand secondary education. Despite this expansion, the ratio of the places available in primary schools has remained one place for nearly every fourteen children.

Why did Uganda achieve so much in educational development compared with many other African countries? It was not because the colonial government did more to develop education in Uganda than elsewhere. Of course, the colonial government has always been proud to quote Uganda, Ghana and southern Nigeria as areas where the British developed African education, but much of the credit goes rather to the missionaries. In countries where missionary effort was slow, African education developed very slowly, and particularly where the countries were poor, the colonial governments did little to develop African education. Much more was achieved in Uganda because Uganda was richer and Africans participated in the growing of cash crops such as coffee and cotton. Today education is no longer restricted to the privileged few.

During the same period, medical services expanded considerably. The first hospitals and dispensaries were founded by missionaries; Mengo Hospital remained for many years the most famous of these hospitals. The missionaries also ran a number of scattered hospitals and other small units. From the earliest period of the protectorate, the foremost department was that of medical services. Its director was originally responsible to the Chief Secretary for the administration of the department and for advice on medical matters generally. At the beginning of the 1950s, the Ministry of Social Services was established to bring about a closer integration of the many different aspects of medical services. Today there are rural dispensaries, district and sub-district hospitals, and mission hospitals. The central hospital is Mulago, wich cost over £3 000 000 to build and has nearly nine hundred beds. It has a medical school attached to it, providing medical training for nearly three hundred students from all over East Africa and beyond.

The beginnings of nationalism

Baganda agents had been removed from north and eastern Uganda as early as 1901, though a few remained until the late 1920s. By the beginning of the 1930s, Baganda agents, wherever they were, were making way for the indigenous chiefs: in Ankole, Kigezi, Toro, Bunyoro and elsewhere. Throughout these areas, a great deal of the reaction to colonial rule was provoked not so much by the British as by their agents, the Baganda. Remotely therefore, these first reactions can be described as the first seeds of nationalism in as much as they were directed against alien rule even though it was represented by the Baganda. For a very long time, Buganda remained the centre of political activity, expressed either against the economic exploitation of the African by European and Indian businessmen or against the chiefs, even against the kabaka himself or against certain policies of the central government. The first signs of political discontent appeared before the 1914–18 war.

The Bamalaki, a semi-religious movement, sprang up and provided the venue for voicing political discontent. Although this was in all appearances a religious movement, like many such movements it also had political aims. The high-water mark of political discontent came early in the 1920s when the Bataka movement nearly forced a revision of the 1900 Buganda Agreement. The Bataka desired a redistribution of land, and inclusion of a clause which would make ancestral land the property of the clans rather than of the individual heads in whose names

324

the land was registered. The kabaka, Sir Daudi Cwa II, sympathised with their case and recommended a revision of the agreement. The colonial government, however, sided with the existing chiefs whose interests were at stake, and advised the Colonial Secretary to reject the kabaka's recommendation.

Political activity further manifested itself in the opposition to an East African federation in the 1920s and 1930s because of the fear that Uganda might become another Kenya—a country dominated by European settlers. The most vocal organs at this time were the Buganda Lukiko, the Young Baganda Association and the Young Basoga Association. During the 1940s, economic and political discontent increased considerably in Buganda. People wanted more participation in the direction of their affairs through more representatives in the lukiko. At the same time they wanted to get rid of the old type of chiefs who seemed to be puppets of the colonial government. Such discontent found an outlet in the Buganda riots of 1945, and also in the assassination of the Buganda Prime Minister, Martin Luther Nsibirwa. From that time onwards events moved fast and the Uganda African Farmers Association conducted a campaign against the exploitation of African farmers by Indian and European businessmen. The agitation culminated in the 1949 riots, which were more serious and better organised than those of 1945. The Africans demanded that they should be allowed to market their own crops and also asked the Kabaka to make the lukiko more democratic by increasing the representative side to sixty members. One factor characterising the riots of the 1940s was that they were confined to Buganda and their immediate target was the Baganda chiefs. This has created the impression that they were local movements having nothing to do with the advancement of Africans in Uganda. What must be remembered, however, is that nationalism had to start somewhere. By fighting against the economic exploitation of farmers, and by denouncing their own chiefs who seemed to be agents of this exploitation, the leaders of the 1945 and 1949 movements sowed the seeds of modern nationalism. But for the time being they were unable to talk in terms of national politics, for they had fewer than six representatives in the only national body, the Legislative Council.

Militant nationalism which brought independence thus took a long time to formulate itself because of a number of factors. The Uganda African, unlike his Kenya counterpart, was never robbed of his land. Although there was forced labour, it was never carried to the same extent as in Kenya or in other countries where there were European settlers. But perhaps the greatest factor militating against a rapid growth of nationalism was the system of indirect rule and lack of a clear policy on the part of the British on the future of Uganda. Indirect rule tended to favour the growth of local autonomy, and the result was that the

British indirectly encouraged federalist tendencies in their administration. Lack of a central political forum for the Africans and the British encouragement of local councils meant that the immediate African interests were with local affairs. But by exposing the economic exploitation of the masses, and by demanding increased representation in the Buganda Lukiko, men of the 1940s lighted the tinder which burst into nationalist flames towards the end of the 1950s. After the 1949 riots, the clock could never be turned back nor even be stopped.

It was Uganda's good fortune at this stage of her political development that at the beginning of the 1950s, there came a governor who was prepared to keep pace with the winds of change. Sir Andrew Cohen had arrived in Uganda in 1952, and early in 1953 proposed constitutional changes in Buganda which if adopted would have led to real representative government. Other parts of the country were also to be affected in varying degrees. In Buganda more power was to devolve on the government through the transfer of a number of responsibilities: primary and junior secondary schools, rural hospitals, agriculture and veterinary services. In order to cope with these new responsibilities, ministries in the kabaka's government were increased by three, and in the lukiko sixty out of eighty members were to be elected, giving it for the first time an elected majority. Sir Andrew's pre-occupation at this stage was to introduce progressive reforms which would give a greater say to the Africans in the running of their own affairs. He at the same time wished to see a steady development of Uganda as a unitary state. But things suddenly took a sharp turn when, in 1953, the kabaka, supported by the lukiko, opposed the idea of an East African federation, proposed in the Secretary of State for the Colonies' speech of 30 June 1953. It was also at this time that the kabaka demanded independence and thereby posed a threat to the existence of the colonial government. Hitherto, the colonial government had used the kabaka as the instrument of suppression of any radicalism in Buganda politics, and even in the reforms proposed by Sir Andrew Cohen the kabaka was still regarded as a promoter of colonial policy. When by his demand for independence Mutesa appeared to assume the role of nationalist leader, and when he attempted to bring the other rulers in the West to his line of thinking, he clearly became a threat to the colonial government. In November, Mutesa II was deposed and deported to Britain, for 'breaking' the Buganda Agreement which required him to cooperate loyally with the protectorate government.

Meanwhile, in 1952, the first modern political party was formed. This was the Uganda National Congress (UNC). Its declared aim was to unite all the peoples of Uganda and to bring independence. The kabaka crisis had given a new and sharper edge to the development of nationalist forces. By unceremoniously deporting the kabaka, Sir Andrew Cohen had made the worst blunder of his political career in Uganda. Overnight, Mutesa became a hero and acquired a measure of popularity which he had not achieved since his accession in 1940. All politically minded people saw the Governor's action as an affront to the African. The UNC had now a clear target: the immediate ending of colonial rule. It denounced the economic exploitation of the African masses by Indians and Europeans, and opposed East African federation. People all over Uganda were becoming more politically conscious. In 1954 the Democratic Party was founded. At about the same time the Progressive Party, the PP, was also formed. But the latter two parties lacked the dynamic drive of the UNC, which had such leaders as Musaazi, Joseph Kiwanuka and Abu Mayanja. The UNC was Uganda's burning spear and remained so until about 1958.

At the central level, important constitutional changes were taking place. Early in 1953, Sir Andrew had announced changes in the composition of the Legislative Council. A Cross Bench of ten unofficial members was to be formed and the representative side was to be increased to twenty-eight, of whom fourteen were to be Africans. These changes were not welcomed by all peoples in Uganda. They were in fact not as radical as some contemporary non-Africans believed; the representative side was only half of the total Council. The entire approach to the affairs of Uganda was still racial: for instance the composition of the council was still in the ratio of two to one to one, and only two Africans were unofficial members of the Executive Council.

Negotiations for the reinstatement of Mutesa II had led to a new agreement, which attempted to define in a more up-to-date manner the political position of Buganda in Uganda. In these negotiations the Baganda asked for the introduction of direct elections. The request was accepted and incorporated in the 1955 Buganda Agreement. Moving with extraordinary swiftness, Sir Andrew Cohen announced in 1956 that direct elections would be held in Buganda as an experiment, but that indirect elections would continue to be held in other areas. But people outside Buganda felt that they too should be given the opportunity of holding direct elections and their demand was accepted by the Governor.

Although it was the Baganda who had first asked for the introduction of direct elections while negotiating the 1955 agreement, they suddenly changed their minds when the time drew near in 1957. The Mengo regime, and the kabaka's government in particular, suddenly realised the political dangers of the ballot box, and therefore opposed the introduction of direct elections 'until certain conditions in the Buganda Agreements' had been fulfilled. Legal fictions were found, such as that the introduction of a Speaker in the Legislative Council was contrary to the agreement of 1955, and expert lawyers from Britain readily made themselves available to argue Buganda's case. This was in fact a way of

327

perpetuating the positions of the old regime in Buganda politics. The new Governor, Sir Frederick Crawford, was extremely cautious when dealing with Buganda affairs. So he let the Baganda have their own way in this matter, and when direct elections were held in 1958 Buganda did not participate. A system of indirect elections, however, was used whereby the lukiko nominated the representatives. It was an effective method of control by the kabaka and the lukiko on these representatives. It was not long in fact before the lukiko recalled its representatives from the Legislative Council. With this act, the kabaka's government, then led by Michael Kintu, withdrew Buganda from the centre of Uganda politics. Other districts where the existing regimes felt threatened by the ballot box followed Buganda and opted for indirect elections. Thus no direct elections were held in Ankole. But Mengo's intransigence did not halt the march of progress, for ten districts participated in the district elections, not counting Bugisu, which demanded fulfilment of certain conditions, and Karamoja, which was a special case.

The introduction of the ministerial system in 1955 and of direct elections of African representatives in 1958 marked the real beginning of political progress in Uganda. After these elections, the Legislative Council consisted of twenty-five representatives, fifteen of whom were Africans. The important feature of the post-1958 Council was that, although there were more official members, the Africans had a majority over non-Africans, and there was also a majority of non-civil servants. The political wind of change had begun to blow hard.

In 1959, the government appointed a committee to consider constitutional changes which would pave the way for self-government and independence. The committee was chaired by Mr J. V. Wild, a civil servant, and in December 1959 it produced its report. The Wild Report recommended the introduction of a common roll and the abolition of the indirect rule system of elections. Throughout the country representation was to be on a population basis. The government accepted nearly all the major recommendations and these led to the first country-wide elections. Meanwhile the political scene had been enlivened by the Uganda National Movement which had been launched early in 1959. It was essentially a political movement but had as many other aims as there were leaders. It declared a trade boycott against non-Africans and very soon had to back its actions by intimidation and violence. Augustine Kamya took over leadership of the movement, thus giving it the mantle of being truly a 'common man's movement'. But it was soon proscribed, its leaders were deported to Karamoja and other parts of northern Uganda, and it finally went underground. The UNM was in many ways a failure for it had neither a programme nor defined aims. However, as the first popular movement in Buganda, it was supported with an enthusiasm which was only exceeded by the Kabaka Yekka Movement launched in 1961.

Meanwhile political parties had multiplied with the intense political activity. The once strong UNC had been bedevilled by party squabbles which led to splits, expulsions and counter-expulsions. By 1960, the strongest splinter group was that which became the Uganda Peoples' Congress, led by A. M. Obote. It carried with it some of the radicalism of the old UNC, but this gradually rubbed off. The only major political parties in Uganda in 1960 were the Democratic Party (DP), and the UPC. The former was greatly aided by a change of leadership in 1958 when Benedicto Kiwanuka succeeded Mugwanya as the leader of the party. But, although these were country-wide political parties, they faced great handicaps in getting themselves established. First of all, Uganda was in many ways an artificial unit containing many different tribes. Throughout the seventy years of British rule, little effort had been made to unify the country and develop it as a single unit. The second difficulty was the relative lack of educated manpower. The majority of the educated people were civil servants who were debarred from all kinds of political activity. The DP had another handicap, for it was suspected of masking a Roman Catholic plot, while the UPC was almost non-existent in Buganda. It was with these difficulties that Uganda's two major political parties confronted each other when in 1961 the first country-wide elections were held.

After the collapse of the Uganda National Movement and other Mengo-backed political parties (such as the United National Party led by Apolo Kironde), the Mengo regime was left without a political party. It was this rather than the 'securing of Buganda's position' which led the kabaka's government in 1960 to boycott the registration of voters and the subsequent election. As a result of the boycott and intimidation, registration in Buganda was very small, which meant that the DP was virtually unopposed and so won the general election with a fairly comfortable majority. The 1961 election opened the way for the first African government headed by the party leader, Benedicto Kiwanuka. Dr Obote led the Opposition. Independence could not be delayed for long and with its approach political activity was intensified throughout the country. Meanwhile, the Mengo regime, realising that they were missing the boat, took steps to correct the unfortunate decision of the previous year. First a party was formed, the *Kabaka Yekka* (King Alone). Its formation provided an outlet for the pent-up emotions of the people of Buganda. A popular movement with a potent weapon in the slogan 'Kabaka Yekka' and the knowledge that it was supported by the kabaka himself, Kabaka Yekka (KY) spread like a wild fire and threatened almost total disaster to the only strong party in Buganda, the Democratic Party. KY, however, was essentially confined to Buganda, having as sole objective the protection of the monarchy. However it won national status when it made an alliance with the UPC and agreed

329

to participate in the constitutional conference which was to produce the Independence Constitution of 1961. One of the major features of the 1961 constitution was the option given to Buganda to nominate its representatives to the National Assembly instead of electing them directly as in other parts of Uganda. As events were to show later, it was dangerous to support the option, because its ultimate aim was to strangle nationalist movements in Buganda. But the immediate aim of ousting the DP served its purpose. In February 1962, elections to the lukiko took place and the DP, the only major party to contest seats with the KY, was soundly thrashed, winning only two of the sixty-eight seats in the new lukiko. Kabaka Yekka took the expected decision and opted for indirect elections to the National Assembly.

Things were now moving fast. Self-government was granted in March, and Mr Kiwanuka became Uganda's first prime minister. One month afterwards, a general election was held to decide which party was to lead Uganda to independence. After its defeat in Buganda, the DP's chances of winning the elections were almost nil. They were defeated outside Buganda by the UPC which joined hands with the KY which, with twenty-one members nominated by the Buganda Lukiko, gave the UPC-KY government a comfortable majority. Dr Obote became the Prime Minister, and in September 1962 led a delegation to London to put the final touches to the Independence Constitution.

Independence and after

On 9 October 1962, Uganda joined the other new nations of Africa as an independent and sovereign state, but there was to be a governor-general and the Queen was to be the Head of State. In the 1962 constitution there were a few points which could only be changed after independence. One of the thorny questions which had been bequeathed to the new government by the colonial power was that of the 'lost counties'. The establishment of British rule had led to the alienation of the counties of Bugangazzi and Buyaga, both of which had been Bunyoro territory then. Although the Banyoro claimed more than the two counties, the government made arrangements to hold a referendum only in those two. This took place in 1964, when the inhabitants of Buyaga and Bugangazzi voted to rejoin Bunyoro. In 1963, Sir Edward Mutesa, the Kabaka of Buganda, was elected the first President of Uganda and Sir Wilberforce Nadiope, the Kyabazinga of Busoga, was elected Vice-President. By the end of 1964, the government had settled the 'lost counties' issue, and Uganda had an African president, though the Queen was in a vague way still regarded also as the Head of State, for Uganda was not yet a republic. Meanwhile the UPC had strengthened its position by crossings from

KY and DP. These crossings from KY deprived the movement of its intellectual wing, and left the masses with no sound leadership. Daudi Ochieng attempted to turn it into a modern political party, but without success. On the surface therefore, the UPC's position seemed formidable, for the party had won practically every district council election, and the only area where they were almost non-existent was still Buganda. Nevertheless, with the frequent crossings from DP and KY, it looked as if Uganda would become a one party state even without legislation.

But all was not well inside the ruling party. Dissensions tore it from top to bottom. The annual delegates' conference which elects the party leaders had to be postponed. By late 1965, there were rumours of a threatened *coup d'etat*, which set the country on edge. Matters came to a head when in January 1966, Daudi Ochieng brought a motion in the National Assembly demanding an investigation of the financial activities of some leading ministers, including the Prime Minister and Deputy Commander of the Uganda Army. These serious allegations led to the appointment of a committee of inquiry which included a number of the leading lawyers of East Africa.

By the end of January 1966, it had become clear that there must be an explosion of some kind. Hence in February, during a cabinet meeting, the Prime Minister, Dr Obote ordered the arrest and immediate detention of five of his ministers. He suspended the constitution and assumed full powers. All this took place before the Committee of Inquiry into Ochieng's allegations had met. The suspension of the 1962 constitution virtually meant the end of the non-executive president and vice-president and it was not long before Sir Edward and Sir Wilberforce had to vacate their offices. The 1962 constitution was finally replaced on 15 April 1966 by a new constitution. The major change was that Dr Obote became the new President. Other important changes affected Buganda and the kabaka's ability to direct political movements in Buganda.

Soon afterwards, tension increased between the central government and the Buganda government. Things came to a head when the lukiko passed a resolution which virtually expelled the central government from Buganda soil. The situation seemed to have reached a point of no return and it exploded on the morning of 24 May 1966, when central government troops invaded and overran the kabaka's palace. The kabaka and some of those within escaped, but very many others were slain.

Meanwhile all political rallies except those of the ruling party were banned. Kabaka Yekka had already been declared illegal and many people were thrown into jail either for alleged rioting during the month of May 1966 or for alleged plotting to overthrow the government. The Kabaka Yekka movement will remain one of the most dramatic and

331

interesting episodes in the history of Uganda. It had been formed for the specific aim of protecting the monarchy. It left Buganda without a kabaka and with the country in a state of emergency.

Further reading

LOW, A. D. 'Uganda: The Establishment of the Protectorate, 1884–1919', *History of East Africa, II*, Oxford Univrsity Press, Oxford, 1963, pp. 57–122.

EHRLICH, C. 'The Uganda Economy 1903–1945', *History of East Africa, II*, Oxford University Press, Oxford, 1965, pp. 395–475.

INGHAM, K. *The Making of Modern Uganda*, Allen and Unwin, London, 1957.

INGHAM, K. *The Economic Development of Uganda*, Report of the International Bank, Baltimore, 1962.

O'CONNOR, A. *The Economic Geography of East Africa*, Bell and Sons, London, 1966.

LOW, A. D. and PRATT, R. C. *Buganda and British Overrule*, Oxford University Press, London, 1960. (See especially pp. 163–178 for valuable comment on indirect rule.)

WILD, J. V. *The Story of the Uganda Agreement*, East African Literature Bureau, Nairobi, 1950.

WILD, J. V. *Report of the Constitutional Committee, 1959*, Uganda Government Printer, Kampala, 1959.

APTER, D. *The Political Kingdom in Uganda*, Oxford University Press, London, 1961.

MITCHELL, P. E. 'Indirect Rule', *Uganda Journal, IV*, 1937, pp. 101–107.

16

Economic and Social Developments before Independence

Cyril Ehrlich

Three interconnected themes can be traced in the economic and social history of East Africa—the growth of its economies, the policies of its governments, and the welfare of its peoples. Under these main headings we can ask a series of questions. What was the nature and extent of economic development during the colonial period? Which goods were produced with what arrangement of productive factors, land, labour, capital, and enterprise? As the economy grew what happened to its structure, what were the main determinants of this evolving pattern, and what ultimately was the legacy inherited by the new independent governments? How did the colonial governments frame and execute social and economic policies, and with how much success? Finally, to what extent and in what sense were people better off during and as a result of all these changes—what happened to their standard of living? A short introductory chapter cannot hope to provide adequate answers to all these questions, but it might perhaps stimulate interest in and indicate the scope of a neglected subject. It may also provide the reader with some useful background knowledge for a better appreciation of the enormous problems of social and economic development facing East Africans today.

Creating a cash economy

At the beginning of our period, in the late nineteenth century, East African economies were simple and poor, based at best on a traditional

333

agriculture which in good seasons provided sufficient food for the home and perhaps for a limited local market. In some privileged areas, such as Buganda, fertile soil and adequate rainfall supported a denser population at a higher and more assured level of subsistence. Elsewhere, nature was frequently less generous, population sparse, and in bad seasons men, unaided by physical capital, starved. An essential first step towards growth, therefore, was the creation of a cash exchange economy, for men do not willingly work to produce more than their immediate requirements, so building up capital and raising their standard of living, unless they can find profitable outlets for these surpluses. Within East Africa, however, such market outlets were severely limited by various aspects of an omnipresent poverty—low incomes and a general lack of cash, poor communications, small populations, and an absence of towns. For these isolated subsistence economies to pull themselves up by their own bootstraps would have been a slow and arduous process, but the opening of the Suez Canal in 1869 and the growth of ocean shipping offered an alternative way of breaking this vicious circle of poverty. A comparison with West Africa's trade links is illuminating. The distance from Lagos to Liverpool is about 4 300 miles [6 920 km]; from Zanzibar to Britain via the Cape is over twice that distance; the Suez Canal lopped 2 000 miles [3 200 km] off the journey. Now East African products could more easily be exported to establish markets overseas, which promised a ready source of income to anyone who could supply suitable goods at competitive prices. The advantages of thus linking East Africa with the international economy were obvious and far reaching, but there was an attendant disadvantage. Thenceforth growth and welfare would depend to a very large extent upon factors lying outside the control of East Africans; while the *quantity* of exports would reflect local circumstances and effort, their *value* would be greatly affected by those world market conditions which still determine the demand for and the price of most East African products. For example, in 1930 the price of coffee dropped from about £120 to £70 a ton; the price of sisal slumped from £40 a ton in 1929 to £20 in the following year, and then to £12. Such dependence upon markets which are notoriously fickle has been frequently deplored, but the admitted defects of this situation when prices fall have been counter-balanced by the enormous benefits of good years like the 1920s and the great boom of the 1940s and early 1950s. Irregular income is better than no income. Moreover, this form of dependence should not be confused with the political dependence imposed by colonial authority. It is, in fact, the prevailing condition of many small independent countries, such as New Zealand and Ireland, whose foreign trade provides a high proportion of their national income, and whose prosperity therefore depends upon their ability to exploit the international economy, which can act as a powerful engine of growth if there is a sufficiently creative response to its manifold opportunities. There are abundant examples of this truth in modern economic history, from the spectacular successes of Denmark and Japan to the more modest but still impressive achievements of Uganda during the decade before 1914 and particularly during the 1920s. The production of viable exports has been the essential basis of whatever material progress East Africans have enjoyed during the twentieth century.

A transport revolution

Before they could benefit from such opportunities, a thorough-going revolution in transport facilities was an indispensable first step. Except on the coast, travel was extremely arduous, a fact that goes far to explain its economic backwardness in the nineteenth century. Water transport was insignificant, draught animals could not survive, and the motor-lorry had not so far appeared. The only form of carriage was the human caravan which was degrading, slow, wasteful of scarce labour, and absurdly expensive. Therefore, only goods which were extremely valuable in relation to their bulk could be afforded transport for any distance: here was a formidable barrier to trade and therefore to development. The obvious answer was to build railways, but the necessary investment would be large, and there was little evidence of a potential traffic that might attract sufficient funds for such an enterprise. The German company which began work on the Tanga-Korogwe railway in 1893 was first in this unenviable field, and its experience was typical of much of the early history of railway building elsewhere in East Africa. Difficult terrain, shortage of skilled labour, inexperience and inefficiency, inadequate materials and machinery, all ensured that progress was costly and slow. By 1896, the line had progressed a mere 27 miles [43 km] to Muhesa, boasted one train a week, and was earning less than a thirtieth of its running costs. The government eventually took over and at vast expense pushed the line on to Korogwe by 1902. Meanwhile, the British had made faster, but arduous and expensive progress with the so-called Uganda Railway.

The detailed history of this and later railway lines is already familiar. What concerns us here is their economic significance. Since there were no clear prospects of profit and, particularly, no known mineral deposits to exploit, railway projects were unattractive to all but the most optimistic investors, and therefore had to be financed out of public funds. Their principal economic effect was to link East Africa with the international economy by enormously reducing inland transport costs. Thus before the coming of the railway the cost of carrying a typical load from Mombasa to Kampala would account for more than half its final price.

The railway and improved transport on Lake Victoria reduced freight costs from England to Kampala by approximately ninety per cent. Deliveries were not merely cheaper, but also faster, more reliable and more regular. All this was of enormous benefit to import and export trade, for regularity and reliability are essential to modern commerce, and reduce the costly necessity of tying up capital in barren stocks. Railways also made an important contribution to urbanisation. Nairobi was born as a railway base in 1899, providing employment, a market for local produce, and general economic stimulus. There were similar if smaller scale developments at Mombasa, Dar es Salaam, and Tabora. Large labour forces were required for construction; in the building of the Tanganyika central line twenty thousand men were employed at peak periods of activity. For the building of the Uganda railway thirty-two thousand workers had to be brought from India (a warning of labour shortages to come). Of these, incidentally, only one-fifth elected to remain after their period of indenture was complete. After their construction, the railways continued to require a large labour force for their operation, administration and maintenance. By the end of our period East African Railways and Harbours, as it was then called, with a staff of some fifty thousand, was by far the largest industrial employer in the region.

The economic significance of the railways was therefore considerable, but it should not be exaggerated. Their extent was limited in relation to the vast area that needed to be opened up. Southern Tanganyika is perhaps the clearest example of this, but it should also be remembered that the so-called Uganda Railway did not actually enter Uganda until the 1920s and did not reach western Uganda until the 1950s. To have done more would have required massive investment which nothing but obsessive philanthropy or megalomania could have called forth. But their limited mileage and inherent inflexibility meant that they failed to provide anything approaching an adequate transport system. It can indeed be argued that the real agents of a transport revolution in East Africa were not the railways but, from the beginning of our period, the bicycle, and during the 1920s, the motor-lorry. The bicycle's contribution to productivity and well-being is self-evident, and makes it one of the most useful items to be found on the import lists. The lorry, financed by innumerable small businessmen, created a flexible transport system and introduced men to machinery—an innovation of far-reaching educational significance. Its impact was particularly beneficial in eastern Uganda where roads were comparatively good and the cotton crop made great demands on the transport system. Elsewhere, roads remained very poor for most of our period, though a great and expensive effort was made to improve them in Tanganyika during the closing years of colonial rule.

Despite their limitations, however, the railways did remove the immediate barrier to East Africa's joining the international economy. The question then was what could be produced that foreigners would buy in sufficient quantities to provide East Africans with a continuous flow of cash income and with foreign exchange to finance desired imports. The existing trickle of exports, consisting of such natural products as ivory and skins, was no base for economic development, and new commercially viable products had to be pioneered. While this was ultimately desirable for everyone's welfare, for the colonial governments it was an immediate *sine qua non*, for without cash incomes men could not pay taxes in a usable form and without cash revenue government could not function. Early attempts to impose taxes led, at best, to the accumulation of a useless collection of animals and produce. The creation of an exchange economy was thus an essential prerequisite for both economic and political development. During the early years of this century even the modest expenditures of the Kenya and Uganda governments were made possible only by grants in aid from Britain, and the administration of Tanganyika was subsidised in similar fashion by Germany. Under pressure to reduce these grants local administrators made considerable efforts to find commercial products and men who would produce them. There was virtually no indigenous industry and no mineral deposits had so far been discovered. Therefore the task was one of agricultural policy and development.

Agricultural policy

Agricultural policy was of vital importance for two simple reasons. First, because agriculture was by far the biggest sector of the economy, and therefore what governments did about it had far-reaching effects upon growth and welfare. Second, because these policies affected or even determined the involvement of Africans in commercial agriculture, and therefore the extent of Africanisation ultimately required when the countries became independent. It should be remembered, of course, that policies were not neat blueprints, imposed after careful planning by a fully informed government. Rather did they emerge as compromises, subject to the delays and pressures of politics, scarcity, and ignorance. Above all, in this as in most aspects of government policy, evolution tended to be slow because it was based upon what has been well described as 'the tranquil assumption of the long-term character of colonial rule'.

The two alternative systems through which commercial crops were produced can be briefly described as 'peasant' and 'plantation' agriculture. Under the first system people already on the land were persuaded or sometimes bullied into adapting their traditional forms of cultivation so as to include the new crops. Uganda's cotton industry is a familiar example of this grafting process by which traditional and exchange economic activities were merged. Under the 'plantation' system large units of land were allotted to immigrants who farmed commercially, employing Africans merely as unskilled labour. In German East Africa much capital, enterprise and skill were thrown into the production of sisal, coffee, and cotton on alienated estates. The Amani research institute, founded in 1902, was typical of the German thoroughness which justified their claim to be 'ahead of British East Africa by a decade in the development of the tropical belt'. In general the choice of system was affected to some extent by the intrinsic qualities and cultivation requirements of different crops, but it was mainly determined by governmental decisions which were in turn influenced by the desire for quick results and by the varying pressures of settler demands. Many crops could be grown under either system, but this fact was usually obscured by special pleading, notably in the case of coffee, which was satisfactorily produced by Africans in Uganda and Tanganyika, while the Kenya government, accepting spurious warnings of crop disease, restricted its cultivation to Europeans.

There were three ways in which governments influenced the pattern of agriculture. First and foremost was the question of white settlement and land alienation, probably the most familiar and certainly the most contentious aspect of colonial policy. Closely linked with this and equally controversial was the 'labour problem'. Existing levels of wages and working conditions were inadequate to attract a sufficient supply of labour for public works, like road building, or for plantations. Governments, therefore, frequently resorted to compulsion, the moral case for which was at least arguable. But planters expected them to exert similar pressures to recruit labour for private employment, where clearly there was no moral case, although 'the dignity of labour' was commonly invoked. Officials reacted to this demand with varying degrees of humanity and circumspection, and missionaries played a notable part in educating British public opinion. The climax of these public airings centred around Kenya's notorious 1921 'Northey circulars', after which officials were unequivocally ordered 'to take no part in recruiting labour for private employment'. But compulsory labour was still occasionally used for public works. In the long run, men's willingness to work on plantations, usually far from their homes, depended less upon government edict that upon the availability of alternative sources of income, a principal factor determining those long distance migrations which are so prominent a feature of African economic life. Here we meet the third form of government influence—the role of agricultural departments. They could serve primarily as information centres for European farmers and planters, as tended to be the case in Kenya and in

German East Africa. Alternatively they could actively promote peasant agriculture; but in so far as they succeeded in this they would further increase the planter's labour difficulties and thus incur their animosity. A remarkable example of this was the career of Simpson, who, as Uganda's Director of Agriculture between 1911 and 1929 devoted his considerable energies to building up the cotton industry, despite limited resources and bitter opposition from planters and sometimes even from his colleagues.

These differences between the relative emphasis given to plantation and peasant agriculture form one of the most significant themes in the economic history of East Africa. In Uganda the economy grew on a solid base of African cotton and coffee. From the outset Indians and Europeans were prominent in the processing and marketing of these crops, and Africanisation was delayed until the emergence of co-operatives in the 1950s. But the grass roots of development were indigenous, and when independence came, comparatively little unscrambling was necessary. Kenya was utterly different. African commercial agriculture did not grow significantly until the 1930s, and even then it was given little encouragement by the government. Not until the 1950s, under the Swynnerton plan, was real progress made; African coffee production, for example, a mere thousand tons in 1954, expanded six-fold during the next five years. In Tanganyika after the defeat of Germany the pace of development slowed down. There were small cases of African cash income in the desert of subsistence and inactivity. Chagga coffee growers, with the ardent support of Dundas, formed a cooperative in 1924, despite strong opposition along familiar lines from European planters, some of whom advocated a transfer of Kilimanjaro to Kenya! Bukoba was another centre of coffee production; but there was little dynamism in the promotion of African commercial agriculture. By far the biggest industry was sisal, grown on alien owned plantations in which the African's role was solely that of an unskilled labourer, with education to be derived from his experience, and few prospects of promotion.

The social disadvantages of plantations were therefore considerable. Their principal economic advantage was the possibility that skilled management might get quick results. Against this, however, management costs tended to be high and inflexible, though Indian firms, where they were allowed to farm, tended to be more efficient in this respect. Such inflexibility was a frequent source of failure in times of depression when peasants proved their greater resilience by retreating a little from cash. The long-term social and political advantages of the peasant system were enormous but entailed certain short-term economic disadvantages. It was usually a slow and difficult task to persuade peasants to change their methods of cultivation. This stubbornness was

339

not always a matter of tradition-bound ignorance in the face of superior scientific knowledge, for traditional methods frequently embodied the inherited wisdom of the past, and the new agricultural 'expert' was not always equipped with knowledge that was relevant to local conditions. Since this problem continues to bedevil traditional agriculture all over the world, despite the huge international resources that have been thrown into development programmes in recent years, it is not surprising that the small, undermanned, and poorly-equipped colonial departments made slow progress with their pioneering efforts. Three criticisms can be made of their policies. First, there was always a tendency to enforce unreasonable quality standards which were unrelated to the costs of attaining these standards and to actual market demands. Second, there was a disproportionate concern for soil erosion which made little sense in an economy where time horizons were short and where land was usually the *least* scarce of all factors of production. Finally, official policies frequently laid great emphasis upon the need to provide an insurance against famine by cultivating such unattractive crops as cassava. Although it was well-intentioned, this policy was fundamentally wrong-headed from a developmental point of view. Instead of encouraging market consciousness and the enlargement of the exchange economy, it 'fastened upon the producer the straitjacket of subsistence production'. The 1955 royal commission's brilliant attack upon this and similar policies is essential reading for those who wish to understand the intricacies of colonial paternalism.

The pattern of development and trade

Our emphasis upon agricultural *policy* is not intended to suggest that governments alone were responsible for economic change. Even in highly centralised economies development rarely takes place simply as a result of a government's aspirations and plans. In colonial East Africa foreign trade was the chief motor driving the economy forward, but the power of this motor had to be harnessed and transmitted throughout society. At times a government could provide such transmission directly, as when the Uganda administration distributed cotton seed and advice to cultivators. But normally the government's task was to provide lubrication for the motor—a monetary system, an apparatus of commercial law, and generally an environment in which men could initiate economic change. In the economic history of many countries such men emerge as leading characters, particularly in times of rapid growth— Arkwright, Carnegie, Ford—and entrepreneurial history is an important branch of the subject. In East Africa most entrepreneurs worked on a small scale, left no records, and are therefore forgotten; only a rare figure like Alidina Visram left his mark. But this anonymity, and later political judgements, should not lead us to underrate the significance of their contribution to economic growth. The value of enterprise and investment in agriculture or mining was self-evident; Williamson's diamonds, for example, were a great contribution to the Tanganyikan economy. By contrast, the trader's role is more obscure. Traders and middlemen were an important group, but their activities, as is common in peasant society, were frequently regarded as parasitic and essentially unproductive. Such criticism stemmed from a basic misunderstanding of the merchant's dynamic role. As a buyer of crops he created markets even in remote areas and injected cash into the economy. By assembling and transporting these small purchases for resale he then provided one of several essential steps on the road to world markets. As a retail trader he made goods available, again in remote areas and in the small quantities desired, which in turn created incentives for further production. If these activities sometimes gave him a power which could be abused, they also demanded skills and the taking of risks which deserved recompense. The fact that Indians tended to be dominant in trade was an additional reason for misunderstanding and mistrust. Towards the end of our period considerable official encouragement and assistance was given to African traders, most notably in Uganda. The expense and many setbacks of such schemes provided fresh evidence that trading was a difficult, skilful, and costly activity.

The emerging pattern of development is shown in the table below which illustrates the parallel growth of foreign trade and government revenue in each of the mainland territories. In Zanzibar the story was even simpler since cloves were far the most important source of income. It will be appreciated that a brief table of this kind can give only the barest outline of the quantitative picture. The following paragraphs will attempt to add some details, but students should supplement the figures by their own research. An investigation into the 1950s, when prices and incomes increased rapidly, would be particularly rewarding and comparatively simple as statistics are readily available.

Foreign trade and government revenue 1911–61

UGANDA

	Exports ($£$m)	Imports ($£$m)	Government revenue ($£$m)	Main export commodities as % total exports	
				Cotton	Coffee
1911	0.3	0.5	0.2	55	1
1921	1.5	not available	0.8	85	6
1931	1.9	1.3	1.4	84	8
1951	47.4	22.1	15.8	62	29
1961	46.0	24.5	22.3	43	36

341

TANGANYIKA

	Exports (£m)	Imports (£m)	Government revenue (£m)	Cotton	Coffee	Sisal
1911	1.1	2.3	0.7	6	6	20
1921	1.1	1.4	0.9	11	13	22
1931	1.6	2.5	1.5	7	15	43
1951	40.5	31.7	11.9	7	11	58
1961	48.6	39.7	21.9	14	14	29

KENYA

	Exports (£m)	Imports (£m)	Government revenue (£m)	Maize	Coffee	Sisal	Tea
1911	0.3	1.1	0.7	8	1	0	0
1921	1.8	not available	1.3	7	21	10	0
1931	2.3	4.3	3.0	18	42	10	1
1951	24.1	50.6	23.4	3	17	29	6
1961	35.3	62.5	46.2	0	30	12	11

Imports consisted of capital equipment and consumer goods, such as textiles and shoes, which improved African standards of living. In this connection the advantages of free trade were significant, for poor consumers benefited greatly from the import, for example, of cheap Japanese manufactured goods. Apart from temporary wartime stoppages, the chief impediment to free trade was the protection afforded to Kenya producers of meat and dairy products, which probably had little effect on African living standards. Only in the final decade of colonial rule was there a determined effort to protect such infant industries as Uganda textiles; this harmed consumers, of course, whatever its ultimate benefits in terms of economic growth and diversification.

Exports were narrowly based upon a few agricultural products which were mostly established before World War I and remained dominant thereafter. Their quantity and value rose steadily through the boom of the 1920s, more slowly during depression in the 1930s, and leaped forward after World War II. Tanganyika, however, was particularly unfortunate in failing to share the prosperity of the 1920s, years when the upsets of defeat and the uncertainties of her status as a League of Nations mandate deterred investment and entrepreneurial activity. Thereafter her rate of growth was slower and the living standards of her people tended to be even lower than elsewhere in East Africa. Another notable difference between the countries lay in their balance of trade—the value of Kenya's imports was always considerably greater than that of her exports. This adverse balance of visible trade was financed in two ways. At various times throughout our period there were relatively large imports of public and private capital from overseas which both reflected and advanced the activities of European and Indian enterprise in Kenya. The second source of income not shown in our table was the invisible exports which arose largely from the position of Nairobi as East Africa's main industrial and commercial centre. The expansion of manufacturing and distribution was particularly rapid in Kenya during the 1950s so that by 1960 they accounted for over twenty per cent of the national income. In Uganda and Tanganyika the proportion was very much lower, and dependence upon world markets was therefore greater.

Education and the colonial legacy

For the first twenty years colonial governments did little to promote education, though a few schools were opened by the Germans. Missionaries were, of course, far more active, but evangelism was their main purpose and the literacy which accompanied it was limited and fortuitous. As governments began slowly to accept responsibility the financial problem became acute, for Africans' thirst for education was far greater than could be quenched by local resources. A typical statement was the memorandum of the Kikuyu Central Association to the Hilton Young Commission which stated their willingness to pay 'cesses for . . . the education of the many and the higher education of the few'. But African incomes were not commensurate with such inspirations. In 1924 the Phelps-Stokes Commission argued that expenditure on education 'had been negligible in comparison with the great needs'. There was progress thereafter, particularly in Uganda, where the education bill increased from £8 000 in 1923 to £88 000 by 1933. Tanganyika was less fortunate. Expenditure rose rapidly after 1925 but the depression enforced severe retrenchment after 1932. By 1934 only ten per cent of children of school age received a regular education, and most of these were offered an insubstantial vernacular course. Even by 1945 the modest proposals of a pre-war committee were rejected as 'far beyond the capacity of the territory'.

After World War II the Colonial Development and Welfare Acts ushered in a far more generous period of aid. Again it was Uganda that set the pace, government expenditure rising from £715 000 in 1950 to over £5 million in 1960. But throughout East Africa the creation of an appropriate system of education proved difficult and elusive. In recent years there has been increasing awareness of the role that education can play in economic development. If costs and curricula are well adjusted to society's resources and needs it can be regarded as investment in man, more profitable and therefore more worthy of sacrifice than many

343

tangible forms of physical capital. Rarely was this truth grasped until the closing years of our period. Education was more often regarded as a matter of social rather then economic policy, even a luxury which might follow, rather than an essential which must precede and accompany development. When its economic effects were considered it was usually within narrow limits of training for those few jobs which Africans were thought capable of handling. The limitations of colonial education arose therefore from a lack of both finance and relevant ideas. As independence approached concepts of education became more generous but not necessarily more appropriate, except in terms of the immediate objective—training an elite for the Africanisation of the civil service. It is arguable that the British were poorly qualified to provide education suitable for a developing society. Their own system was elitist—fine in quality, deficient in quantity—and export models tended to be caricatures of the domestic product. This was most evident at the university level where costs, standards, and to some extent even curricula, were ill-adapted to East Africa's long term needs. It would be unreasonable and anachronistic to castigate them for this. Africans demanded 'the best' and to a remarkable degree this was given, as defined by the British. But the legacy for the independent nations of East Africa was not wholly beneficial.

What, in conclusion, can be said about growth and welfare during the colonial era? What was the colonial legacy? Except for a few isolated pockets of subsistence the region had joined the international economy and was enjoying some of its benefits. If progress appeared slight after sixty years, it could be remarked that the period was short by the standards of economic growth, and that it had been interrupted by two wars and a great depression. Clearly Uganda was best prepared for independence. Real income per head of the African population was higher, though there were serious regional inequalities. The economy was firmly based on African activity so little economic unscrambling was necessary. In Kenya, African incomes were lower but the economy was more diversified. Africanisation of commercial agriculture and the civil service had at last begun, but the former was impoverished by a half century of neglect, and recruitment to the latter was difficult and costly because of its size and sophistication. Tanganyika's economic inheritance was least enviable. After 1947 the groundnut scheme had done nothing, and an ambitious road programme little, to overcome a harsh geographical environment. By any standards of measurement she remained one of the poorest countries in tropical Africa.

But if the colonial experience had wrought only modest changes in terms of economic growth, it had stimulated wholly new conceptions of human welfare. This gulf between performance and aspiration was the principal and unenviable inheritance of East Africa's new leaders.

344

Further reading

EHRLICH, C. 'The Uganda Economy 1903–1945', V. Harlow and E. M. Chilver (Eds) *History of East Africa, II*, Oxford, Clarendon Press, 1965.

EHRLICH, C. 'Some Social and Economic Implications of Paternalism in Uganda', *Journal of African History*, 1963.

EHRLICH, C. 'Some Aspects of Economic Policy in Tanganyika 1945–1960', *Journal of Modern African Studies*, July 1964.

EHRLICH, C. 'Some Antecedents of Development Planning in Tanganyika', *Journal of Development Studies*, 1966.

ELKAN, W. *The Economic Development of Uganda*, Oxford University Press, 1961.

HENDERSON, W. O. 'German East Africa, 1884–1918', Harlow and Chilver (Eds) *op. cit.*

POWESLAND, P. C. 'History of the Migration in Uganda', in A. I. Richards (Ed.) *Economic Development and Tribal Change*. Cambridge, Heffer, 1954.

WRIGLEY, C. C. *Crops and Wealth in Uganda*, E.A.I.S.R., Kampala, 1959.

WRIGLEY, C. C. 'Kenya: The Patterns of Economic Life, 1902–1945', Harlow and Chilver (Eds) *op. cit.*

The Gross Domestic Product of the Protectorate of Zanzibar 1957–1961, E.A.C.S.O., 1963.

The Gross Domestic Product of Uganda 1954–1959, E.A.C.S.O., 1961.

Domestic Income and Product in Kenya, Nairobi, 1959.

17

Independent East Africa

Ali A. Mazrui

As independence approached, the term 'East Africa' in the political sense shrank in meaning. It then referred to the area consisting of Uganda, Kenya, Tanganyika and Zanzibar. A different colonial background had, by the 1950s, effectively separated Rwanda and Burundi from the historical stream of the region.

In this chapter then, we shall use the term 'East Africa' in its narrow sense. Tanganyika attained independence on 9 December 1961, to be followed by Uganda on 9 October 1962. On 10 December 1963, Zanzibar too emerged into nationhood, to be followed by Kenya two days later.

A month after attaining independence, Zanzibar had a major revolution. The dynasty of sultans on the island was overthrown, and a socialist era was inaugurated. In April of the same year Zanzibar united with Tanganyika to form the United Republic of Tanzania.

In broader terms, the story of East Africa as a whole since independence has been a complicated struggle for national unity within each country, for economic growth, for social justice, and for regional cooperation between the different countries.

In accounts of modern East Africa there is sometimes a tendency to leave the question of regional unity until the end, and in discussions of regional unity to underestimate the contribution of Uganda to East African integration. This chapter proposes to resist both tendencies.

We shall discuss the question of regional unity first and concentrate on the role of Uganda. Our concern here is not with the issue of who

346

is disrupting East African unity but on how that unity came to be there in the first place, and the latter question involves a major historical dimension. The role of Uganda in giving East Africa a recognisable personality is crucial in this, and since we have to be selective in so short a chapter, it is pre-eminently to this issue that we shall first devote our attention.

Uganda's role in Pan-Africanism

There are few countries whose geographical position has had as big an effect on their political history as has the position of Uganda on the history of eastern Africa as a whole. It has sometimes been argued that Uganda is among the least Pan-African of the countries of East and Central Africa. If Pan-Africanism is defined in terms of strict ideological commitment, this accusation is not entirely unfounded. In the movement since independence to form an East African federation, Uganda's enthusiasm for unification has not been striking. Julius Nyerere once offered to delay Tanganyika's independence if that would help achieve East African federation, and Mzee Kenyatta and his colleagues started negotiating in earnest about how best to achieve that goal. Uganda leaders were, however, suggesting that unless their country was assured her sovereignty, there was no question of her joining an East African federation. This was no different from saying that Uganda did not want to join an East African federation. We must therefore face up to the fact that Uganda has not been in the forefront of Pan-African militancy.

And yet perhaps it is true that some are born Pan-African, some become Pan-African, and others have Pan-Africanism thrust upon them. It is not entirely clear into which category Uganda would fall. What is clear is that by a series of geographical and historical accidents, and by some acts of deliberate policy, Uganda has indeed made a decisive contribution to greater unity along the eastern seaboard of the African continent. Discussing this would be meaningless without reference to East Africa before independence. In an analysis of this kind, there is an iron law of historical continuity which cannot be avoided.

Uganda's contribution to East African integration took a variety of forms. First, it was Uganda's strategic position more than anything else which ensured that East Africa as a whole was ruled by Great Britain and not by another colonial power or combination of powers. As I hope to demonstrate, the fact that Uganda, Kenya and Tanzania were jointly ruled by Britain was itself an important contribution to East African unity. A related element in Uganda's enforced Pan-Africanism is that she is situated at the head of the Nile waters. A third factor is that Uganda, being landlocked, might be increasingly forced to explore new forms of

347

access to her neighbours. A fourth factor in Uganda's Pan-African role is her situation in a sensitive area of Afro-Arab relations, a matter of concern for the continent as a whole. The fifth factor in Uganda's contribution to greater integration in this region hinges on the role of Makerere. This institution of higher learning was closely associated with the emergence of a regional intellectual elite in East Africa which shared a language of political discourse and which is helping to shape the destiny of the three countries of East Africa.

Let us now take a closer look at these factors. In what way did Uganda's strategic attractiveness for Britain later help the cause of East African unity? It would be impossible to grasp the full implications of this first point unless we stopped being naive about the effects of European imperialism in Africa at large. We often think of imperialism as being an exercise in a policy of 'divide and rule'. This view is not entirely false, but it is only one side of the imperial coin. The truth is that if the imperialists divided (as a policy) in order to rule, they also united (in effect) in the very act of ruling. Their intention might very often have been to divide people against people, but administrative convenience frequently resulted in uniting territory with territory. The very momentum and logic of imperial expansion meant adding this piece to that piece of land. But the pieces of land were not empty—they had people on them. And so by putting two pieces of land together they sometimes brought two tribes together in the process.

The natural tendecy of imperialism is to prevent the unification of its subjects; and yet an equally natural tendency of imperialism is to prevent an excessive fragmentation of its territory. During the colonial period, the Belgian government, for example, did not want to see the Congolese united. Yet they did not split up the Congo into a number of small colonies because they wanted the landmass of the Congo to remain one territorial unit. And so it was not until immediately after independence that the Belgians were prepared to encourage Katanga, under Tshombe, to secede from the rest of the Congo. In fact Belgian attempts at Balkanisation came at the time of Belgian withdrawal rather than before. In other words, Balkanisation is an imperialist device, characteristic more of imperial retreat than of imperial expansion.

This view finds further support in French Africa. For as long as France was in effective colonial control, her preference was for large administrative areas. But as soon as nationalistic trouble was on the horizon, the French decided on greater administrative decentralisation. Two huge federations of French West Africa and French Equatorial Africa were ultimately split up into nearly a dozen little sovereign states. Again a policy of Balkanisation, or territorial 'divide and rule', was more evident in the era of decolonisation than in the days of militant annexation.

And yet, of all the colonial powers, Britain has been the most reluctant to Balkanise her former colonies in the process of withdrawal. British territorial units of administration in Africa were hardly ever as big in size as the old Belgian Congo or the two federations of French West Africa and French Equatorial Africa. Britain did not similarly indulge in blatant Balkanising tricks when she was retreating from Africa either; on the contrary, British policy at the time of imperial withdrawal endeavoured to prevent territorial fragmentation. Both in Nigeria and in East Africa, British diplomacy in the course of imperial disengagement aimed at keeping things together. In East Africa, Britain was so keen on federation that her enthusiasm had to be restrained— lest she should embarrass Pan-African federalists like Nyerere. The East African leaders were so conscious of British keenness to see an East African federation that they even took advantage of it in order to get early independence for Kenya. The East African leaders asked Britain to give Kenya independence before the end of 1963—so that Kenya could join a federation. And Britain responded positively. This old hand at the game of 'divide and rule' was now converted to a policy of 'withdraw and unite'.

The moral of all this is that imperialism is not a purely divisive force. On the contrary, where East Africa is concerned, the most unifying single factor has been that the three countries were all ruled by the same imperial power. If Uganda had been ruled by France, Kenya by Britain, and Tanganyika by yet another imperial power, the cause of East African unity would have been twice as difficult. Ugandans would have felt as distant from Kenyans as they do today from Congolese. It was of great relevance for East African integration, not only that all three countries came to fall under the same colonial power, but also that the colonial power happened to be Britain rather than either France or Belgium, both of which had also had designs on this region of Africa in the course of the great imperial scramble. Britain even brought forward the independence of British Somaliland to enable it to unite with Italian Somaliland to form the sovereign state of Somalia. All this does not necessarily mean that British rule in East Africa was a good thing. But it does mean that East Africa might easily have had a more divisive colonial power than she actually had.

But in what way was Uganda decisive in ensuring that East Africa was ruled by Britain? Precisely by virtue of her strategic attractiveness. It is not often remembered that the British government was for a while reluctant to take over Uganda, in spite of pressures from missionaries in Uganda asking for the establishment of a protectorate. Nor was Britain convinced by the arguments of the Imperial British East Africa Company regarding the commercial and economic potential of the region. What sealed the fate of Uganda was the Nile Valley doctrine of the British

349

Foreign Office that whoever controlled the source of the Nile could easily control Egypt as well. A special British commissioner, who was sent to Uganda to assess the advantages of British intrusion, argued in his report to the British government that Uganda was 'the natural key to the whole of the Nile Valley' and had to be 'protected' by Britain or fall into the hands of other powers. The doctrine of the unity of the Nile became a crucial consideration in the European scramble for Africa. As two distinguished British historians have recently put it, 'almost everything in Africa north of the Zambesi River was to hinge on it'.

When Britain finally decided to establish a protectorate in Uganda, the fate of the rest of East Africa was also sealed. The road to Uganda from the East African coast was through what later came to be known as Kenya; and so the idea of building a railway to the lakes became an important factor in Britain's Uganda policy. The very legislation authorising the building of the railway was called the Uganda Railway Bill. The British government, without an adequate survey, incurred the great expense of building this railway link to the source of the Nile. Why? The answer which came from the British Foreign Minister at the time was this: 'We did so with a perfect consciousness of what we were doing, and for the sake of speed . . . . There were considerations of a very cogent character which induced us to desire to finish, at the earliest period possible, what was practically our only access to those regions.'

Having built a railway line, Britain wanted to make it pay; that was the beginning of the policy of encouraging white settlers to come and settle in Kenya. In other words, British interest in Kenya came only as a result of British interest in Uganda. And the fate of both Kenya and Uganda then became intertwined.

Tanganyika had to wait until the end of the First World War before it could be taken out of German hands. But why was it then handed over as a mandate to the British by the League of Nations? In the final analysis, the reason was because Britain was already occupying the contiguous areas of Kenya and Uganda. And so the fate of Uganda, in the long run, affected the fate of Tanganyika too. That all three countries were ruled by the same imperial power helped their sense of community. Otherwise Nyerere today might have been a German-speaking African, or a French-speaking African with a Belgian background. Moreover, there would have been no East African Common Market or Common Services Organisation but for the accident of the British hegemony in East Africa.

Since then, Uganda's place at the head of the Nile waters has had other Pan-African implications. Two of the most important dams in Africa are affected—the Owen Falls Dam at Jinja and the Aswan Dam in Egypt. These waters could easily give rise to serious disputes between the countries which share the River Nile. But it is also possible for the old doctrine of the Unity of the Nile now to serve the new ideal of the Unity of Africa. Certainly the great potential of hydro-electric power in Uganda is already making a contribution to the electrification of neighbouring countries. An even greater contribution of this kind might be possible in the future.

Uganda's landlocked position makes her excessively dependent on Kenya. This is not by itself a bad thing, but every country must try to have more than one good access to the outside world. And just as Zambia is now seeking a new rail link, as well as a possible road connection with Tanzania, so might Uganda have to explore new forms of communication with her neighbours. Her very situation as a landlocked country has a Pan-African dimension. It emphasises for her the need for better and better communications and greater commercial intercourse with her neighbours.

Then there is Uganda's position on the border with the Sudan. It has often been pointed out that one of the worst clashes which could happen in Africa is a deep cleavage between Arab Africa and black Africa. Such a cleavage would not only destroy the Organisation of African Unity but could shake the continent in more profound ways. It happens that the most fragile point of Afro-Arab relations is precisely on the border between Uganda and the Sudan. There are ethnic ties between southern Sudanese and the Ugandans on the border; and with significant numbers of refugees from southern Sudan in Uganda, sympathies could easily lead some Ugandans into supporting the cause of the rebellion in southern Sudan. If this were to lead to an open military clash between Uganda and the Sudan, or even strong tension centring on the racial issue, the whole fabric of trans-Saharan cordiality in the African continent might be in serious danger. But the Ugandan government has so far resisted all temptations which might endanger Pan-African cordiality at this vital level, taking the position that to condemn secessionism in Katanga and to support it in southern Sudan would be racialistic. In the words of a former Minister, Sam Odaka, 'We cannot denounce racialism in southern Africa and support it when it comes to southern Sudan.' In the very discipline that Uganda has exercised on this issue, she has critically safeguarded the viability of the Organisation of African Unity.

Finally, there is Makerere's contribution to East Africa's integration. Until the eve of independence Makerere was, in effect if not in name, the 'University of East Africa'. It was the top institution of higher learning in the region, and helped to produce a regional intellectual elite. As independence approached, many potential leaders in each of the three East African countries passed through Makerere. These included two who were to be heads of government—Milton Obote and Julius Nyerere —and a significant proportion of the cabinets of the three governments on attainment of independence. Leadership in the struggle for independ-

351

ence was a crucial factor. So, too, among the new African civil servants who were taking up key administrative positions throughout East Africa, the Makerere contribution was often critical and decisive. Among the forces which have helped to give East Africa a sense of political and intellectual integration must surely be included the role of Makerere in producing a regional intellectual elite at a vital moment in the history of the three countries.

All these factors add up to give Uganda a Pan-African status in the history of this part of the continent. Very often Uganda has been Pan-African in spite of herself—a definite case of greatness being thrust upon her. What remains to be seen is whether Uganda can now assume her unifying destiny with greater intent and deliberation.

Internal unity and equality

But regional unification, though a major part of the politics of East Africa for many years, is far from being the only theme of significance. The story of independent East Africa has also included the struggle for internal unity, economic development and social justice.

On internal unity, the basic issue has been to find a suitable compromise between love for one's tribe and loyalty to one's nation. These two emotions are sometimes opposed to each other, but need not be; just as a man need not stop loving his family in order to love his country, so he need not renounce his tribe in order to be patriotic. But the problem in East Africa—as in much of the rest of the continent—has been one of trying to find a suitable balance.

The question of what kind of party-system a country should have is linked to this issue of potentially conflicting loyalties. A two-party system has been suspect in Tanzania, because it was regarded as symbolic of class antagonism, and in Kenya, because it could become a symptom of tribal antagonism. In Tanganyika, Nyerere argued that the Anglo-American systems of government were based on a division between the haves and the have-nots, and the party structure reflected that division; Tanganyika should therefore have only one national movement—the Tanganyika African National Union (TANU). But what kind of choice would the people have at election time if there were only one party? On the recommendation of a special presidential commission which took evidence from the people on what system of government was best suited to the country, Tanzania in 1965 launched the great experiment of competitive elections within the single party. Members of TANU contested the same seats against each other—and several ministers lost their seats. It was a great innovation in combining the principle of government by consent with a one-party structure. The second such elections held in 1970 had the smoothness of a routine.

Kenya's experiment was different. It rested first on a refusal to outlaw opposition parties. Kenya preferred a one-party structure, but not by legal decree. The first opposition party which Kenya had after independence was the Kenya African Democratic Union (KADU). But the division between this party and the preponderant Kenya African National Union (KANU) was complicated by tribal suspicions. Mr Ronald Ngala, the leader of the smaller party, later decided to dissolve his own party and join forces with KANU. The country then had a *de facto* one-party state until Mr Oginga Odinga and his colleagues withdrew from KANU in 1965 to form a new radical party, the Kenya People's Union (KPU). But the KPU was, in turn, banned following shooting incidents in Kisumu when President Kenyatta visited the town in October 1969. But the party system in Kenya continued to be flexible, at least from a legal point of view.

The party situation in Uganda has also been flexible. On attainment of independence Uganda was ruled by a pragmatic alliance between Buganda's Kabaka Yekka and Dr Obote's Uganda People's Congress. In opposition was the Democratic Party. But the ruling alliance lasted only until Dr Obote felt strong enough to do without his Kabaka Yekka partners. During the rest of 1964 Uganda seemed to be on the way towards becoming a one-party state. Crossing the floor in parliament to join the UPC became so common that it appeared to be only a matter of time before the opposition parties liquidated themselves. The climax was the crossing of the Leader of the Opposition, Mr Basil Bataringaya, in December 1964 with several other members of the Democratic Party.

Yet in the course of 1965 new divisions began to appear in Uganda, some of these within the UPC itself. A new confrontation also developed between Buganda and the central government. But by the end of May 1966 the central government under Dr Obote had prevailed. Sir Edward Mutesa, former Kabaka of Buganda and former President of the country, had left for England. Yet the main task had yet to be completed—that of devising a new political arrangement in Uganda which would assure national unity, including Buganda participation. For this great task the basis was to be the new constitution which Dr Obote introduced in April 1966. In the meantime the country continued to have more than one party, the UPC and the DP, and pragmatic flexibility continued to be the essential policy of Dr Obote's government. This situation ended abruptly with the attempted assassination of the President in December 1969. All opposition parties were banned. The UPC felt vindicated in the resolution it had already passed in favour of a one-party system. Obote followed this up with a special electoral scheme for competitive elections under a one-party umbrella. The scheme brought in the innovation of each Member of Parliament standing in four constituencies, one in each of the four regions of Uganda.

But in addition to these problems of regional and national unity, each East African country was engaged in a struggle to devise the best means of economic development and the best methods of assuring social justice. These too were, of course, connected with national goals within each country and we cannot understand them without looking at national values. If one were to choose the three most important values influencing policy and political behaviour in independent East Africa, one would probably list those of equality, development and unity as basic. And of these three, perhaps the oldest in the history of African political movements is the value of *equality*. Today the problem of equality in East Africa is connected with policies of trying to Africanise the economies, as well as with attempts to control the development of great inequalities of income between citizens. But before independence, the idea of equality was at the root of the growth of nationalism itself.

In previous chapters, attention has already been drawn to the history of African resistance to colonial rule. In this chapter, we hope to show how the idea of equality during the colonial period gradually determined the kind of national values which East Africa was to have after independence. National values in East Africa are still fluid and changeable, but the theme of equality is definitely there. We might begin by looking at its origins, and then trace the development of racial integration in East Africa. Of the countries of East Africa, the one which experienced racial segregation at its most elaborate was Kenya. Many of the illustrations of the early history of the idea of equality in East Africa may therefore best be drawn from Kenya's experience. But much of this experience was shared to some degree by other parts of East Africa, and indeed by much of the rest of the continent.

Equality and segregation

Ideas of equality in Africa had indigenous origins as well as external sources. The latter included the impact of Christianity and the principle of human neighbourliness, and that of Islam which sometimes demonstrated greater racial toleration than was achieved by most Christian churches in Africa. Internally, there was the historical background of the African who, partly because of relative isolation from other races in the past, and partly because of certain values of fellowship and hospitality within the tribal ways, had not accumulated as many racial prejudices as the paradoxically more 'cosmopolitan' white man. Latest among the channels through which the ideas of equality have entered Africa is that of European socialism—of Marxism, the British Labour Party and other shades of belief.

Africa has not, of course, been the only area of the world which has witnessed a denial of the principles of equality on grounds of racial differences. The United States in particular has had a continuing racial and constitutional crisis on the issue of civil rights for black Americans. Yet segregation in Africa has sometimes had more complex and varied consequences than even in the United States. In education, for example, the segregation of colonial East Africa was not simply between white schools and non-white schools. Among government schools or government-aided schools in the region as a whole, there were those which were exclusively for Europeans, those for Indians, those solely for Arabs and those for Africans. In addition there were private schools for groups within groups. Among these were Goan schools (for that section of the Asian population which came from former Portuguese Goa), and Aga Khan schools (for those of the Indian Muslim community who were followers of the Aga Khan). Christian Mission schools were also segregated. The late Tom Mboya, himself a product of a Catholic African school in Kenya, was known to complain that missionaries had condoned the colonial order in Africa 'to the point of complying with such things as segregated schools and segregated churches'.

As pressures in East Africa mounted for school integration, the usual argument advanced against it was that integration was bound to 'level down educational standards'. The European schools were the best in the country. If they were to be 'immediately flooded' with children from poorly educated or completely illiterate non-white families, 'the result would not be to bring up the Africans to the level of Europeans, but to bring down European standards of education to the level of the poorest and crudest schools of the nation'. This, it was contended, was a wasteful way of achieving equality. It was like the philosophy sometimes attributed to socialism by its critics—that 'if everybody cannot become rich then everybody must become poor'. Such a philosophy of bringing down the educational standards of East Africa's white population was, so the argument went, short-sighted and misguided for a region which needed highly skilled local people even if they should happen to have a white skin.

Comparing this with the American experience, one detects a different kind of reasoning from that which was used in the United States to support segregated schools before the great Supreme Court decision in 1954. Until that year, the American constitution had been interpreted as meaning that people could be segregated and still be equal. Black Americans could have separate schools from whites, provided the black schools were comparable in quality and facilities with schools for white children. This whole principle came to be known as the 'separate but equal' condition of segregation under the American Constitution.

Segregationist arguments in old Kenya, however, rested on a fundamentally different premise—that the standards of the segregated schools were *not* equal, with the admission that the European schools were superior, and that this superiority was on no account to be sacrificed at the altar of the Goddess of Abstract Equality if Kenya was to make the most of her resources of personnel, regardless of race.

In 1954, while Kenya was in the agony of the Mau Mau insurrection, the United States was changing its mind about the principle of 'separate but equal'. The American Supreme Court decided that the very insistence on segregation implied inequality between races. In any case the segregation in schools had resulted in standards which were *not* equal. With that Supreme Court decision, the American civil rights revolution of the mid-twentieth century was launched.

Five years later it was East Africa's turn to start a reappraisal of its own segregationist tradition. Against the thesis that the standards of the region's best schools should not be sacrificed 'for the sake of an abstract-tion', it was now contended that a temporary lowering of the standards of European schools in East Africa was not too high a price to pay for getting the next generation of East Africans to grow up together into less racially-conscious citizens. It was not too high a price to pay for a new East Africa in which no child eager for the best education that the country had to offer would be driven to wish that it had a racially different set of parents.

The segregationists in East Africa have failed. Even the region's best European schools have now embarked on some degree of integration. That in some cases the integration was for a while little more than a 'token', in spite of African independence, is a measure of African patience when a principle has already been accepted. That the Africans have wanted integration at all shows how grossly exaggerated was the assertion sometimes made that African independence would just 'reverse the colour bar'. This assertion might apply to the question of who is permitted to wield political power. Africans might insist on ruling the country to the exclusion of other races. The claim might also be proved correct in certain areas of economic activity—that instead of Europeans and Asians being the economically privileged or dominant section of Kenya's population, discrimination might now be applied to give the Africans a chance to shift the balance of economic power.

Yet the phrase 'Africa's reversal of the colour bar' is still a distortion. It implies a continuation of *social* segregation, as well as a shift in political and economic advantage. One just cannot see the African insisting, as the colonial white man did before him, on segregated schools for Africans, segregated hotels and dancing halls, or segregated restaurants and residential areas. To put it crudely, one cannot imagine the African insisting on a mere exchange of public lavatories. For the African to concede racial segregation at the social level would be to defeat the whole object of African self-assertion. The African government in Kenya—

356

unlike its colonial predecessor—therefore makes a virtue of racial mixture rather than of racial separation. And who knows what greater racial toleration might in time emerge out of this greater social intermingling?

By 1960 the shape of the new East Africa, even in the heart of settler-Kenya, was beginning to be discernible. Racially exclusive hotels were disappearing. Scholarships for study abroad were no longer in racial quotas. The doctors were planning to merge European, Asian and African medical associations which had so far been separate. There was soon to be a determined policy to introduce as many Africans as possible into the higher ranks of the civil service. Scales of salaries according to race— regardless of similarity of work or identity of qualifications—had already been abandoned. The White Highlands in Kenya, for decades reserved exclusively for white settlers and prospective white immigrants, were soon to be legally no longer 'white'. The Kenya Regiment Training Centre was about to accept its first non-European recruits. The new electoral roll in Kenya, following the first Lancaster House conference of 1960, had not only been substantially integrated, but had also allowed for an elected African majority in the legislature. Even the lavatories were beginning to lose the familiar signs of 'European' and 'Non-European'. And where the signs were still hanging, they could be ignored with impunity. It was symbolic that even such small details of personal intimacy were beginning to conform with the integrationist principles of the new East Africa.

Self-help and ideological toil

But, after independence, new problems of inequalities have presented themselves. It is one thing to narrow the gulf between Africans on one side and Europeans and Asians on the other. But what about the danger of creating new gulfs between Africans themselves? Is there not a possibility of some Africans getting richer too rapidly after independence while others remain poor? Is there not a danger of creating class distinctions between Africans themselves?

One safeguard against this danger is a national ethos which puts a premium on frugality and hard work. Within East Africa the best exponent of such a policy has so far been Tanzania. It is a policy which seems to have deep roots in the ideologies of Tanzania's leaders and has had a consistent history since the country approached independence.

In *Ujamaa: The Basis of African Socialism*, Nyerere claims that in traditional Africa everyone was a worker—a 'worker' not merely as distinct from employer but also as distinct from 'loiterer' or 'idler'. It is not certain that this is a justified interpretation of life in traditional Africa. What is certain is that Tanzania has tried from the outset to utilise the the concept of *work* as a slogan for national mobilisation.

357

There was first the neat motto of '*Uhuru na Kazi*' or 'Freedom and Work', and then, on independence, came the programme of self-help. Apparently self-help was first considered during discussions on the Three Year Plan envisaged for 1961 to 1964. Some of the external aid expected had not materialised and it appeared more important than ever that a scheme of self-help should be devised. When the Regional Commissioners took office in March 1962, Mr Rashidi Kawawa, then Prime Minister, explained to them the government's desire to get the people to participate in projects which they could undertake without government finance, such as roads and houses. How useful self-help schemes have been economically is not clear, but the idea had other functions apart from economic ones. As Dr Joseph Nye, Jr, once put it in an article in *Transition*:

'Self-help also allowed the Tanganyika government to release the energies of those who had participated in the struggle for independence, and later to increase the number involved in the political process . . . . While no figures are available it is a generally accepted impression that a greater part of the population has been involved in self-help, and it might be called their first contact with "the Tanganyika Nation".'

A later manifestation of the ideology of hard work in Tanzania was in regard to farms. If again we go back to Nyerere's formulation of his socialism in *Ujamaa* we see the following argument:

'Those of us who talk about the African way of life and, quite rightly, take pride in maintaining the tradition of hospitality which is so great a part of it, might do well to remember the Swahili saying: "*Mgeni siku mbili; siku ya tatu mpe jembe*" or, in English, "Treat your guest as a guest for two days; on the third day give him a hoe".'

For not developing their Arusha farms fully, some Europeans there were later to have their farms taken away from them. They were '*wageni siku ya tatu*'—and they had failed to accept the challenge of the *jembe* or hoe. Indeed, the challenge of 'toil' as an ideological concept confronted the native as well as the foreigner. And the concept of toil has now become part of the ambition of maximum utilisation of the nation's resources. On 15 February 1965, the government of Tanzania once again reiterated the following policy:

'Because of the significant part which the agricultural economy had played in the past, and because of the increased role which it is to continue to play, the government attached great importance to land and its use. It was the greatest single asset at the disposal of the country, and the government was therefore determined to see that those who had been given land, both indigenous and non-indigenous people, should develop it fully and properly, in the interest of the nation.'

In some ways, this preoccupation with hard and rational work is one of the more attractive aspects of the national ethic of Tanzania. In the

358

struggle for independence the compelling slogan was 'uhuru'—but Nyerere soon turned it into 'uhuru na kazi'. Now the call is for 'socialism' —and the new motto has perhaps become 'socialism and sweat'.

Then, in October 1966, came the new National Service in Tanzania, requiring university graduates and products of other major educational institutions to join the National Service for two years and participate in nation-building activities. Here again was an instance of 'ideological toil'—the use of the idea of 'work' as a basis of national commitment and self-reliance.

The culmination of this ethic was the Arusha Declaration of February 1967 which required frugality and self-denial from everyone connected with government. Every person in authority had to be a worker or peasant in essential status. If he owned an extra house and rented it to a tenant, he had become a landlord and was in danger of losing his status as essentially a worker. But this policy of self-denial by all those in authority, at both national and local levels of government, was phased out a little. Total renunciation of such worldly goods by those in authority could be done gradually over a relatively short span of time. But, at any rate, the idea of self-denial had now become a necessary qualification for holding public office.

Also arising out of the Arusha Declaration was the decision of the government of Tanzania to nationalise the banks and then other industries in the country. It was both an assertion of central control of the economy and an attempt once again to narrow the possibility of class privilege in the country.

Nationalisation and socialism

The taking over of banks and other industries in Tanzania, when juxtaposed with renewed declarations of economic policy in both Kenya and Uganda, presents interesting differences in conception.

Two senses of *nationalisation* are becoming effectively operative in East Africa. In one sense—that of Tanzania—'nationalisation' has the usual Western meaning. It means putting economic resources under the control of the state.

But there is another sense of 'nationalisation'—and that is putting economic resources under the control of *nationals*. In the latter sense, the resources might indeed be transferred from foreign hands to the hands of nationals—but not necessarily to the hands of the State. President Kenyatta's major speech at the state opening of Kenya's parliament on 15 February 1967 was a reaffirmation of the latter sense of nationalisation —an increasing participation in the economy by nationals of the country.

Linked to the above distinction are also two senses of *public ownership*. One sense of 'public ownership'—that of Tanzania—is the usual Western one. An industry comes under state ownership. But there is another sense of 'public ownership'—that of trying to make sure that the shares of an industry are owned widely by ordinary members of the public themselves and not by the state. The House of Manji in Kenya, until then a family business, converted itself on 16 February 1967 into a public company and was going to issue forty-five per cent of its shares to the public. But how could it be ensured that this forty-five per cent was not simply bought by another rich man? Mr Mwai Kibaki, Kenya's Minister for Commerce and Industry at the time, announced that the issue of shares to the public would be handled by his Ministry to ensure that they were available to as wide a section as possible all over Kenya. Prospective buyers would be able to obtain application forms from district officers anywhere in the country.

Mr Kibaki emphasised that the purpose of the Ministry's help in the distribution was to ensure that the shares were available to all Kenyans, not just to people in Nairobi and substantial investors outside. The shares were expected to sell at a par value of twenty shillings and the issue was expected to begin on 1 June. There was also to be a free issue of shares, sixty per cent of which would go to African women who had been employees of the House of Manji.

This particular experiment of the House of Manji encountered difficulties, but the basic policy of the Kenya Government remained the same. The Kenya sense of public ownership was, in some ways, the more novel of the two we have discussed. In order to grasp this point fully, we have to relate it once again to the kind of equality which African national-ism has cherished so far. In their struggle against European rule, Africans did indeed aspire to bring about a world in which no African individual counted for less than an individual from another race. And while they were struggling for that world, African nationalists before independence tried to make sure that no individual African counted for more than another African either. But independence has now posed new dilemmas. The ideal of maintaining equality between Africans themselves in a particular country has sometimes come into conflict with the ideal of creating equality between Africans and other races. The former ideal of equality between Africans should presumably dictate a policy aimed against the emergence of an African commercial class. But, in East African conditions, such a policy could mean leaving the profits of the private sector of the economy exclusively to non-indigenous entrepre-neurs. Africans in Kenya might then remain equal in poverty between themselves—while the inequalities of income between them on one side and the Asians and Europeans on the other were allowed to persist.

The government of Kenya seems to have rejected, for the time being, this solution. In April 1965, for example, Kenya's Minister for Commerce and Industry at the time urged the non-African businessmen to identify themselves with African aspirations by inviting Africans to buy shares in their enterprises. Minister Kiano said: 'While we do not discriminate against non-Africans in Kenya, the spirit of give and take should prevail.' The late Tom Mboya also repeated the same theme as a reminder to those concerned. Similar attempts to increase African participation in commerce were made in Uganda.

The Kenya Government Sessional Paper on African Socialism also included a bias towards such a policy. It appeared that what was being urged by the Kenya Government was not so much African socialism as the Africanisation of capitalism. And yet for many Kenyans—as indeed for many Africans elsewhere—African socialism had to include the Africanisation of the rudimentary capitalism which had already emerged. There is certainly a great keenness in Kenya and, to some extent, in Uganda that there should be greater African participation in commerce. But is this 'equality'? Kenya's Minister for Commerce and Industry has described it as a process of narrowing 'the wide gap between Africans and non-Africans in commerce and trade'. Uganda's Ministers have made similar appeals to non-African businessmen—that they should try and get more and more African shareholders. But, while the gap between black East Africans and non-indigenous East Africans is being narrowed, new gaps between black East Africans themselves again might be created.

Marxist purists might argue that this is not socialism. But the significant thing about socialist thought in a place like Kenya is not its relationship to Marxism, not even what it expounds in a documentary; it is what it seems to take for granted. In an ethnically pluralistic society, the first task of socialism, according to this school, is not to abolish class distinctions altogether but to prevent class distinctions from coinciding with ethnic differences. The problems of class distinctions can be reduced by 'social mobility'. This is the ability of a person to move from one class to another. The very creation of an African business class would be proof that social mobility can be engineered or manipulated by government policy.

Uganda's 'Rubicon of radicalism'

For a while Kenya and Uganda were like-minded on these issues. Uganda's legislation on trade licensing and on control of immigration was greatly influenced by the preceding Kenyan legislation. Uganda's commitment to the Africanisation of commerce, though less publicised than Kenya's, seemed to share the same characteristics.

Uganda's policy to create an indigenous business class has not been abandoned altogether, but it has been sharply qualified by important new ideological developments.

Under the leadership of President A. Milton Obote Uganda entered the 1970s with a commitment to pursue a socialistic path of development. It was on May Day 1970 that the Rubicon of radicalism seemed to have at last been crossed. Obote announced that from then on all the export and import business would be transacted by para-statal bodies. The oil companies would, however, continue to import and distribute oil and other petroleum products. Yet from that day the government would acquire 60 per cent of the shares of every oil company operating in Uganda. (Some modifications were later made after negotiations with the oil dealers.)

The Kampala City Council, together with the trade unions in Kampala, would acquire 60 per cent of the shares in the Kampala and District Bus Services. Outside Kampala the district administration, the urban authorities, the co-operative unions and the trade unions, in each of the regions, would acquire 60 per cent of the shares of the bus companies based in those regions.

The Ugandan economy rested on coffee, cotton and copper. Coffee and cotton were produced, processed and marketed by the growers, as well as the public bodies controlled by Government. But from that May Day of 1970 the Uganda Development Corporation would increase its share-holding in Kilembe Mines to 60 per cent.

The workers and the para-statal bodies would, from then on, acquire 60 per cent of the shares in every important manufacturing industry and plantation. 'Lastly,' said President Obote, 'I would wish to announce that from today the Government will acquire 60 per cent of the shares of every bank, credit institution and insurance company operating in Uganda. The 60 per cent shares which have today been acquired by the people of Uganda in the various economic centres I have announced will be paid for, over a period, from the profits made by the companies concerned.'

For more than a year Uganda had been expecting some important socialistic measure to be taken by Obote. True to his style, he had first let loose a trial balloon with a declaration that his government intended to move to the left. A lot of speculation started, later fed by the establishment of a Ministry of National Service. Was Obote going to embark on wide nationalisation measures? Again, true to his style, Obote seemed at first to be soft-pedalling. In a major address to Parliament at the beginning of 1969 Obote argued that the left was a direction, rather than a specific revolutionary stopping point. Uganda had been moving to the left since independence in any case, given that the acquisition of independence was itself in the leftward direction.

And then Dr Obote issued *The Common Man's Charter* in October 1969. The charter did deepen the rhetoric of radicalism, but all indications still seemed to suggest that Obote was, on the one hand, eager to prepare the public for important changes; and, on the other, apprehensive about prematurely alienating important sectors of that public, and indeed of members of his own cabinet. The word 'socialism' in Uganda has never evoked quite the same enthusiastic response that it has done in some other African countries. On the contrary, an important part of Ugandan opinion has remained deeply suspicious of socialism. While the kingdom of Buganda survived, one important reason for suspecting socialism lay, quite simply, in its presumed anti-royalist tendencies. There was a fear that if the socialists captured power, they would proceed to abolish the monarchies.

Obote, in the initial stages of independence scrupulously assured the kings that their future was in no danger. Indeed, we have seen how he even concluded an alliance with Kabaka Yekka, a party of Buganda committed to the preservation of kingship and the autonomy of Buganda. The alliance lasted from independence in 1962 until 1964, when Obote felt strong enough to do without the support of Kabaka Yekka. But the principle of kingship was still not touched. Indeed, one of the anomalies of Uganda in the African context was that it had for a while a presidential system which was not a republican system. Most other former British colonies in Africa, upon devising a system with a president at the top, *ipso facto* became republics. They had severed their last links with a British monarch. In Uganda, on the other hand, the link with the British monarch was cut in 1963, but the presidential system which emerged looked, in part, to the indigenous kings for candidates to occupy the presidency. The first President of Uganda was also the Kabaka, or King, of Buganda.

Tensions between President Mutesa and his Prime Minister Obote started fairly early, and seemed to be moving towards a crisis. The crisis erupted in 1966. Obote and a few of his colleagues were accused of misappropriating gold and ivory from the rebels in the Congo; Obote in turn later accused Mutesa of sounding foreign powers for military assistance to subvert the purposes of the Ugandan Constitution in order to strengthen his own power on a national scale.

In swift moves Obote also turned on five of his colleagues in the cabinet, whose loyalty seemed to have been compromised. These were detained. He then suspended the Constitution, relieved Mutesa unilaterally of his constitutional presidency, and appointed himself as the first executive president of independent Uganda. Events culminated in a confrontation between the kabaka's guards and the troops of the central government at the kabaka's palace. The palace fell, the kabaka fled to England, and Obote proceeded to try to restructure Uganda more in his own image.

363

The first major reform came the following year in 1967 with the abolition of all four kings of Uganda. The new constitution strengthened the power of the executive president, and inaugurated an era of true republicanism.

In the old days the royalists had feared that socialism would bring republicanism. But in fact the sequence was reversed—republicanism was now leading on to socialism. The move was not immediate. The first era of self-congratulation centred on the new republican status of the nation. But gradually Obote began to think about taking the next step on the long road towards his preferred ideology.

There was no doubt that Obote personally had been socialistic from quite early. But his style of leadership had included a marked tendency towards reconciliation. And the chief characteristic of such a style was a capacity to find areas of compromise between otherwise antagonistic viewpoints and a readiness to define the boundaries of political accommodation. Throughout his political career in independent Uganda Obote had, in fact been portrayed by his critics as a leftist, even as a communist. The royalists exaggerated Obote's leftism because they feared its republican implications; but, in addition, many religious Ugandans feared Obote's radical orientation because they assumed that it included ungodliness and anti-religious tendencies. For much of his political career Obote had felt it necessary to allay such fears, especially those which associated socialism with anti-clericalism. And then in 1969 and 1970, as he was groping towards the full consolidation of his socialistic ideas, he was anxious to ensure that there should be no misunderstanding as to his ultimate motivation. He ended the speech of nationalisation on May Day 1970 with the words 'Fellow citizens, I have decided upon the matters I have told you, "for God and my country".'

The coup of January 1971

Then on 25 January 1971, a military coup was announced on Radio Uganda. Dr Milton Obote was away attending a conference in Singapore when fighting erupted in Uganda. Before he boarded the plane on the first stage of his journey to Uganda, Obote was informed of the fighting which was under way. After the next stop on the flight back he knew the worst. He had been overthrown.

Major-General Idi Amin, whom Obote himself had groomed and appointed to command the armed forces, took over power. Amin asserted that a mutiny in the armed forces had very quickly escalated into a military challenge which had resulted in the ousting of Milton Obote. In Buganda the coup was greeted with spontaneous and almost hysterical rejoicing. There was little doubt that the Baganda had felt oppressed under Obote since 1966. On 25 January 1971, it was not clear if the new regime would be any more tolerant of the Baganda than the previous one. But at the very minimum the new coup signified two things—it signified that the man who had ousted Mutesa was no longer in power, and it also signified that the north was no longer solidly united in national politics. These two facts, from a Ganda point of view, were themselves a gain over the previous situation.

But it turned out that General Amin wanted to conciliate the Baganda. Almost immediately following the coup he promised to bring back the body of Sir Edward Mutesa for a state funeral in the land of his ancestors. He lifted the state of emergency in Buganda, which had operated since 1966. And although he proclaimed that the soldiers had no intention of changing the republican status of Uganda, Amin nevertheless permitted the Baganda for a while to discuss the implications of that statement and to make out a case for change. The restoration of the kabakaship became an issue which gathered in public import at least until the ninth anniversary of Uganda's independence on 9 October 1971, when Amin at last took up a firmer position against it.

Meanwhile Mutesa's body was brought back and buried with full military and state honours. The titles 'prince' and 'princess', which had been out of use since the new constitution proclaimed by Obote in 1967, were now heard again. Kings were no more, but princes were still in existence. Prince Badru Kakungulu, the former kabaka's uncle, was now once again publicly referred to as 'Prince Badru'. And Ronald Mutebi, Mutesa's favourite son, was formally recognised as Mutesa's heir in everything but the kabakaship, and was now once again publicly referred to as 'Prince Ronald Mutebi'.

The situation in Uganda remained somewhat uncertain politically for quite a while after the coup, and relations between Uganda and her neighbours occasionally deteriorated.

Was the new coup going to reverse some of the changes which Obote's regime had brought into being? As we have noted, the republican status of the country was after all to remain unchanged. That very fundamental point provided a continuity between Obote's policies after 1966 and the policies of the military regime. The nationalisation measures in the economy were modified, but not rescinded. What did disappear was the rhetoric of socialism and the 'move to the left'. By a curious destiny it was replaced by a rhetoric of 'action under God'.

In a sense, what was happening was a substitution of religious symbolism for ideological symbolism as a basis for national unification. Amin saw himself as a person who would at last rescue Uganda from the sectarianism and religious tensions inherited from the competitive proselytism of the missionaries from back in the 1890s. Amin was even in favour of establishing a Ministry of Religious Affairs, but was then persuaded to reduce it to a Department of Religious Affairs under a permanent secretary. Amin spoke with religious leaders periodically, and even organised a major religious conference at which the different denominations discussed the points which divided them internally and in relation to other denominations. Committees for Protestants, Catholics, Moslems and others were each chaired by a minister. The ministerial chairmanship was itself a measure of the seriousness of the enterprise.

The Moslems and the Protestants were deeply divided within themselves, and one way of handling the divisions in the case of the Moslems turned out to be the idea of establishing an Islamic Council as a policy-making body for all Moslems in Uganda. The Protestants found it harder to be re-united, but in general an atmosphere of ecumenicalism was purposefully promoted by the new military government. There was even a report that Amin intended to train two of his sons to be Roman Catholic priests, although Amin himself was a Moslem. This account was given by the Acting Chief Justice, himself a Roman Catholic, but was never publicly confirmed or denied by Amin himself. Whether the plan was serious or merely a gesture of religious broadmindedness, it was certainly symptomatic of the ecumenical spirit pursued by the new government. Obote's secular ideology as a basis for national unification had indeed for a while been replaced by Amin's sacred symbolism as a route towards national reconciliation.

And yet the two approaches—the secular and the sacred—need not be mutually exclusive. It may well turn out that Uganda will seek a synthesis of secular inspiration and religious commitment in the years ahead.

Conclusion

There is no doubt that Tanzania, Kenya and Uganda in different ways are seeking the elusive ideal of social justice. We cannot as yet be sure which is the most effective way. Tanzania seeks to eliminate economic classes, but there is a risk that she might eliminate economic creativity at the same time. Tanzania has so far tried to create a system which enables every individual to be politically involved. But what about the economic involvement of each individual in the life of the nation? If the state runs everything, can an individual achieve his economic best?

Kenya, on the other hand, would like to increase African participation in commerce and thus give to the African individual a chance to become an effective economic agent in his own right. But this too has had its risks. Opportunities for individual achievement in the economy entail the danger of some inequalities growing in the days ahead. The Ugandan experiment under Obote shared attributes with both Kenya and

Tanzania.

But East Africa will not innovate unless it is prepared to take some calculated risks. Perhaps it is good for the region as a whole that there are several bold experiments taking place at the same time. The different party systems within each country, the different solutions to tribal problems, the varying relationships between the civil service and the government, and the divergent routes towards equality and social justice, all go to give East Africa a certain richness and inventiveness. In some ways the three countries are drifting apart; in other ways they stand to gain by the lessons of those experiments which are going on independently in each country. Perhaps the cause of East African regional integration is not dying after all; it is merely undergoing the pangs and agonies of profound transformation.

Further reading

APTER, D. E. *The Political Kingdom in Uganda*, Princeton University Press, Princeton, 1961.

CLIFFE, L. (Ed.) *One Party Democracy*, East African Publishing House, Nairobi, 1967.

GERTZEL, CHERRY *The Politics of Independent Kenya, 1963–1968*, East African Publishing House & Heinemann, 1970.

MAZRUI, A. A. *On Heroes and Uhuru-Worship*, (Chapters 2, 5 and 6), Longman, London, 1967.

MAZRUI, A. A. *Violence and Thought* (Chapters 1, 2, 6, 7, 10 and 12), Longman, London, 1969.

NYERERE, J. K. *Freedom and Unity*, Oxford University Press, Dar es Salaam, 1966.

NYERERE, J. K. *Freedom and Socialism*, Oxford University Press, Dar es Salaam, 1969.

NYE, J. S. Jr. *Pan-Africanism and East African Integration*, Oxford University Press, London and Nairobi, 1966.

OBOTE, A. M. *The Common Man's Charter* and its Four Appendices, Government Printer, Entebbe, 1970.

ROSBERG, C. G. Jr. and NOTTINGHAM, J. *The Myth of Mau Mau: Nationalism in Kenya*, East African Publishing House, Nairobi, 1967.

ROTHCHILD, D. and ROGIN, M. Uganda in *National Unity and Regionalism in Eight African States*, Ed. G. M. Carter, Cornell University Press, Ithaca, N.Y., 1966, (pp. 337–440).

ROTHCHILD, D. (Ed.) *Politics of Integration: An East African Documentary*, East African Publishing House, Nairobi, 1968.

TORDOFF, W. *Government and Politics in Tanzania*, Nairobi: East African Publishing House, Nairobi, 1967.

GHAI, Y. P. and MCAUSLAN, J. P. W. B. *Public Law and Political Change in Kenya*, Oxford University Press, 1970.

East African Royal Commission 1953–55 Report, 1955.

The Arusha Declaration, Government of Tanzania, Dar es Salaam, 1967.

Economic Planning and its Application to African Socialism, Kenya Government, Nairobi, 1965.

Treaty for East African Cooperation, Nairobi, 1967.

ROBSON, P. and LEYS, C. (Eds) *Federation in East Africa: Problems and Opportunities*, Oxford University Press, London, 1965.

GHAI, D. P. and VAN ARKADIE, B. The East African Economies in (Eds) Robson, P. and Lury, D. A. *The Economies of Africa*, George Allen and Unwin, London, 1969.

NYERERE, J. *Education for Self-Reliance*, Dar es Salaam, 1967.

Second Five Year Development Plan, Tanzania.

Development Plan: 1970–74, Kenya.

Development Plan, Uganda.

18

Some Aspects of Social and Economic Progress and Policies in East Africa, 1961 to 1971

D. P. Ghai

East African countries have been independent for nearly a decade. This period has been marked by far-reaching social and economic change throughout East Africa. The pre-independence societies and economies of East Africa had been moulded into a distinctive pattern by the long years of colonial rule. They reflected the interests of the imperial power and the associated dominant groups. With the attainment of independence, new forces and ideas came to the fore, presaging major social and economic changes. The changes which have unfolded themselves in the 1960s will appear in the historical context as the beginning of a continuing process of adaptation of colonial structures and institutions to the new pressures and ideologies set in motion by the decolonisation of East Africa. They can be fully understood by reference not only to the configuration of the internal power structure of the post-independence period but also to the external constraints and pressures exerted on the East African countries.

In the early years of the post-independence period, there was a certain similarity in the social and economic policies pursued by the three countries. But with the passage of years there have emerged major differences in the manner in which each of the countries is responding to its social and economic problems. And within individual countries there have been marked and sudden changes of policies. Thus a study of the East African experience over the past decade provides rich and illuminating contrasts in the common endeavour at modernisation of societies through deliberate social and economic planning.

The purpose of this chapter is to focus on some aspects of the leading social and economic developments in the East African countries in the sixties. Since many of them flow directly from the structures created in the colonial period, it is necessary to sketch in the relevant outlines of the social and economic system as it existed in the twilight of the colonial era. This is followed by a discussion of some of the main themes of public policy in the post-independence period: Africanisation, economic growth, diversification, strategies of development and the East African economic relations. The concluding section looks at the main issues in social and economic policy in the seventies.

The colonial heritage

In East Africa, as in other parts of the colonial world, colonial rule created some characteristic social and economic structures. Before its conquest by the imperial powers, the East African region had an economy characterised by subsistence production and consumption with very limited exchange of goods and services. The introduction of colonial rule resulted in the creation and growth of a cash economy linking the East African region with the outside world. This typically took three forms: the growth of cash crops by African peasant farmers for export to the outside world, principally the metropolitan powers; the development of agricultural and mineral products for export by European plantation and mining companies; and the creation of modern commercial, industrial and agricultural enterprises by immigrant settlers from Europe and Asia.

Although most parts of the East African region experienced all three types of activities, the dominant path of economic expansion took different forms in different countries. At one extreme was Uganda where the basis of the cash economy was laid by the growth of cash crops—cotton and coffee—by millions of small-scale peasants scattered all over the country. Kenya was at the other extreme where at the height of colonialism virtually the entire agricultural cash production was monopolised by European farmers and plantations. As in most comparisons of this nature, Tanzania was somewhere in the middle with a more balanced mixture of African peasant and European settler and plantation production of cash crops.

In the non-agricultural sectors—transportation, construction, commerce and industry—the ownership and management of enterprises was in all three countries virtually exclusively in the hands of Europeans and Asians. The African participation in the modern economy, with the exception of cash crops production in Uganda and Tanzania, largely took the form of provision of unskilled wage labour.

370

The structure of East African economies on the eve of independence displayed characteristics typical of an underdeveloped economy: the dominance of agriculture, the limited development of industry, heavy reliance on exports of primary products and on imports of capital goods and consumer manufactured goods. There were, however, some structural differences in the economies of the three countries: at one extreme was Tanzania with the highest reliance on production and export of agricultural and mineral products, a very narrow industrial sector, and least development of the physical and human infrastructure —roads, railways, ports, electricity, education and health services. Kenya had relatively the most diversified economy, with significant manufacturing, commérce, banking, insurance and transportation. Uganda was somewhere in between. The relatively higher development of the Kenya economy was due in the main to two factors: first, as will be shown later, Kenya served in many ways as the commercial and industrial centre of East Africa, thus deriving income from the provision of manufactured goods and services such as commerce and transportation, to the other two countries. Secondly, the higher development of its manufacturing and commercial sectors was due to the demand for these products created by the heavy concentration of high income immigrant communities in Kenya in relation to the other two countries.

The structure of the economy paralleled the organisation of society along racial lines, with its hierarchical division of skills, lines of responsibility and levels of income. The overwhelming majority of Africans survived at bare subsistence levels; their main source of income being either small family farms, using low-productivity techniques of production, or unskilled wage employment in farms, factories, shops and government service. The only exceptions were a handful of prosperous farmers in Uganda and in the Kilimanjaro and Lake Districts of Tanzania. To these should be added a sprinkling of Africans employed either as clerks, teachers and nurses in the public services, or in the lower supervisory and junior technical grades in private commerce and industry.

The middle level manpower in the public services and in commerce and industry was supplied by Asians, who also monopolised small scale commerce and industry. A tiny fraction of the Asian population was able to rise to high levels of affluence through income from large scale industry, commerce and agriculture, or from property and successful practice in the professions—law, medicine, engineering and architecture.

At the apex of the hierarchical pyramid came the Europeans, monopolising the top jobs with high income levels in public services as well as in modern commerce and industry. In addition, a substantial number derived high incomes from farming, business and the professions.

The racial stratification of society along economic lines was created

371

by the colonial authorities and buttressed by numerous rules and regulations as well as by differential provision of public social and economic services. In Kenya for instance, which was the most racially segregated of the three countries, Africans were prevented by legislation from growing cash crops, thus forcing them to seek employment at low wages on European farms and plantations. Asians were restricted from engaging in economic activities outside scheduled urban areas. There was a strict racial segregation of residential areas in cities, and differential salary structures in both the public and private sectors of the economy for Europeans, Asians and Africans. In the other two countries, racial discrimination was never carried to such extremes, but the public policy, whether in terms of per capita expenditure on health and education, or on economic infrastructure such as roads and electricity, almost always favoured the Europeans with Africans coming at the bottom.

It was not until well after the Second World War that it became a deliberate policy of the colonial administration to improve the standards of living of the great mass of the East African population through some sort of social and economic planning. This is particularly true of Kenya, for in the other two countries the colonial administrations did not have to contend with a powerful lobby of European settlers who felt their interests threatened by a diversion of resources to the betterment of African standards of living through modernisation of their agriculture. The decade preceding independence saw some expansion of educational and health services for Africans, intensification of extension and credit services for farmers in Uganda and Tanzania, and the beginnings of a modern agricultural system for Africans in Kenya. But these efforts were limited in scope and certainly fell far short of the scale necessary to cope with the magnitude of the problem created by decades of colonial neglect.

At the same time, the basic assumption of development policy was that apart from modernisation of African agriculture, the only pattern of economic expansion was through the infusion of foreign capital and skills for the creation of industrial and commercial enterprises. The public policy was thus designed to attract European capital and immigrants into East Africa. This policy was reasonably successful in Kenya in the 1950s as large inflows of private capital and European immigrants created boom conditions for most of this period. But there was relatively little trickling down of the benefits of economic expansion to the great majority of Africans. In Uganda and Tanzania this policy of encouraging foreign capital and skills for the development of the economy does not seem to have had any significant impact.

The role of the government in the establishment, ownership and operation of enterprises was severely limited. There was indeed a plethora of rules and regulations bearing on the economic life of the country but their main objective was either as in Kenya the protection of the vested interests of European farmers, or the paternalistic, often misguided, sheltering of Africans from the competitive impact of the modern economy. Only in Uganda towards the end of the colonial rule was any significant attempt made through the publicly-owned Uganda Development Corporation to promote a range of large-scale, modern, agricultural, industrial and mining enterprises.

Before discussing the changes brought about by independence, we must consider the economic cooperative arrangements in East Africa. During the colonial period, a high degree of economic coordination and integration had emerged among the three East African countries. Since the early 1920s, the three countries constituted a virtual common market: with the exception of some agricultural products, there was free trade in all local products and a common external tariff on imports originating from outside East Africa. The three countries formed a monetary union, with a common currency issued by the East African Currency Board. The structure of income and excise taxes was identical. In combination with a well-developed transport system, these arrangements resulted in relatively high and rapidly expanding inter-territorial trade. Economic cooperation was further cemented by the operation of certain vital services such as railways, airways, posts and telecommunications, higher education, research institutes, and collection of income, customs and excise taxes, by single East African authorities. This impressive degree of economic integration functioned under the overall authority at first of the Conference of East African Governors and subsequently the Authority of the East African Common Services Organisation. Because the headquarters of most of these services were concentrated in Kenya which also had a more developed economy, the major benefits of these cooperative arrangements tended to flow to Kenya, strengthening its already established position as the governmental, industrial and commercial heart of East Africa.

Priorities after independence

The general picture presented above—underdeveloped economies with large subsistence sectors, heavy reliance on production and export of primary products, limited development of non-agricultural sectors, racial divisions coinciding neatly with economic functions, beginnings of social and economic planning for the benefit of the masses, a high degree of economic integration with a strong bias in favour of Kenya—constitutes an essential background for an understanding and appraisal of developments in the first decade of independence. Independence paved the way for the articulation and implementa-

373

tion of the aspirations and interests of the African majority. The tasks before the independent African governments were clear—greater control and ownership of the economy, increased African participation in the modern society and the economy, rapid economic growth, a vast expansion of social and economic services, and a reconstruction of the basis of East African economic cooperation to ensure an equitable distribution of benefits. If these tasks were to be carried out, the governments had to play a more active and wider role in the management of social and economic affairs. The sixties therefore witnessed an unparalleled expansion in the size and functions of the public sector in all the three countries. The first priorities were Africanisation of public services and the economies, and greater local and state control and ownership of key enterprises in the modern sector of the economy.

Africanisation

It has already been noted that on the eve of independence there was a marked lack of African participation in the modern sector of the East African economies. It has been calculated that towards the end of the fifties, Africans claimed two-thirds of the monetary Gross Domestic Product of Uganda, half of the Tanganyika product and only one-third of the Kenya product. The concentration of economic power and wealth in the hands of a tiny alien minority was ethically wrong and politically explosive. All three governments, therefore, sought to bring about a rapid increase in African share and participation in the modern sectors of the economy. In the early years of independence, the policies pursued in the three countries were largely similar but in recent years Tanzania has moved sharply away from the policies aimed at creating an African business class and in the direction of creating a socialist economy with public ownership of the larger enterprises in the field of agriculture, commerce, banking, manufacturing and construction. Before coming to these developments, we shall trace the Africanisation policies in the three countries in the years immediately following independence.

The problem of ensuring a larger African role in the economy has been tackled on four fronts. The first stage everywhere was the Africanisation of the political system, which marked the emergence and dominance of African political parties, African representatives in national legislatures, and African ministers and heads of governments. This was followed by rapid Africanisation of the civil services in the three countries. The process of Africanisation of civil services, both at the higher and at the middle ranks, involved crash training programmes and extremely rapid promotion for African officers. It also involved replacement of expatriate officers, which was facilitated by generous compensation retirement terms for expatriates. The fact that Britain was prepared to finance the costs of Africanisation directly and indirectly through loans to East African governments materially assisted the orderly progress of structural change in a major national institution. The achievement is all the more striking when it is remembered that it was carried out at a time when the governments in all three countries were assuming new and complex responsibilities.

The progress made in the localisation of public services in the three countries since independence can be documented by a few figures. In Tanzania, for example, only about a quarter of the total posts in the senior and middle grades were held by citizens in 1961; this proportion had risen to 86 per cent by 1970. Likewise in Kenya, at the time of independence, only one post in seven of the higher ranks of the civil service was held by a citizen. Even in the lower executive and technical grades less than half of the staff were citizens. Already by the end of 1966, well over half of the higher ranks, and an average of three-quarters of the executive and technical grades had been Africanised. The process of replacing foreign with citizen officers has been proceeding apace in the last five years. Uganda also has experienced a similarly rapid Africanisation of its public services.

The current position, therefore, is that the process of localisation of middle grades of the civil service is virtually completed in all three countries except in certain posts requiring skills which continue to be in short supply such as stenography. Likewise, the higher administrative posts are almost completely localised. It is only in the technical and professional posts that localisation has proceeded at a slow pace due mainly to a lack of local persons with the necessary training and skills. With the anticipated expansion in the numbers of East Africans trained in professional and technical lines, there should be a material acceleration of localisation of these posts over the next five years.

The third area in which the East African governments have pressed ahead with Africanisation is agriculture. Kenya was faced with the most acute problem in this respect. In the past, the cash agricultural sector was completely dominated by European settlers. As the land issue had been at the root of most of Kenya's troubles in the past, it was necessary to find a satisfactory solution to it in the interests of stability and growth. As is well known, the problem was tackled by a massive resettlement of African farmers on the erstwhile European farms in what was known as the 'White Highlands'. Between 1960 and 1968, more than 800 000 hectares of former European farms had been taken over for 'high density' and 'low density' settlement schemes and for large government and cooperative farms. In addition, many large farms have been bought privately by Africans either as individuals, partnerships or companies. In all, about 45 000 African families had been settled on these farms. The cost of the entire exercise, of land purchase, settlement, and development loans to African farmers has run into millions of pounds.

An important aspect of Africanisation relates to the processing, marketing and distribution of agricultural produce, in which the main instrument for Africanisation in all three countries has been the co-operative movement. Over the years, cooperatives have tended to control an increasing share of the processing and marketing of agricultural products. The governments have aided this process by providing cheap credit, training facilities and generally preferential treatment for cooperatives. In Uganda by the early sixties the cooperatives and individual growers controlled the marketing and ginning of the entire cotton crop. Coffee curing and marketing, which until the fifties were largely in the hands of non-Africans, had been firmly placed in the hands of cooperatives by 1966. Likewise, greater control was secured on the marketing of minor cash crops through the creation of the Agricultural Produce Marketing Board. In Tanzania, cooperatives had played a more important role from an earlier period, particularly in the Chagga area. The official policy has been to place the marketing and processing of all agricultural products as soon as possible in the hands of cooperatives. This policy has been vigorously carried out in the sixties, and one crop after another has been taken over by cooperatives. At the national level, state-controlled marketing boards have been set up in all three countries to give the governments greater control over the marketing of agricultural products.

The fourth aspect of Africanisation relates to increased African share in commerce and industry. Since 1963 major efforts have been made by the East African governments to increase national and African share in the activities of these sectors. The inclination in the earlier period was to rely on special programmes of training and credit and the voluntary efforts of non-African businesses to step up the rate of Africanisation. But apparently these efforts proved inadequate to achieve Africanisation at a satisfactory rate. Thus in recent years, new policies relying on administrative measures have been adopted to force the pace of Africanisation in these sectors.

Three sorts of measures have been employed in the East African countries to accelerate Africanisation in commerce and industry. In the first place, all the three countries have introduced legislation under which non-citizens are required to obtain work permits before they can take up a job. The permits are issued by the government only if no suitable citizens are available to do the job. Furthermore, these permits are issued for fairly short periods, generally ranging from six months to two years during which time the employer is expected to train local persons to take over from non-citizens. These measures have had a marked impact on the acceleration of the localisation of jobs in commerce and industry in all the three countries.

The second measure used in Kenya and Uganda has been to require non-citizen businessmen to obtain trade licences. Under the Trade Licensing Acts of Kenya and Uganda, certain areas, which in effect include all areas outside the main shopping centres of a few large cities, are reserved exclusively for citizens. Non-citizen traders are allowed to operate there only if they are granted a licence, which is given for one year at a time. It is only in the non-scheduled areas, which have been steadily shrinking, that non-citizens are allowed to carry on their trade. The second provision of the Acts restricts trade in certain commodities to citizens only, irrespective of their location. These Acts have been in operation for less than four years in Kenya and two in Uganda, but already they have had substantial impact, especially in Kenya, in accelerating Africanisation of commerce and transport in smaller towns and urban areas.

In Tanzania, as has already been stated, the policy since 1967 has been to discourage the emergence of an African capitalist class and the emphasis has been placed on localisation through state and cooperative ownership and management of business. The wholesale trade has been nationalised and state and cooperative retail outlets are being encouraged.

The third instrument of localisation in all the three countries has been the establishment of state-owned trading corporations which are vested with the responsibility of importing all or specified goods from abroad and distributing them to African traders. In Tanzania, the State Trading Corporation has the monopoly of imports and their wholesale distribution. In Uganda, the National Trading Corporation is charged, among other things, with the responsibility of distributing goods as far as possible through African traders. In Kenya, likewise the Kenya National Trading Corporation has monopoly rights in the import and distribution of certain commodities; and it assists African businessmen by granting them distributive rights in these commodities. Other state institutions, such as the Industrial and Commercial Development Corporation and the National Housing Corporation in Kenya, and the Uganda Development Corporation, assist African businessmen to establish new enterprises or extend and diversify the old ones.

The cumulative impact of all these measures has been to increase substantially African participation in commercial and industrial sectors. But since they have been in operation for a relatively short period of time, their full impact will only be felt in the seventies.

Economic growth, diversification and strategies of development

Another major objective of economic policy in the post-independence period has been the achievement of high rates of economic growth and the diversification of the economy in terms of reduced dependence on primary products and widening of external economic relations. The former is necessary for a steady rise in the standard of living of the people as well as for expansion of social and economic services. The latter is required for the long run structural transformation of the economy as well as for reducing dependence for trade, foreign private investment and aid on single or a narrow range of sources.

The objective of accelerated economic growth has been pursued in a number of ways. The machinery of government is constantly being geared to cope with rapid economic expansion. Soon after independence, ministries of planning were created in all three countries to give greater cohesion and importance to developmental effort. This was followed by the publication of comprehensive and ambitious development plans in the three countries—Tanzania and Kenya in 1964 and Uganda in 1966. These plans attempt to accelerate growth and allocate investment resources within the framework of nationally agreed social and economic goals. Since independence a major effort has been made by the three countries to extract increased internal resources for development through taxation and domestic borrowing. At the same time the search for external sources of capital and technical assistance has been intensified.

All these efforts have borne fruit in significant acceleration of growth in the years since independence. The years immediately preceding independence were characterised for a variety of reasons by slow growth, stagnant public revenues, constant or falling exports, and large outflows of private capital. There was a sharp reversal of these trends after independence. The output of goods and services has increased at a rate of 6–7 per cent in Kenya, and around 5 per cent in Uganda and Tanzania. In evaluating this performance, it should be borne in mind that these results were achieved at a time when the East African countries were attempting to carry through fundamental changes in their economies and societies: liquidation of colonial racial structures, rapid Africanisation of civil services, agrarian revolution in Kenya, and socialist transformation in Tanzania. In addition, Uganda had to contend with persistent political crisis throughout this period.

Inevitably, slower progress has been made with respect to diversification of the economy. The share of subsistence activities in the East African economies has been falling gradually in the sixties, and that of manufacturing, construction and public services has been rising. Likewise, there has been limited diversification of exports. On the whole, however, the structure of the East African economies has not changed significantly over the past decade. On the other hand, there has been greater progress in the diversification of external economic relations.

378

Before independence, the United Kingdom was overwhelmingly important in terms of trade, aid and foreign investment. The attainment of independence enabled the East African countries to broaden their economic links with the outside world. Although Britain continues to be the single most important trading partner, her relative position has declined considerably. Other countries such as Japan, Germany, the USA and socialist countries have greatly expanded their trade with East African countries. In addition, substantial trade links have been forged with neighbouring African countries, particularly Zambia. In the same way, the British role as a source of foreign private investment has declined and that of Japan, Western European countries and the USA has gone up correspondingly.

The greatest change has occurred in the field of foreign aid. International agencies like the United Nations Development Programme and the World Bank, which played an insignificant role during the colonial days, are now becoming the major sources of aid and technical assistance to the East African countries. Following the agreement on Tan-Zam railway, China has become the largest aid donor to Tanzania. The Scandinavian countries have also become major sources of development assistance to the East African countries. Japan, the United States and the European Economic Community countries have also stepped up their aid efforts in the East African region.

The past decade has also been marked by the evolution and definition of distinct strategies of development in the East African countries. Before independence, the main focus of nationalist activity was the liberation of the country from colonial rule; very little systematic thought was given to the problems of social and economic reconstruction. In the post-independence period, the governments have been forced to define their positions and policies on such important matters as the role of private and public enterprise in the economy, foreign private investment, and the patterns of growth and distribution of income and wealth.

In 1967 came a decisive turning point in Tanzania's strategy of development. Before that, although the government was committed in a general way to building a socialist society, the First Five Year Development Plan continued to emphasise the role of the private sector, both local and foreign, in the development of the economy. The publication of the Arusha Declaration in 1967 was followed by a sweeping nationalisation of all the major enterprises in agriculture, manufacturing, banking, insurance, construction, and export-import trade. In subsequent years, other economic activities and assets such as wholesale trade and urban properties have been brought under public ownership. This has been accompanied by a reorientation of the development effort towards rural areas. At the same time a series of measures has been taken to reduce inequalities of income between wage earners and peasant farmers on the one hand, and between high and low income employees on the other. Thus Tanzania enters the seventies with the key enterprises firmly under public ownership and with substantial progress made towards an egalitarian society.

The blueprint of Kenya's strategy for development is contained in the Sessional Paper on African Socialism published in 1965. It has been further elaborated and concretised in the successive development plans. Kenya has committed herself to seeking economic development primarily through reliance on a mixed economy, operating under the overall economic management of the state but with incentives and safeguards for private investment, whether local or foreign. Although encouragement is given to the private sector, the state has progressively increased its participation in the ownership and management of directly productive enterprises. Through a network of parastatal bodies, the government has obtained partial ownership of a wide variety of enterprises in the field of manufacturing, construction, transportation, trade, tourism, etc. In recent years the government has sought equal or majority ownership in some of the basic industries such as petroleum, electricity, and banking. Although the official policy is to promote a more equitable distribution of income and wealth, the measures taken to bring this about have been relatively weak. Consequently, while the economy has been on a strong upward trend since independence, inequalities of income and wealth have persisted.

In Uganda, as has already been noted, there was a very extensive state participation in agriculture, manufacturing and mining through the Uganda Development Corporation in the colonial days. After independence, the corporation was used to extend public ownership to a number of new and existing enterprises. The official policy continued, as in Kenya, to place reliance on a mixed economy. A major departure from this policy was foreshadowed in the government paper on 'The Common Man's Charter' which called for nationalisation of all major enterprises in the country. This was followed in May, 1970, by a decree nationalising a wide range of firms covering the entire spectrum of the economy. While these measures were being implemented, Obote was overthrown in a military coup in January, 1971. The new government in Uganda has reaffirmed its faith in a mixed economy, and has sought to attract private investment to the country. Some of the earlier measures of nationalisation have been reversed, but it is too early to say what the final picture will be like.

East African economic unity

It was noted earlier that in the colonial era the East African countries had achieved a high degree of economic integration. It is to their great credit, and especially to that of Tanzania which was the first to attain independence, that they agreed, unlike certain West and Central African countries, to extend these cooperative arrangements beyond the colonial era. But this cooperation has not been without its problems and continuing controversy. The source of various problems which have arisen can be traced to two root causes.

Firstly, the extent of economic integration achieved in East Africa on the eve of independence could only be sustained if each country was prepared to surrender sovereign control over certain crucial instruments of economic policy such as fiscal, monetary and commercial policies. With the attainment of independence, it was merely a matter of time before differences in economic policies and plans and a desire to exercise greater control over the economy created powerful pressures for greater economic autonomy. The only alternative to this was the surrender of political sovereignty in an East African Federation. This, unfortunately, despite honest and dedicated attempts, has failed to materialise. Meanwhile, the differences in social and economic organisation and policies have become even sharper.

Secondly, the operation of supranational economic institutions inevitably results in unequal distribution of benefits and costs. The fact that during the colonial era Kenya was the principal beneficiary of such arrangements created demands in Tanzania and Uganda for certain modifications in their working.

The story of the retreat from economic cooperation in the years immediately preceding and following independence is well known. There were complaints in the late fifties from the then Tanganyika, and to a smaller extent from Uganda, that Kenya had reaped most of the benefit from the expansion of the manufacturing industry stimulated by the common market. This resulted in the appointment of the Raisman Commission in 1960 to study the working of the common market and common services. Its recommendations led to the creation of the 'distributable pool' whose purpose was to finance some of the services of the East African Common Services Organisation and also to redistribute revenue from Kenya to Uganda and Tanganyika as compensation for the unequal distribution of benefits from the operation of the common market. This apparently was not considered adequate compensation for Tanzania's continuing and increasing trade deficit with Kenya. Renewed pressure from Tanzania led in 1964 to the negotiation of the 'Kampala Agreement' which made important inroads into the working of the common market in East Africa.

Under the agreement, the countries with a deficit in their trade balance were permitted to impose quota restrictions on imports from the surplus countries in the common market. Tanzania, and to a lesser extent Uganda, made immediate use of this provision to impose restrictions on a wide range of imports from Kenya. This had the effect of slowing down the expansion of inter-state trade among the East African countries over the period 1966 to 1968. In the monetary field also, after the failure to reach agreement on a Federal Central Bank for the whole of East Africa, the three countries proceeded in June, 1965, to introduce separate central banks each with its own currency.

Concerned at the drift towards disintegration of economic cooperation, the three heads of states in 1965 appointed a commission, known as the Philip Commission, to review the entire range of economic relations among the three countries. Their report formed the basis of the Treaty for East African Cooperation signed by the three heads of states in June, 1967. The treaty is a historic document in the annals of East African cooperation and its adoption did much to reverse the disintegration of East African economic unity of the preceding four years. The main achievements of the treaty were the creation of a series of East African councils composed of ministers from the national governments to oversee and plan the development of the common market and common services, and the rearrangement of the latter to ensure equitable diffusion of benefits from economic cooperation. The former provided a mechanism for a regular discussion of the outstanding problems and future developments of the East African Community by the representatives of the national governments, and the latter was essential for its long-run stability. The treaty abolished the quantitative restrictions on trade among the partner states and replaced them with transfer taxes to enable the less developed members to build up their industry and thus reduce imbalances in trade. It also provided for the establishment of the East African Development Bank, which was charged, among other things, to promote a balanced development of industry in the member states. Finally, it provided for the decentralisation and relocation of the headquarters of the common services to ensure their equitable distribution. In this connection the most important development was the movement of the headquarters of the East African Community from Nairobi to Arusha.

The new framework for economic cooperation brought into being by the treaty has done much to solve the old problems and to create opportunities for fruitful collaboration in a number of new areas. In the four years of its existence, the East African Community has made substantial progress in the achievement of the objectives laid down in the treaty: accelerated, harmonious and balanced development of the region for the benefit of the people of East Africa. In 1971, the community faced severe strains, and indeed a challenge to its very existence, as a result of political tensions between Uganda and Tanzania, arising from the overthrow of the Obote regime in Uganda. But the very crisis facing the community has evoked a powerful resurgence of sentiment in favour of East African unity and the present indications are that the current difficulties, like those of the past, will be successfully surmounted.

A look ahead into the seventies

In the 1960s the East African countries were largely concerned with the reconstruction of their societies and economies in accordance with national ideologies. As they enter the second decade of independence, the priorities for the 1970s are becoming clearer. In the concluding section, it is intended to touch on them selectively.

The major priority in the seventies must be the acceleration of economic growth, since this is a precondition for the fulfilment of practically all the other social and economic goals proclaimed by the East African countries. Unless they can achieve growth rates of a minimum 6 per cent per annum in the seventies, the fulfilment of people's aspirations for improved social and economic conditions will become extremely difficult. There are three main pre-requisites for sustaining high rates of growth over the coming decade: political stability, a favourable international environment, and vigorous domestic efforts. Without political stability, no kind of organised activity is possible. The experience in the sixties in other parts of Africa has shown that political instability can thwart the most promising situations.

The international environment is important because the East African countries are so closely integrated into the world economy through flows of trade, investment and financial and technical assistance. The sixties did not provide a particularly favourable external environment for the development efforts of the developing countries. Unless flows of development assistance are greatly accelerated within the framework of a liberalised and expanding world trade, the achievement of high rates of economic growth by the East African countries will become extremely difficult. Finally, no development effort can succeed unless it is firmly based on domestic initiative. This in turn requires mobilisation of internal resources, pursuit of rational economic policies, and above all an equitable sharing of the sacrifices essential for rapid growth.

The last point brings us to the second priority for the seventies: rapid economic growth must be accompanied by a fairer distribution of fruits of growth. In the East African context, this requires above all that the major effort must be directed at the alleviation of rural poverty. Not only must a substantial part of investment resources but a growing share of public social and economic services must be channelled into rural areas to reach the poorer peasants.

383

A related aspect of this problem is the need to expand rapidly opportunities for productive employment in both the rural and urban areas. In the sixties, there was a significant deterioration in unemployment, especially urban unemployment. This problem can only be solved within the context of a comprehensive development strategy embracing wages and incomes policies, use of appropriate technology, family planning and population control, accelerated rural development, and reform of the educational and training systems. Educational reform is fundamental to many of the pressing social, economic and political problems facing the East African countries. One of the achievements of the sixties was a massive expansion of secondary and higher education throughout East Africa, but relatively little effort was made to restructure the educational system to relate it to the requirements of the local economy and society. In the seventies, it will be necessary to introduce a number of urgent reforms into the educational systems in East Africa.

Firstly, the schools must be made, much more than they have been in the past, the instruments for the transmission of nationally desirable values and attitudes. Secondly, a new network of training centres must be created both in urban and rural areas for imparting elementary skills to primary school leavers in such subjects as agriculture, animal husbandry, woodwork and metalwork, mechanical training to construct and repair simple tools and consumer goods, construction, sewing, tailoring, and basic clerical functions. This is necessary to equip vast numbers of primary school leavers with rudimentary skills to enable them to create gainful employment for themselves. Thirdly, instruction in technical, vocational and professional subjects must be integrated into the secondary school system, to alleviate the existing shortage in middle level manpower in these fields and to equip secondary school leavers with skills which will enable them to find employment. Finally, the present system of teaching and examination must move away from emphasis on learning by rote and the accumulation of a mass of facts to a system which will develop the creative, critical and innovative abilities of students. If significant progress is made in these directions in our educational system in the 1970s, a real breakthrough will have been made in solving some of the most critical social, economic and political problems that are likely to confront the East African countries with increasing urgency over the coming years.

Further reading

East Africa Royal Commission Report, 1955.
African Socialism and its Application to Planning in Kenya, 1965.

C. LEYS and P. ROBSON (Eds) *Federation in East Africa: Opportunities and Problems*, Nairobi, 1965.

Treaty for East African Cooperation, Nairobi, 1967.

The Arusha Declaration: Socialism and Self-Reliance, Dar es Salaam, 1967.

B. VAN ARKADIE and D. GHAI, 'The East African Economies', in R. Robson and D. Lury (Eds) *The Economies of Africa*, London, 1968.

Development Plan: Kenya, 1970–1974.

Development Plan: Tanzania, 1970–74.

Development Plan: Uganda, 1970–75.

Biographical Notes

EDWARD A. ALPERS, A.B. (*Harvard*), PH.D. (*London*) is Assistant Professor of African History at the University of California, Los Angeles. He has contributed articles to the *Uganda Journal, Azania,* and *Aspects of Central African History,* ed. T. O. Ranger (1967). He wrote a pamphlet,—*The East African Slave Trade*—for the Historical Association of Tanzania. A former lecturer in History at the University of Dar es Salaam, he is now revising his thesis on Yao Trade in East Central Africa for publication.

NORMAN R. BENNETT, A.B. (*Tufts*), M.A. (*Fletcher School—Tufts*), PH.D. (*Boston*), is Assistant Professor of History and Research Associate in the African Studies Programme of Boston University. He first visited East Africa in 1959; in 1962 he was visiting lecturer at Kivukoni College, Dar es Salaam. He is the author of *Studies in East African History* (1963) and editor of *New England Merchants in Africa: A History through Documents, 1802 to 1865* with George E. Brooks, Jr. (1965), and *Leadership in East Africa. Six Political Biographies* (1968)—all published by the Boston University Press. He has contributed to the *Journal of African History, Tanzania Notes and Records, African Affairs,* and *Makerere Journal.* He is editor of the American *African Studies Bulletin.*

F. J. BERG, B.A. (*Michigan*), M.A., PH.D. (*Wisconsin*) is Assistant Professor of History at Colgate University. In 1966, he spent ten months in Kenya carrying out work for his dissertation while affiliated with the University of Nairobi as a Research Associate of the Department of History.

386

H. N. CHITTICK, M.A., F.S.A., was educated at Rugby School and Cambridge University, with intervening war service in the Intelligence Corps. He graduated in 1949, was subsequently called to the Bar and took a postgraduate Diploma in Archaeology. He assisted on various excavations in the Middle East during 1951–52. From 1952–56 he was Curator of Museums in the Republic of Sudan, and carried out fieldwork, mostly on the Christian period. In 1956 he was elected Fellow of the Society of Antiquaries of London. He was later appointed to set up the Antiquities Department in Tanganyika, carried out a general survey of antiquities of the country and began excavations on the coast. In 1961 he was appointed Director of the British Institute in East Africa. He completed excavations at Kilwa in 1965 and began work in the Lamu region in 1966. He is the Editor of *Azania*, and the author of *Ghazali, A Monastery in the Northern Sudan*, with P. L. Shinnie (1961), *Kisimani Mafia* (1961), and numerous reports and articles in journals.

DAVID WILLIAM COHEN, B.A., PH.D., graduated in history from the University of Wisconsin in 1965, having also studied social anthropology at the London School of Economics and Political Science, 1963–64. He undertook field work on the pre-colonial history of Busoga in 1966–67 and was awarded a Ph.D. by the University of London, following study at the School of Oriental and African Studies. He was appointed to the faculty of John Hopkins University in 1968 and has returned to Uganda to continue field work on the early history of the northern coastlands of Lake Victoria, having been awarded a John Simon Guggenheim Fellowship for 1971–72. His volume, *The Historical Tradition of Busoga: Mukuma and Kintu*, was published in 1972 by the Clarendon Press.

CHRISTOPHER EHRET, B.A. (*University of Redlands*), M.A., PH.D. (*Northwestern University*), is Assistant Professor of History at the University of California, Los Angeles. He was a Research Associate at the Universities of Nairobi and Dar es Salaam in 1967. He was previously engaged in research on the early history of the Highland Nilotes, as Foreign Area Fellow in East Africa. His particular interest is developing linguistic evidence as a source for writing history. He is the author of *Southern Nilotic History: Linguistic Approaches to the Study of the Past*, Northwestern University Press, 1971; *Ethiopians and East Africans: The Problem of Contacts*, E.A.P.H. (forthcoming).

DR CYRIL EHRLICH is a graduate of the London School of Economics. In 1952 he joined the staff of Makerere College where he introduced the subject of economic history and pioneered its application to East Africa, lecturing extensively in Africa, Britain and the United States. He has published several articles in learned journals and has contributed to the

Oxford History of East Africa. In 1961 he left Makerere for the Queen's University, Belfast, where he is now Senior Lecturer in Economic History, but has returned to East Africa several times to research and examine at the University.

DHARAM GHAI, was born in Kenya where he received his secondary education at the then Duke of Gloucester School. He studied at Oxford and Yale where he took his Ph.D. in Economics. He has taught at Makerere University and the University of Nairobi. He was a Visiting Research Fellow at the Economic Growth Centre, Yale University 1965–66, and with the Pearson Commission Secretariat in 1968–69. He is now Research Professor and Director of the Institute for Development Studies, University of Nairobi. He has written extensively on the development problems of Africa. He is Editor of *Eastern Africa Economics Review*, and an Associate Editor of *East Africa Journal*.

JOHN ILIFFE is a graduate of the University of Cambridge. He carried out research in East Africa in 1961–63 and received a doctoral degree from Cambridge in 1965. He then returned to the University College, Dar es Salaam in 1965, to lecture in history and to write on German administration in East Africa, the Maji Maji rising, and Tanzanian nationalism. He is now a Lecturer in History at the University of Cambridge.

J. A. KIERAN, B.A. (*Liverpool*), Ph.D. (*London*), is a former Senior Lecturer in History at the University of Nairobi. He has done extensive research on missionary activity in 19th century East Africa. He is the author of a chapter on East African history in *The Natural Resources of East Africa*, edited by W. T. W. Morgan (Oxford University Press, 1969).

ISARIAH N. KIMAMBO, M.A., Ph.D. (*Northwestern University*), is Professor and Head of Department, the University of Dar es Salaam. He is also the Chief Academic Officer of the University. He is the author of *A Political History of the Pare of Tanzania*, c. *1500–1900*, Nairobi, E.A.P.H., 1969; Editor with A. Temu, of *A History of Tanzania*, Nairobi, E.A.P.H., 1969; as well as several articles on various aspects of East African history.

M. S. M. KIWANUKA was educated at Namilyango College, Royal College, Nairobi, Makerere University College, Kampala and at the School of Oriental and African Studies, London University. He graduated with a B.A.(Hons) in History in 1962 and got his Doctorate in 1965 at London University. He has been on the History staff at Makerere University College since 1965. He was a Visiting Associate Professor at Northwestern University and Duke University, U.S.A. He has also lectured in many universities in the U.S.A. He is a former President of the Uganda Society and a member of many learned societies. He has published many articles and reviews and a number of monographs as well as the following books: *Mutesa of Uganda: A Short Biography* (East African Literature Bureau, 1967), *The Kings of Buganda* (Editor), Nairobi, E.A.P.H., 1971; *A History of Buganda: From the Foundation of the Kingdom to 1900*, Longman, 1971.

ALI MAZRUI was born in Mombasa, Kenya, in 1933. His early education was at the Government Boys' School, Mombasa, and at Huddersfield College of Technology. He obtained a B.A. with distinction from the University of Manchester, an M.A. from Columbia University, New York, and a D.Phil. from the University of Oxford. He has also been a Rockefeller Foundation Fellow and Visiting Professorial Scholar at the Universities of Chicago, California (Los Angeles), Harvard and Singapore, and at the Indian School of International Studies, New Delhi. He has lectured in Britain, Holland and Sweden, and is now Professor and Head of the Department of Political Science at Makerere University, Uganda. Dr Mazrui's published works include *Towards a Pax Africana*, *The Anglo-African Commonwealth*, and *On Heroes and Uhuru Worship*.

B. A. OGOT, DIP.ED. (*E.A.*) M.A. (*St Andrews*), PH.D. (*London*), is Professor of History, Director of the Institute of African Studies and Deputy Vice-Chancellor of the University of Nairobi. He started his career as Tutorial Fellow at Makerere University College in 1959–60 and was then awarded a Rockefeller Research Fellowship to the School of Oriental and African Studies, London University. In 1961 he became Research Fellow at the British Institute of History and Archaeology in East Africa, and lectured in history at Makerere University College from 1962–64. In 1965 he became Senior Lecturer and Chairman of the History Department of University College, Nairobi, and was at the same time Director of the Cultural Division of the Institute for Development Studies. He is the Founder Member and National President of the Historical Association of Kenya and is a member of many other learned societies. His published works include *East Africa, Past and Present* (Ed.), *A Place to Feel at Home* with F. B. Welbourn (1966), and *A History of the Southern Luo Peoples, 1500–1900* Vol. I (1967). He has several other works in progress and has contributed articles to numerous books and journals. He is the Editor of *East Africa Journal* and *Transafrican History Journal*.

FRANCIS OJANY was educated at the Government School, Kisii, and Alliance High School. He graduated from Makerere University College in 1960 with a B.A. Honours Degree in geography, with history as a subsidiary subject. In 1960 he was awarded a Commonwealth Scholarship for postgraduate work in geomorphology, and in 1963 gained his M.A. Degree at the University of Birmingham. He subsequently returned to the University of Nairobi, where he is now Senior Lecturer in Geography. With Dr R. B. Ogendo, he has written *Kenya: A Study in Physical and Human Geography*, soon to be published by Longman.

MERRICK POSNANSKY, Professor of Archaeology at the University of Ghana, was in East Africa from 1956–67 and was latterly Director of African Studies at Makerere University College. He was previously Curator of the Uganda Museum and Assistant Director of the British Institute of History and Archaeology in East Africa. He has excavated widely in East Africa on both Stone and Iron Age sites; his most notable excavations being at Lanet in Kenya, Bigo and Magosi in Uganda, and Nyabusora in Tanzania. He was editor of *Prelude to East African History*.

J. E. G. SUTTON, M.A. (*Oxon.*) PH.D. (*East Africa*), is Senior Lecturer in History and Archaeology at the University of Dar es Salaam. Formerly, as a research student of the British Institute of History and Archaeology in East Africa and of Makerere College, he undertook a field survey with excavations of the archaeology of the western highlands of Kenya. The results of this work and its bearing on the history of the Kalenjin and other peoples of the region are explained in several articles, notably in volume I of *Azania* (1966). He is also author of the first paper of the Historical Association of Tanzania, *The East African Coast: An Historical and Archaeological Review* (1966).

G. S. WERE, B.A. Hons. (*Wales*), PH.D. (*Wales*), was educated at the Royal Technical College, Nairobi, the University College of North Wales, Bangor, and the School of Oriental and African Studies, London University. He is currently Senior Lecturer in History at the University of Nairobi. He is the author of *A History of the Abaluyia of Western Kenya: c. 1500–1930, Abaluyia Historical Texts*, and *East Africa through a Thousand Years*, with D. Wilson, and Editor of *Journal of Eastern African Research and Development*.

Index

DT
21

Published by Longman Kenya Ltd., P.O. Box 45925, Shell and BP House (2nd floor), Harambee Avenue, Nairobi, and Printed by Kenya Litho Ltd., P.O. Box 40775, Changamwe Road, Nairobi, Kenya.